# Kamisama Kiss

uzuki

# HARACTER

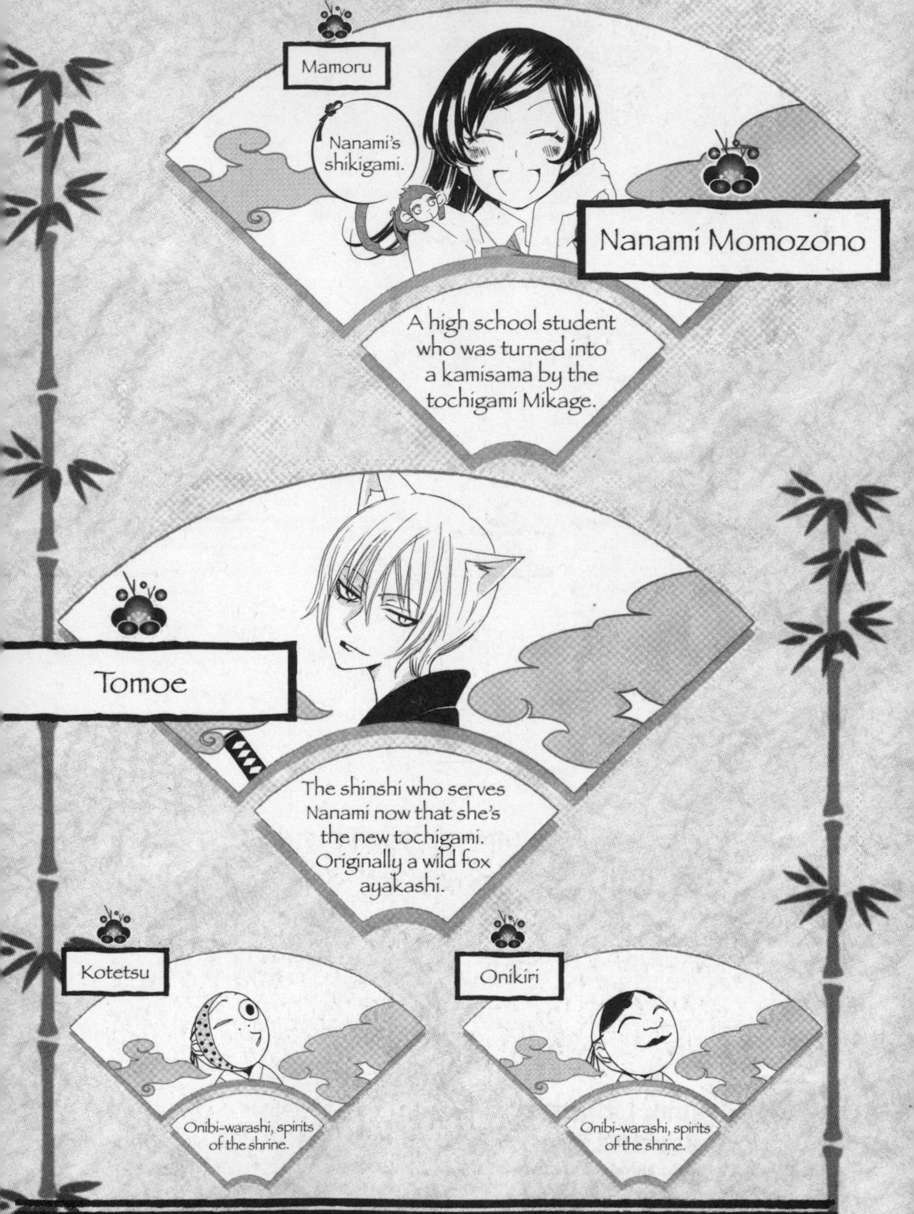
Mamoru
Nanami's shikigami.
Nanami Momozono
A high school student who was turned into a kamisama by the tochigami Mikage.
Tomoe
The shinshi who serves Nanami now that she's the new tochigami. Originally a wild fox ayakashi.
Kotetsu
Onibi-warashi, spirits of the shrine.
Onikiri
Onibi-warashi, spirits of the shrine.

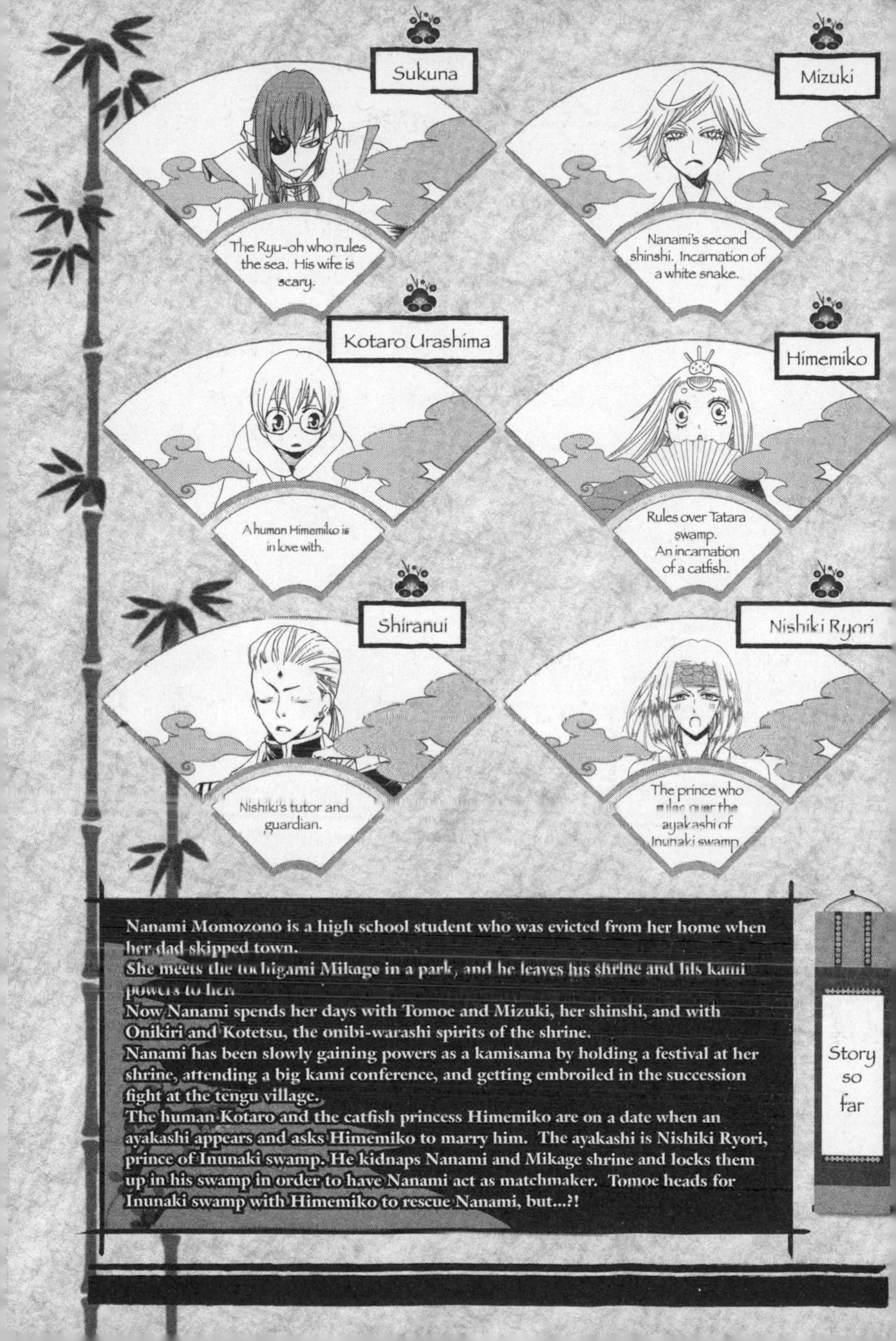
Mizuki
Nanami's second shinshi. Incarnation of a white snake.
Sukuna
The Ryu-oh who rules the sea. His wife is scary.
Himemiko
Rules over Tatara swamp. An incarnation of a catfish.
Kotaro Urashima
A human Himemiko is in love with.
Nishiki Ryori
The prince who rules over the ayakashi of Inunaki swamp.
Shiranui
Nishiki's tutor and guardian.

Story so far

**Nanami Momozono is a high school student who was evicted from her home when her dad skipped town.**
**She meets the tochigami Mikage in a park, and he leaves his shrine and his kami powers to her.**
**Now Nanami spends her days with Tomoe and Mizuki, her shinshi, and with Onikiri and Kotetsu, the onibi-warashi spirits of the shrine.**
**Nanami has been slowly gaining powers as a kamisama by holding a festival at her shrine, attending a big kami conference, and getting embroiled in the succession fight at the tengu village.**
**The human Kotaro and the catfish princess Himemiko are on a date when an ayakashi appears and asks Himemiko to marry him. The ayakashi is Nishiki Ryori, prince of Inunaki swamp. He kidnaps Nanami and Mikage shrine and locks them up in his swamp in order to have Nanami act as matchmaker. Tomoe heads for Inunaki swamp with Himemiko to rescue Nanami, but...?!**

# Kamisama Kiss

## Volume 13
## CONTENTS

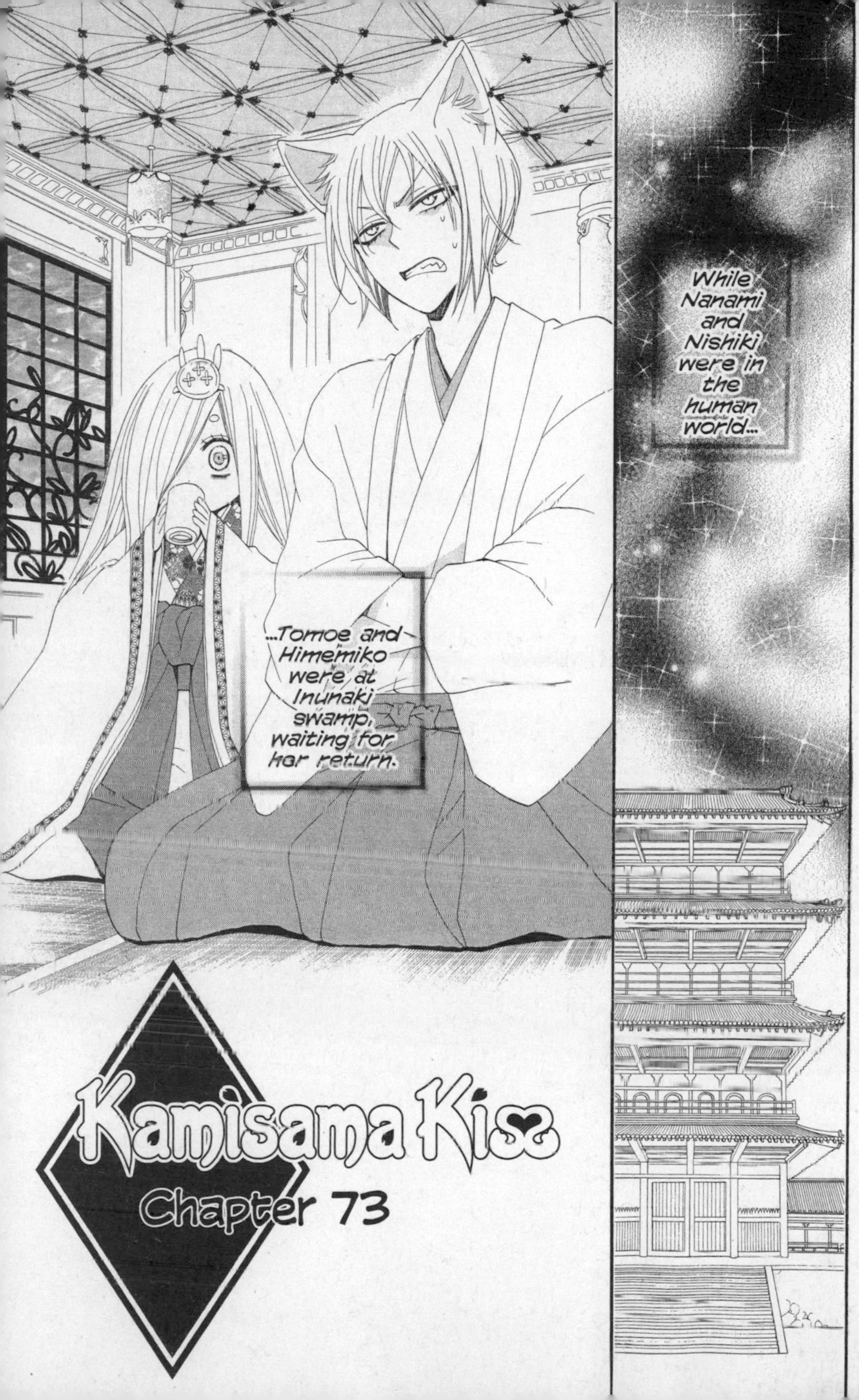
While Nanami and Nishiki were in the human world...
...Tomoe and Himemiko were at Inunaki swamp, waiting for her return.
Kamisama Kiss
Chapter 73

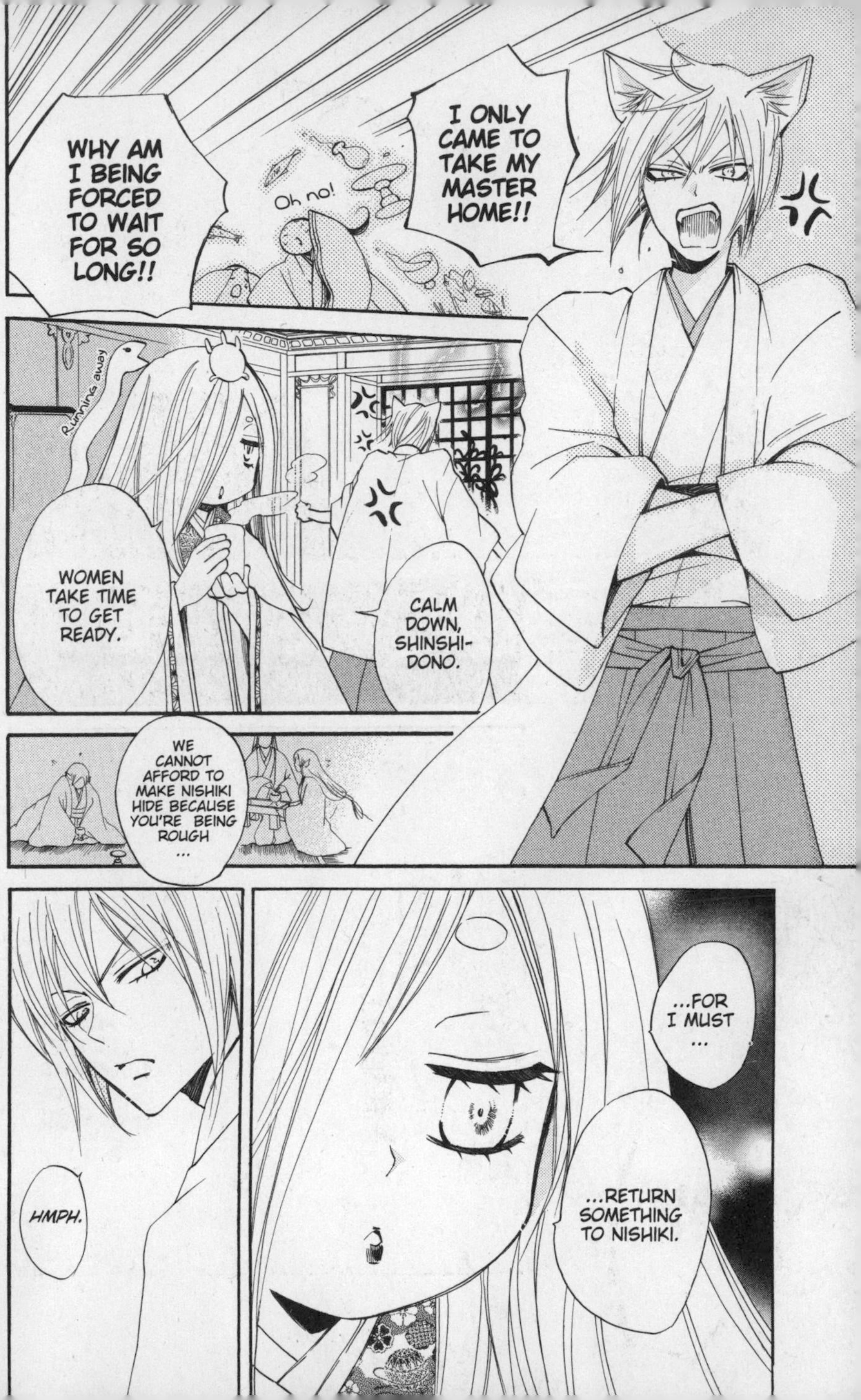
I ONLY CAME TO TAKE MY MASTER HOME!!
Oh no!
WHY AM I BEING FORCED TO WAIT FOR SO LONG!!
CALM DOWN, SHINSHI-DONO.
Running away
WOMEN TAKE TIME TO GET READY.
WE CANNOT AFFORD TO MAKE NISHIKI HIDE BECAUSE YOU'RE BEING ROUGH ...
...FOR I MUST ...
...RETURN SOMETHING TO NISHIKI.
HMPH.

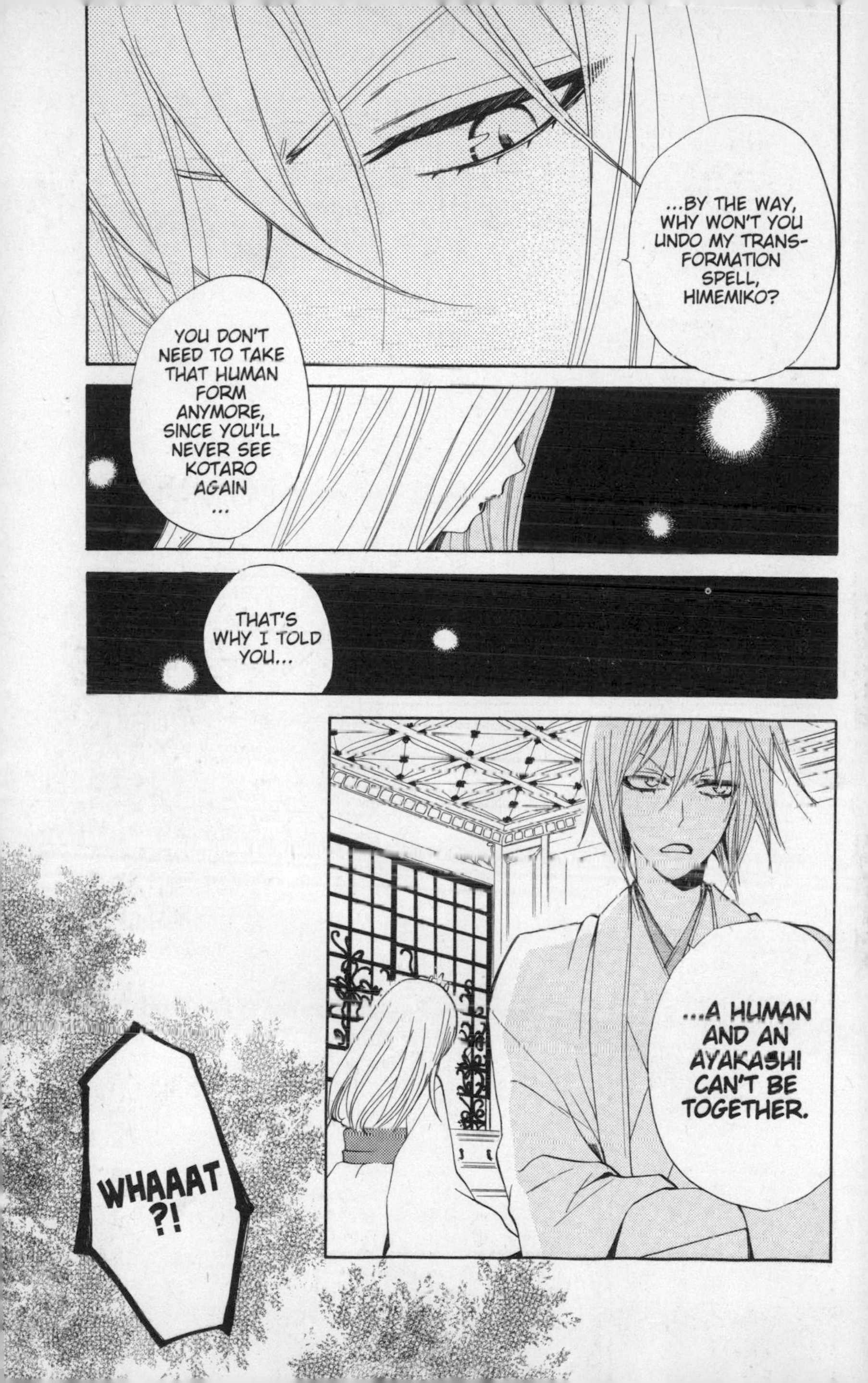
...BY THE WAY, WHY WON'T YOU UNDO MY TRANS-FORMATION SPELL, HIMEMIKO?
YOU DON'T NEED TO TAKE THAT HUMAN FORM ANYMORE, SINCE YOU'LL NEVER SEE KOTARO AGAIN ...
THAT'S WHY I TOLD YOU...
...A HUMAN AND AN AYAKASHI CAN'T BE TOGETHER.
WHAAAT ?!

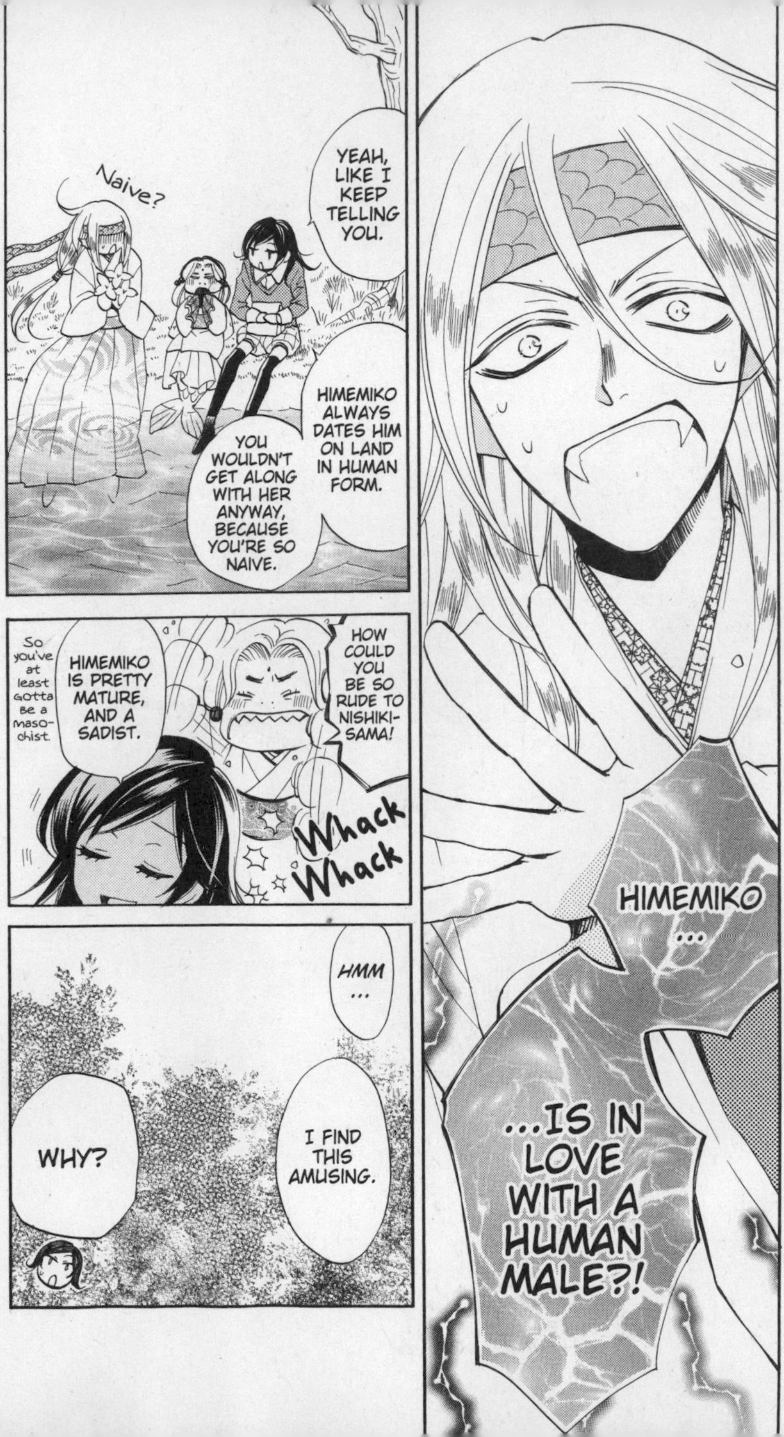
HIMEMIKO ...
...IS IN LOVE WITH A HUMAN MALE?!
YEAH, LIKE I KEEP TELLING YOU.
HIMEMIKO ALWAYS DATES HIM ON LAND IN HUMAN FORM.
YOU WOULDN'T GET ALONG WITH HER ANYWAY, BECAUSE YOU'RE SO NAIVE.
Naive?
HOW COULD YOU BE SO RUDE TO NISHIKI-SAMA!
HIMEMIKO IS PRETTY MATURE, AND A SADIST.
So you've at least gotta be a maso-chist.
Whack Whack
HMM ...
I FIND THIS AMUSING.
WHY?

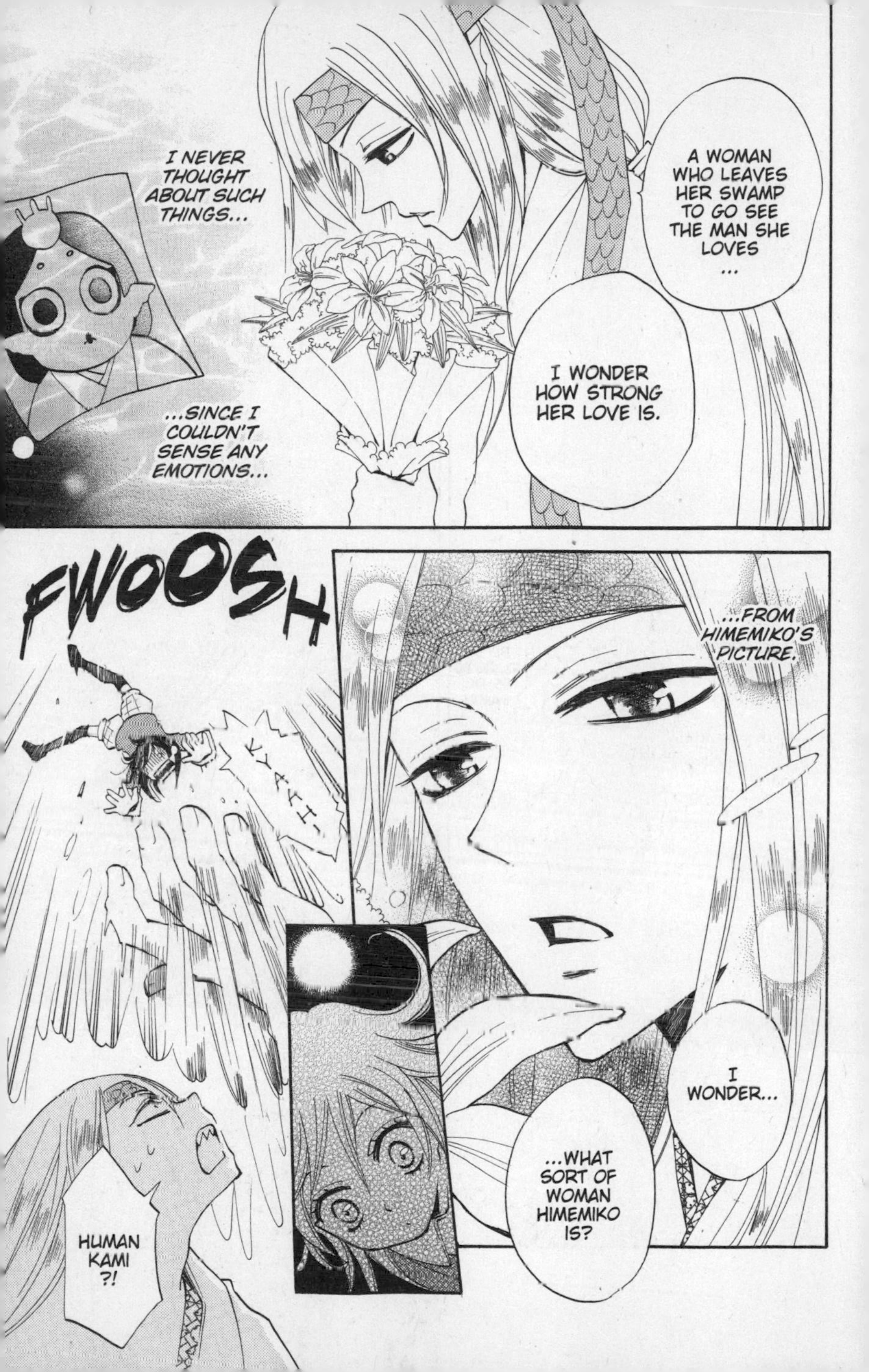
A WOMAN WHO LEAVES HER SWAMP TO GO SEE THE MAN SHE LOVES ...
I WONDER HOW STRONG HER LOVE IS.
I NEVER THOUGHT ABOUT SUCH THINGS...
...SINCE I COULDN'T SENSE ANY EMOTIONS...
...FROM HIMEMIKO'S PICTURE.
I WONDER...
...WHAT SORT OF WOMAN HIMEMIKO IS?
FWOOSH
KYAKI-
HUMAN KAMI ?!

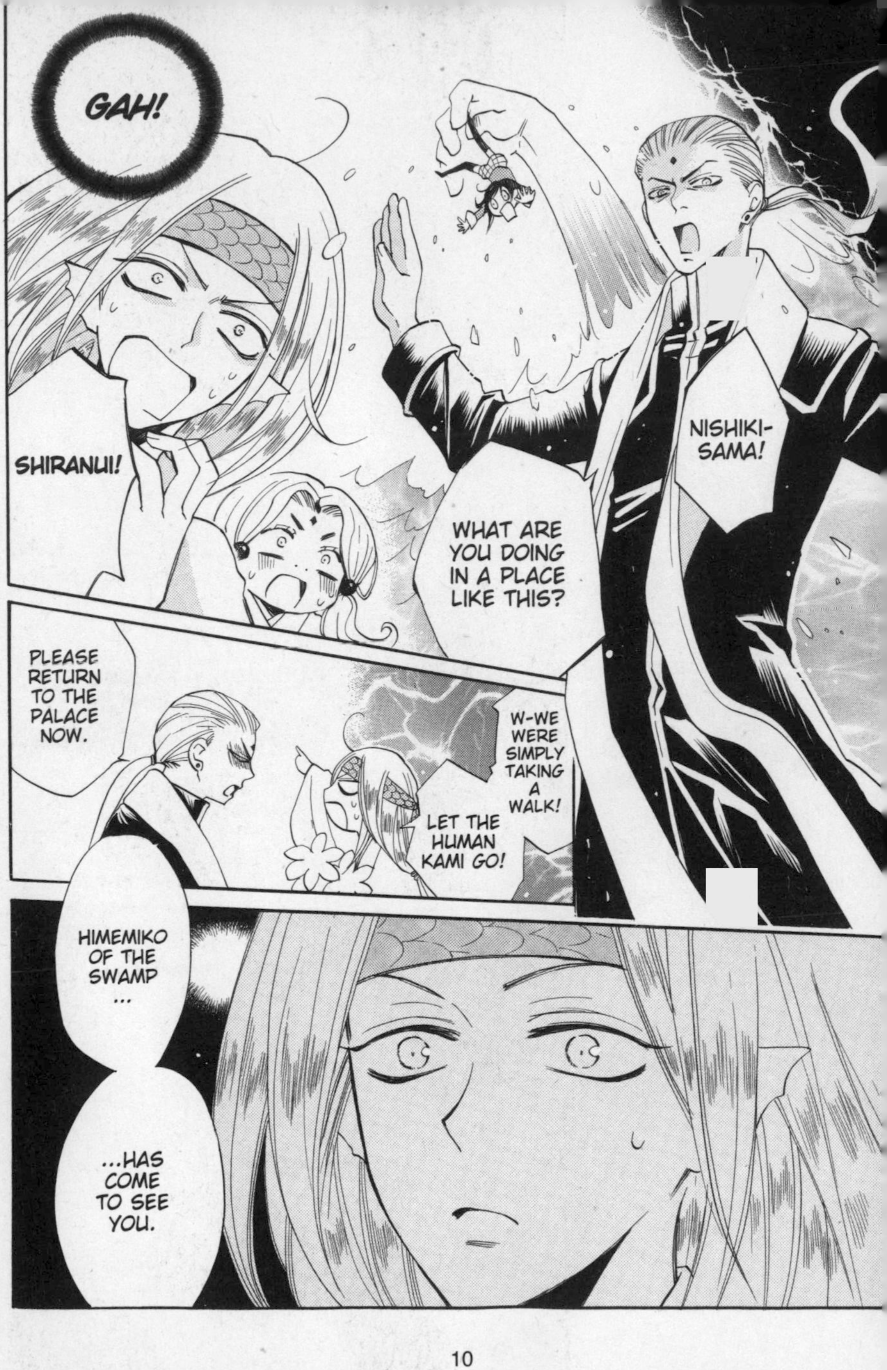
NISHIKI-SAMA!
WHAT ARE YOU DOING IN A PLACE LIKE THIS?
GAH!
SHIRANUI!
W-WE WERE SIMPLY TAKING A WALK!
LET THE HUMAN KAMI GO!
PLEASE RETURN TO THE PALACE NOW.
HIMEMIKO OF THE SWAMP ...
...HAS COME TO SEE YOU.

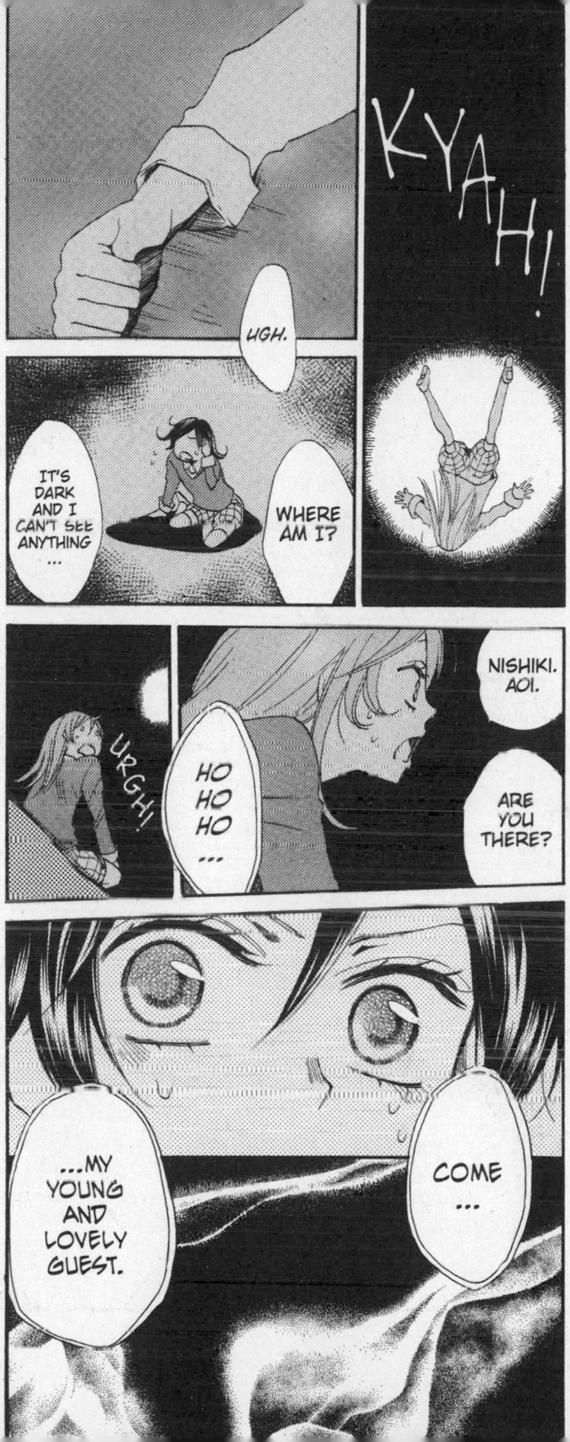
KYAH!
UGH.
WHERE AM I?
IT'S DARK AND I CAN'T SEE ANYTHING ...
NISHIKI. AOI.
ARE YOU THERE?
HO HO HO ...
URGH!
COME ...
...MY YOUNG AND LOVELY GUEST.

Hello!

Thank you for picking up volume 13 of Kamisama Kiss!

I hope you enjoy reading it.

A Kamisama Kiss drama CD got made for the first time! There are two versions of the Japanese volume 13, a special version with the drama CD, and the regular version.

For the first time. For the first time. I'm so happy!

See you later.

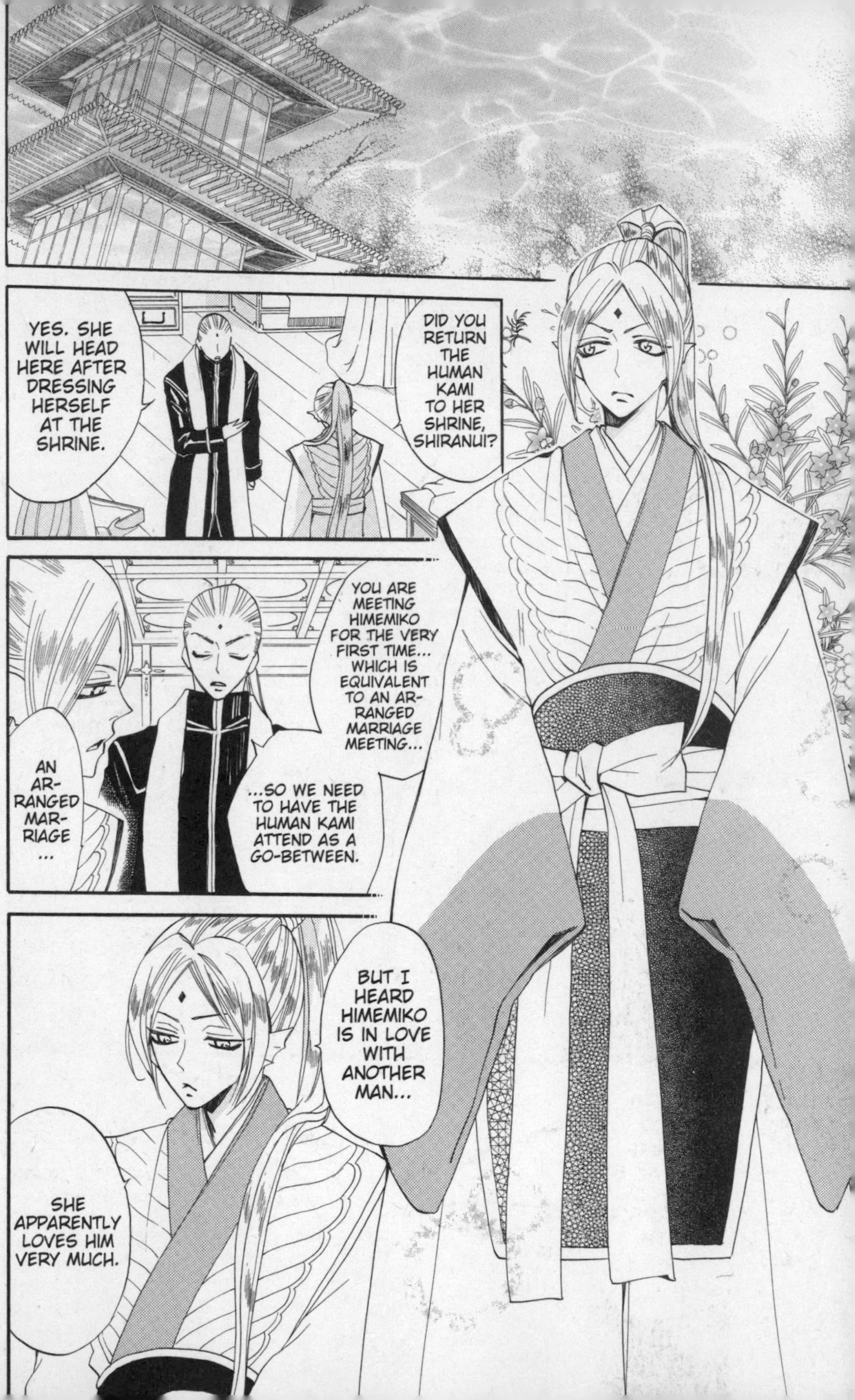
DID YOU RETURN THE HUMAN KAMI TO HER SHRINE, SHIRANUI?
YES. SHE WILL HEAD HERE AFTER DRESSING HERSELF AT THE SHRINE.
YOU ARE MEETING HIMEMIKO FOR THE VERY FIRST TIME... WHICH IS EQUIVALENT TO AN AR-RANGED MARRIAGE MEETING...
...SO WE NEED TO HAVE THE HUMAN KAMI ATTEND AS A GO-BETWEEN.
AN AR-RANGED MAR-RIAGE ...
BUT I HEARD HIMEMIKO IS IN LOVE WITH ANOTHER MAN...
SHE APPARENTLY LOVES HIM VERY MUCH.

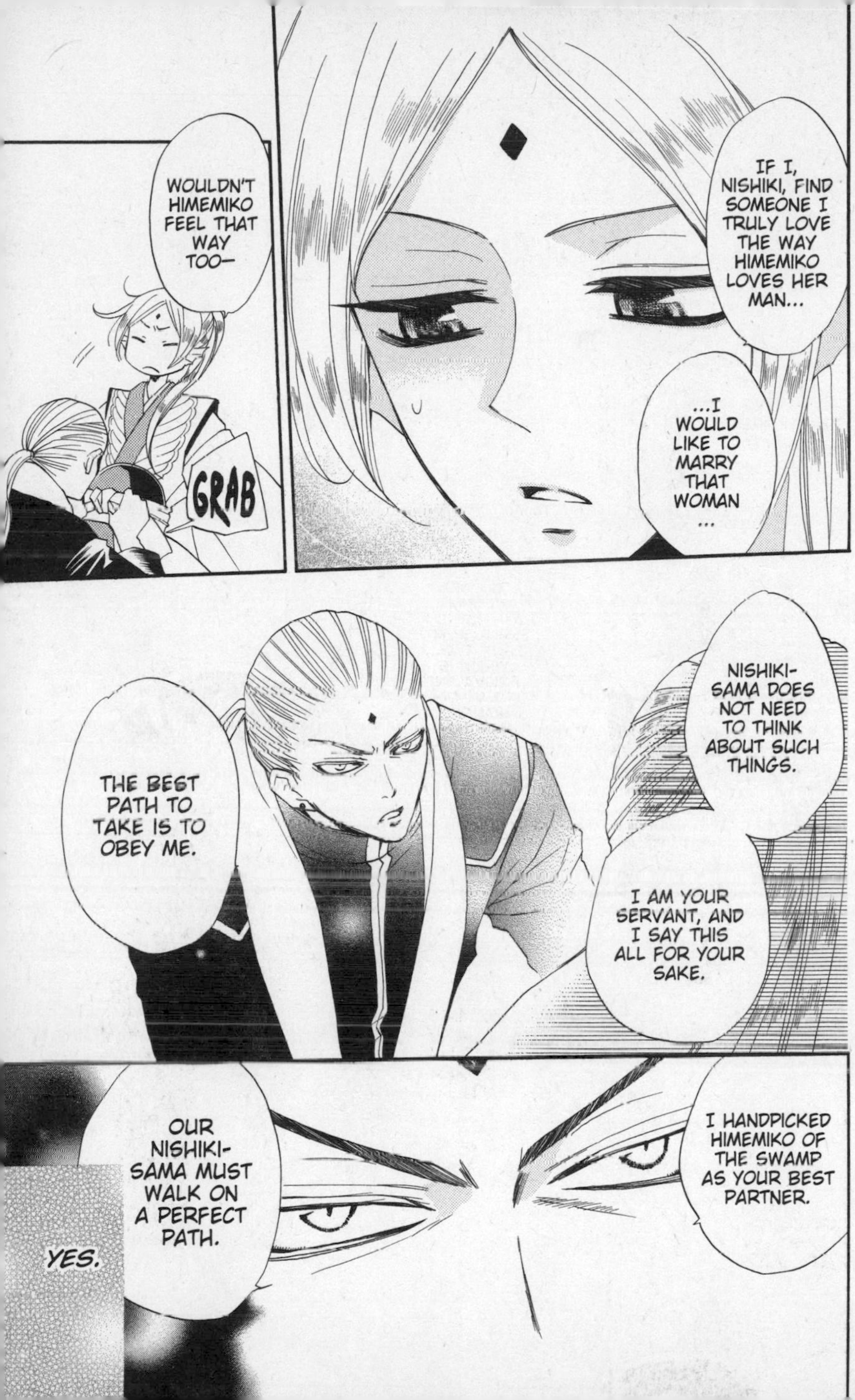
IF I, NISHIKI, FIND SOMEONE I TRULY LOVE THE WAY HIMEMIKO LOVES HER MAN...
...I WOULD LIKE TO MARRY THAT WOMAN ...
WOULDN'T HIMEMIKO FEEL THAT WAY TOO—
GRAB
NISHIKI-SAMA DOES NOT NEED TO THINK ABOUT SUCH THINGS.
I AM YOUR SERVANT, AND I SAY THIS ALL FOR YOUR SAKE.
THE BEST PATH TO TAKE IS TO OBEY ME.
I HANDPICKED HIMEMIKO OF THE SWAMP AS YOUR BEST PARTNER.
OUR NISHIKI-SAMA MUST WALK ON A PERFECT PATH.
YES.

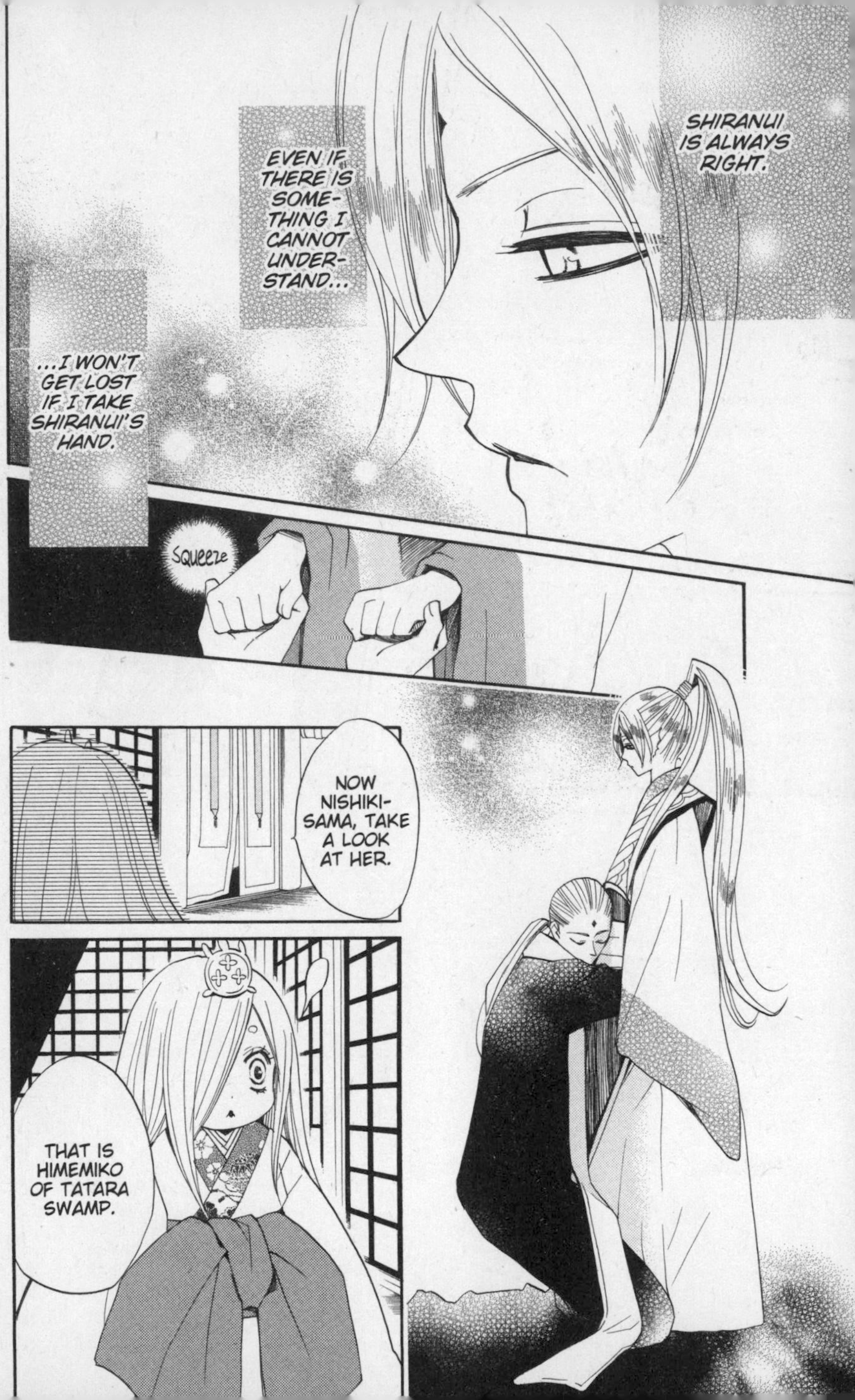
SHIRANUI IS ALWAYS RIGHT.
EVEN IF THERE IS SOME-THING I CANNOT UNDER-STAND...
...I WON'T GET LOST IF I TAKE SHIRANUI'S HAND.
Squeeze
NOW NISHIKI-SAMA, TAKE A LOOK AT HER.
THAT IS HIMEMIKO OF TATARA SWAMP.

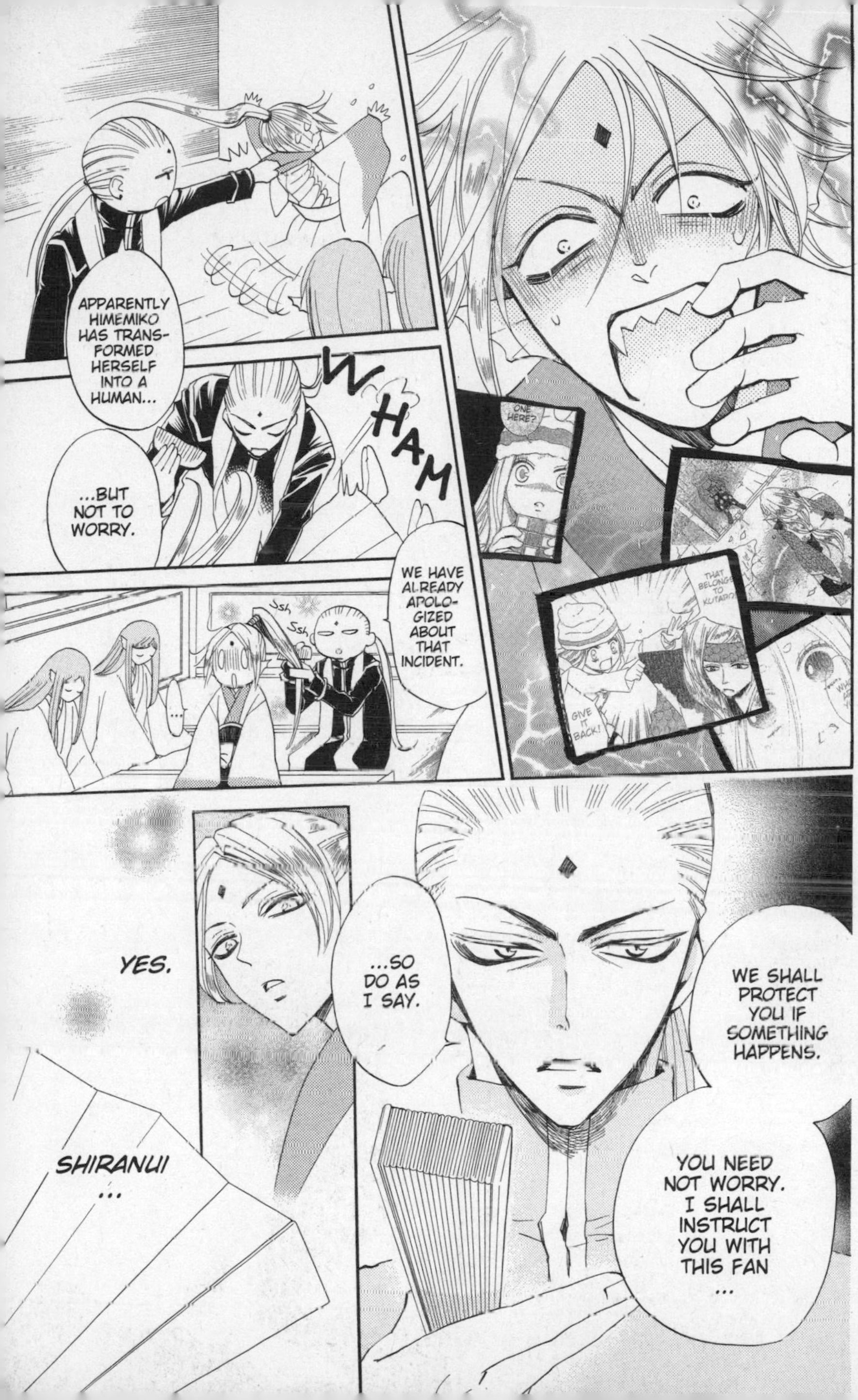
ONE HERE?
GIVE IT BACK!
APPARENTLY HIMEMIKO HAS TRANS-FORMED HERSELF INTO A HUMAN...
WHAM
...BUT NOT TO WORRY.
WE HAVE ALREADY APOLO-GIZED ABOUT THAT INCIDENT.
Ssh Ssh
...
WE SHALL PROTECT YOU IF SOMETHING HAPPENS.
YOU NEED NOT WORRY. I SHALL INSTRUCT YOU WITH THIS FAN ...
...SO DO AS I SAY.
YES.
SHIRANUI ...

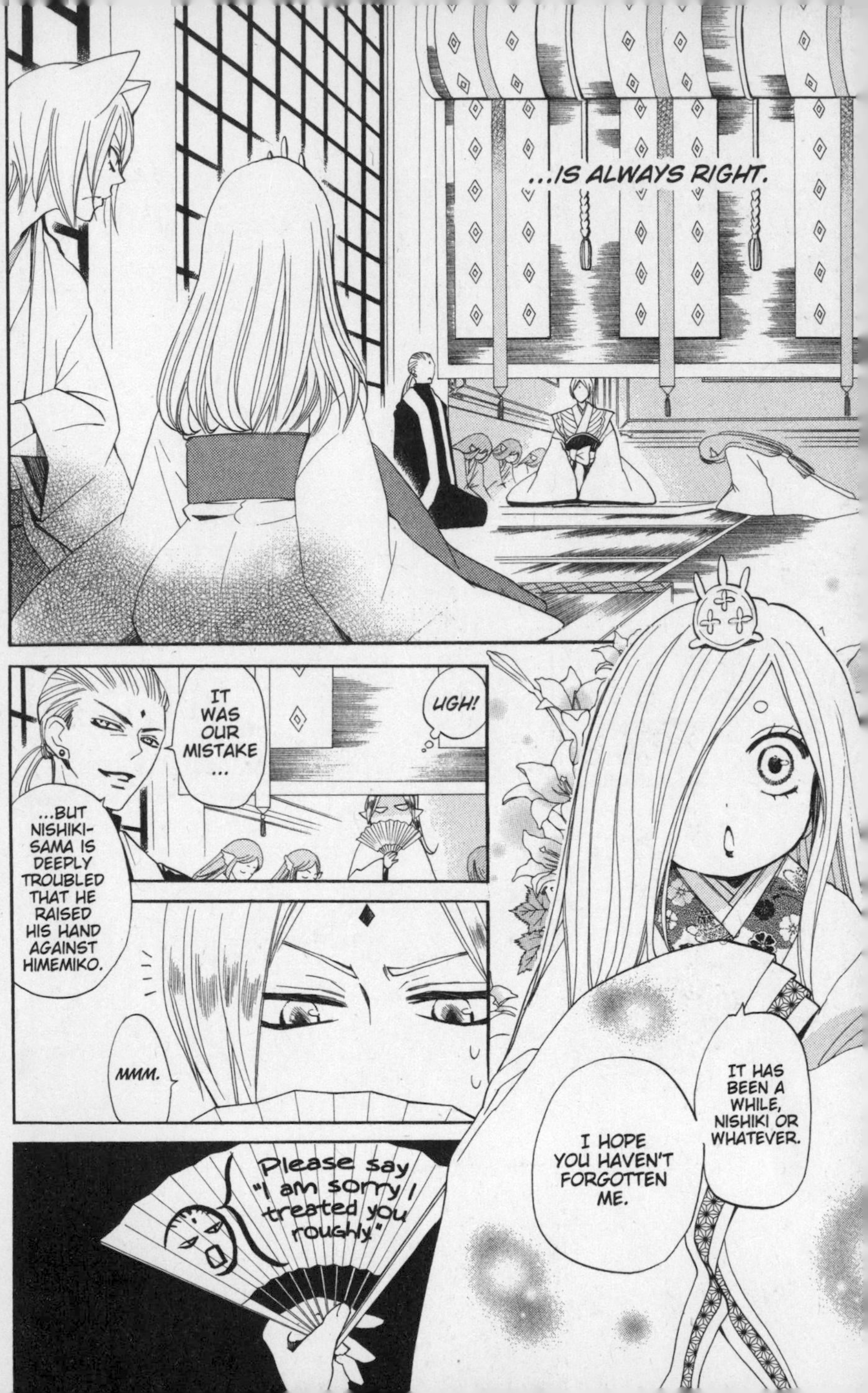
...IS ALWAYS RIGHT.
IT HAS BEEN A WHILE, NISHIKI OR WHATEVER.
I HOPE YOU HAVEN'T FORGOTTEN ME.
UGH!
IT WAS OUR MISTAKE...
...BUT NISHIKI-SAMA IS DEEPLY TROUBLED THAT HE RAISED HIS HAND AGAINST HIMEMIKO.
MMM.
Please say "I am sorry I treated you roughly"

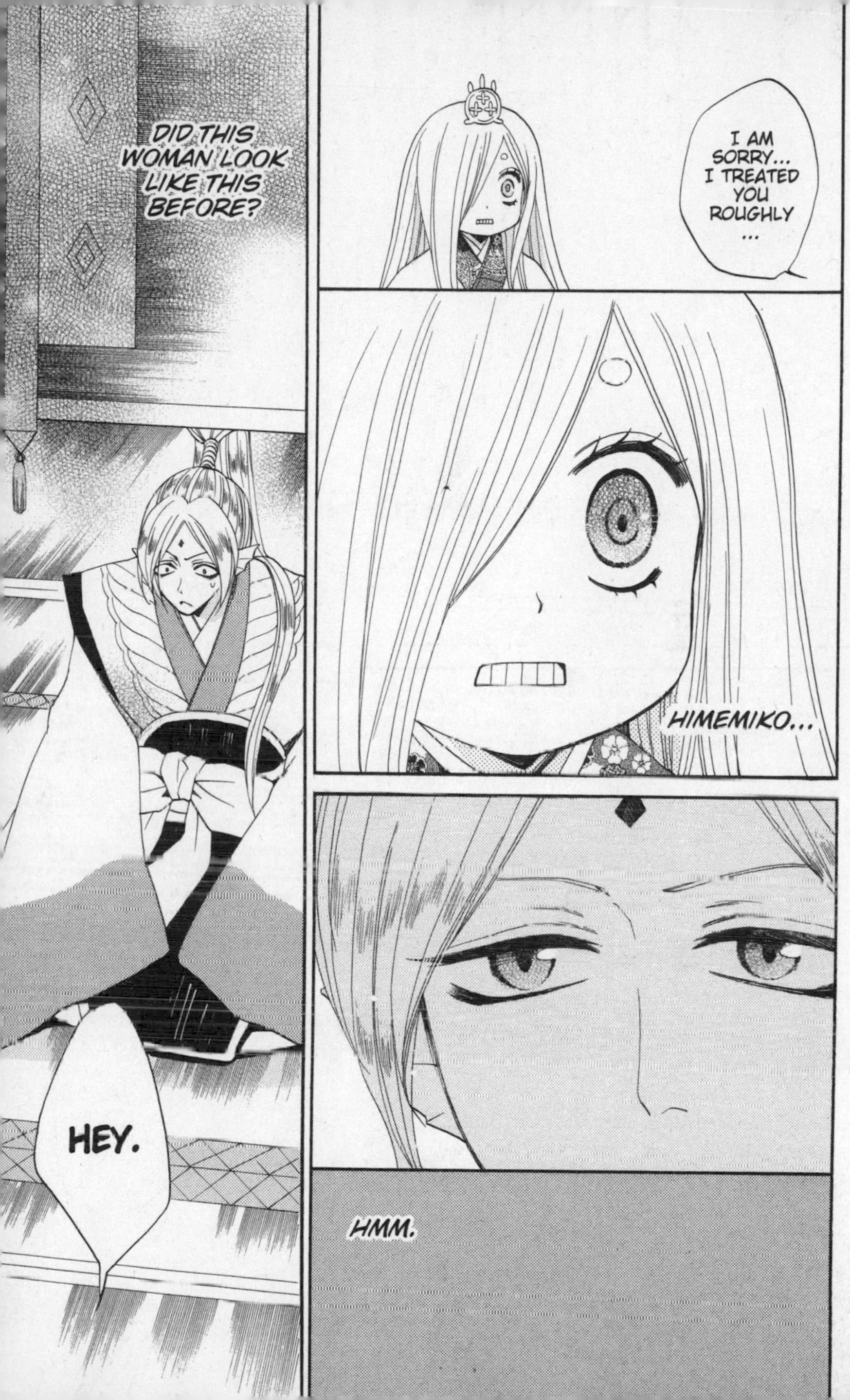
I AM SORRY... I TREATED YOU ROUGHLY...
HIMEMIKO...
HMM.
DID THIS WOMAN LOOK LIKE THIS BEFORE?
HEY.

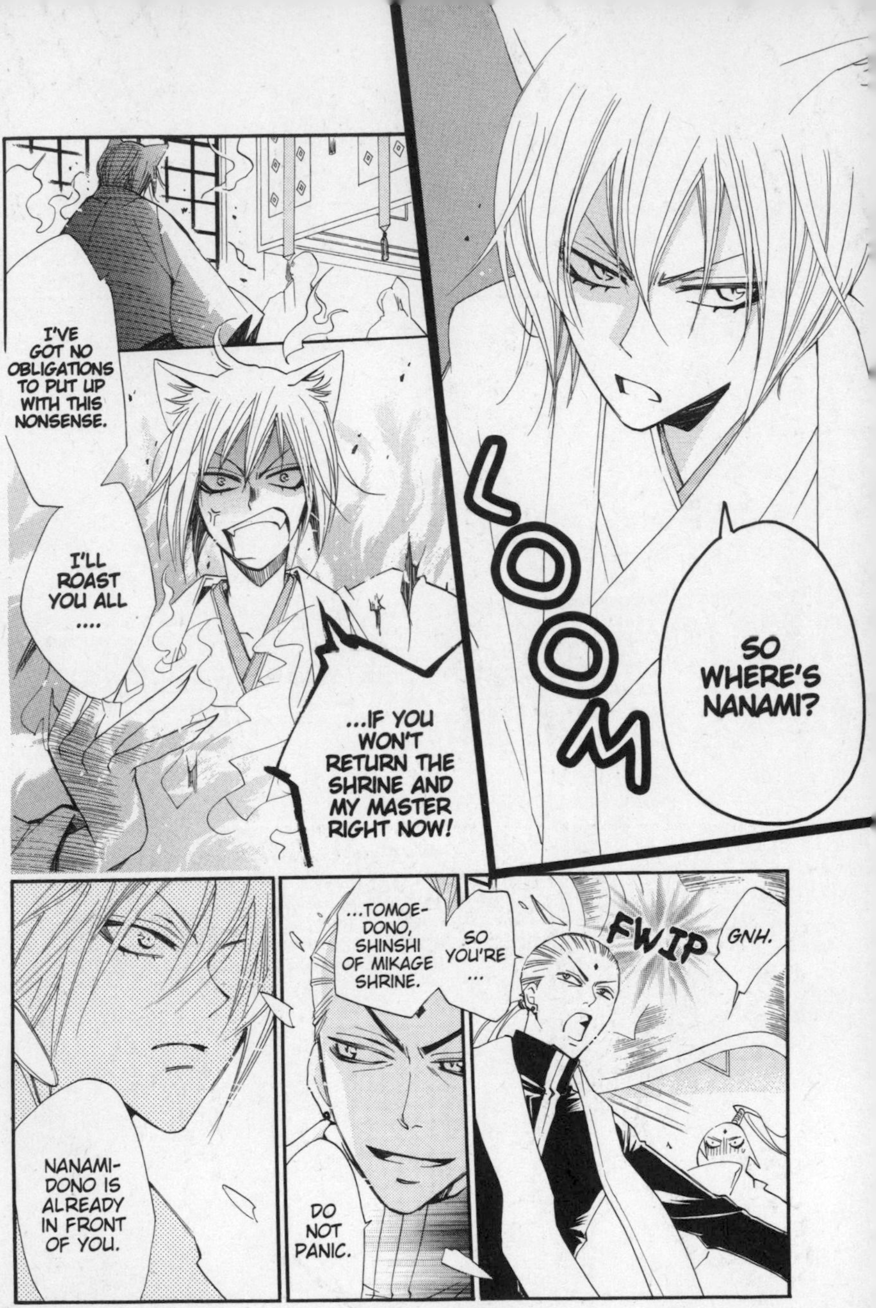
LOOM
SO WHERE'S NANAMI?
I'VE GOT NO OBLIGATIONS TO PUT UP WITH THIS NONSENSE.
I'LL ROAST YOU ALL ....
...IF YOU WON'T RETURN THE SHRINE AND MY MASTER RIGHT NOW!
GNH.
FWIP
SO YOU'RE ...
...TOMOE-DONO, SHINSHI OF MIKAGE SHRINE.
DO NOT PANIC.
NANAMI-DONO IS ALREADY IN FRONT OF YOU.

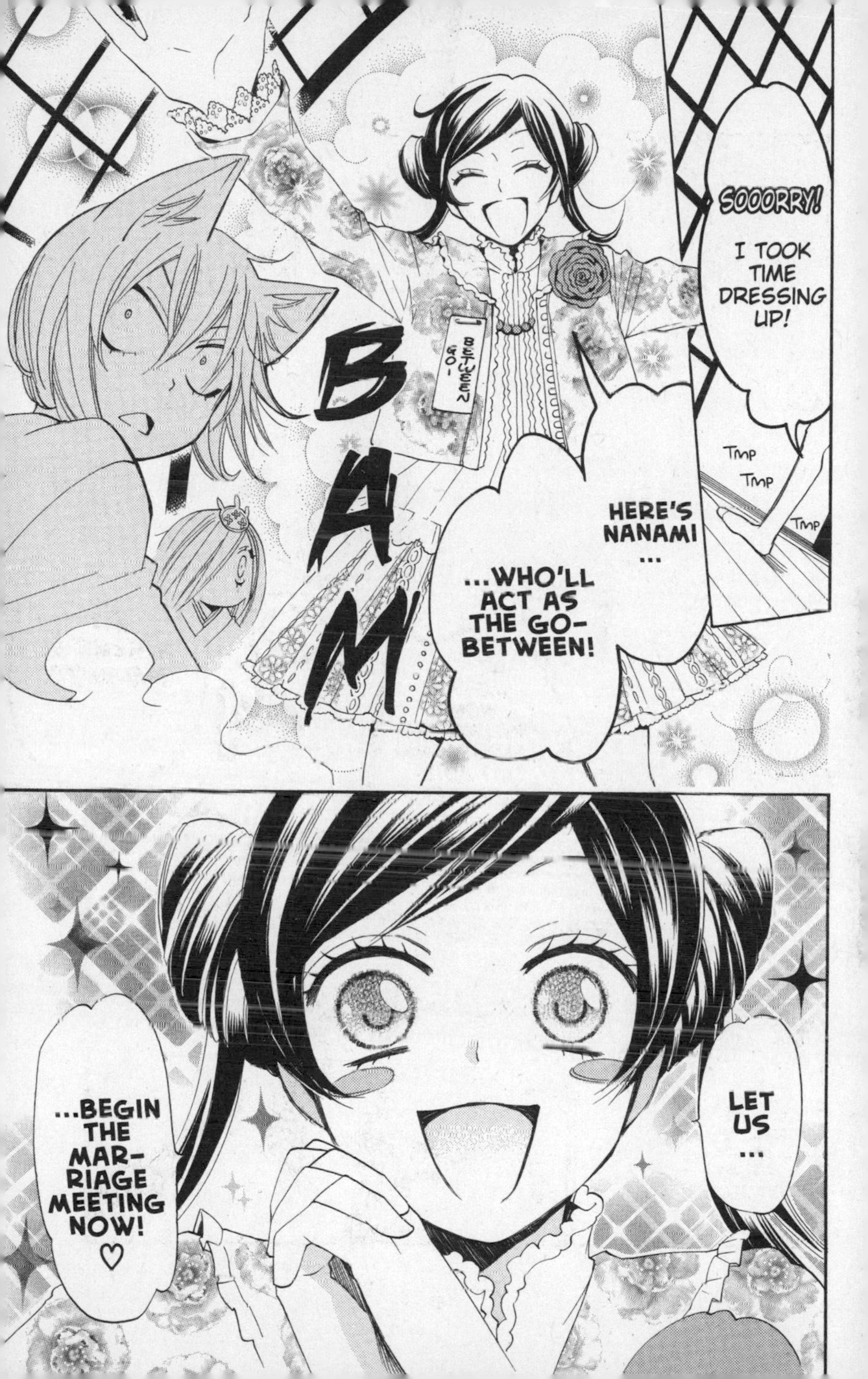
SOOORRY!
I TOOK TIME DRESSING UP!
Tmp Tmp Tmp
HERE'S NANAMI ...
...WHO'LL ACT AS THE GO-BETWEEN!
GO-BETWEEN
BAM
LET US ...
...BEGIN THE MAR-RIAGE MEETING NOW! ♡

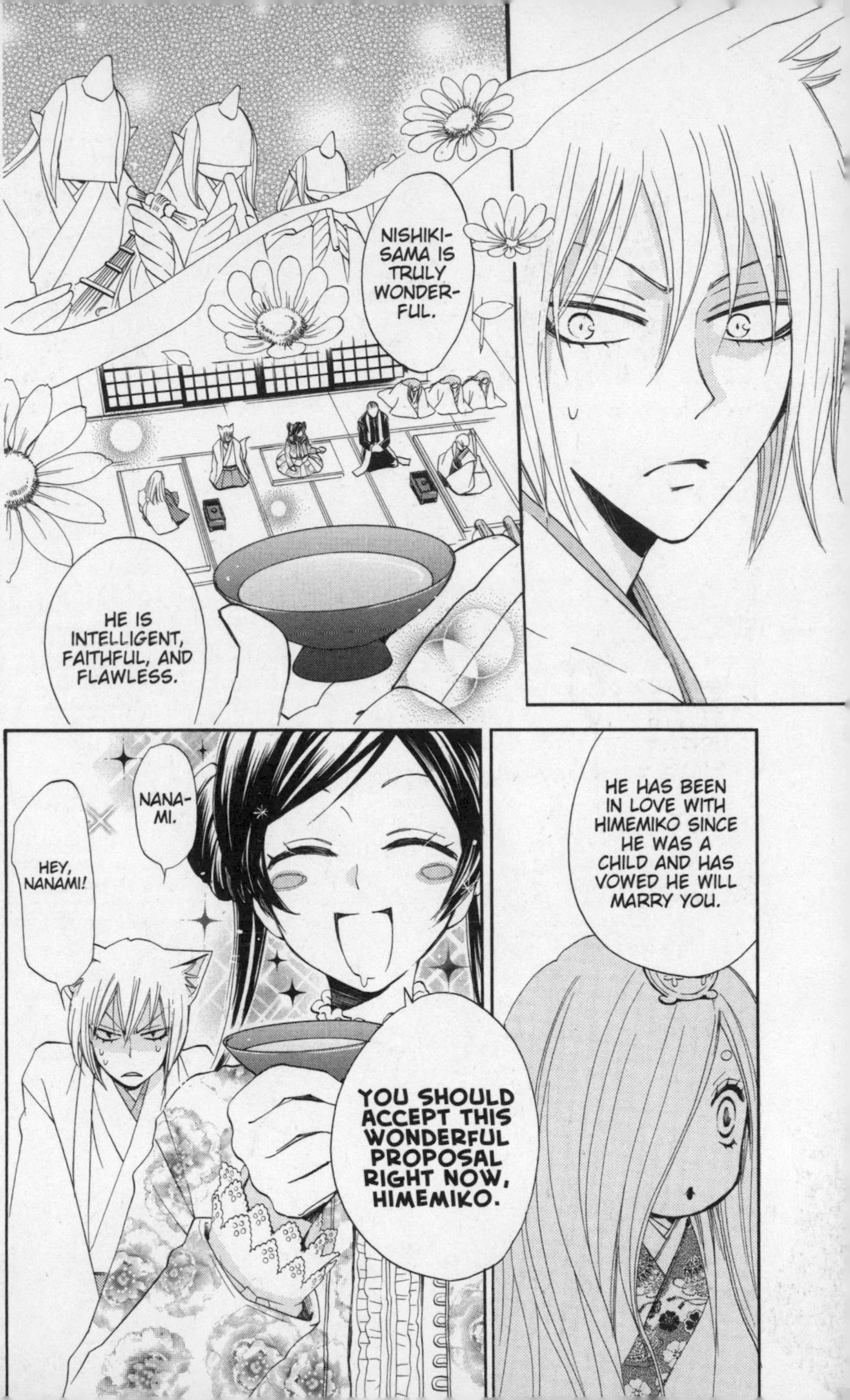
NISHIKI-SAMA IS TRULY WONDERFUL.
HE IS INTELLIGENT, FAITHFUL, AND FLAWLESS.
HE HAS BEEN IN LOVE WITH HIMEMIKO SINCE HE WAS A CHILD AND HAS VOWED HE WILL MARRY YOU.
YOU SHOULD ACCEPT THIS WONDERFUL PROPOSAL RIGHT NOW, HIMEMIKO.
NANAMI.
HEY, NANAMI!

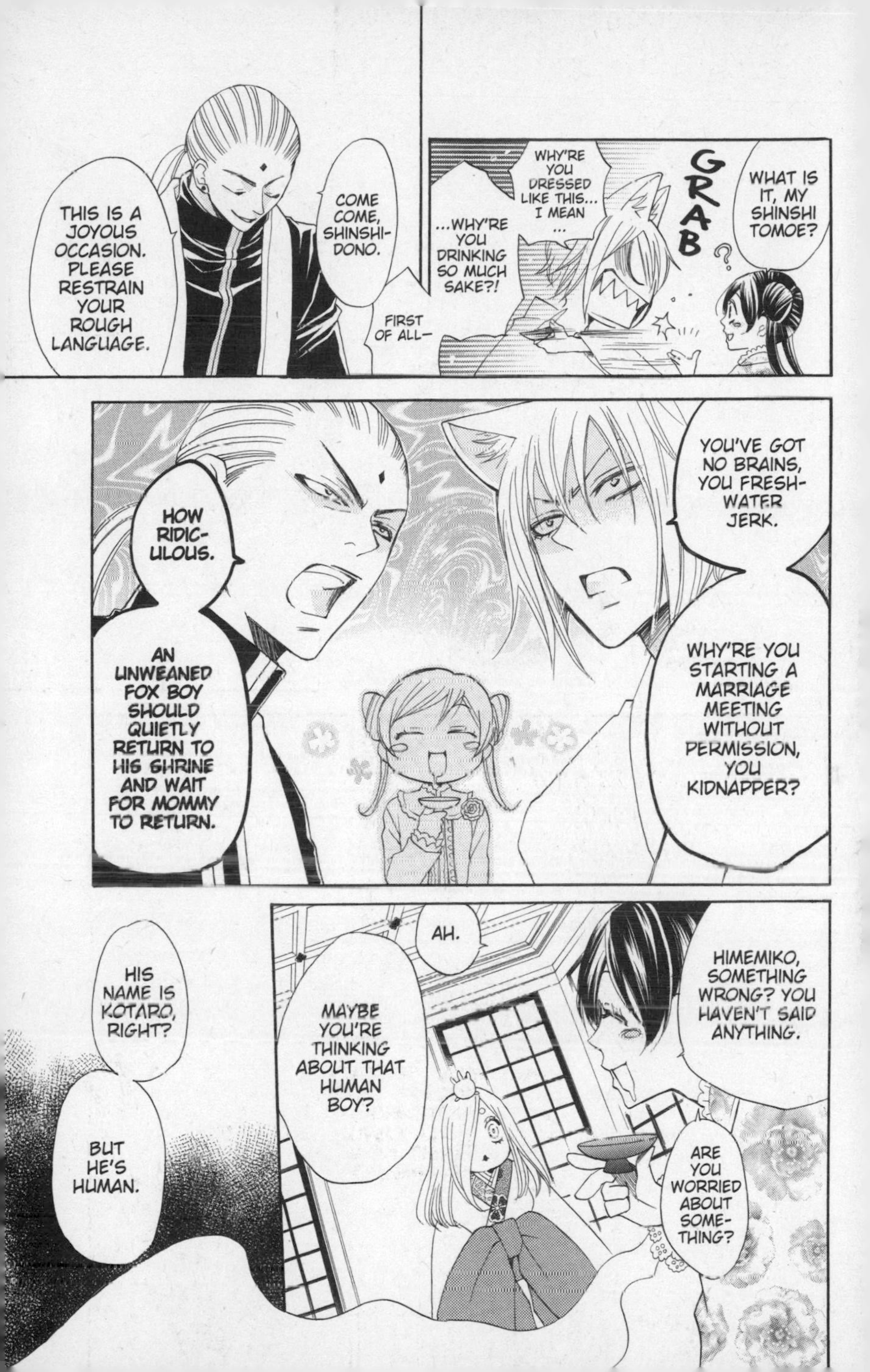
WHAT IS IT, MY SHINSHI TOMOE?
GRAB
WHY'RE YOU DRESSED LIKE THIS... I MEAN ...
...WHY'RE YOU DRINKING SO MUCH SAKE?!
FIRST OF ALL—
COME COME, SHINSHI-DONO.
THIS IS A JOYOUS OCCASION. PLEASE RESTRAIN YOUR ROUGH LANGUAGE.
YOU'VE GOT NO BRAINS, YOU FRESH-WATER JERK.
WHY'RE YOU STARTING A MARRIAGE MEETING WITHOUT PERMISSION, YOU KIDNAPPER?
HOW RIDIC-ULOUS.
AN UNWEANED FOX BOY SHOULD QUIETLY RETURN TO HIS SHRINE AND WAIT FOR MOMMY TO RETURN.
HIMEMIKO, SOMETHING WRONG? YOU HAVEN'T SAID ANYTHING.
ARE YOU WORRIED ABOUT SOME-THING?
AH.
MAYBE YOU'RE THINKING ABOUT THAT HUMAN BOY?
HIS NAME IS KOTARO, RIGHT?
BUT HE'S HUMAN.

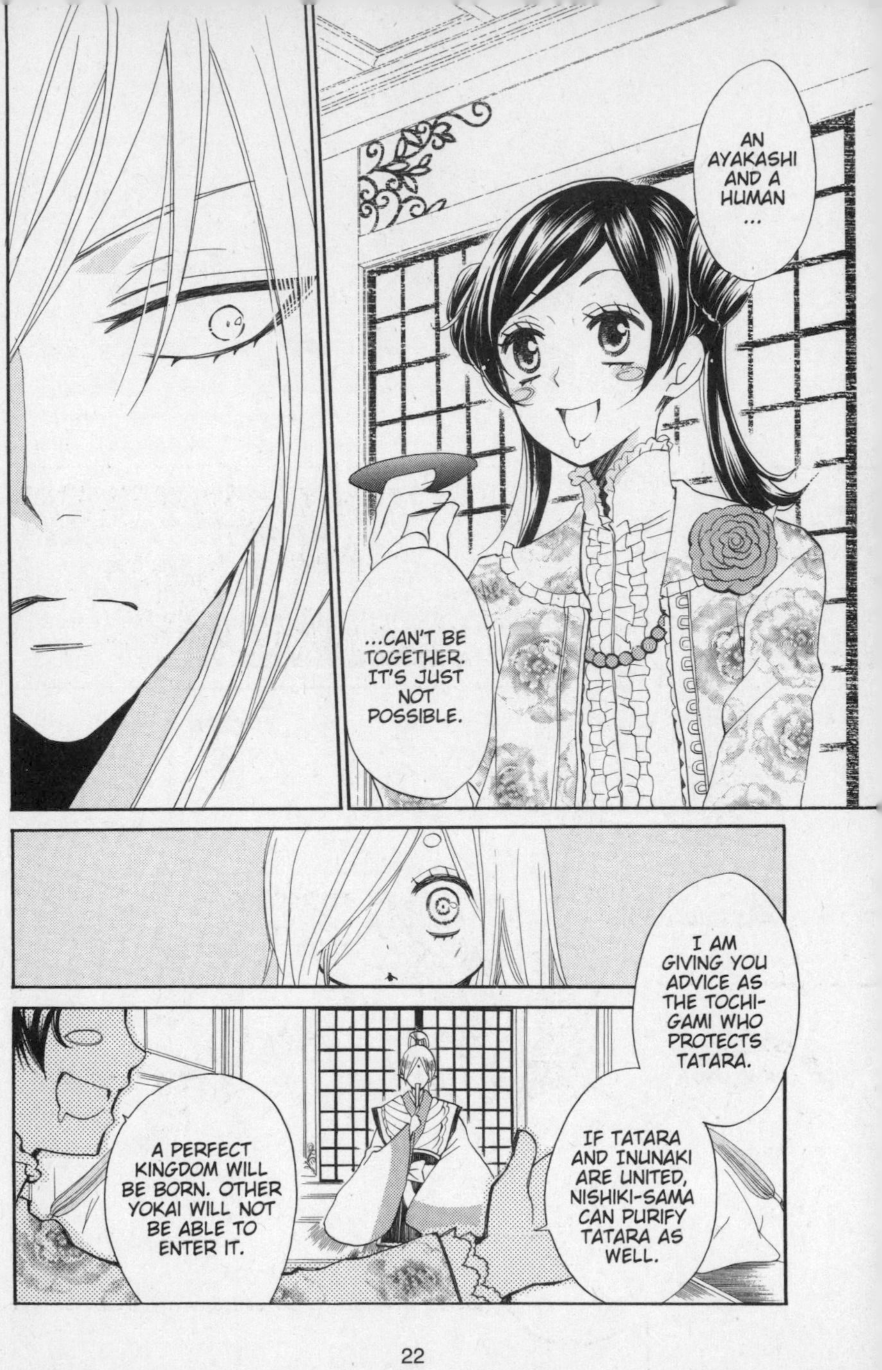
AN AYAKASHI AND A HUMAN ...
...CAN'T BE TOGETHER. IT'S JUST NOT POSSIBLE.
I AM GIVING YOU ADVICE AS THE TOCHI-GAMI WHO PROTECTS TATARA.
IF TATARA AND INUNAKI ARE UNITED, NISHIKI-SAMA CAN PURIFY TATARA AS WELL.
A PERFECT KINGDOM WILL BE BORN. OTHER YOKAI WILL NOT BE ABLE TO ENTER IT.

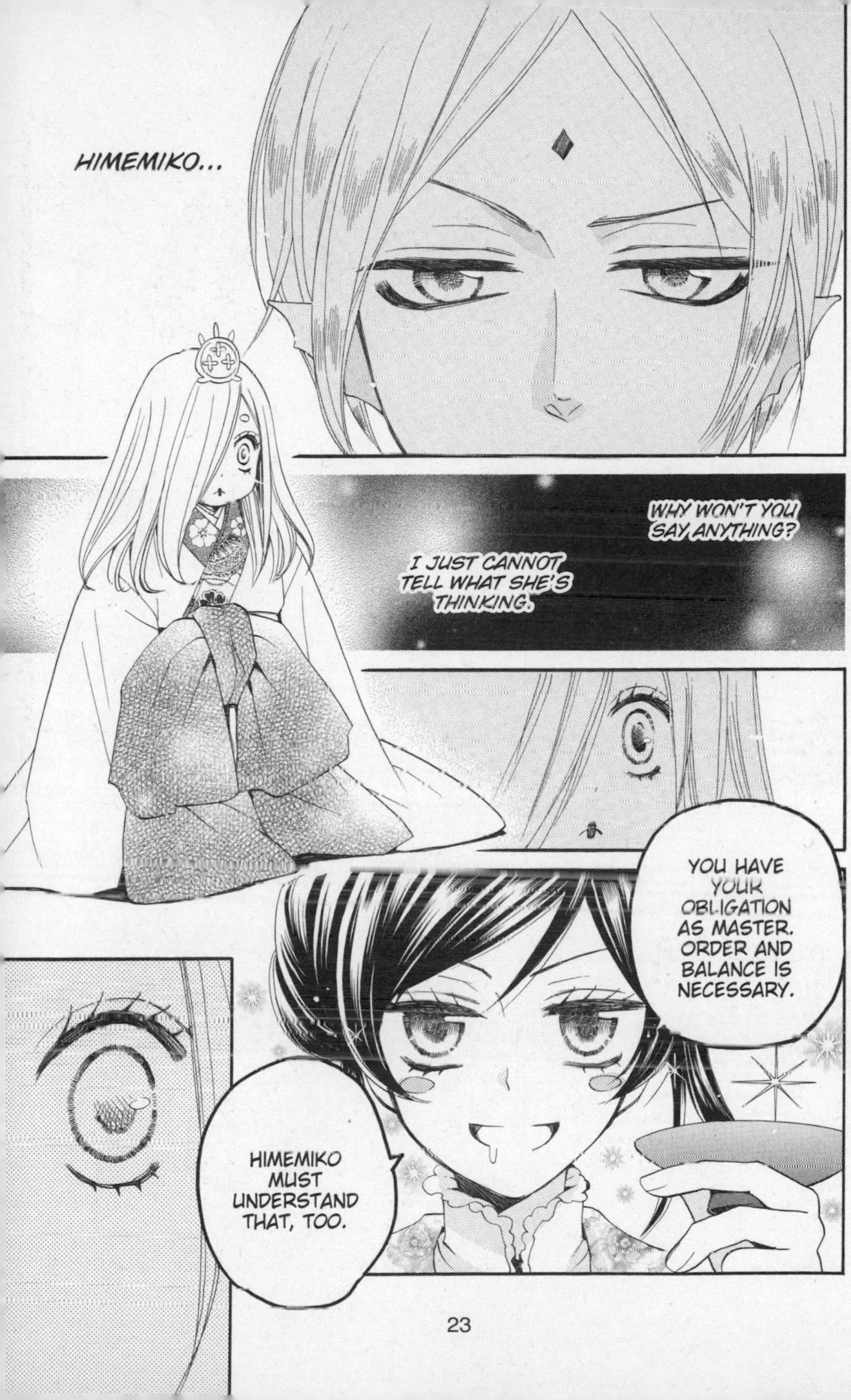
HIMEMIKO...
WHY WON'T YOU SAY ANYTHING?
I JUST CANNOT TELL WHAT SHE'S THINKING.
YOU HAVE YOUR OBLIGATION AS MASTER. ORDER AND BALANCE IS NECESSARY.
HIMEMIKO MUST UNDERSTAND THAT, TOO.

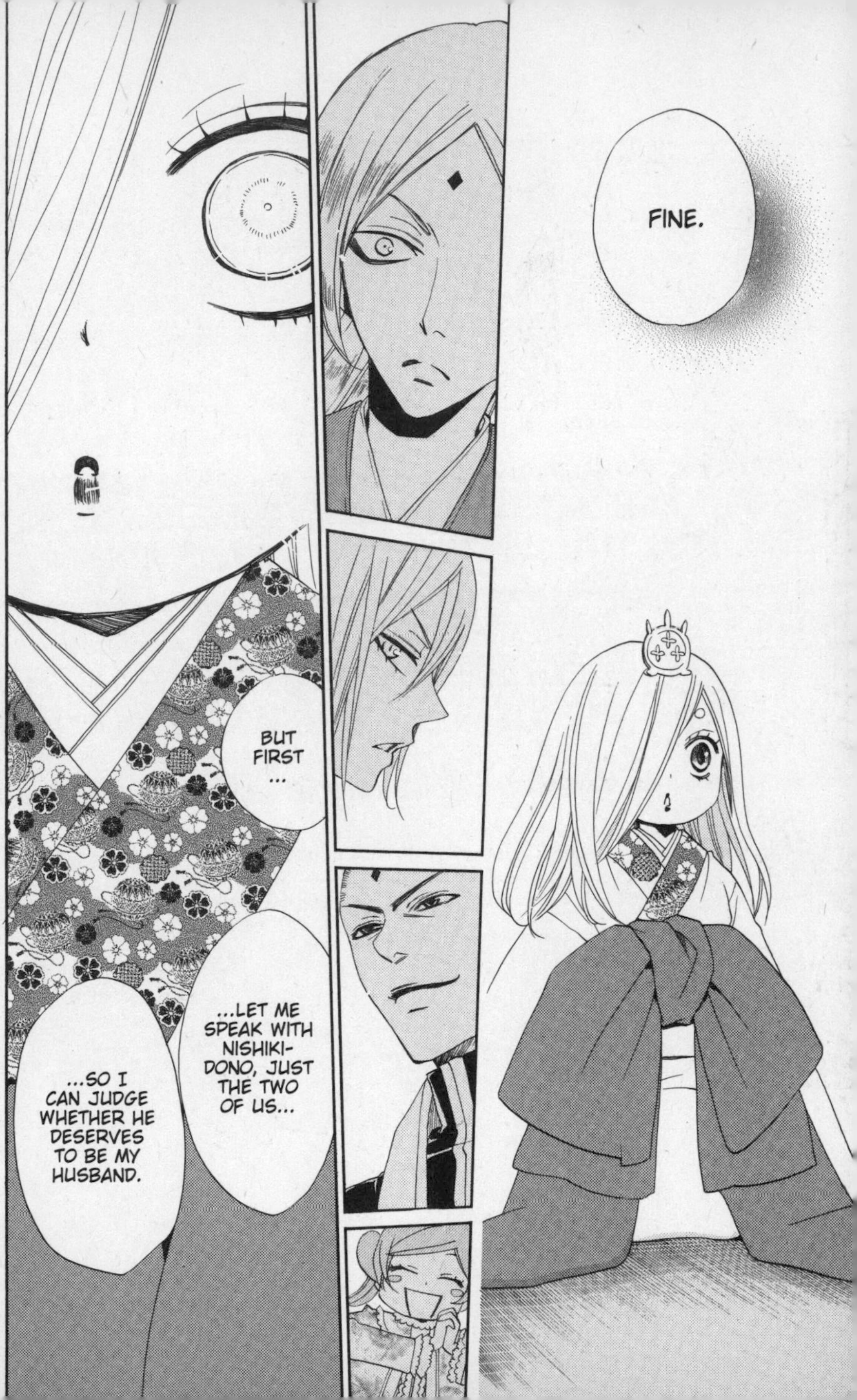
FINE.
BUT FIRST ...
...LET ME SPEAK WITH NISHIKI-DONO, JUST THE TWO OF US...
...SO I CAN JUDGE WHETHER HE DESERVES TO BE MY HUSBAND.

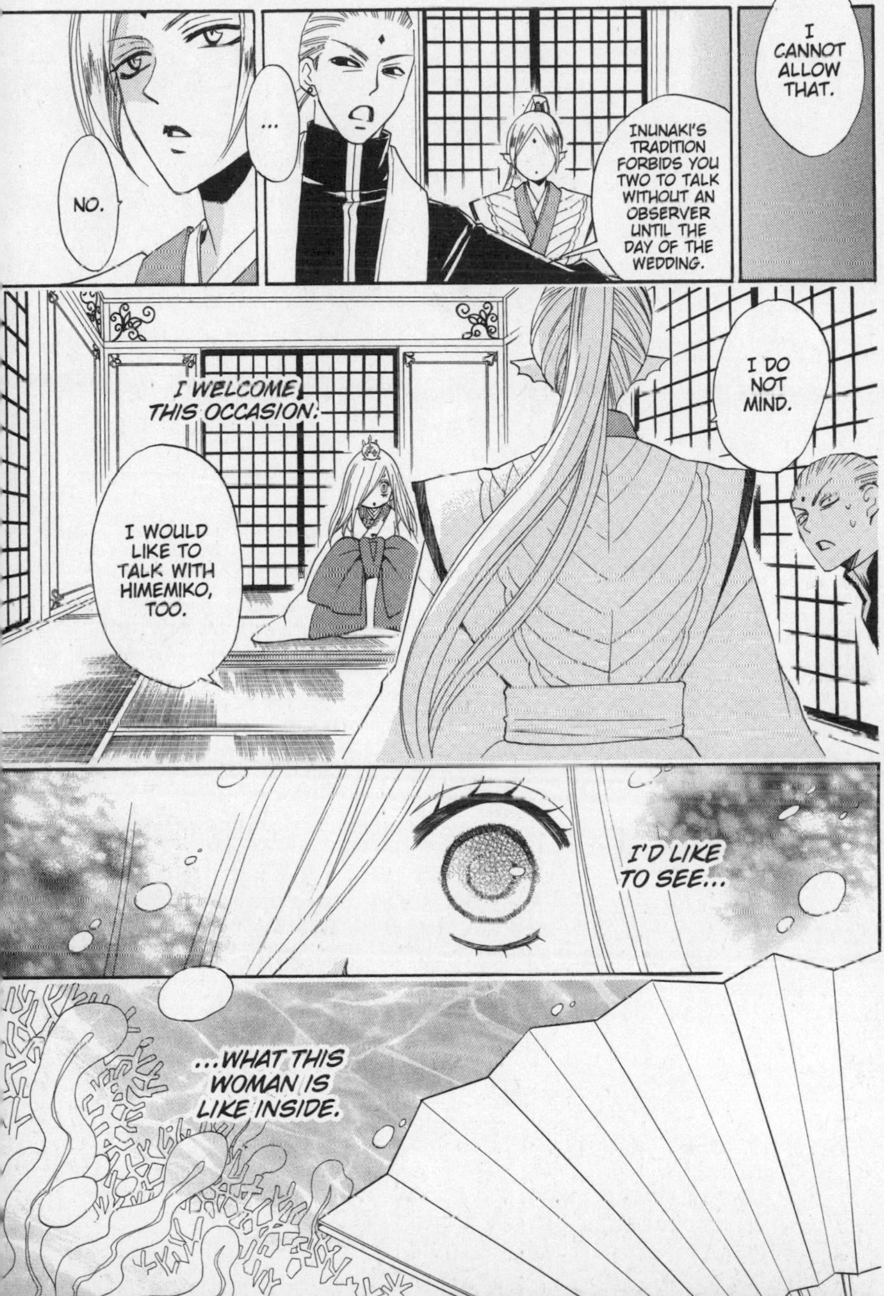
I CANNOT ALLOW THAT.
INUNAKI'S TRADITION FORBIDS YOU TWO TO TALK WITHOUT AN OBSERVER UNTIL THE DAY OF THE WEDDING.
...
NO.
I DO NOT MIND.
I WELCOME THIS OCCASION:
I WOULD LIKE TO TALK WITH HIMEMIKO, TOO.
I'D LIKE TO SEE...
...WHAT THIS WOMAN IS LIKE INSIDE.

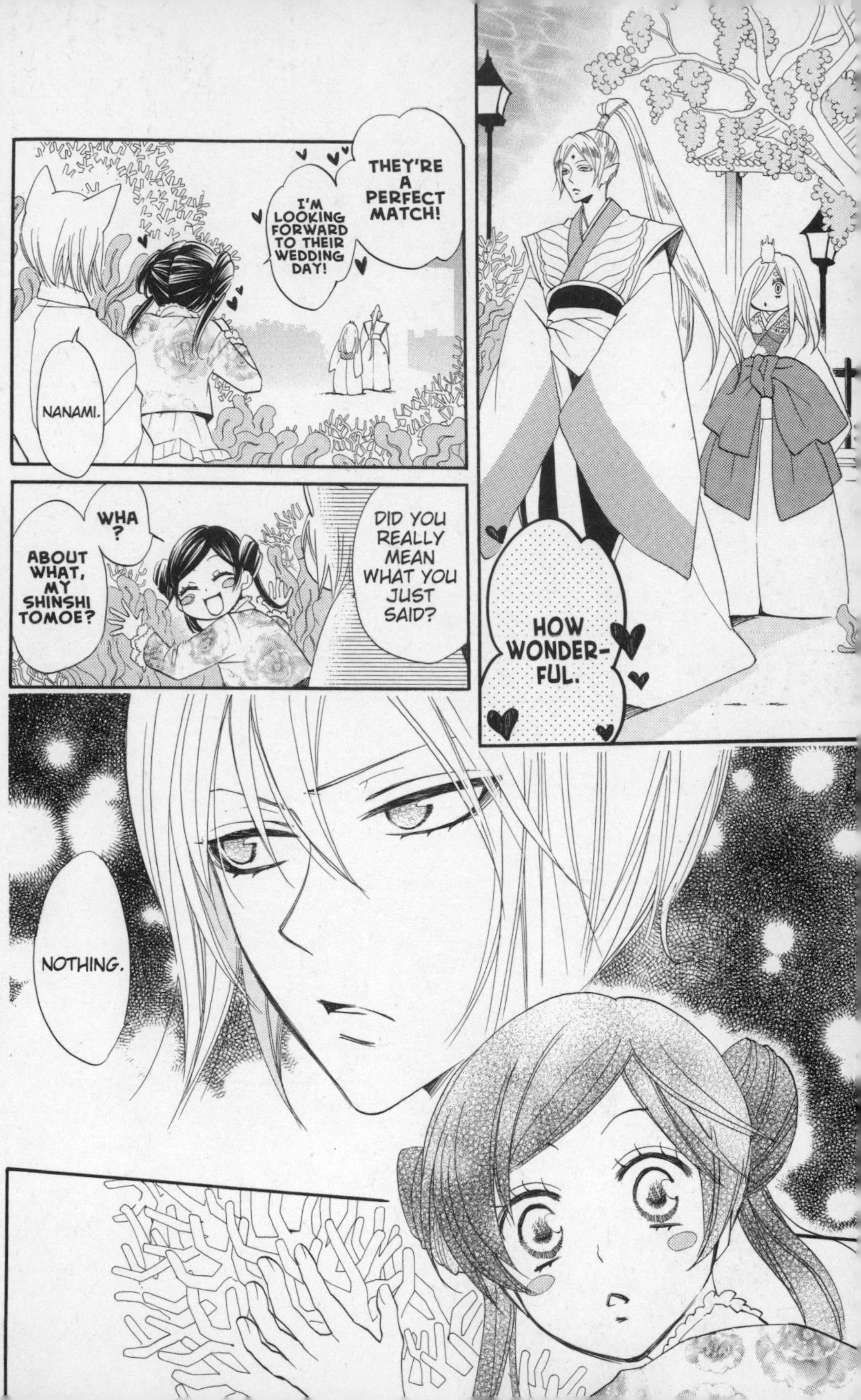
HOW WONDERFUL.
THEY'RE A PERFECT MATCH!
I'M LOOKING FORWARD TO THEIR WEDDING DAY!
NANAMI.
DID YOU REALLY MEAN WHAT YOU JUST SAID?
WHA?
ABOUT WHAT, MY SHINSHI TOMOE?
NOTHING.

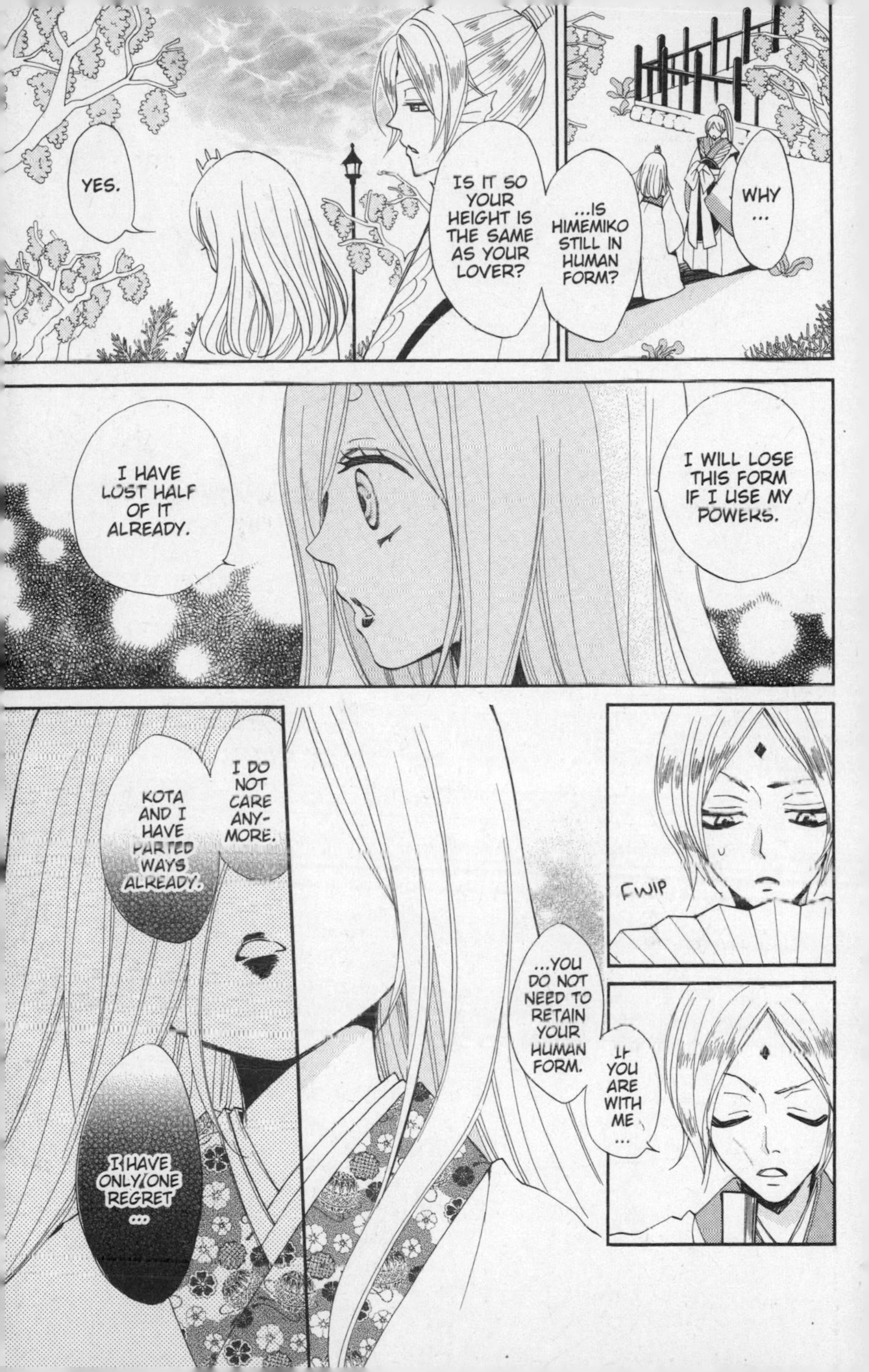
WHY ...
...IS HIMEMIKO STILL IN HUMAN FORM?
IS IT SO YOUR HEIGHT IS THE SAME AS YOUR LOVER?
YES.
I WILL LOSE THIS FORM IF I USE MY POWERS.
I HAVE LOST HALF OF IT ALREADY.
FWIP
IF YOU ARE WITH ME ...
...YOU DO NOT NEED TO RETAIN YOUR HUMAN FORM.
I DO NOT CARE ANYMORE.
KOTA AND I HAVE PARTED WAYS ALREADY.
I HAVE ONLY ONE REGRET ...

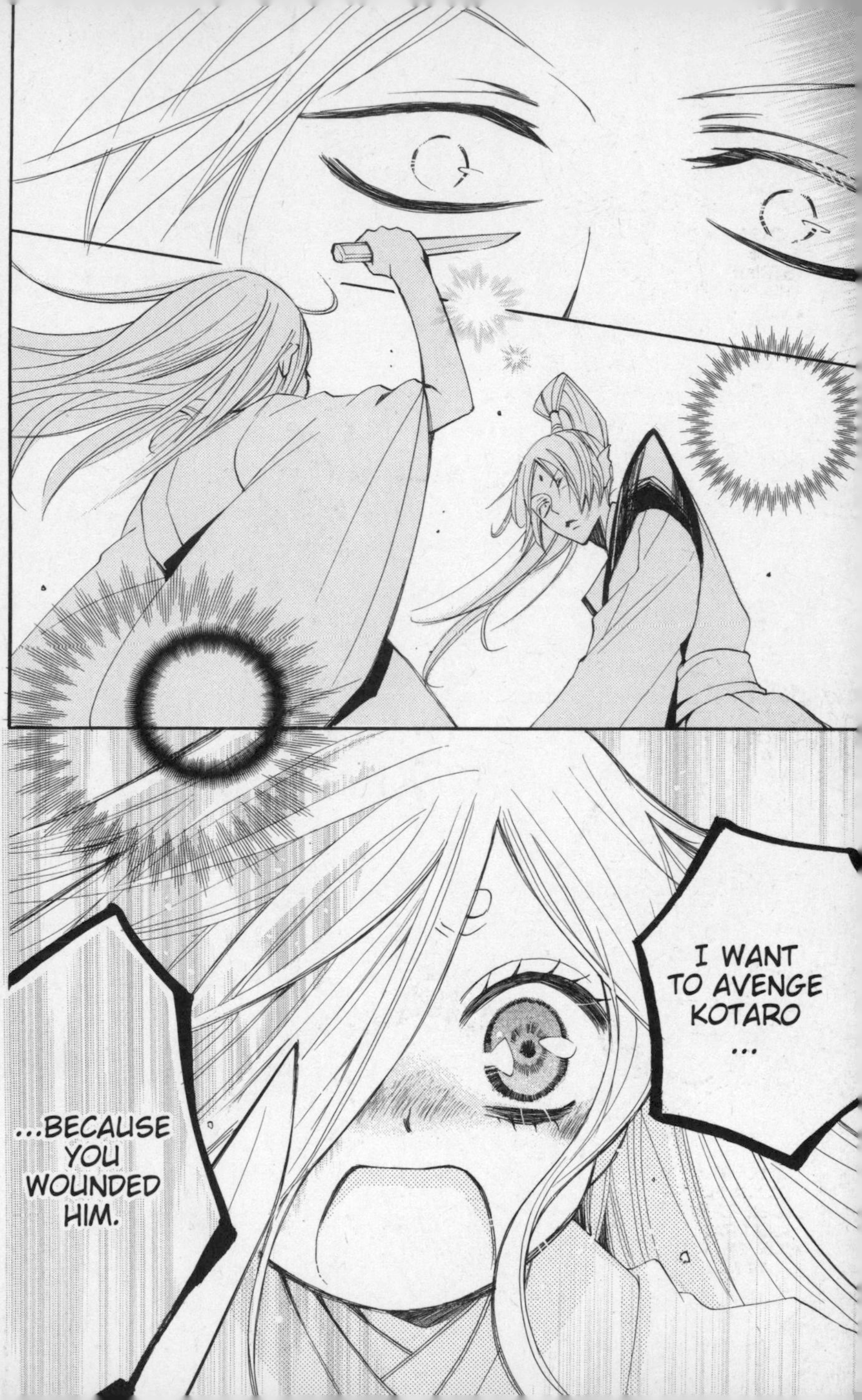
I WANT TO AVENGE KOTARO ...
...BECAUSE YOU WOUNDED HIM.

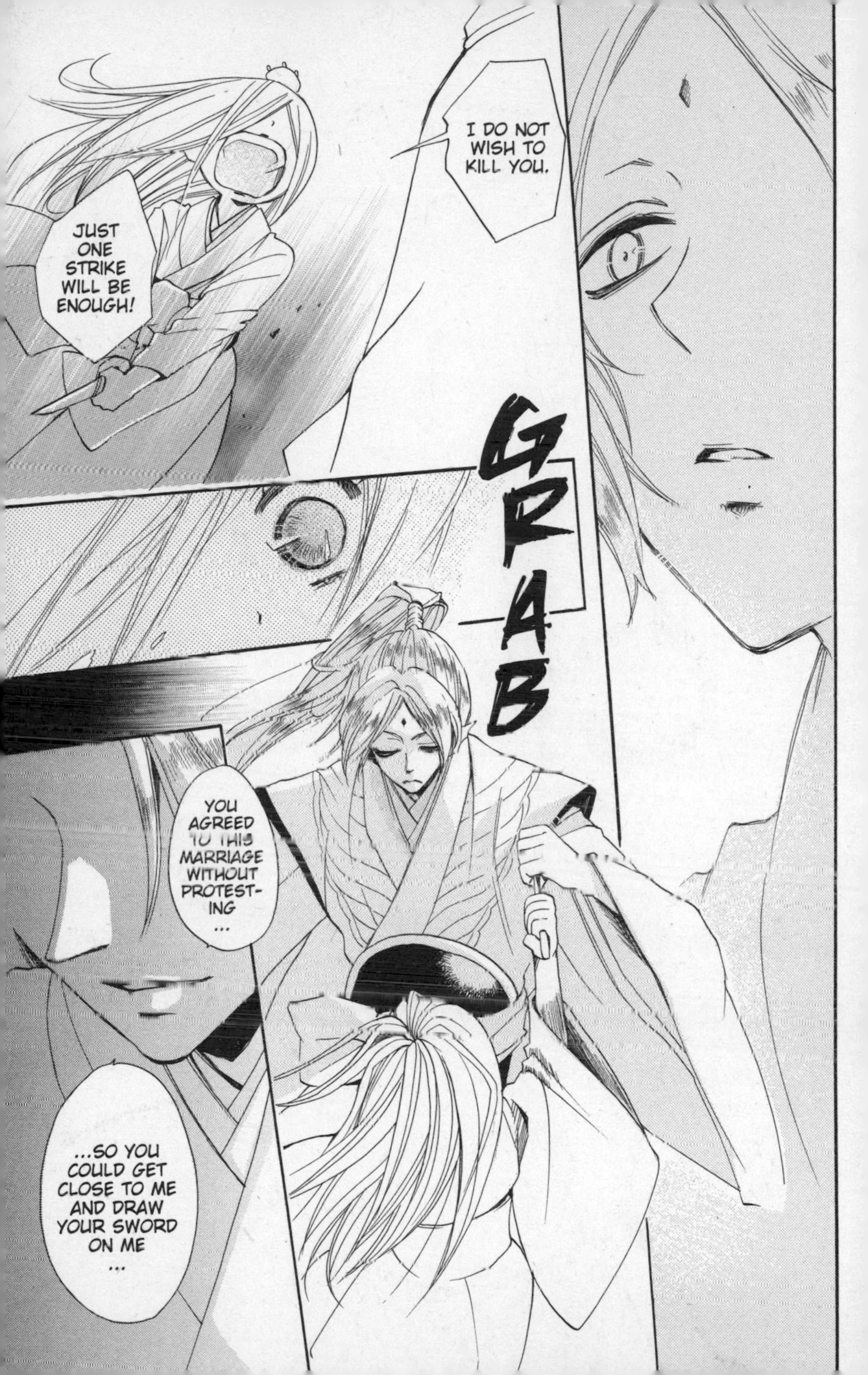
I DO NOT WISH TO KILL YOU.
JUST ONE STRIKE WILL BE ENOUGH!
GRAB
YOU AGREED TO THIS MARRIAGE WITHOUT PROTEST-ING...
...SO YOU COULD GET CLOSE TO ME AND DRAW YOUR SWORD ON ME...

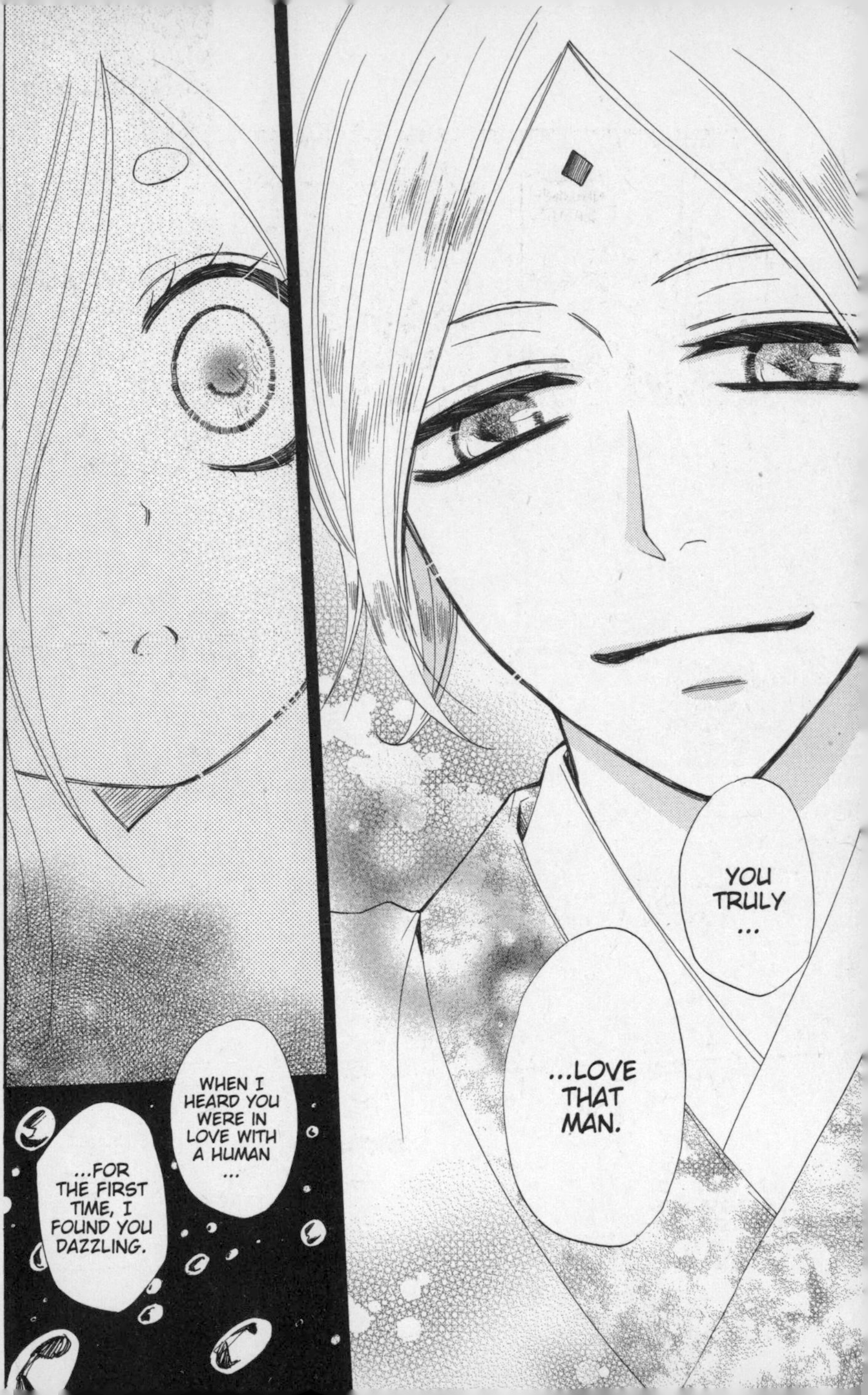
YOU TRULY ...
...LOVE THAT MAN.
WHEN I HEARD YOU WERE IN LOVE WITH A HUMAN ...
...FOR THE FIRST TIME, I FOUND YOU DAZZLING.

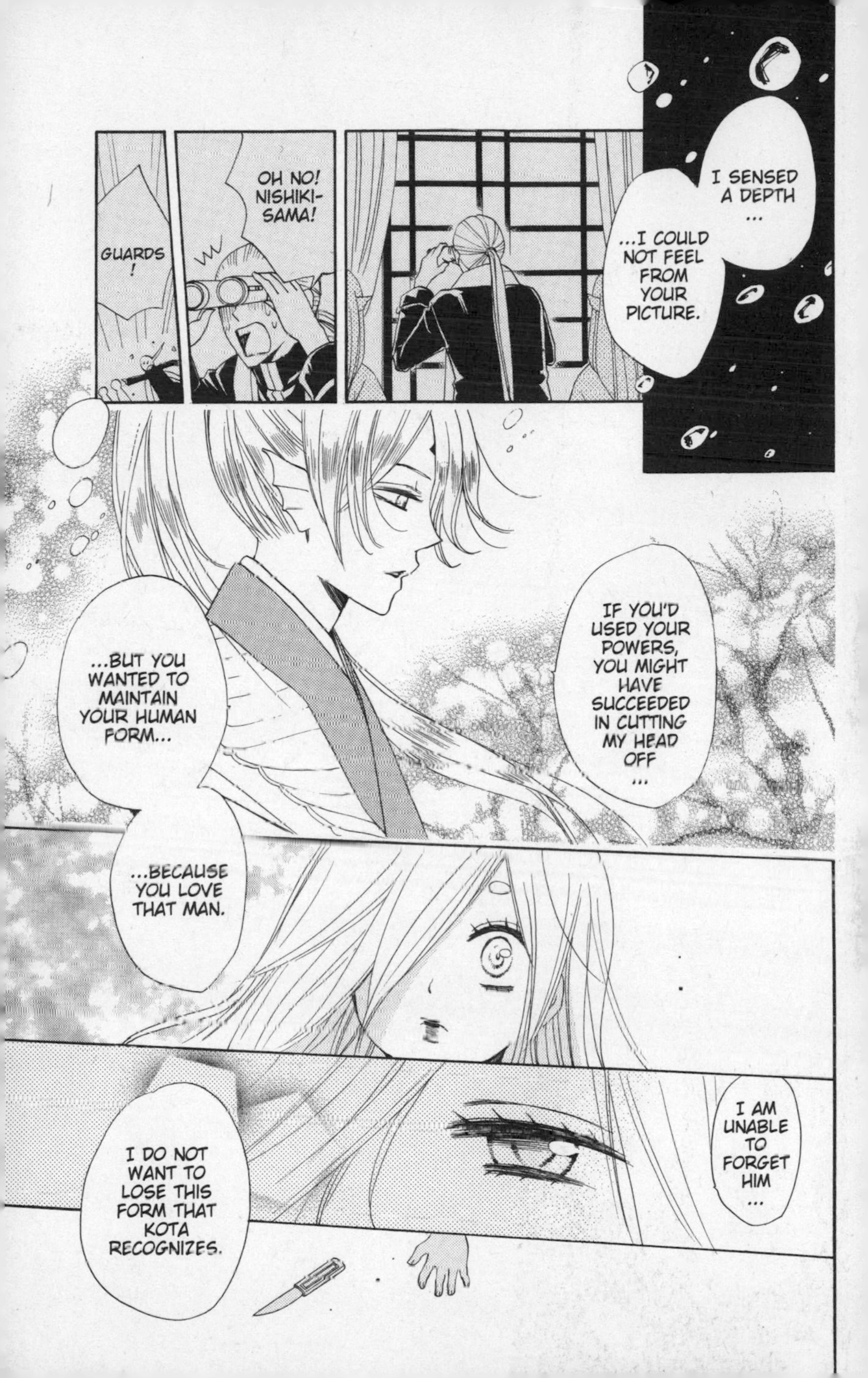
I SENSED A DEPTH ...
...I COULD NOT FEEL FROM YOUR PICTURE.
OH NO! NISHIKI-SAMA!
GUARDS !
IF YOU'D USED YOUR POWERS, YOU MIGHT HAVE SUCCEEDED IN CUTTING MY HEAD OFF ...
...BUT YOU WANTED TO MAINTAIN YOUR HUMAN FORM...
...BECAUSE YOU LOVE THAT MAN.
I AM UNABLE TO FORGET HIM ...
I DO NOT WANT TO LOSE THIS FORM THAT KOTA RECOGNIZES.

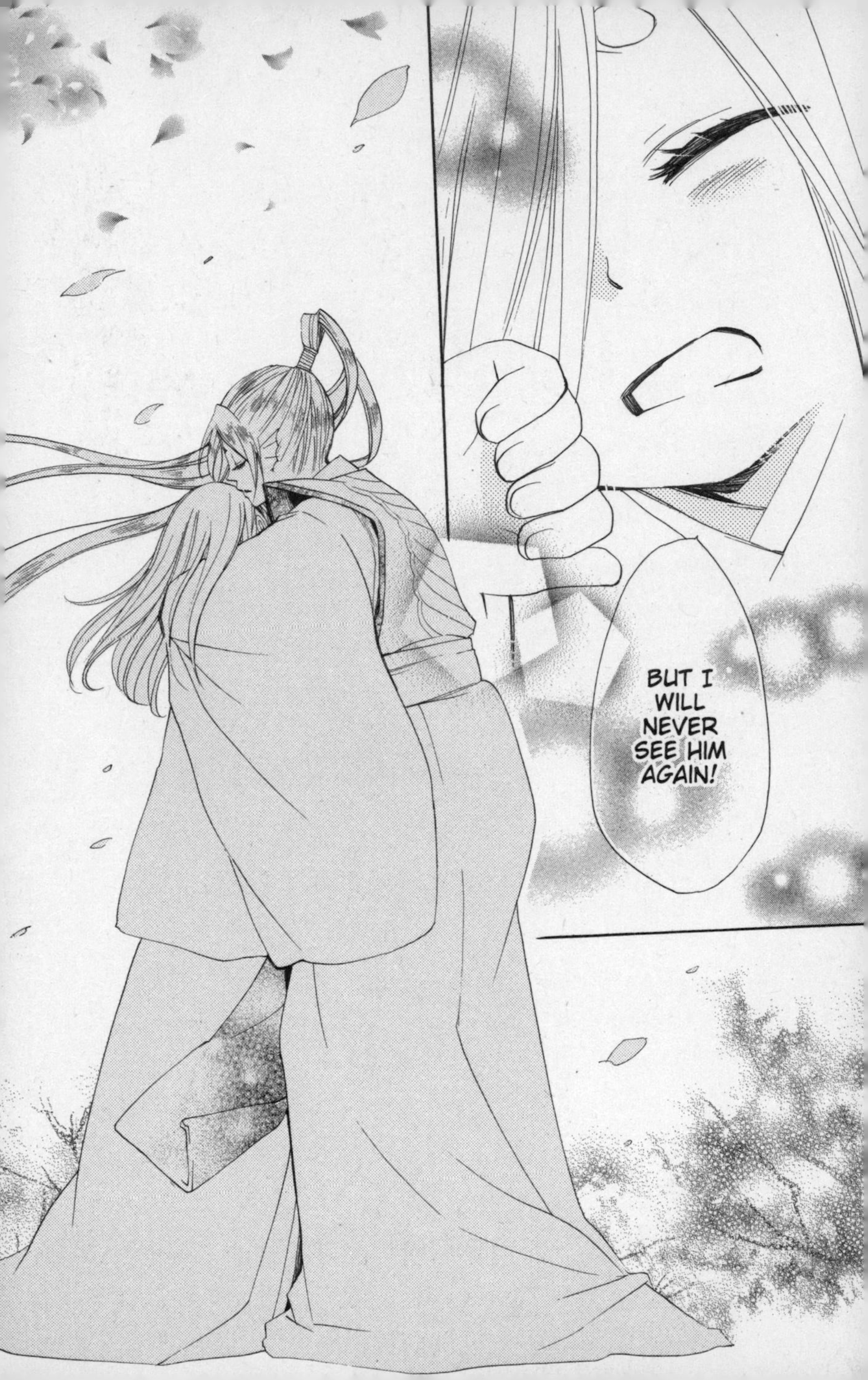
BUT I WILL NEVER SEE HIM AGAIN!

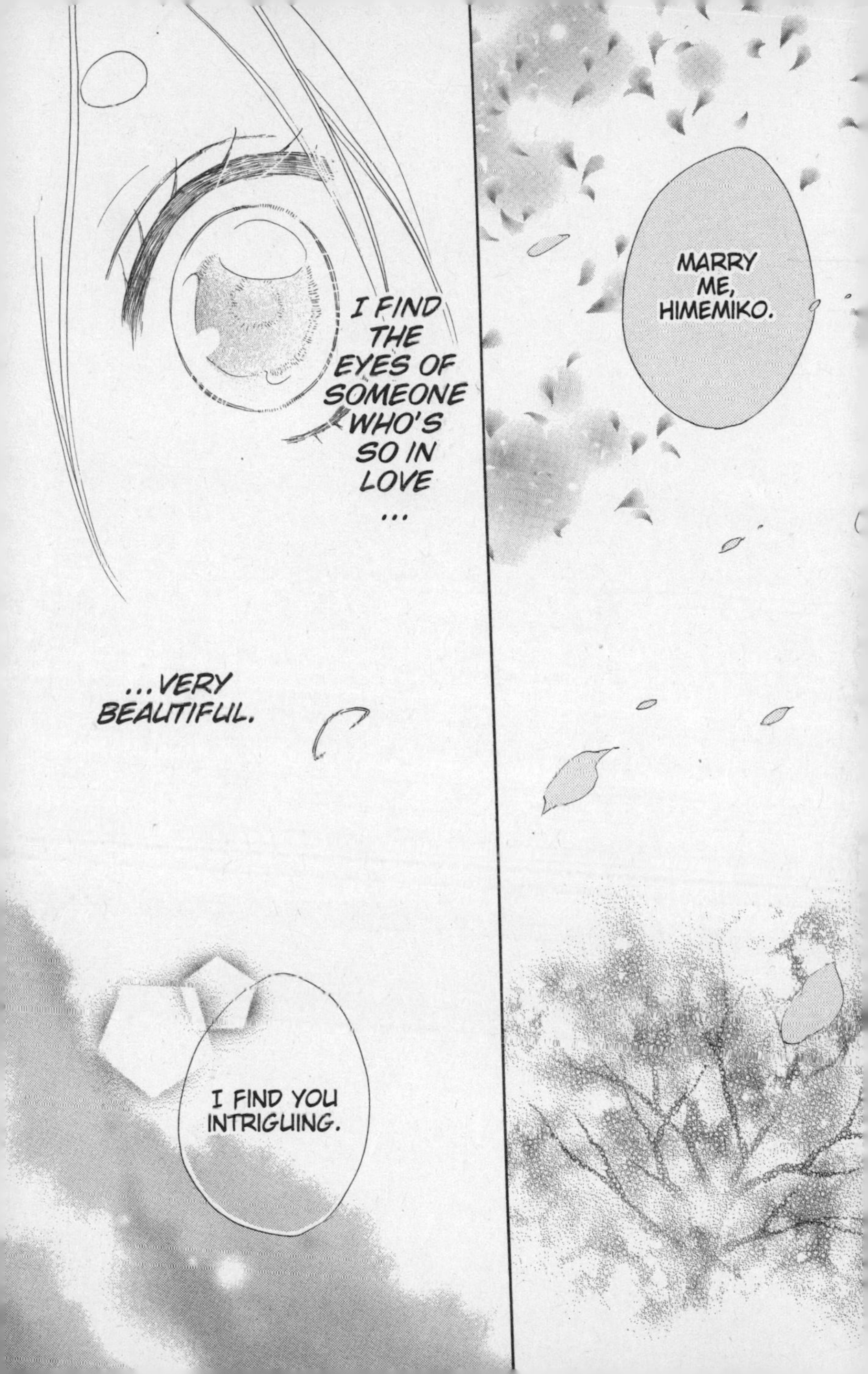
MARRY ME, HIMEMIKO.
I FIND THE EYES OF SOMEONE WHO'S SO IN LOVE...
...VERY BEAUTIFUL.
I FIND YOU INTRIGUING.

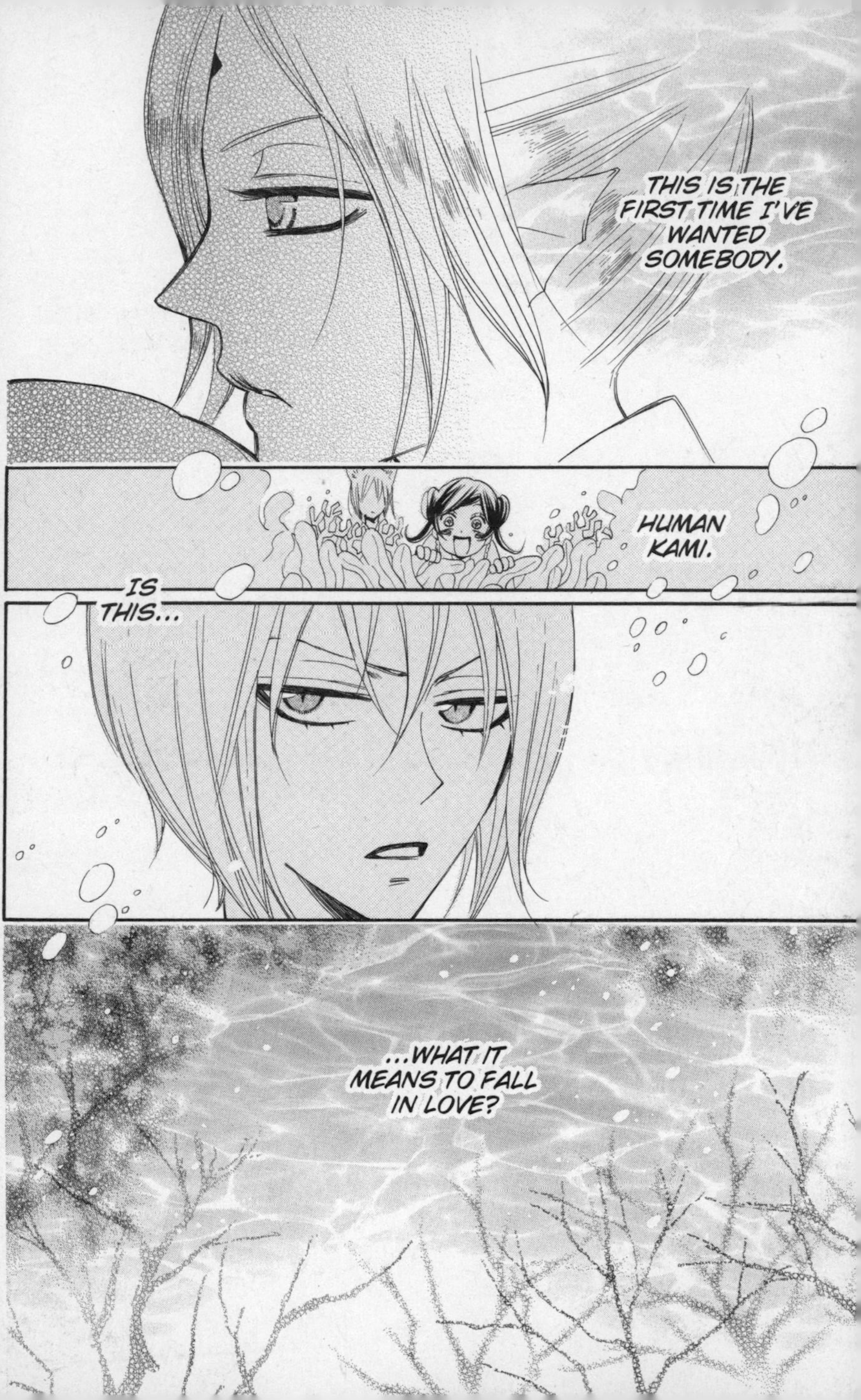
THIS IS THE FIRST TIME I'VE WANTED SOMEBODY.
HUMAN KAMI.
IS THIS...
...WHAT IT MEANS TO FALL IN LOVE?

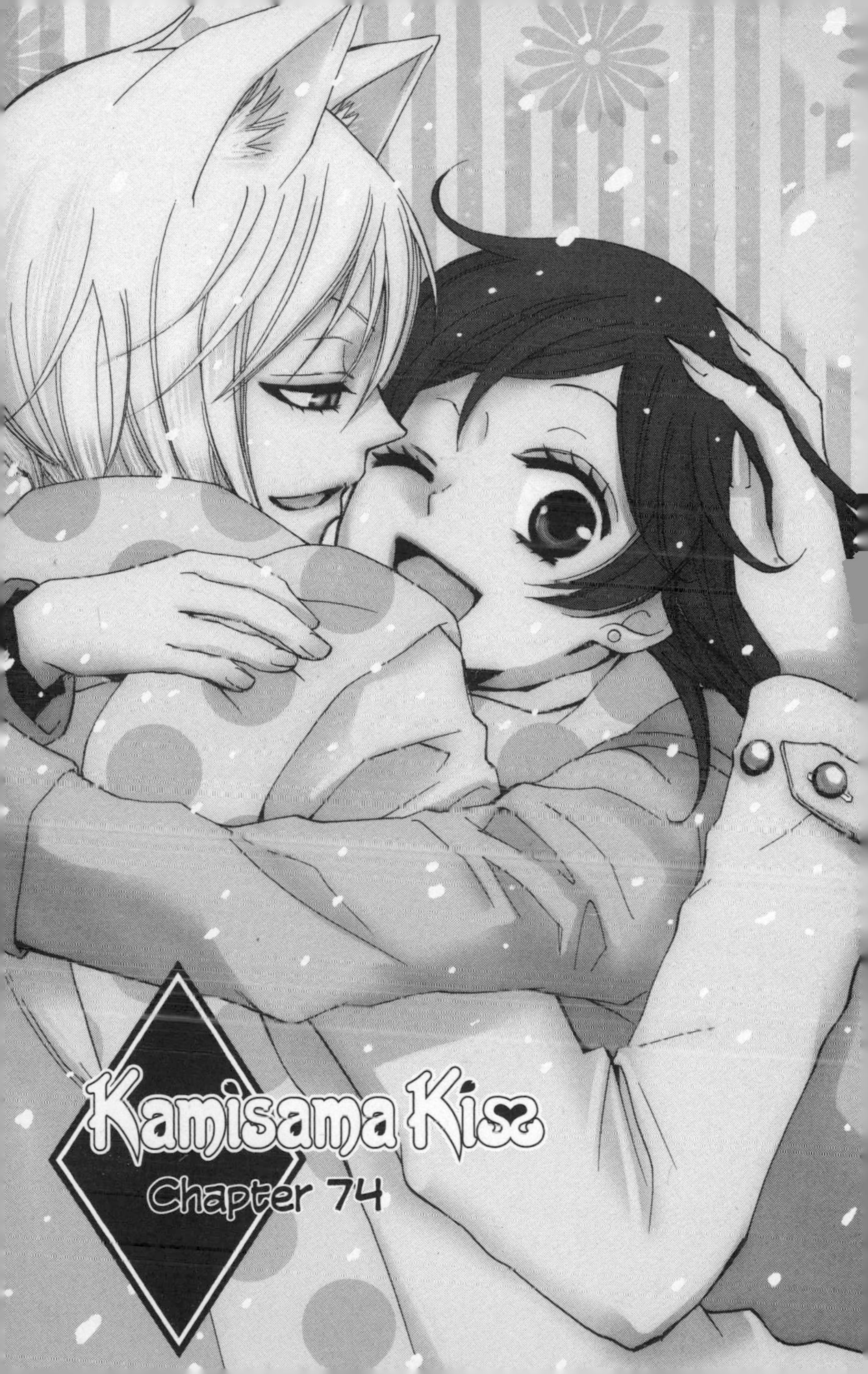
Kamisama Kiss
Chapter 74

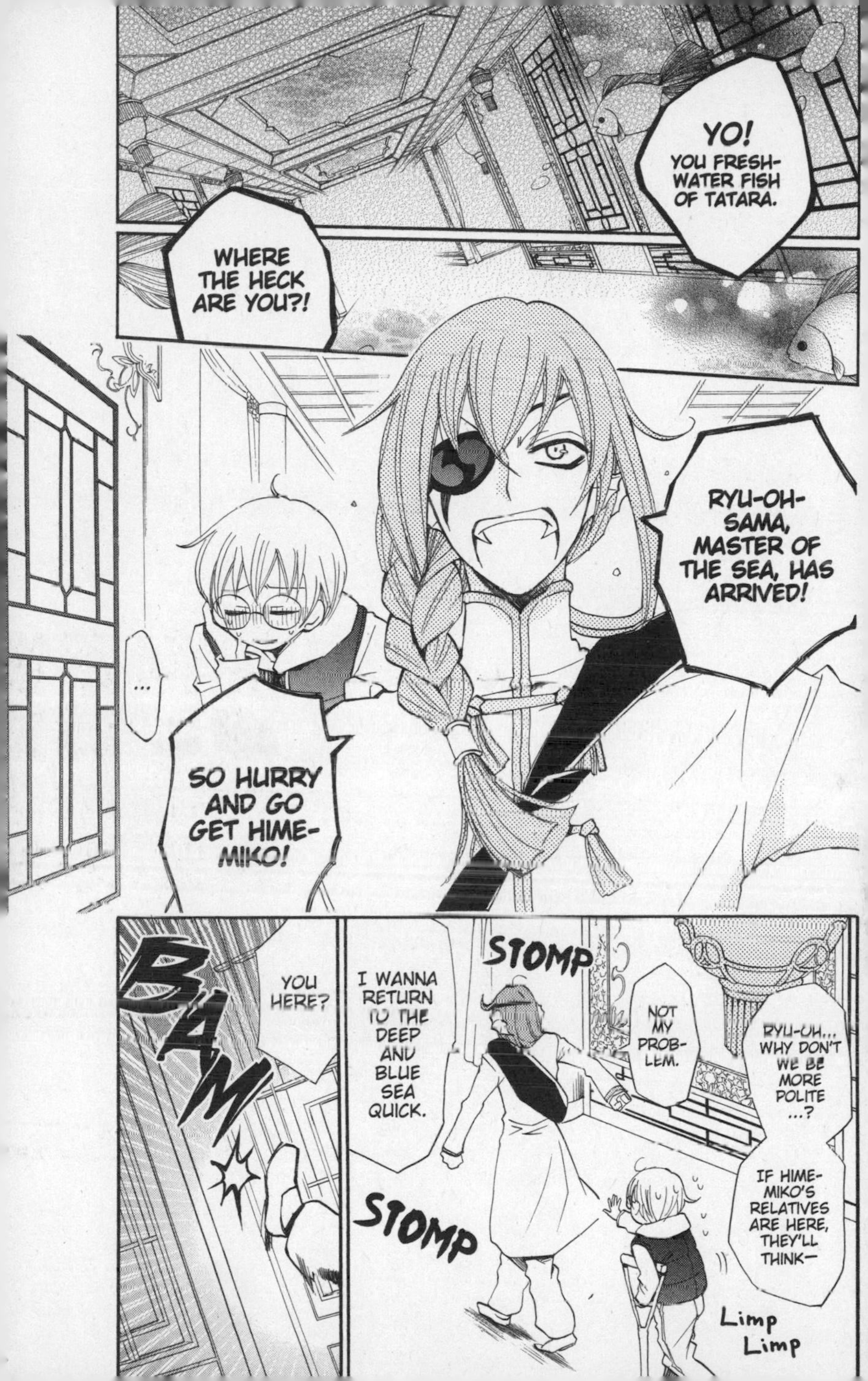
YO!
YOU FRESH-WATER FISH OF TATARA.
WHERE THE HECK ARE YOU?!
RYU-OH-SAMA, MASTER OF THE SEA, HAS ARRIVED!
...
SO HURRY AND GO GET HIME-MIKO!
STOMP
RYU-OH... WHY DON'T WE BE MORE POLITE ...?
NOT MY PROB-LEM.
I WANNA RETURN TO THE DEEP AND BLUE SEA QUICK.
IF HIME-MIKO'S RELATIVES ARE HERE, THEY'LL THINK—
STOMP
Limp Limp
YOU HERE?
BAM

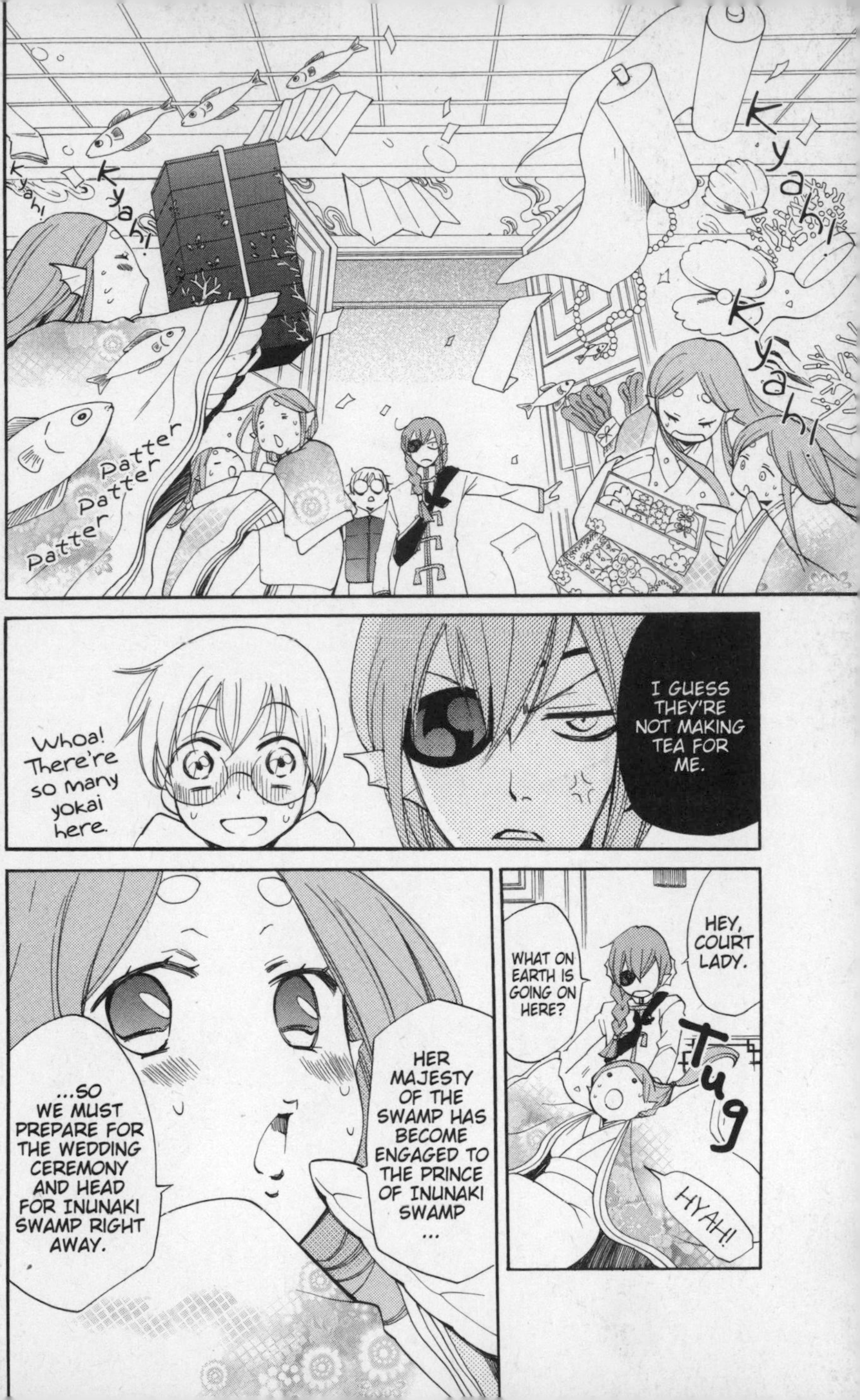
Kyah! Kyah!
Kyah! Kyah!
Patter Patter Patter
I GUESS THEY'RE NOT MAKING TEA FOR ME.
Whoa! There're so many yokai here.
HEY, COURT LADY.
WHAT ON EARTH IS GOING ON HERE?
Tug
HYAH!
HER MAJESTY OF THE SWAMP HAS BECOME ENGAGED TO THE PRINCE OF INUNAKI SWAMP ...
...SO WE MUST PREPARE FOR THE WEDDING CEREMONY AND HEAD FOR INUNAKI SWAMP RIGHT AWAY.

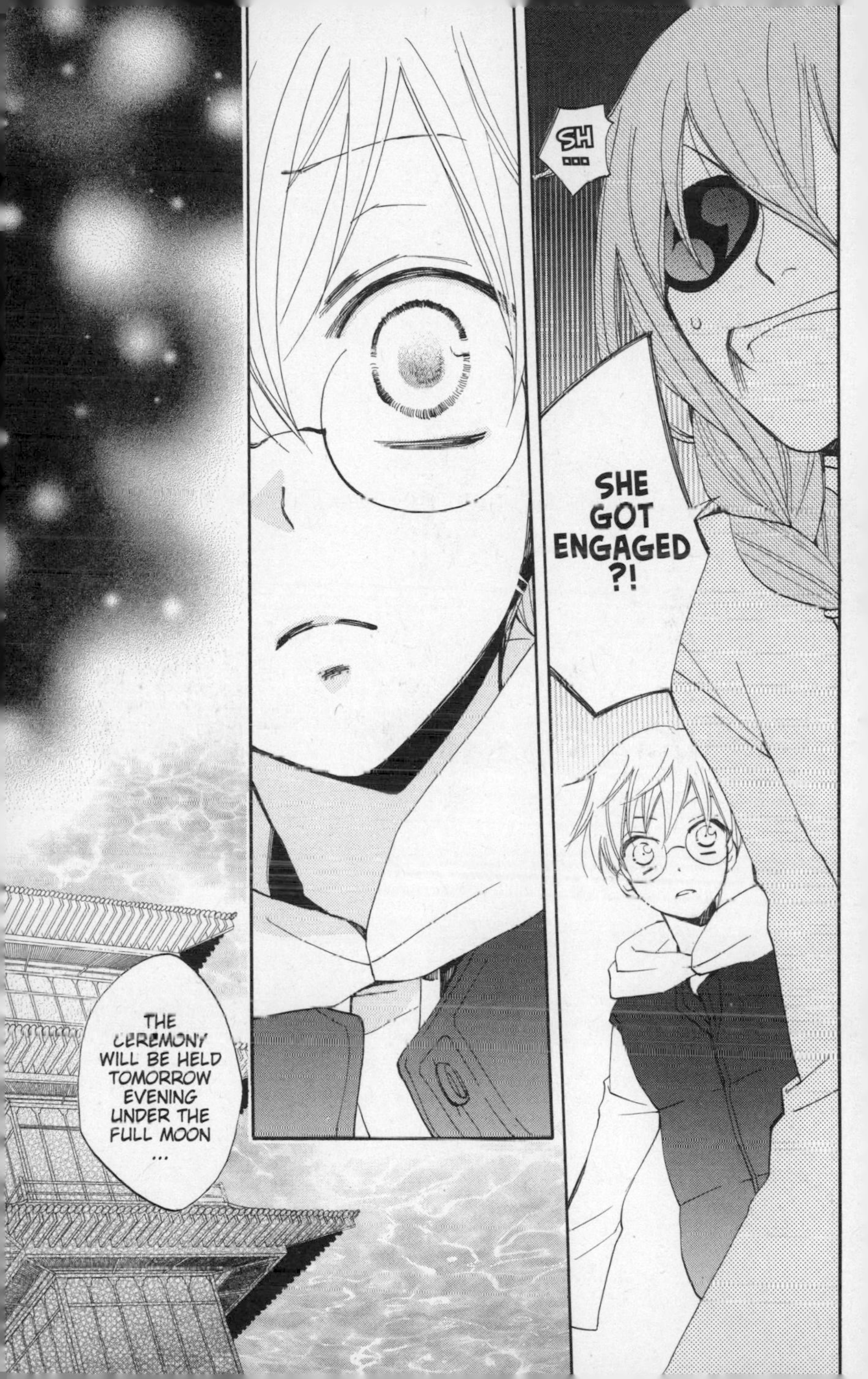
SH ...
SHE GOT ENGAGED ?!
THE CEREMONY WILL BE HELD TOMORROW EVENING UNDER THE FULL MOON ...

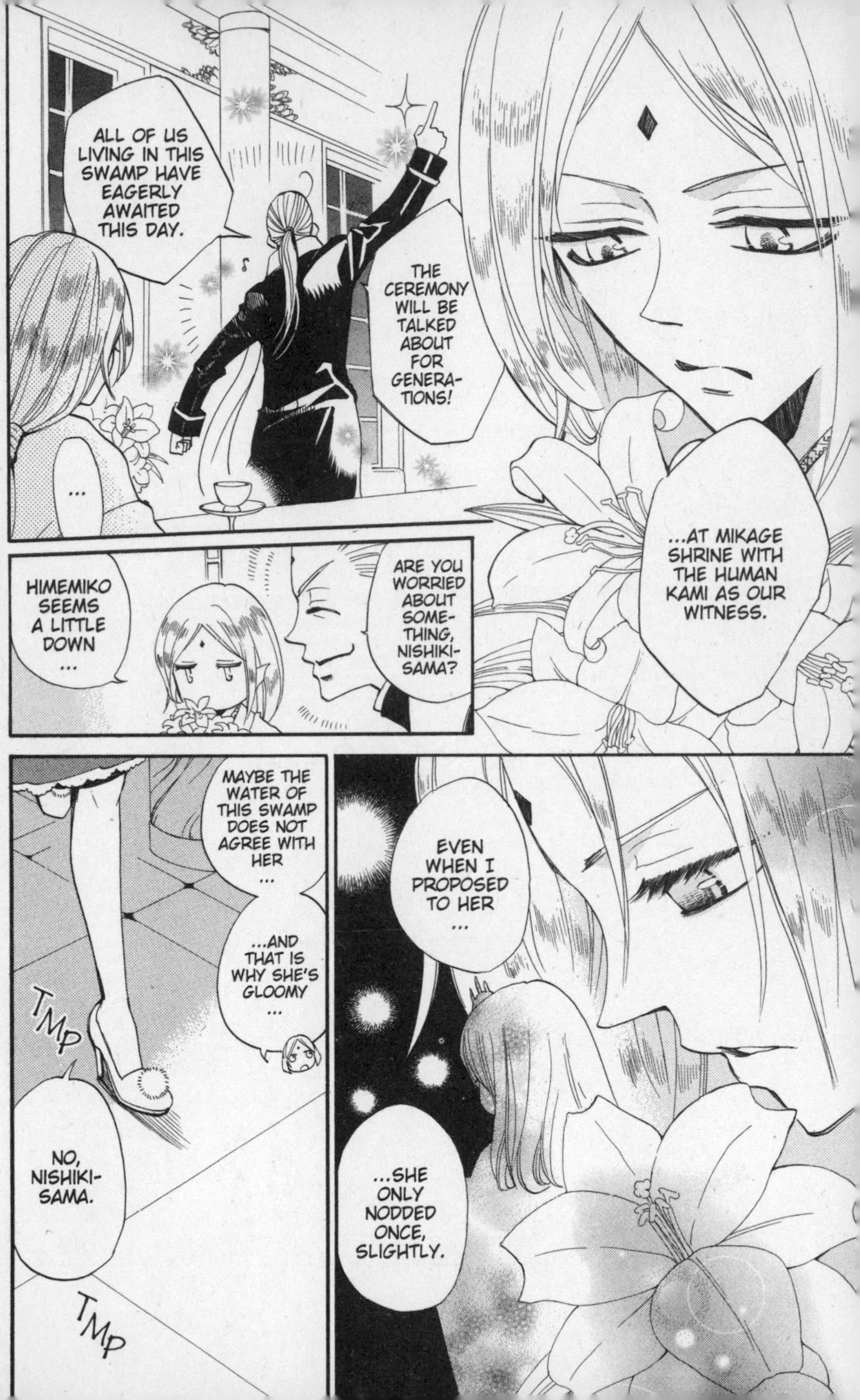

...AT MIKAGE SHRINE WITH THE HUMAN KAMI AS OUR WITNESS.
ALL OF US LIVING IN THIS SWAMP HAVE EAGERLY AWAITED THIS DAY.
THE CEREMONY WILL BE TALKED ABOUT FOR GENERATIONS!
...
ARE YOU WORRIED ABOUT SOME-THING, NISHIKI-SAMA?
HIMEMIKO SEEMS A LITTLE DOWN ...
EVEN WHEN I PROPOSED TO HER ...
...SHE ONLY NODDED ONCE, SLIGHTLY.
MAYBE THE WATER OF THIS SWAMP DOES NOT AGREE WITH HER ...
...AND THAT IS WHY SHE'S GLOOMY ...
TMP
NO, NISHIKI-SAMA.
TMP

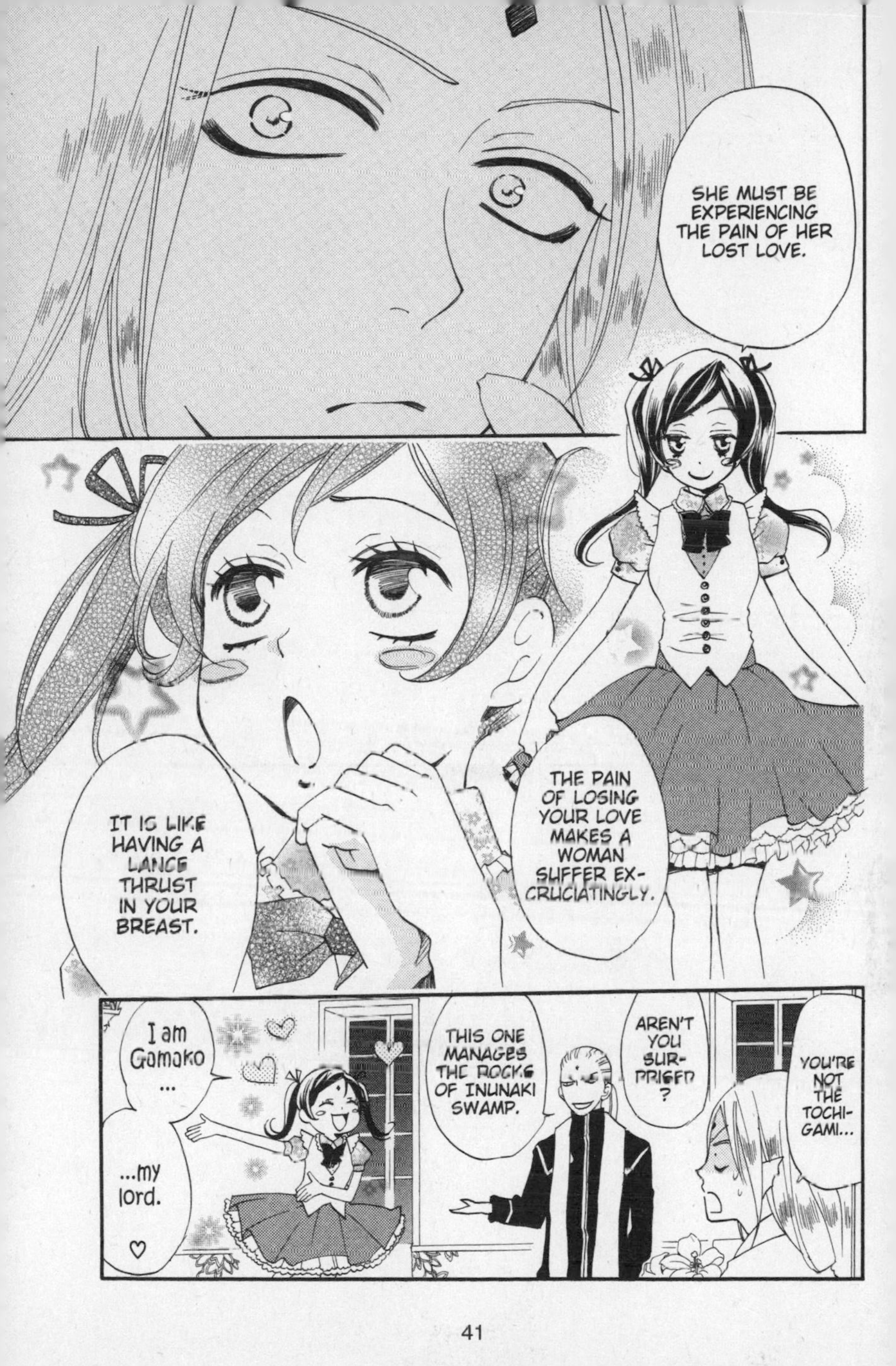
SHE MUST BE EXPERIENCING THE PAIN OF HER LOST LOVE.
THE PAIN OF LOSING YOUR LOVE MAKES A WOMAN SUFFER EX-CRUCIATINGLY.
IT IS LIKE HAVING A LANCE THRUST IN YOUR BREAST.
YOU'RE NOT THE TOCHI-GAMI...
AREN'T YOU SUR-PRISED?
THIS ONE MANAGES THE ROCKS OF INUNAKI SWAMP.
I am Gamako ...
...my lord. ♡

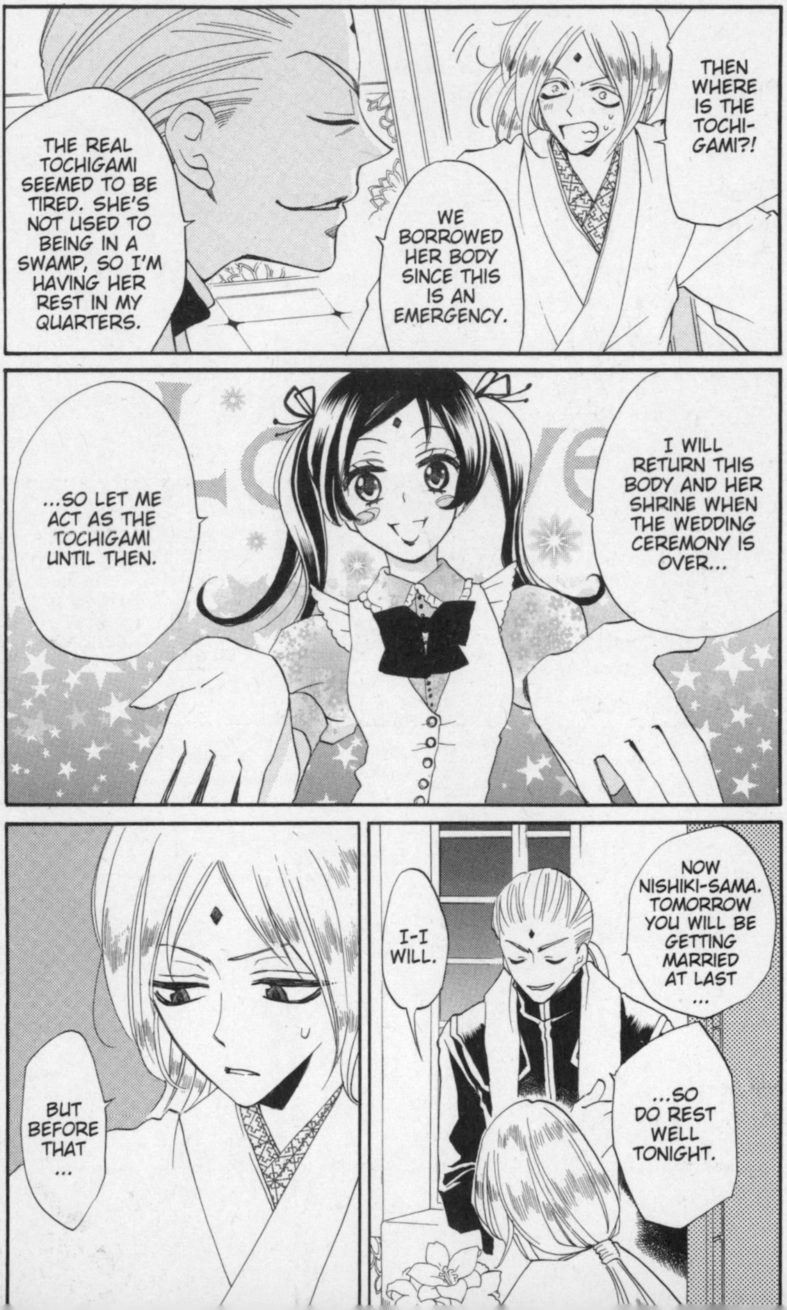
THEN WHERE IS THE TOCHIGAMI?!
WE BORROWED HER BODY SINCE THIS IS AN EMERGENCY.
THE REAL TOCHIGAMI SEEMED TO BE TIRED. SHE'S NOT USED TO BEING IN A SWAMP, SO I'M HAVING HER REST IN MY QUARTERS.
I WILL RETURN THIS BODY AND HER SHRINE WHEN THE WEDDING CEREMONY IS OVER...
...SO LET ME ACT AS THE TOCHIGAMI UNTIL THEN.
NOW NISHIKI-SAMA. TOMORROW YOU WILL BE GETTING MARRIED AT LAST ...
I-I WILL.
...SO DO REST WELL TONIGHT.
BUT BEFORE THAT ...

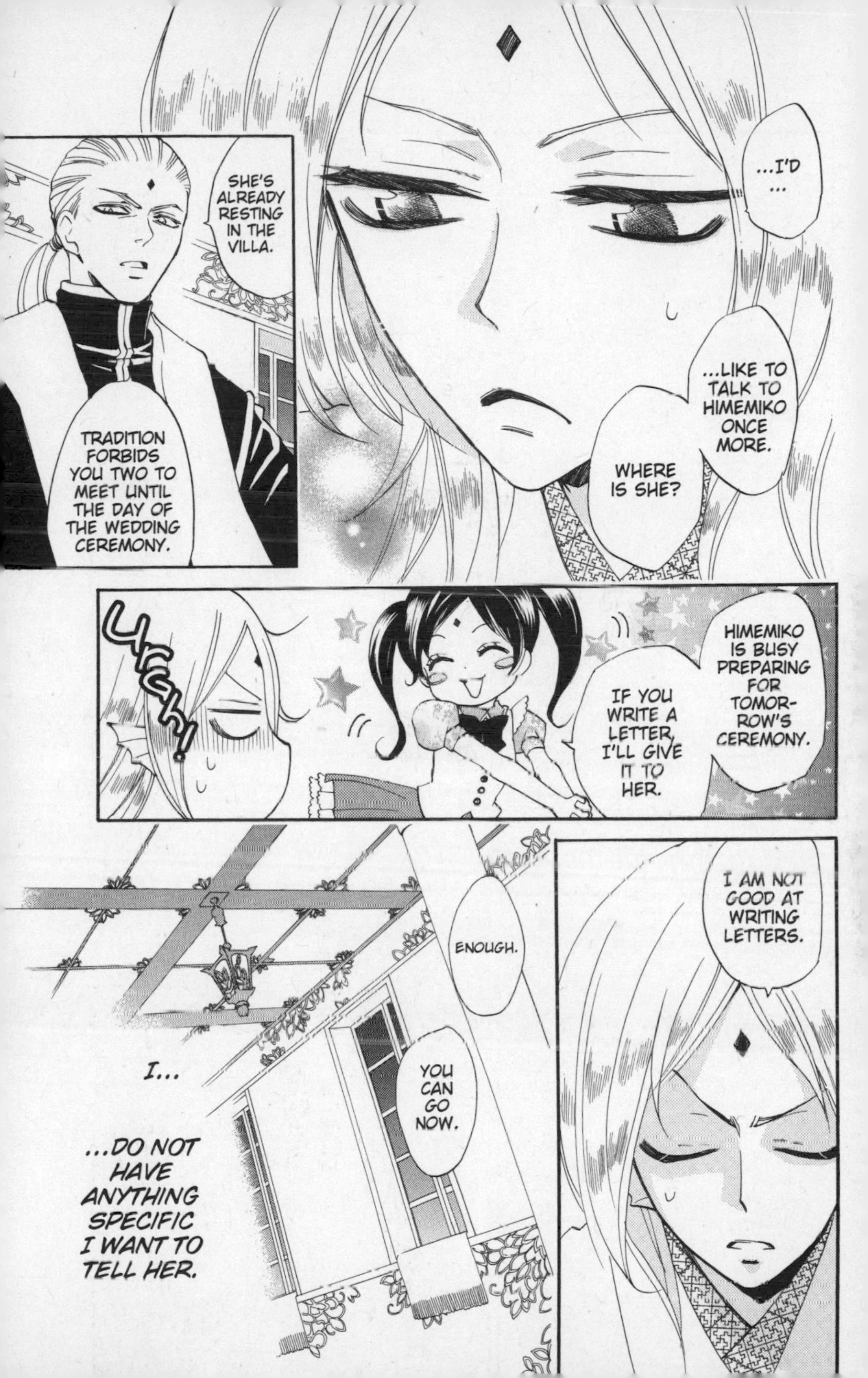
...I'D ...
...LIKE TO TALK TO HIMEMIKO ONCE MORE.
WHERE IS SHE?
SHE'S ALREADY RESTING IN THE VILLA.
TRADITION FORBIDS YOU TWO TO MEET UNTIL THE DAY OF THE WEDDING CEREMONY.
HIMEMIKO IS BUSY PREPARING FOR TOMOR-ROW'S CEREMONY.
IF YOU WRITE A LETTER, I'LL GIVE IT TO HER.
Urgh!
I AM NOT GOOD AT WRITING LETTERS.
ENOUGH.
YOU CAN GO NOW.
I...
...DO NOT HAVE ANYTHING SPECIFIC I WANT TO TELL HER.

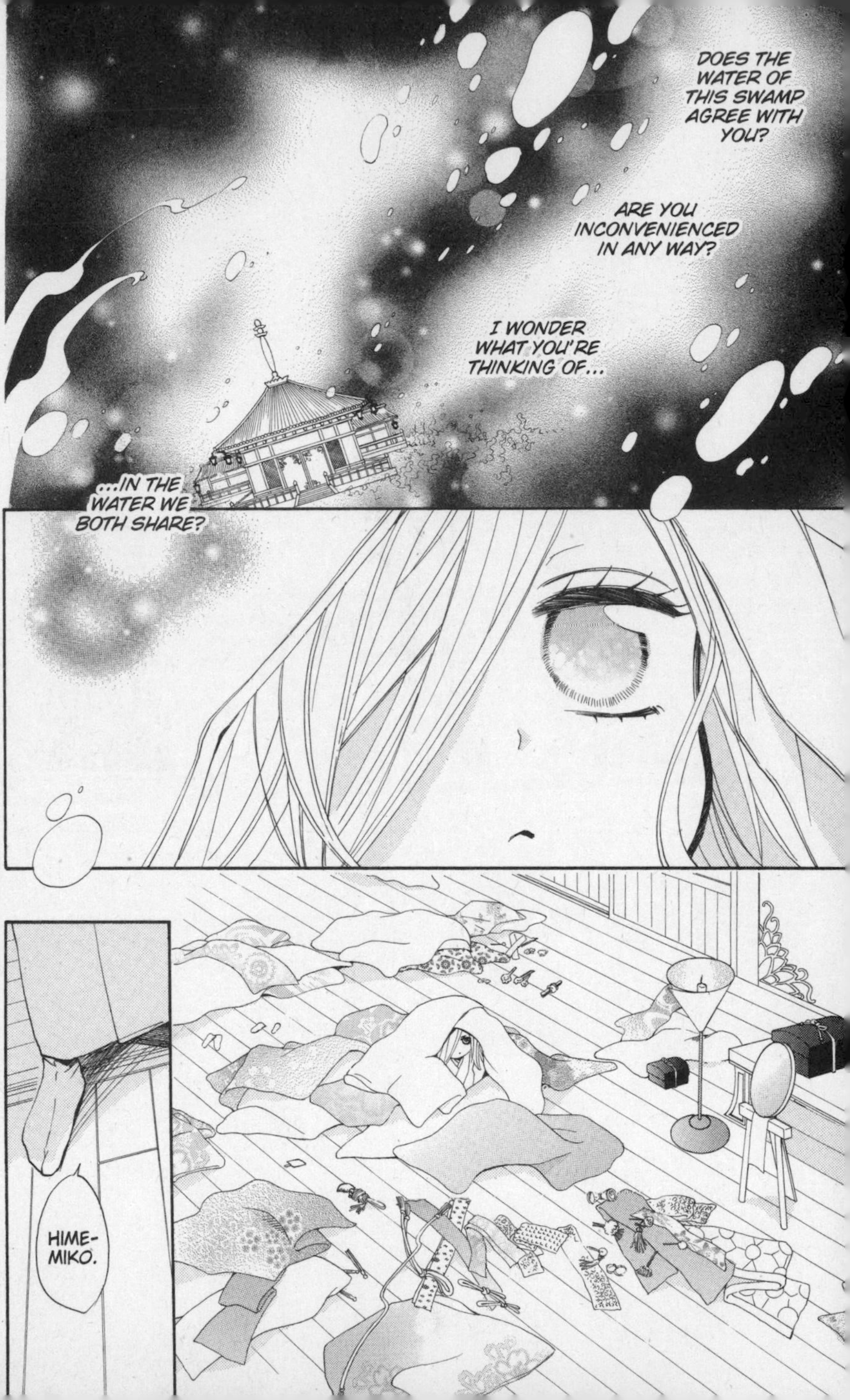
DOES THE WATER OF THIS SWAMP AGREE WITH YOU?
ARE YOU INCONVENIENCED IN ANY WAY?
I WONDER WHAT YOU'RE THINKING OF...
...IN THE WATER WE BOTH SHARE?
HIME-MIKO.

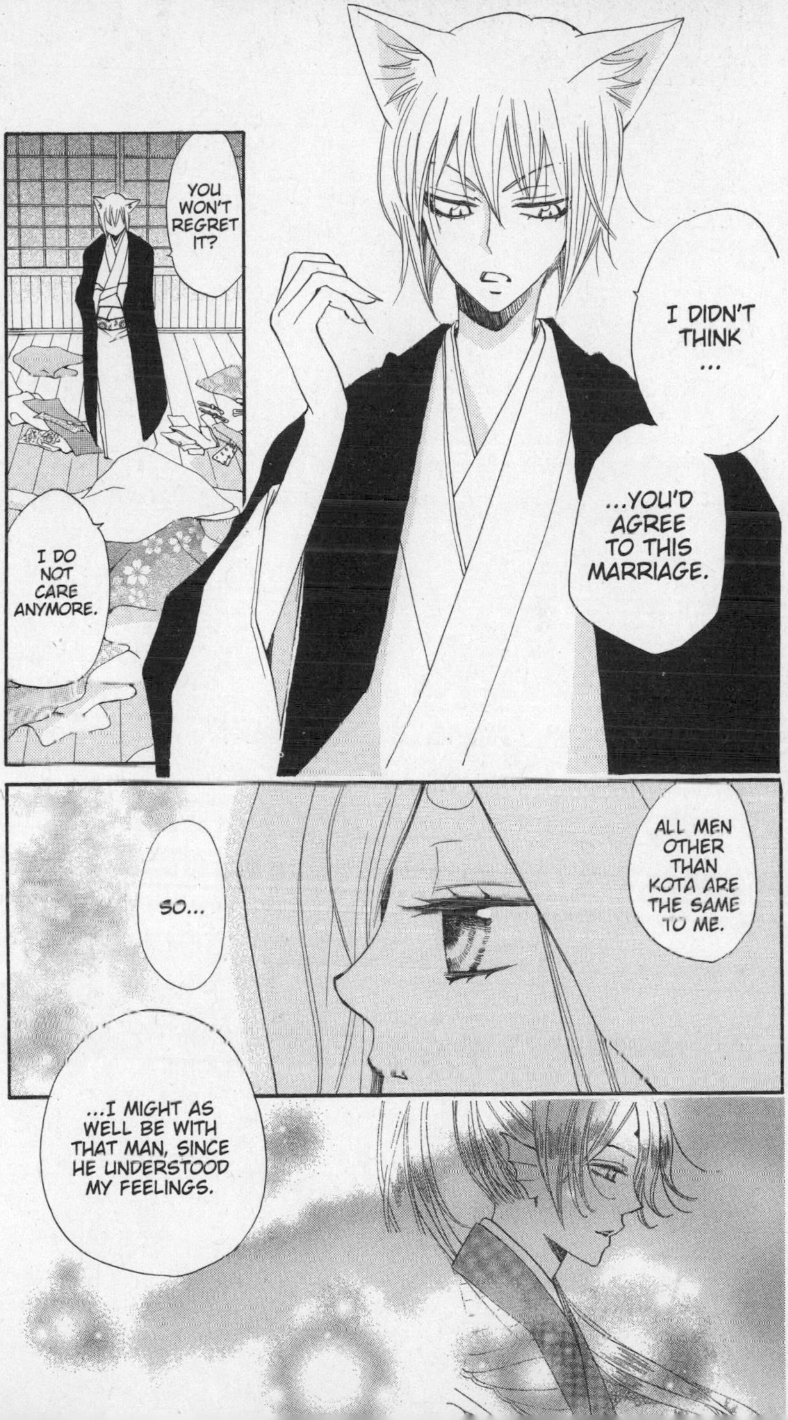
I DIDN'T THINK ...
...YOU'D AGREE TO THIS MARRIAGE.
YOU WON'T REGRET IT?
I DO NOT CARE ANYMORE.
ALL MEN OTHER THAN KOTA ARE THE SAME TO ME.
SO...
...I MIGHT AS WELL BE WITH THAT MAN, SINCE HE UNDERSTOOD MY FEELINGS.

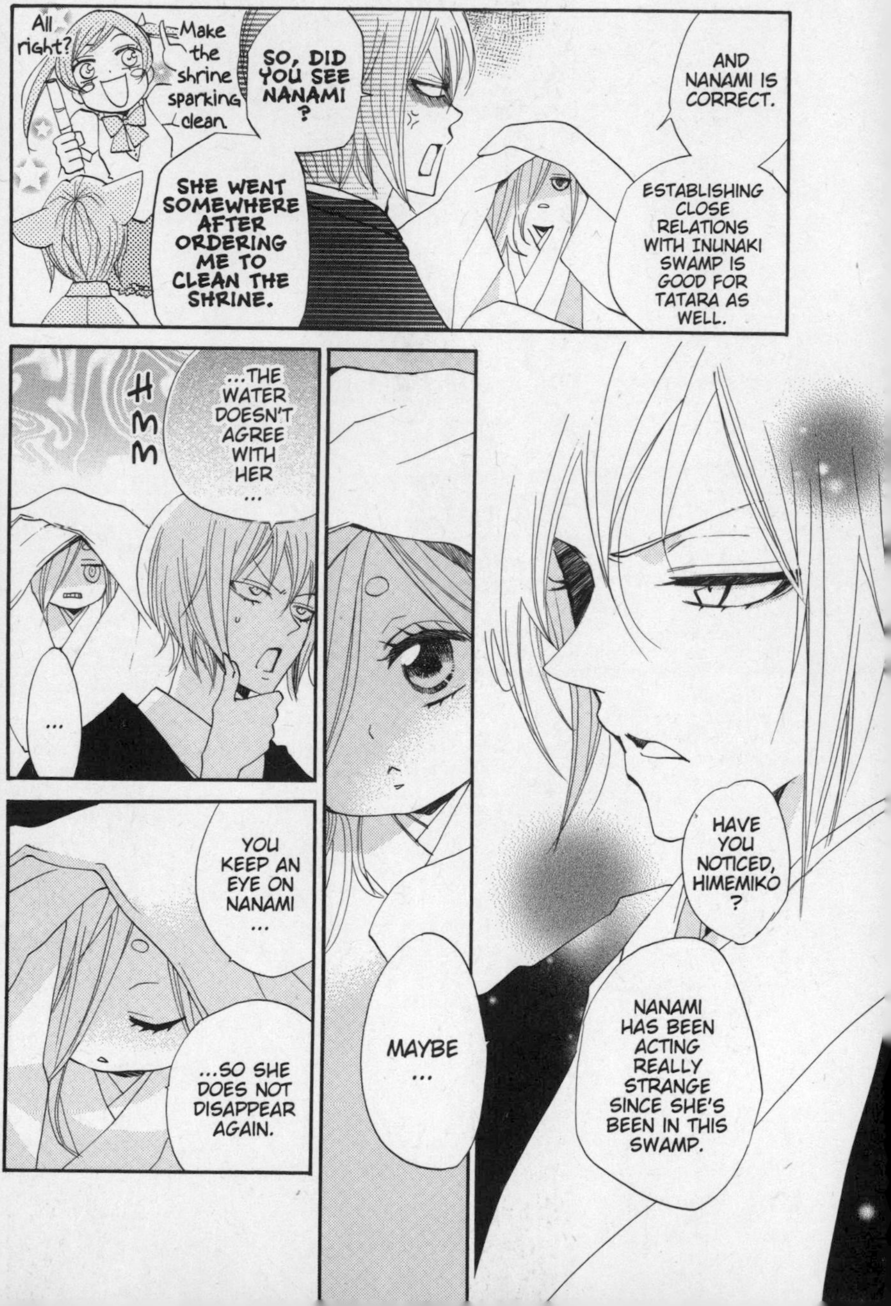
AND NANAMI IS CORRECT.
ESTABLISHING CLOSE RELATIONS WITH INUNAKI SWAMP IS GOOD FOR TATARA AS WELL.
SO, DID YOU SEE NANAMI?
Make the shrine sparking clean.
All right?
SHE WENT SOMEWHERE AFTER ORDERING ME TO CLEAN THE SHRINE.
HAVE YOU NOTICED, HIMEMIKO?
NANAMI HAS BEEN ACTING REALLY STRANGE SINCE SHE'S BEEN IN THIS SWAMP.
MAYBE...
HMM
...THE WATER DOESN'T AGREE WITH HER...
...
YOU KEEP AN EYE ON NANAMI...
...SO SHE DOES NOT DISAPPEAR AGAIN.

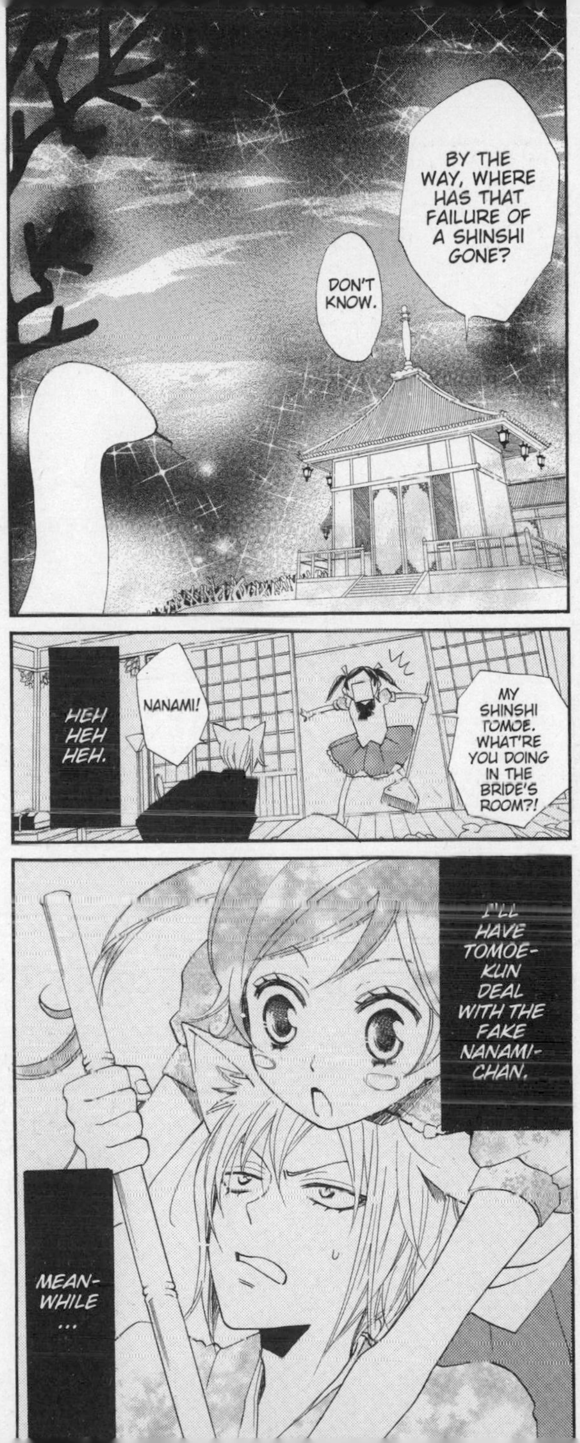
BY THE WAY, WHERE HAS THAT FAILURE OF A SHINSHI GONE?
DON'T KNOW.
MY SHINSHI TOMOE. WHAT'RE YOU DOING IN THE BRIDE'S ROOM?!
NANAMI!
HEH HEH HEH.
I'LL HAVE TOMOE-KUN DEAL WITH THE FAKE NANAMI-CHAN.
MEAN-WHILE ...

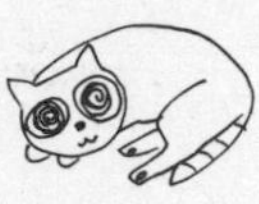

I moved recently.

This is the fifth time I've moved since becoming a mangaka.

I noticed how dirty the rooms were after taking the furniture and everything out of my previous place...

I thought I had always cleaned it well, but I realized it wasn't enough at all...

Now I've changed my ways and am doing my best to clean thoroughly.

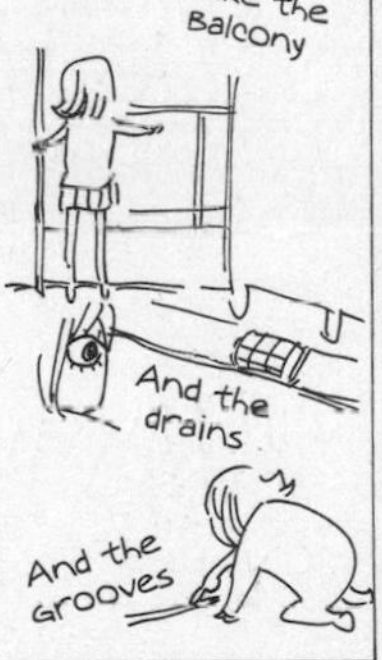
Like the Balcony
And the drains
And the grooves

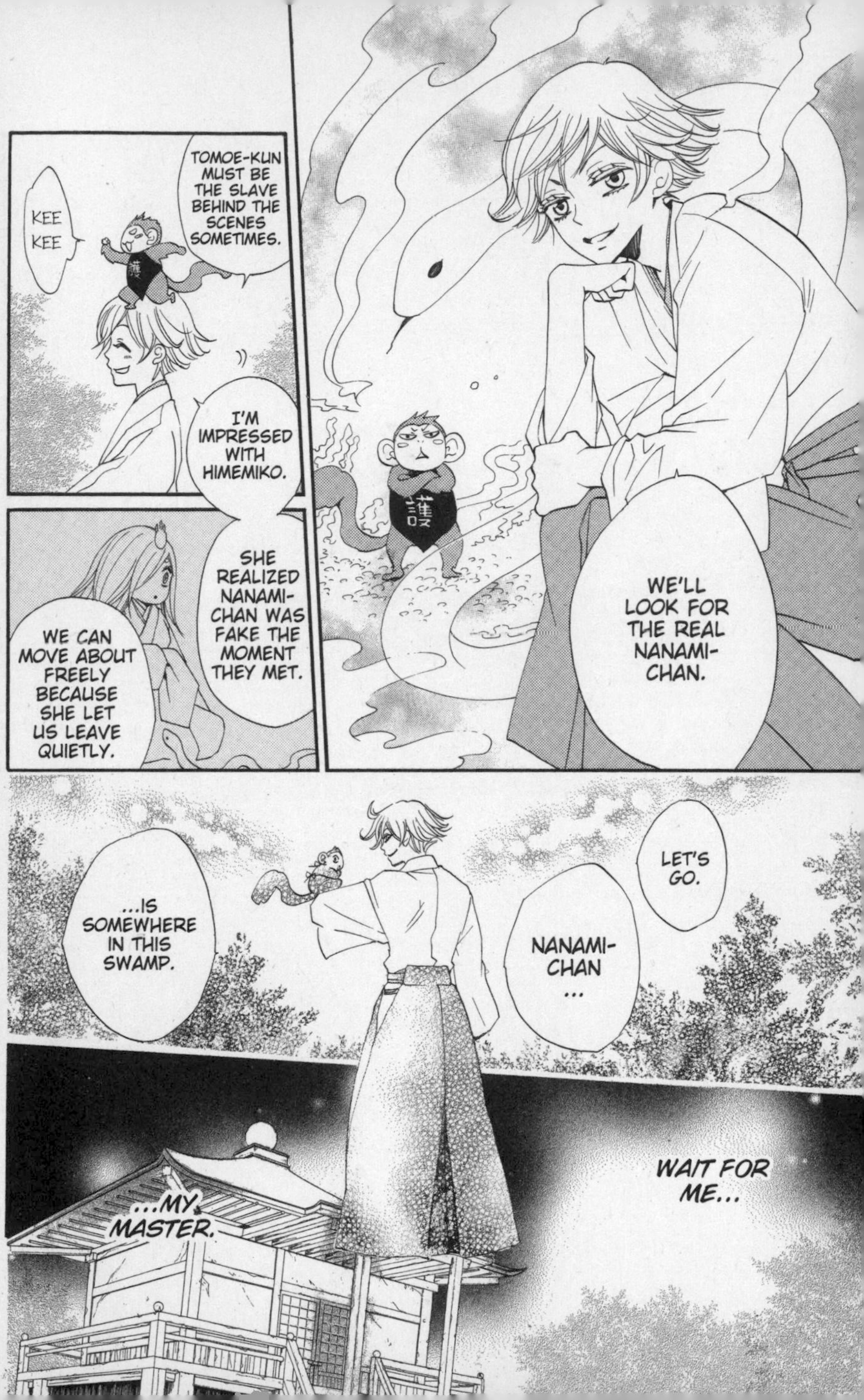
WE'LL LOOK FOR THE REAL NANAMI-CHAN.
TOMOE-KUN MUST BE THE SLAVE BEHIND THE SCENES SOMETIMES.
KEE KEE
I'M IMPRESSED WITH HIMEMIKO.
SHE REALIZED NANAMI-CHAN WAS FAKE THE MOMENT THEY MET.
WE CAN MOVE ABOUT FREELY BECAUSE SHE LET US LEAVE QUIETLY.
LET'S GO.
NANAMI-CHAN...
...IS SOMEWHERE IN THIS SWAMP.
WAIT FOR ME...
...MY MASTER.

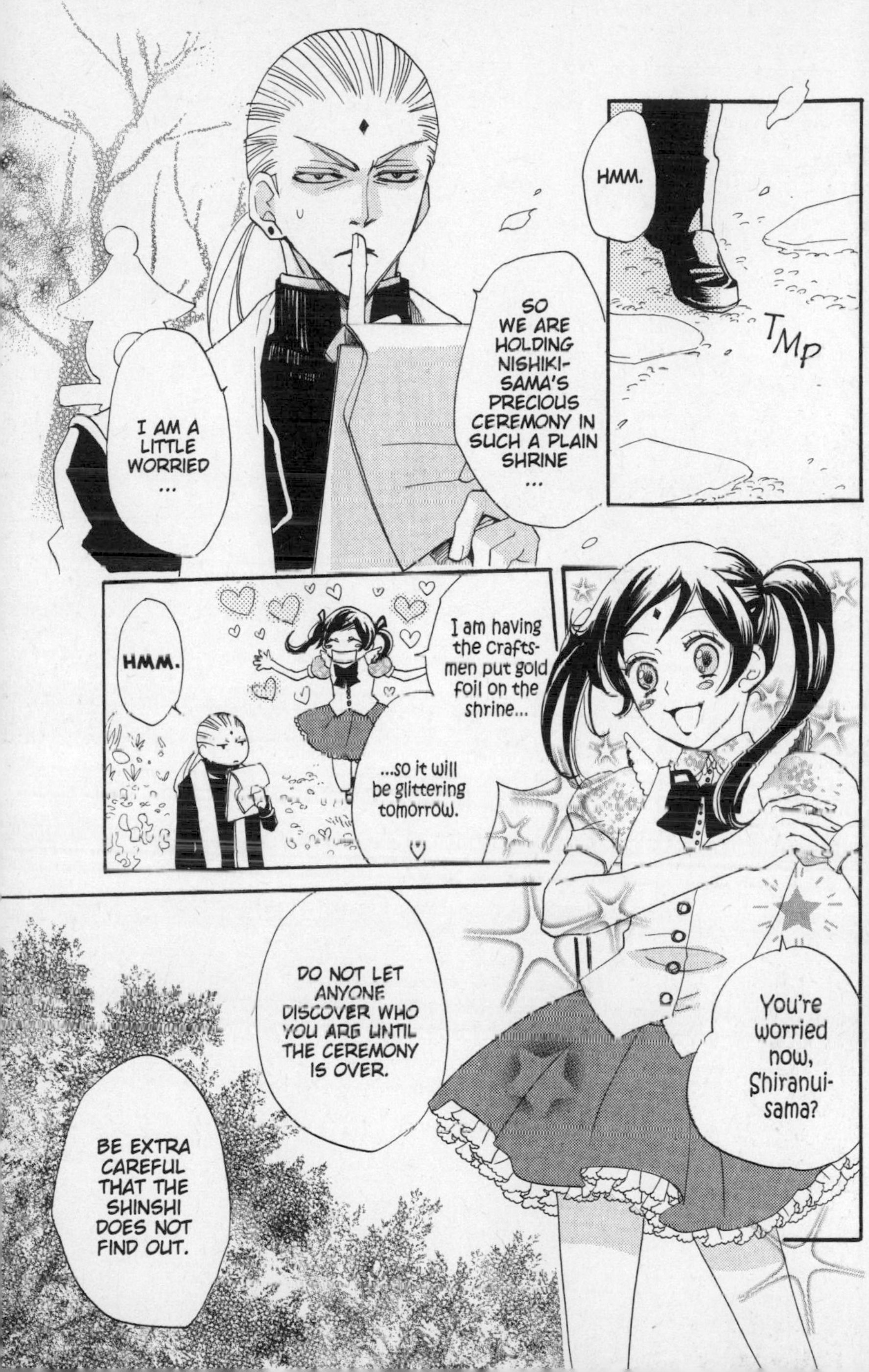
HMM.
TMP
SO WE ARE HOLDING NISHIKI-SAMA'S PRECIOUS CEREMONY IN SUCH A PLAIN SHRINE ...
I AM A LITTLE WORRIED ...
You're worried now, Shiranui-sama?
I am having the crafts-men put gold foil on the shrine...
...so it will be glittering tomorrow.
HMM.
DO NOT LET ANYONE DISCOVER WHO YOU ARE UNTIL THE CEREMONY IS OVER.
BE EXTRA CAREFUL THAT THE SHINSHI DOES NOT FIND OUT.

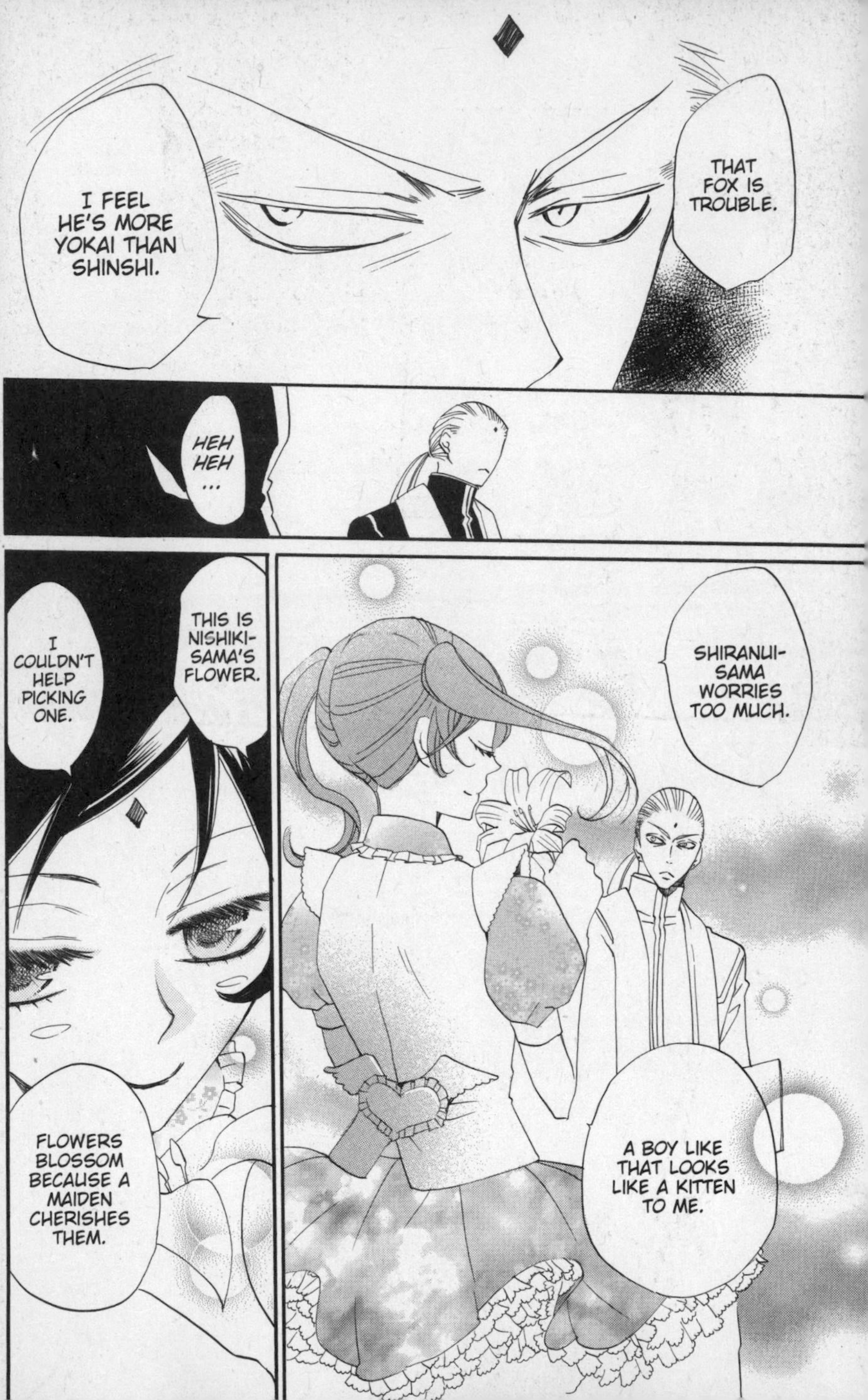
THAT FOX IS TROUBLE.
I FEEL HE'S MORE YOKAI THAN SHINSHI.
HEH HEH ...
SHIRANUI-SAMA WORRIES TOO MUCH.
A BOY LIKE THAT LOOKS LIKE A KITTEN TO ME.
THIS IS NISHIKI-SAMA'S FLOWER.
I COULDN'T HELP PICKING ONE.
FLOWERS BLOSSOM BECAUSE A MAIDEN CHERISHES THEM.

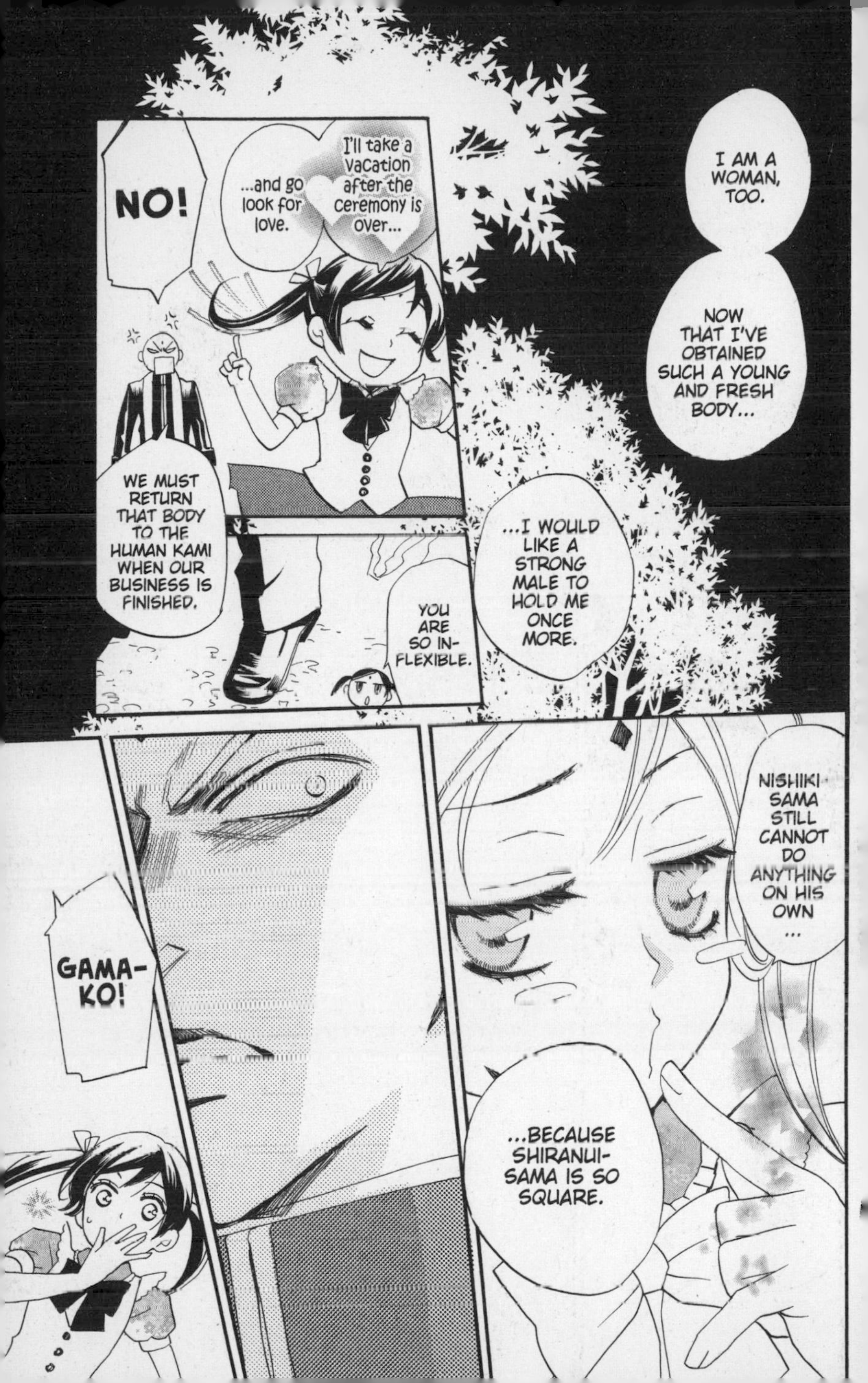
I AM A WOMAN, TOO.
NOW THAT I'VE OBTAINED SUCH A YOUNG AND FRESH BODY...
...I WOULD LIKE A STRONG MALE TO HOLD ME ONCE MORE.
I'll take a vacation after the ceremony is over...
...and go look for love.
NO!
WE MUST RETURN THAT BODY TO THE HUMAN KAMI WHEN OUR BUSINESS IS FINISHED.
YOU ARE SO IN-FLEXIBLE.
NISHIKI-SAMA STILL CANNOT DO ANYTHING ON HIS OWN ...
...BECAUSE SHIRANUI-SAMA IS SO SQUARE.
GAMA-KO!

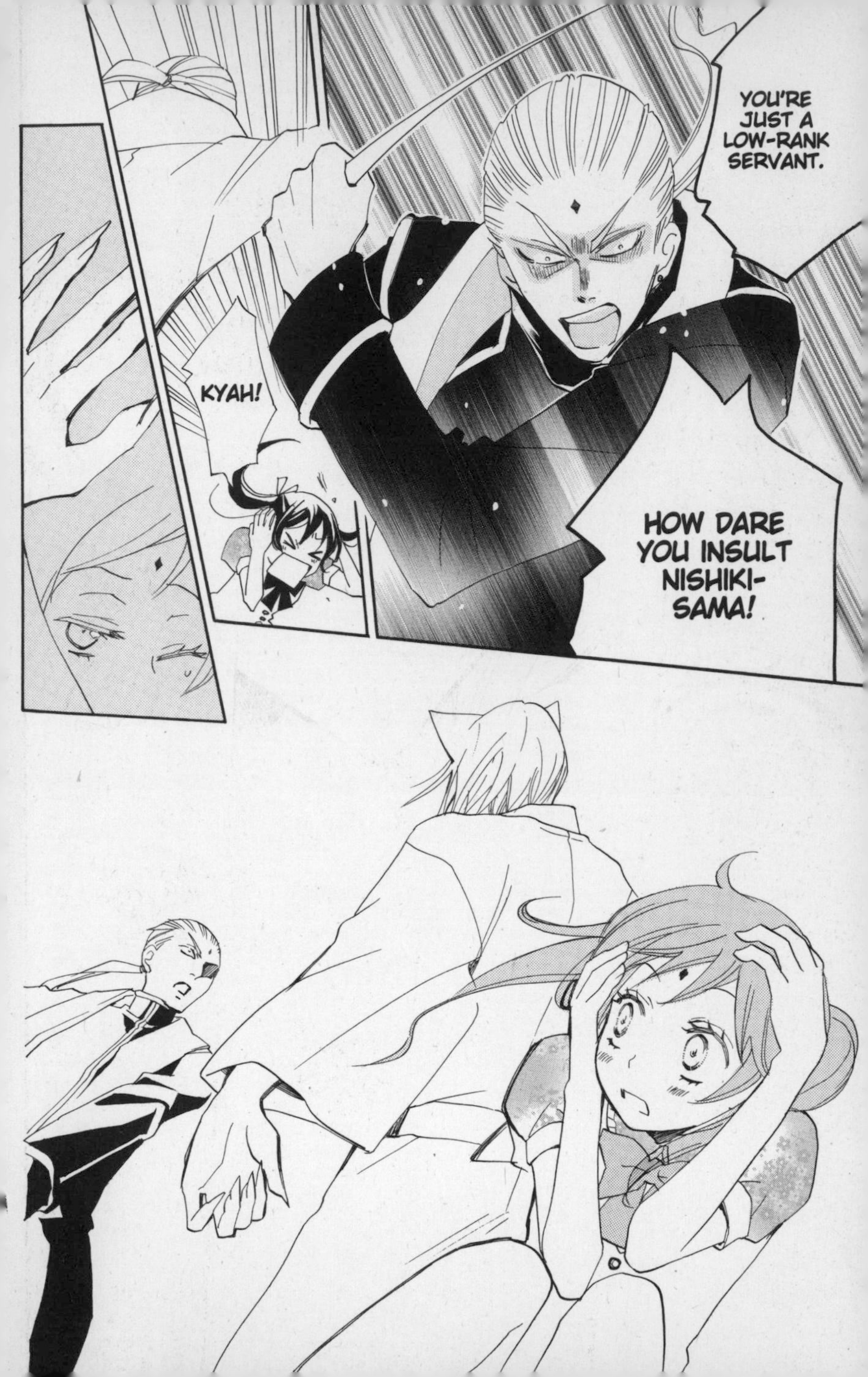
YOU'RE JUST A LOW-RANK SERVANT.
HOW DARE YOU INSULT NISHIKI-SAMA!
KYAH!

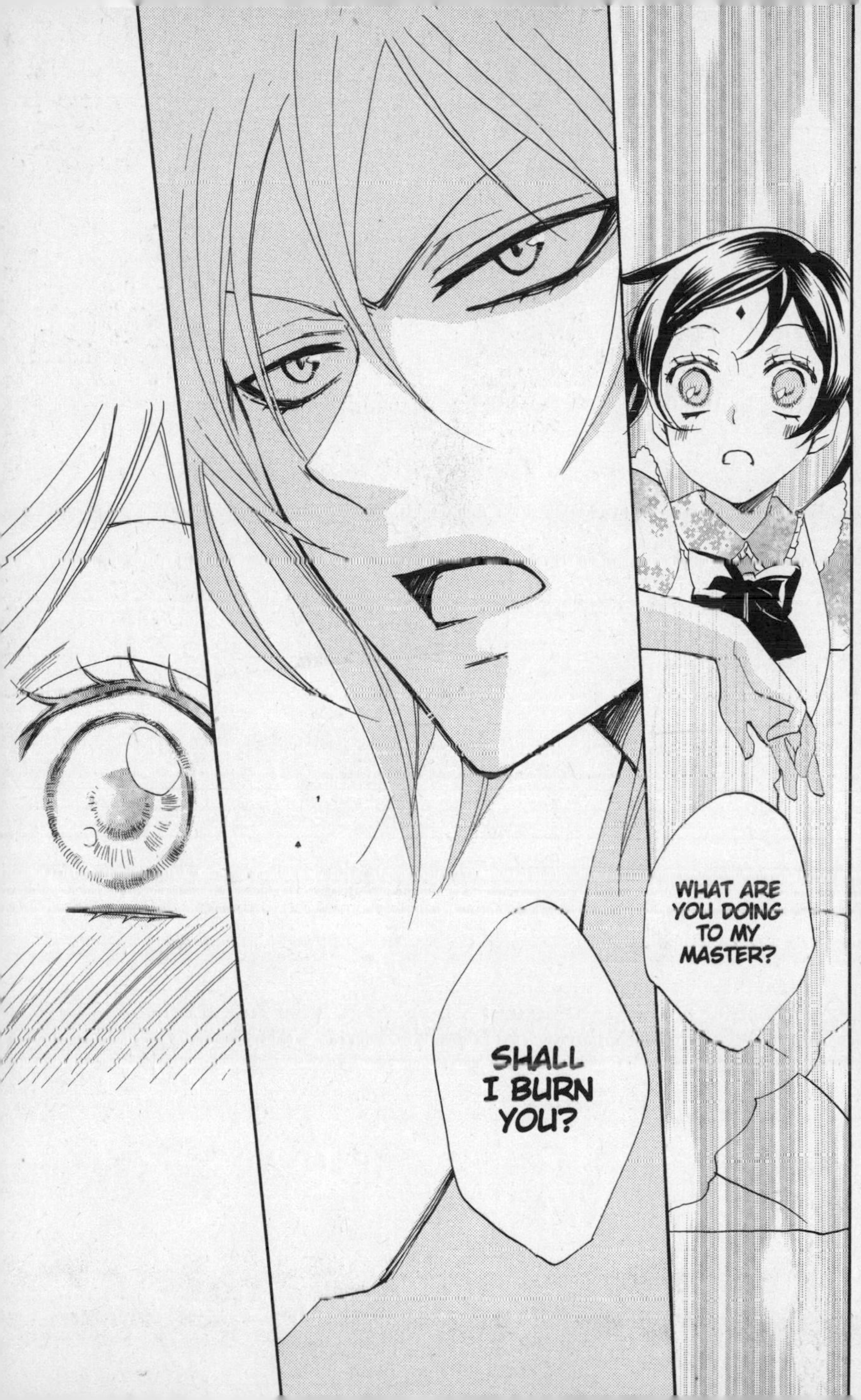
WHAT ARE YOU DOING TO MY MASTER?
SHALL I BURN YOU?

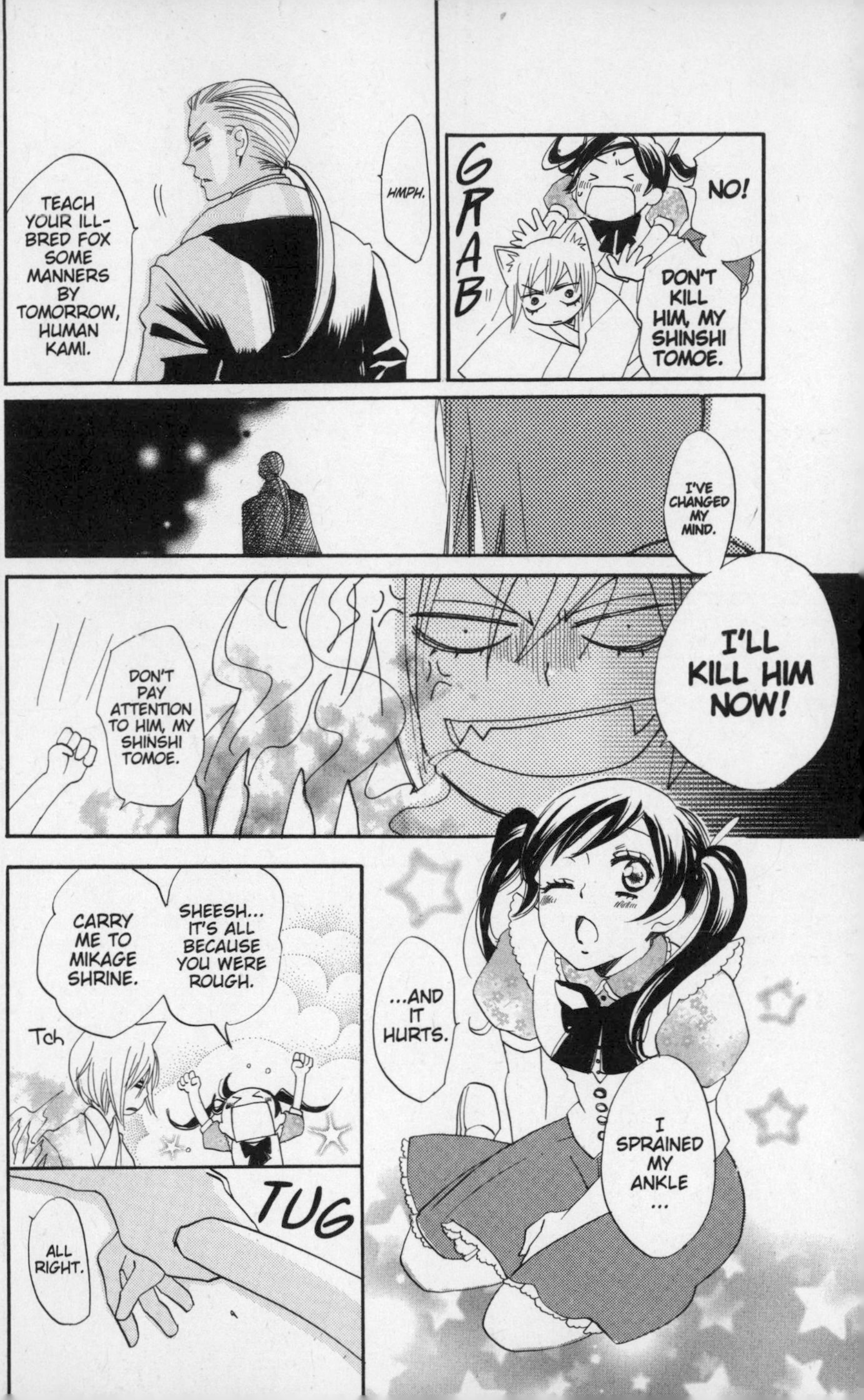
GRAB
NO!
DON'T KILL HIM, MY SHINSHI TOMOE.
HMPH.
TEACH YOUR ILL-BRED FOX SOME MANNERS BY TOMORROW, HUMAN KAMI.
I'VE CHANGED MY MIND.
I'LL KILL HIM NOW!
DON'T PAY ATTENTION TO HIM, MY SHINSHI TOMOE.
I SPRAINED MY ANKLE ...
...AND IT HURTS.
SHEESH... IT'S ALL BECAUSE YOU WERE ROUGH.
CARRY ME TO MIKAGE SHRINE.
Tch
TUG
ALL RIGHT.

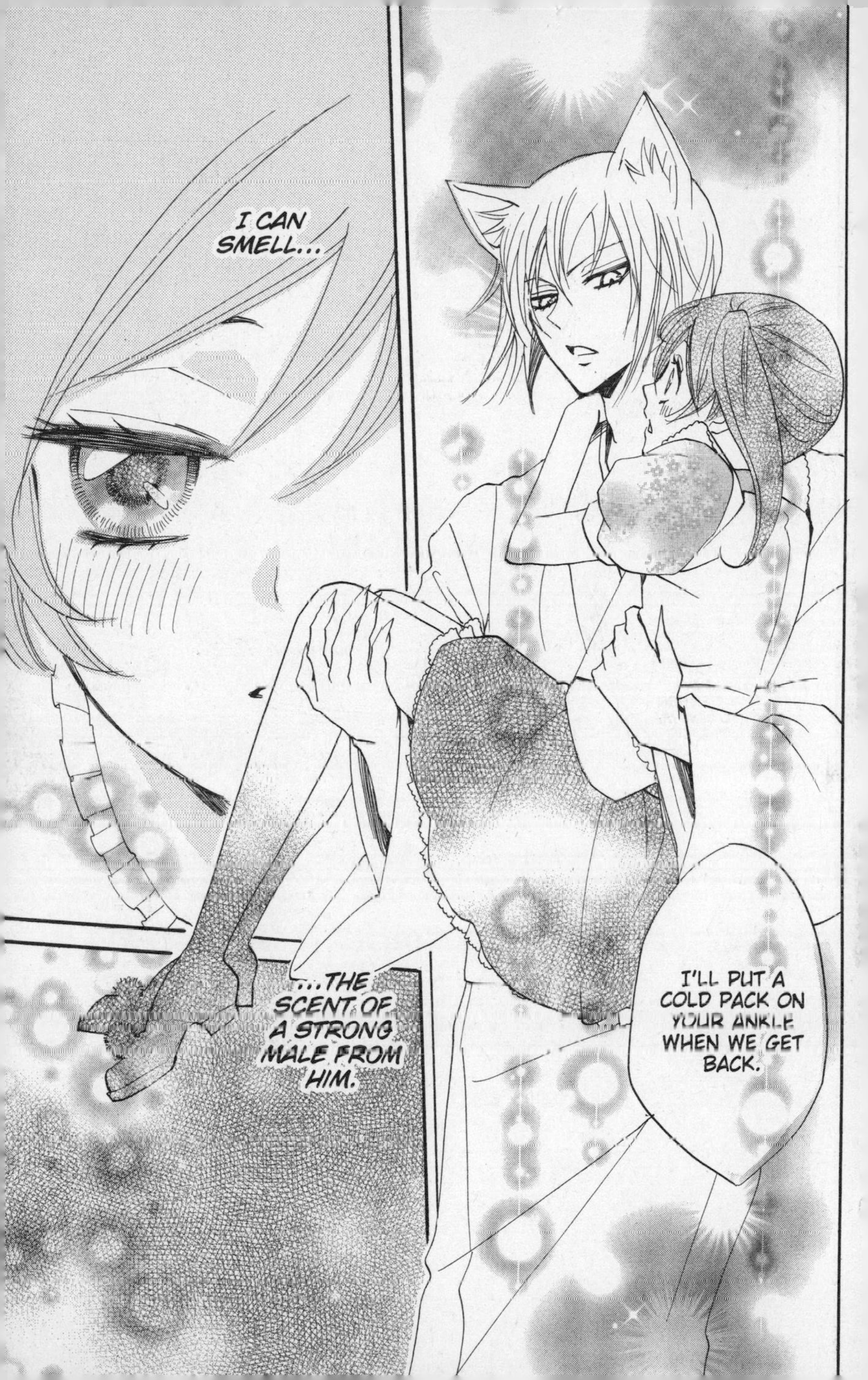
I'LL PUT A COLD PACK ON YOUR ANKLE WHEN WE GET BACK.
I CAN SMELL...
...THE SCENT OF A STRONG MALE FROM HIM.

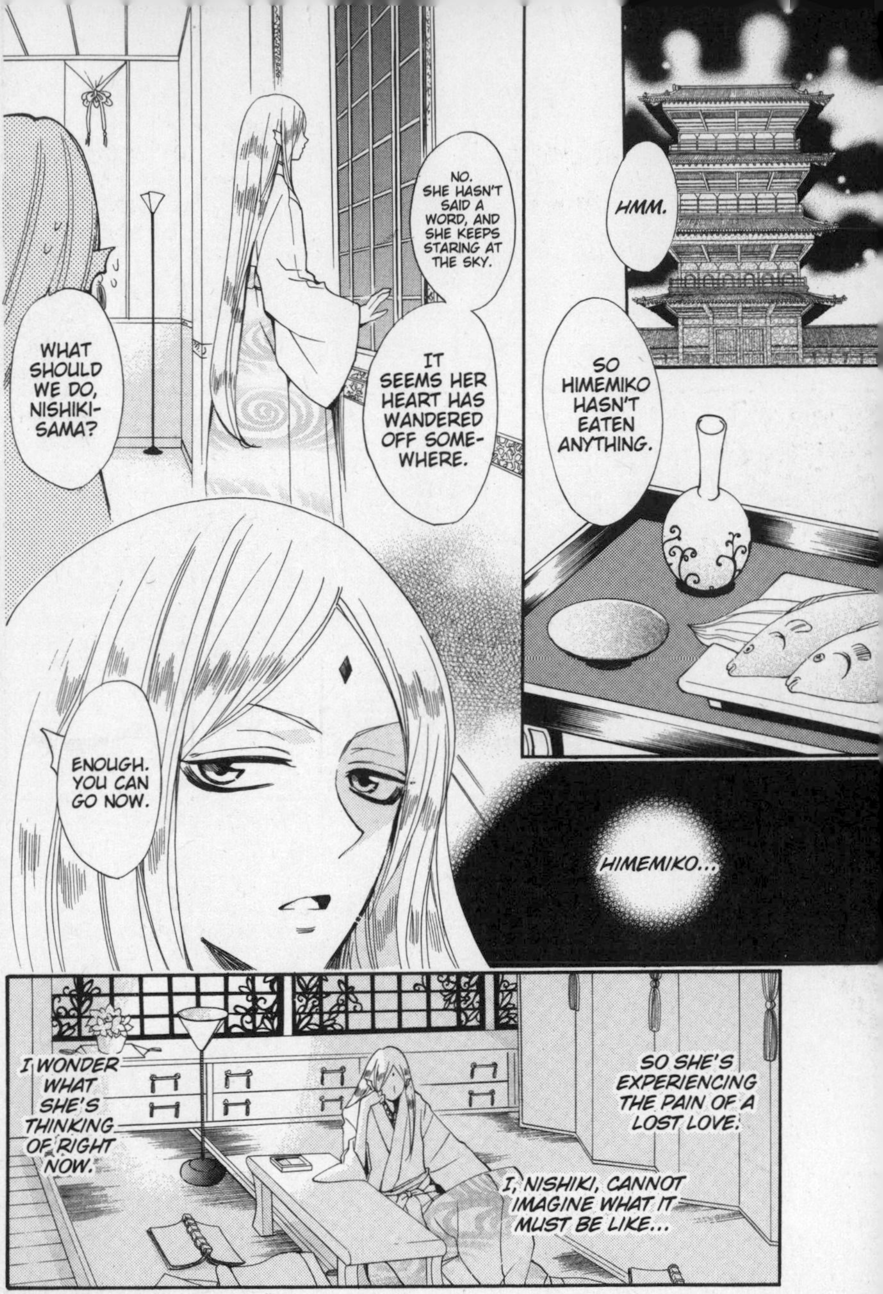
HMM.
SO HIMEMIKO HASN'T EATEN ANYTHING.
NO. SHE HASN'T SAID A WORD, AND SHE KEEPS STARING AT THE SKY.
IT SEEMS HER HEART HAS WANDERED OFF SOME-WHERE.
WHAT SHOULD WE DO, NISHIKI-SAMA?
HIMEMIKO...
ENOUGH. YOU CAN GO NOW.
SO SHE'S EXPERIENCING THE PAIN OF A LOST LOVE.
I, NISHIKI, CANNOT IMAGINE WHAT IT MUST BE LIKE...
I WONDER WHAT SHE'S THINKING OF RIGHT NOW.

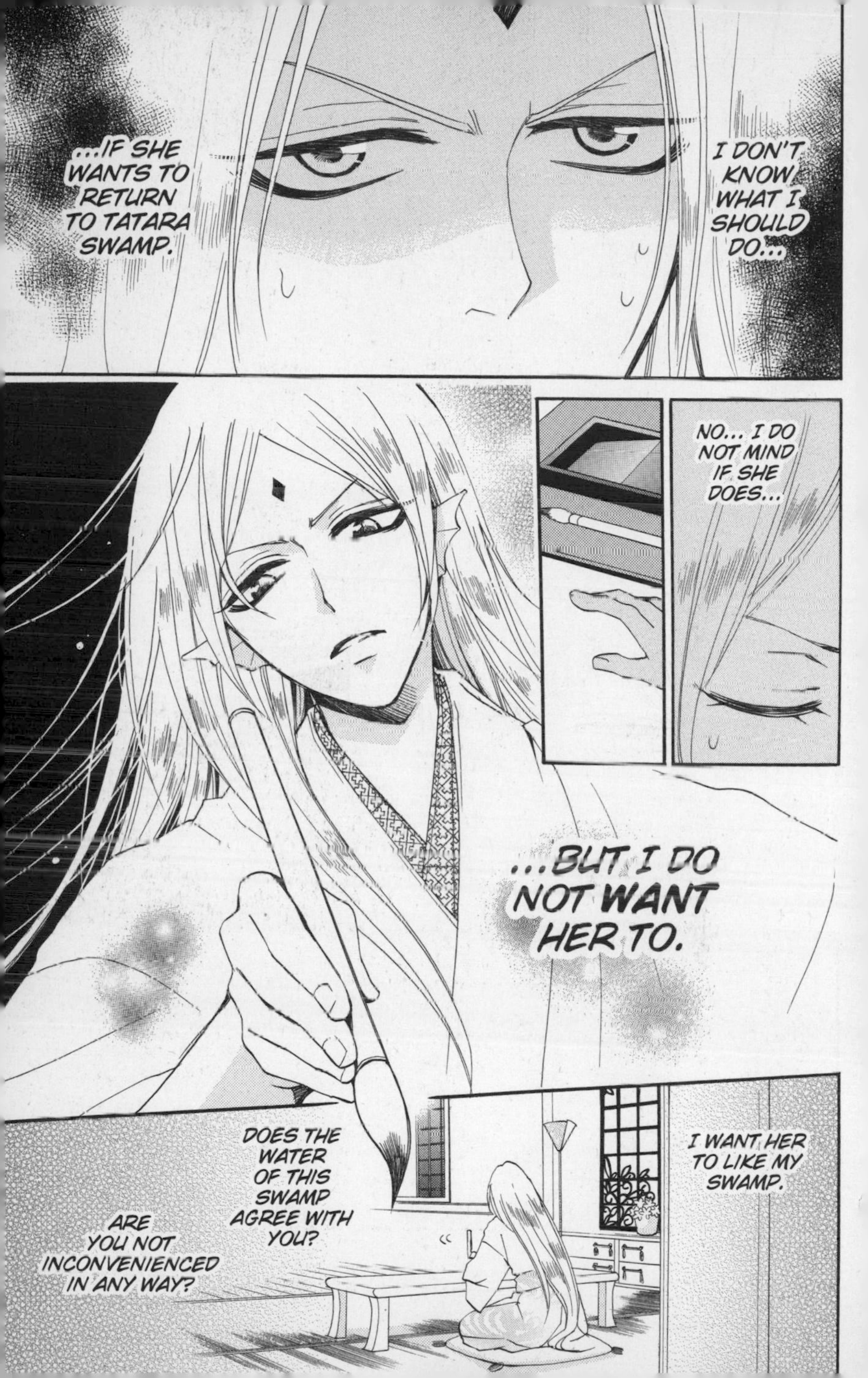
I DON'T KNOW WHAT I SHOULD DO...
...IF SHE WANTS TO RETURN TO TATARA SWAMP.
NO... I DO NOT MIND IF SHE DOES...
...BUT I DO NOT WANT HER TO.
I WANT HER TO LIKE MY SWAMP.
DOES THE WATER OF THIS SWAMP AGREE WITH YOU?
ARE YOU NOT INCONVENIENCED IN ANY WAY?

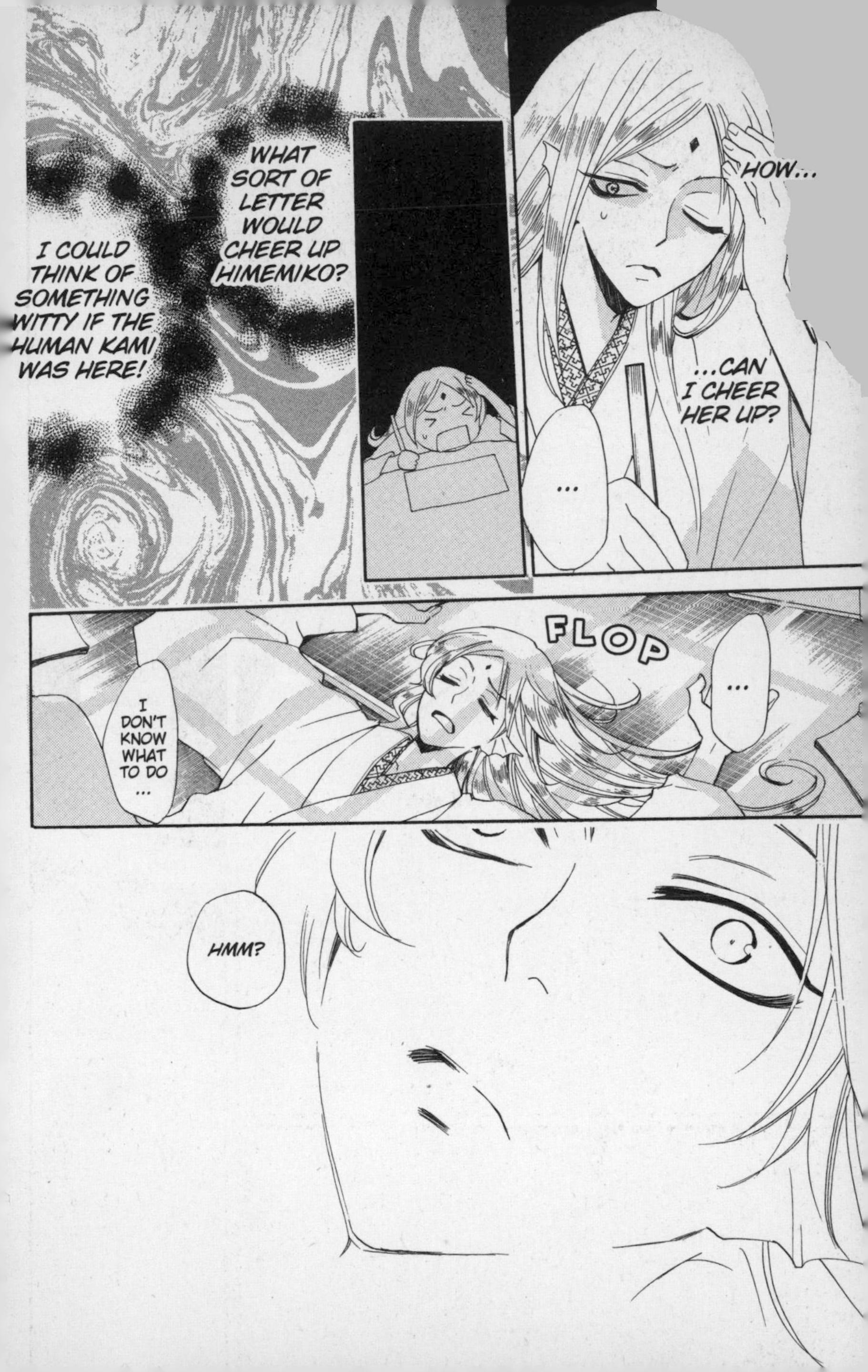
HOW...
...CAN I CHEER HER UP?
...
WHAT SORT OF LETTER WOULD CHEER UP HIMEMIKO?
I COULD THINK OF SOMETHING WITTY IF THE HUMAN KAMI WAS HERE!
FLOP
...
I DON'T KNOW WHAT TO DO ...
HMM?

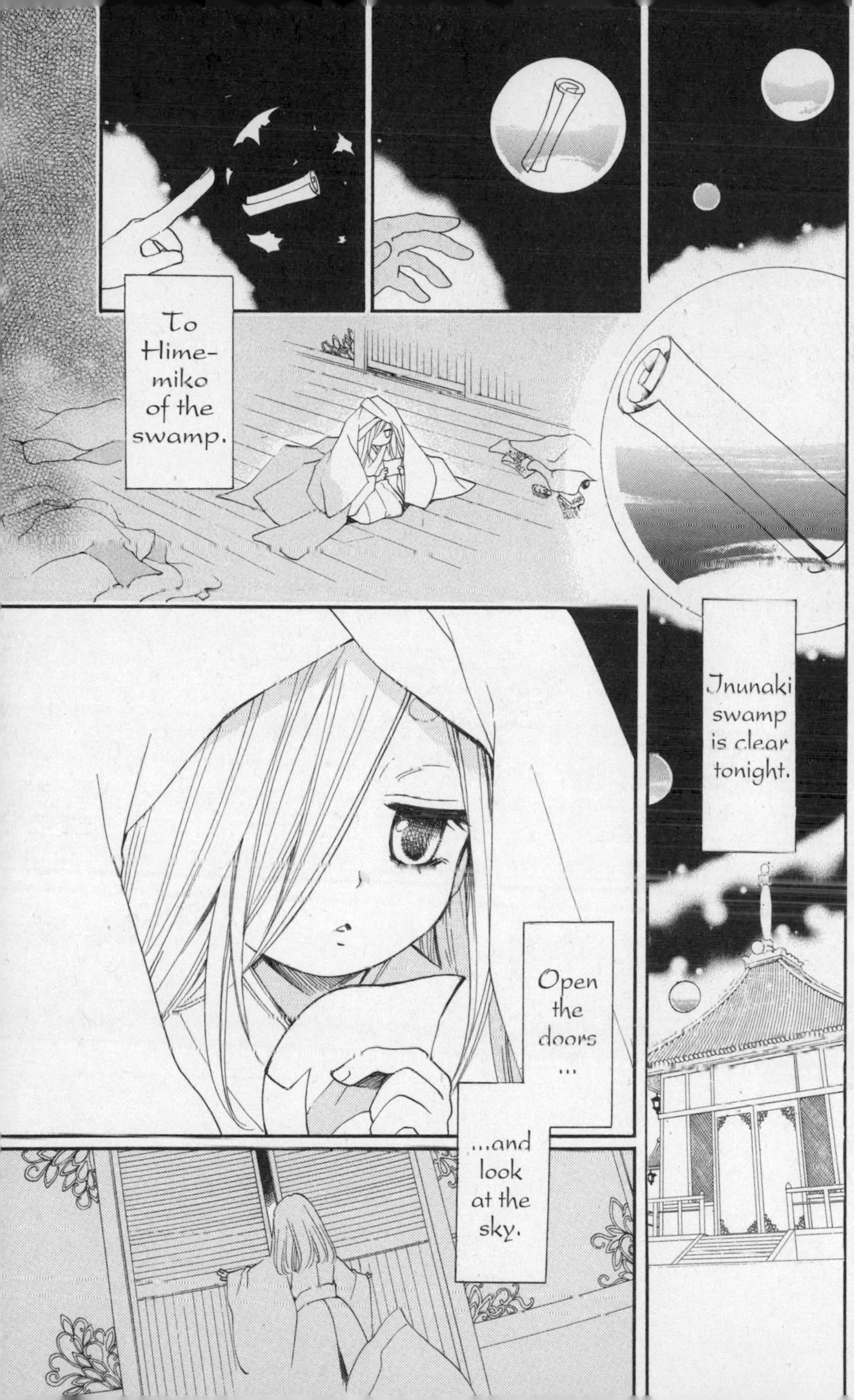
To Hime-miko of the swamp.
Inunaki swamp is clear tonight.
Open the doors ...
...and look at the sky.

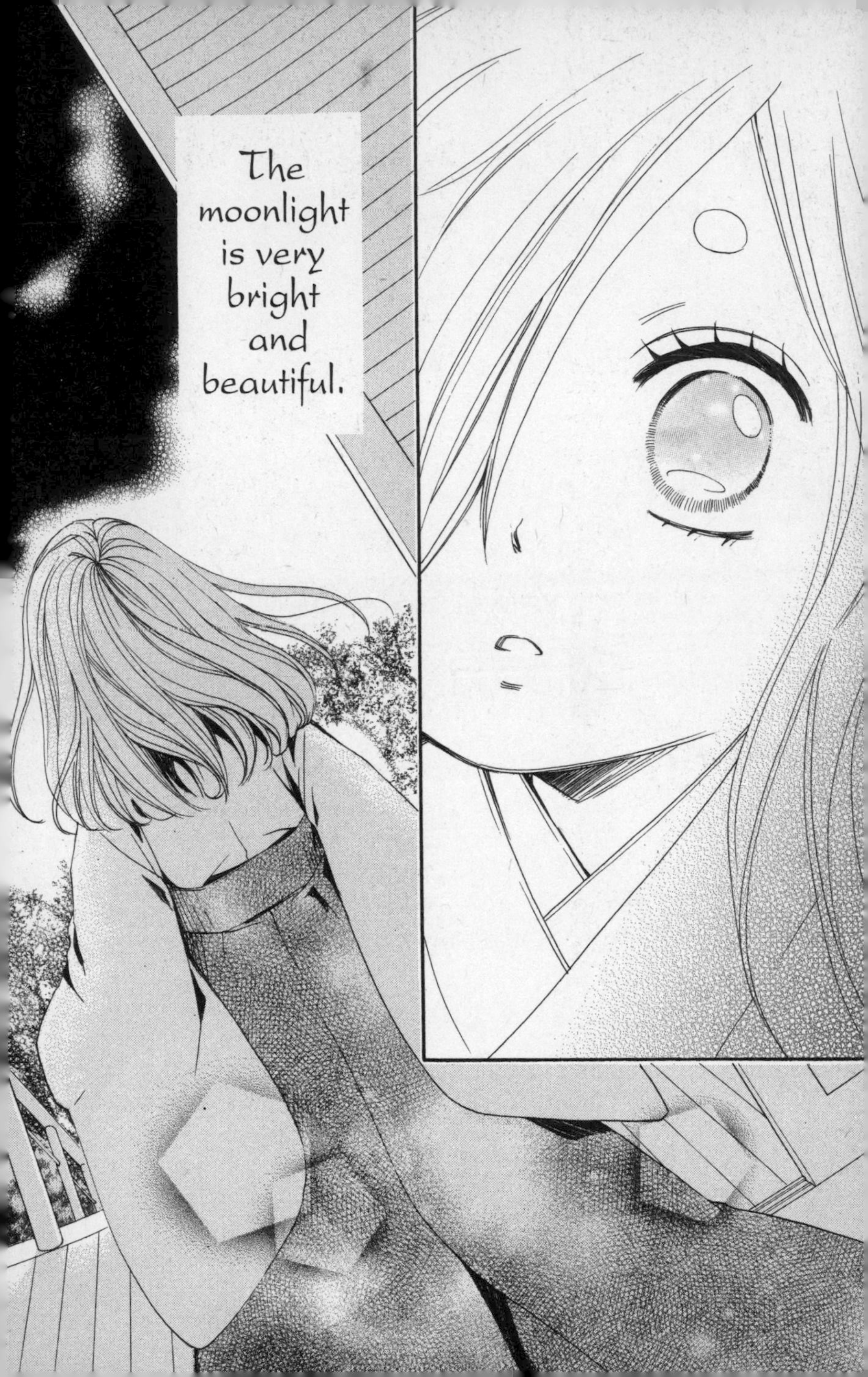
The moonlight is very bright and beautiful.

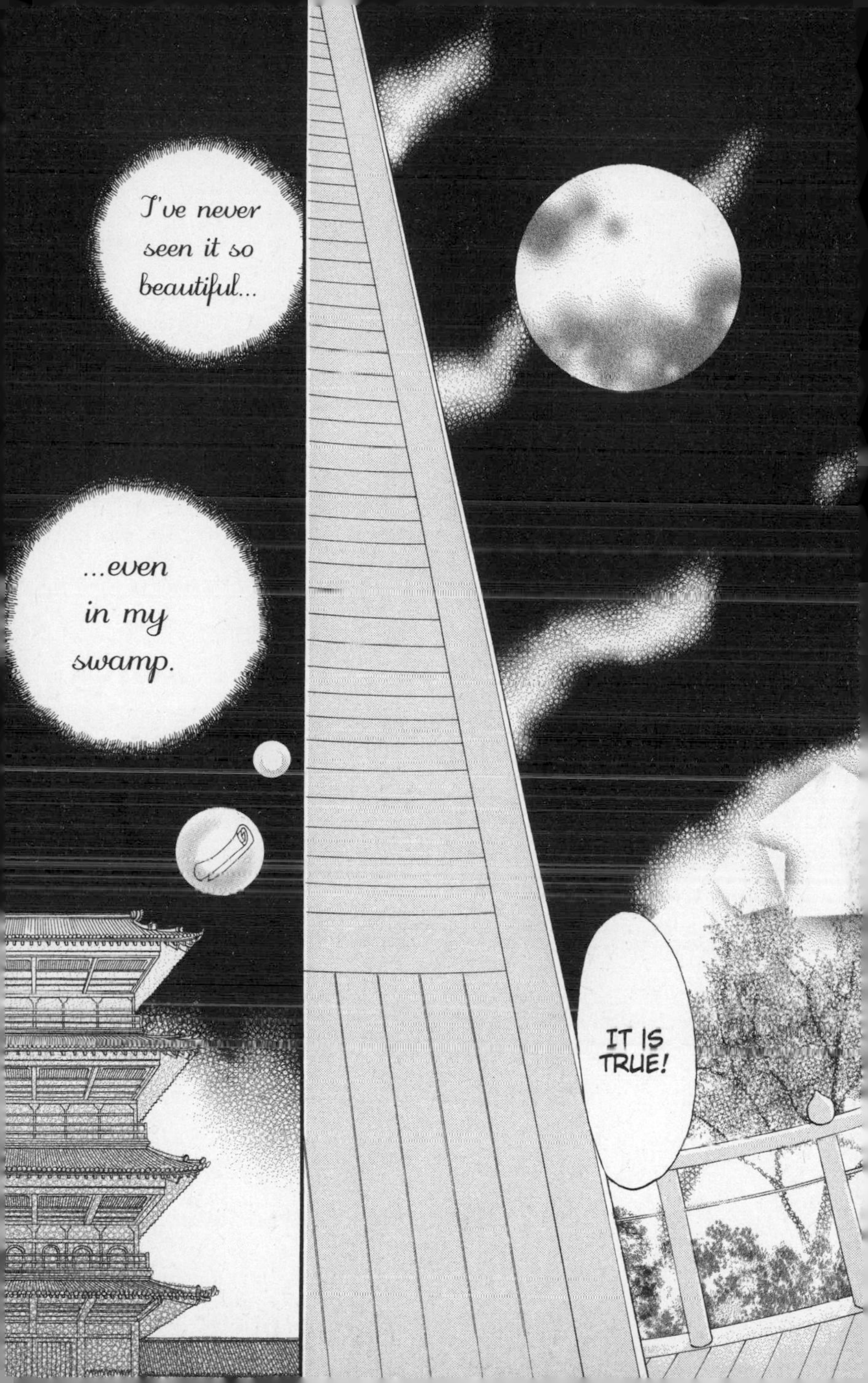
IT IS TRUE!
I've never seen it so beautiful...
...even in my swamp.

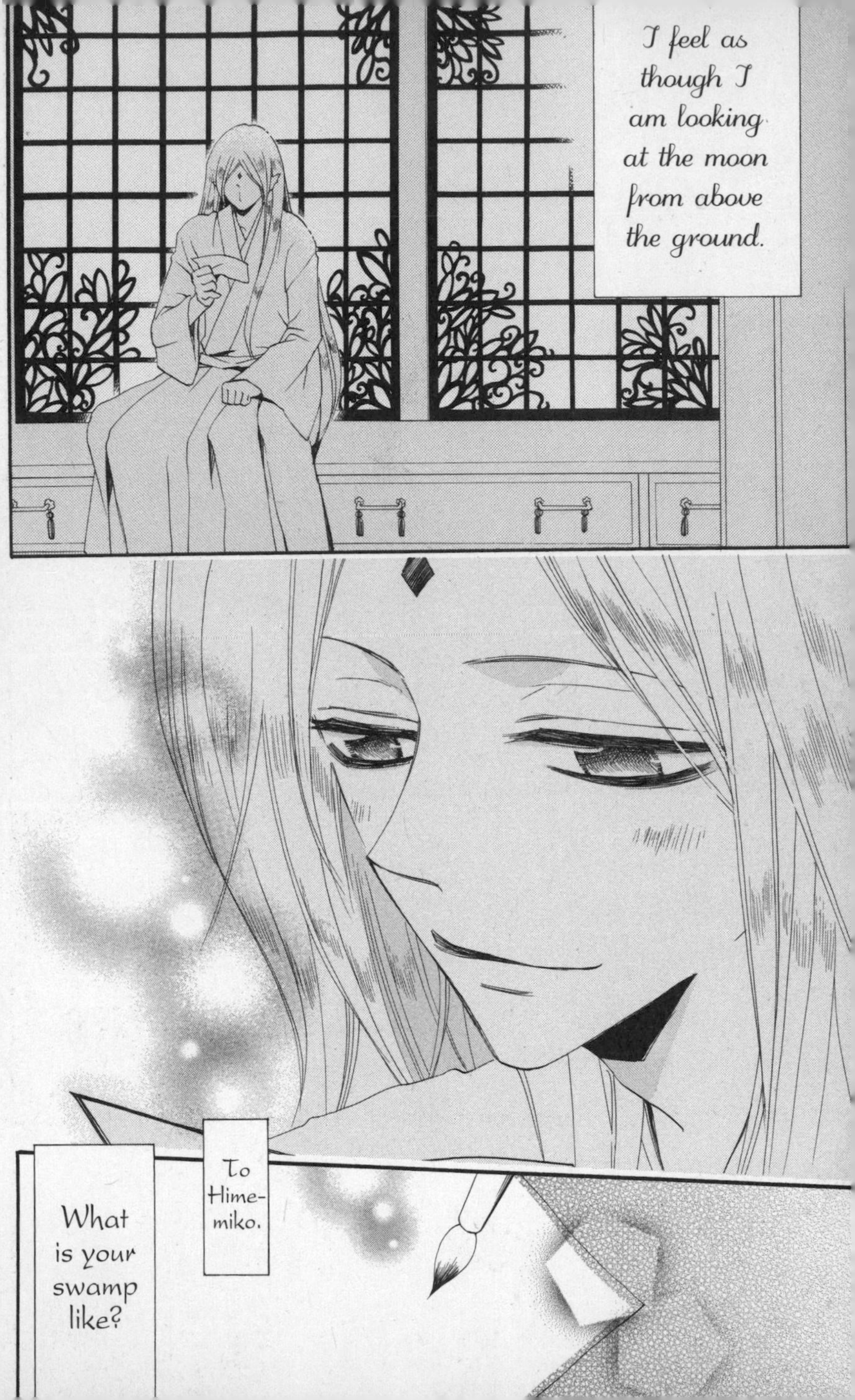
I feel as though I am looking at the moon from above the ground.
To Hime-miko.
What is your swamp like?

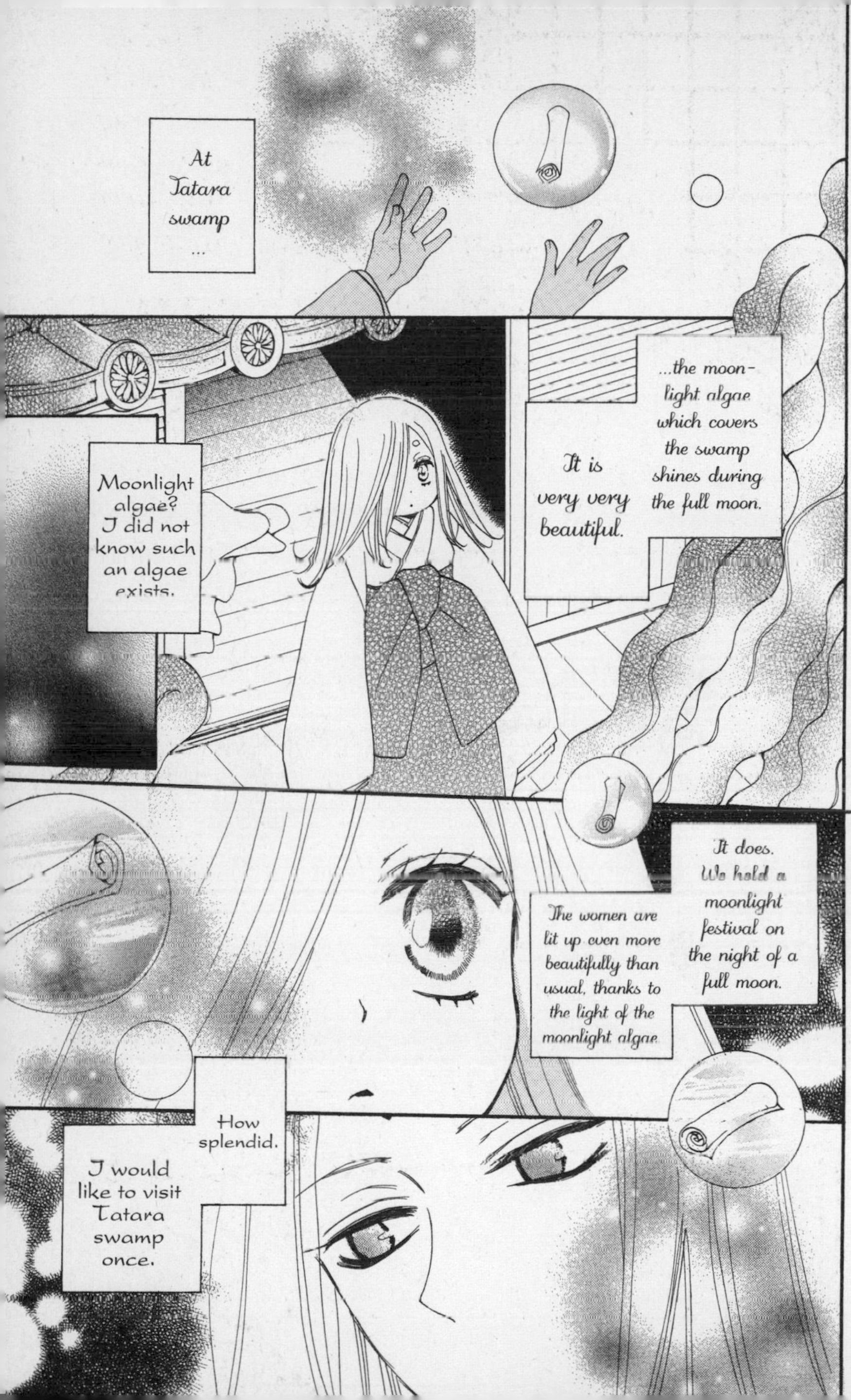
At Tatara swamp ...
...the moon-light algae which covers the swamp shines during the full moon.
It is very very beautiful.
Moonlight algae? I did not know such an algae exists.
It does. We hold a moonlight festival on the night of a full moon.
The women are lit up even more beautifully than usual, thanks to the light of the moonlight algae.
How splendid.
I would like to visit Tatara swamp once.

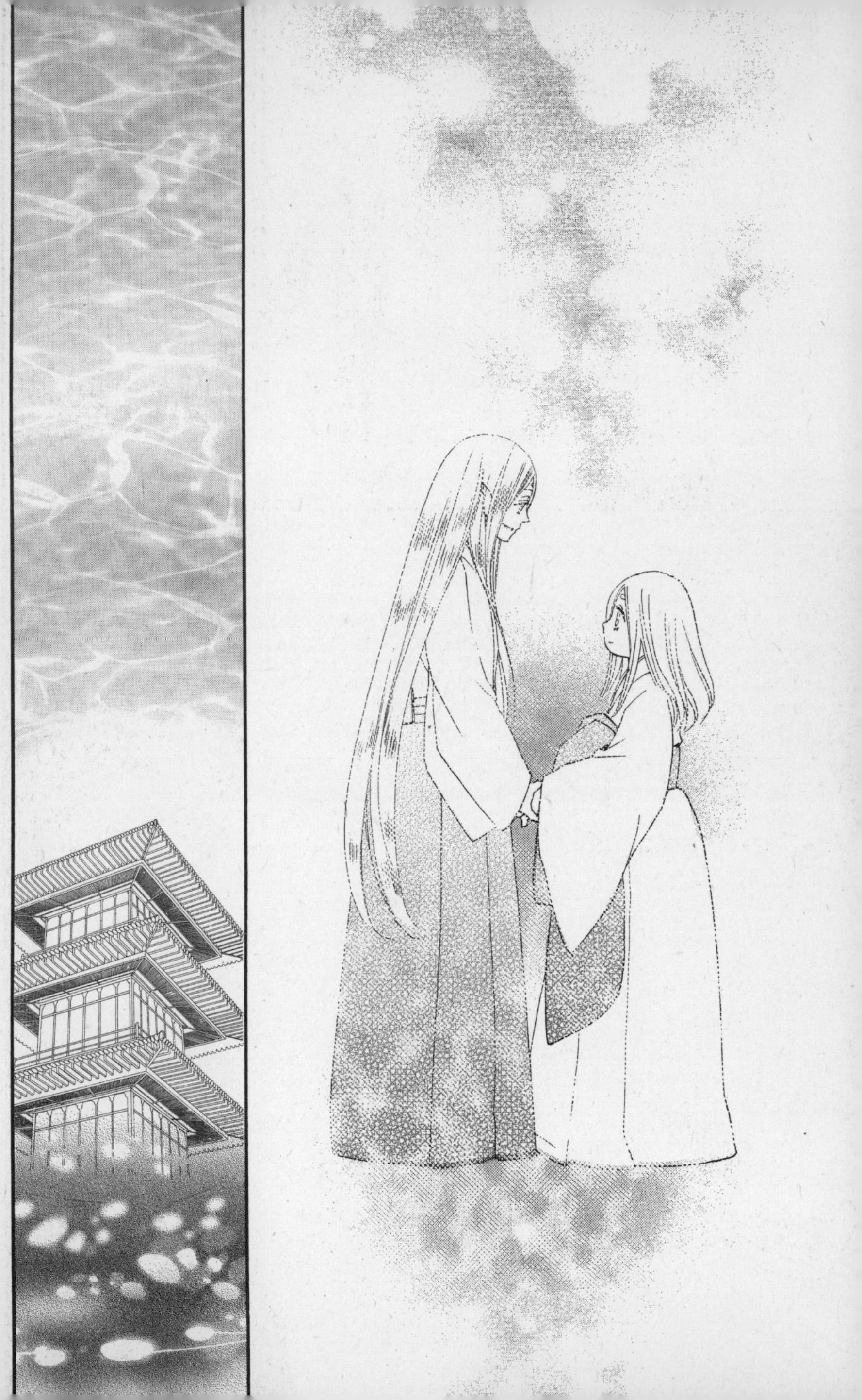

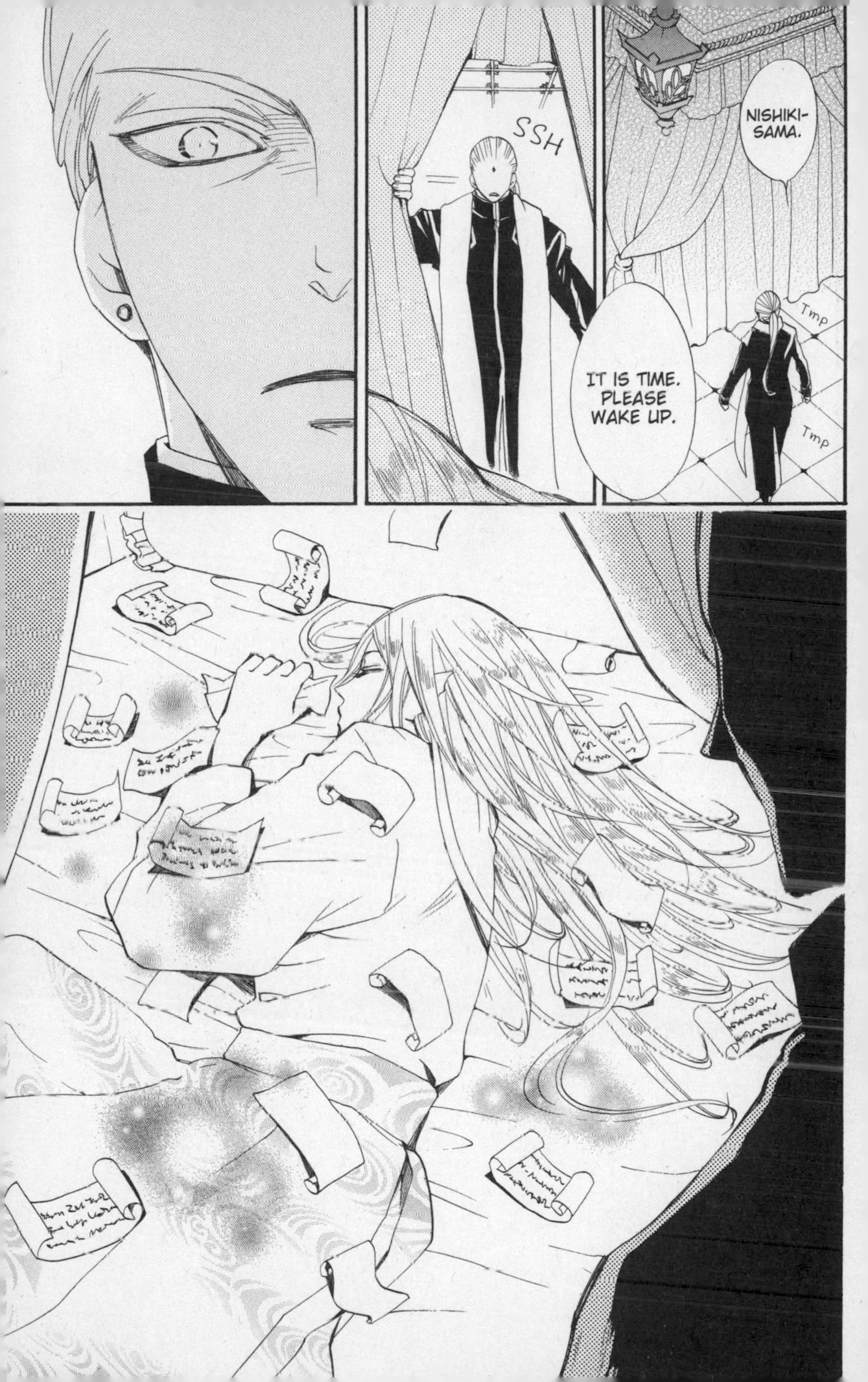
NISHIKI-SAMA.
Tmp
IT IS TIME. PLEASE WAKE UP.
Tmp
SSH

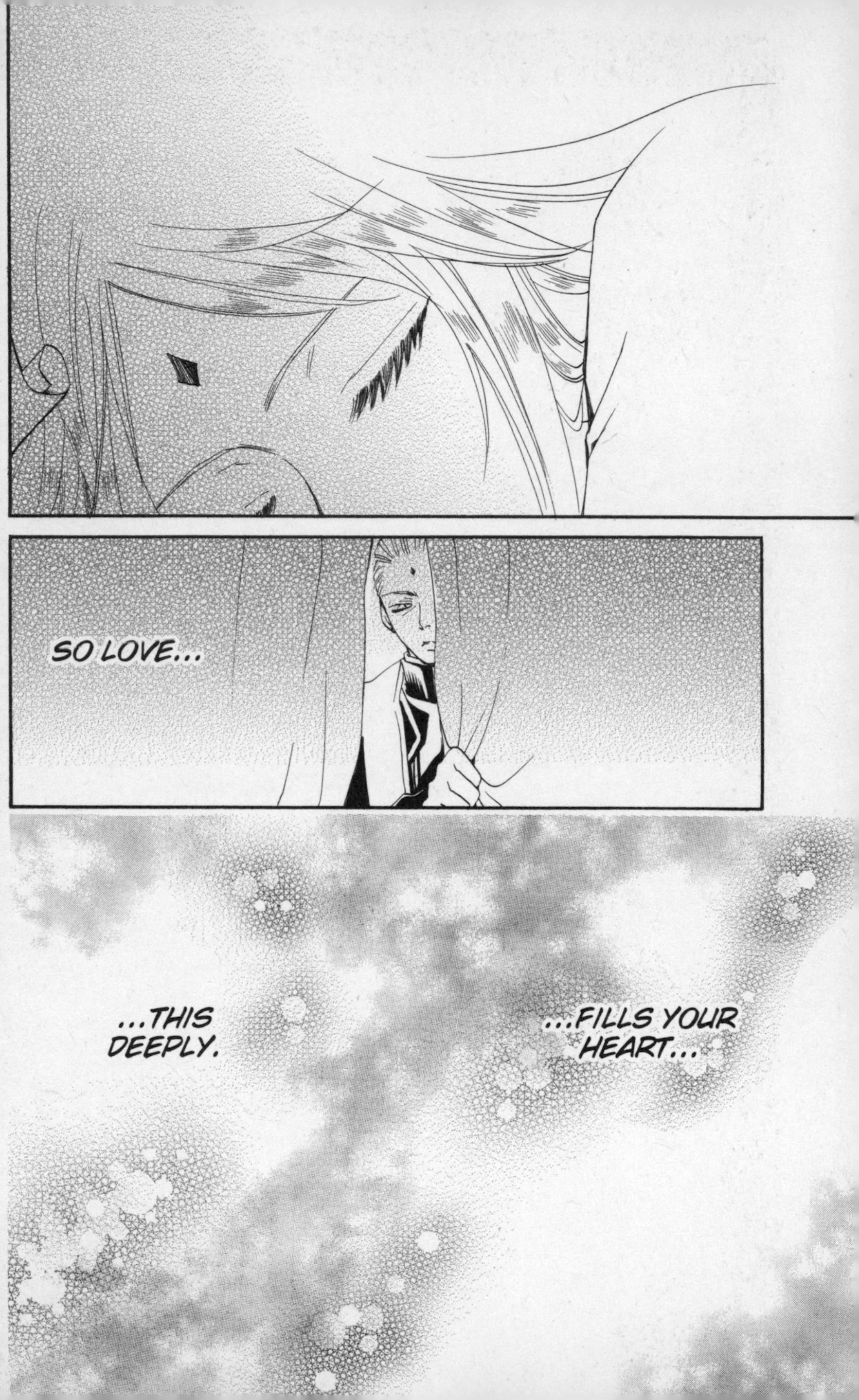
SO LOVE...
...FILLS YOUR HEART...
...THIS DEEPLY.

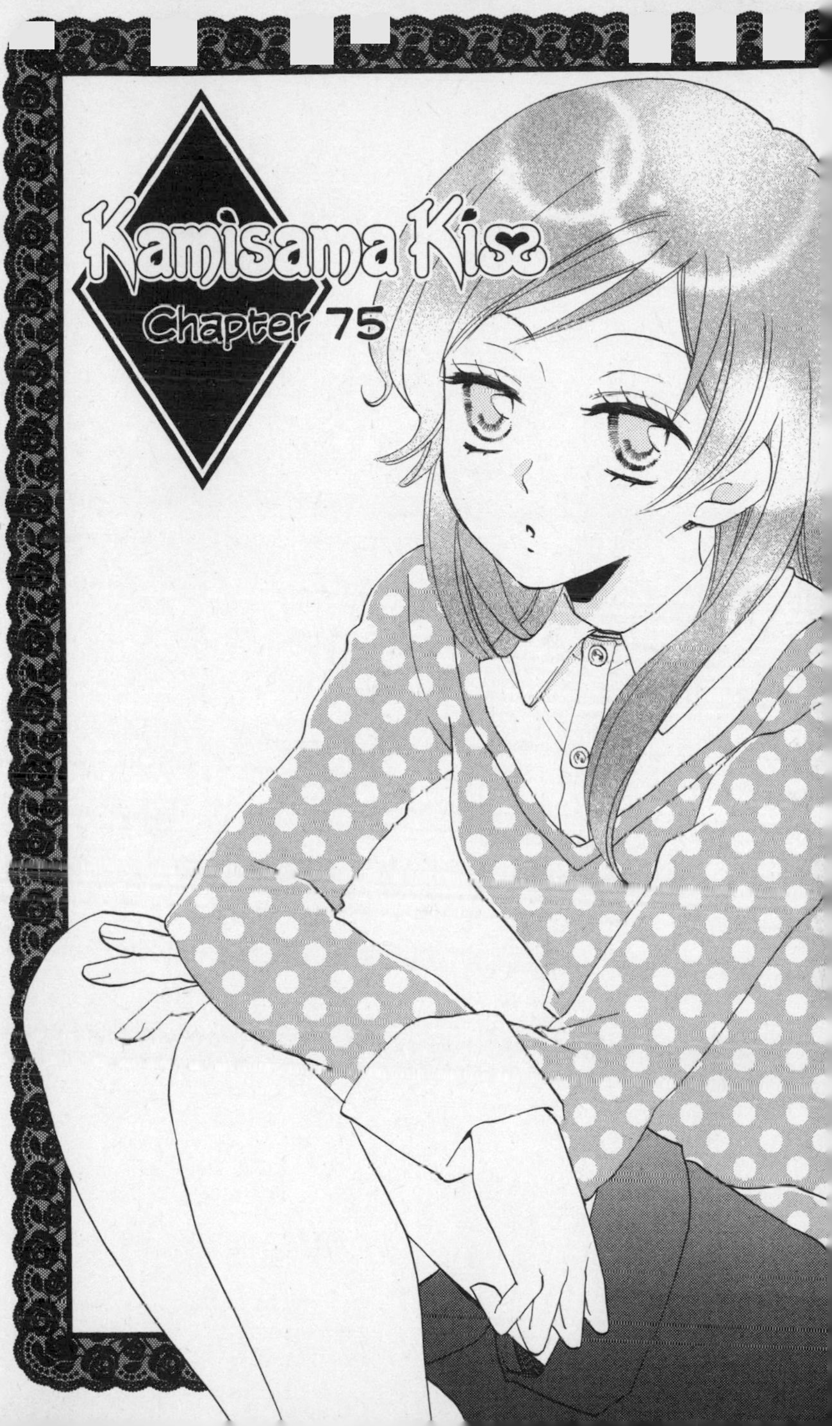
Kamisama Kiss
Chapter 75

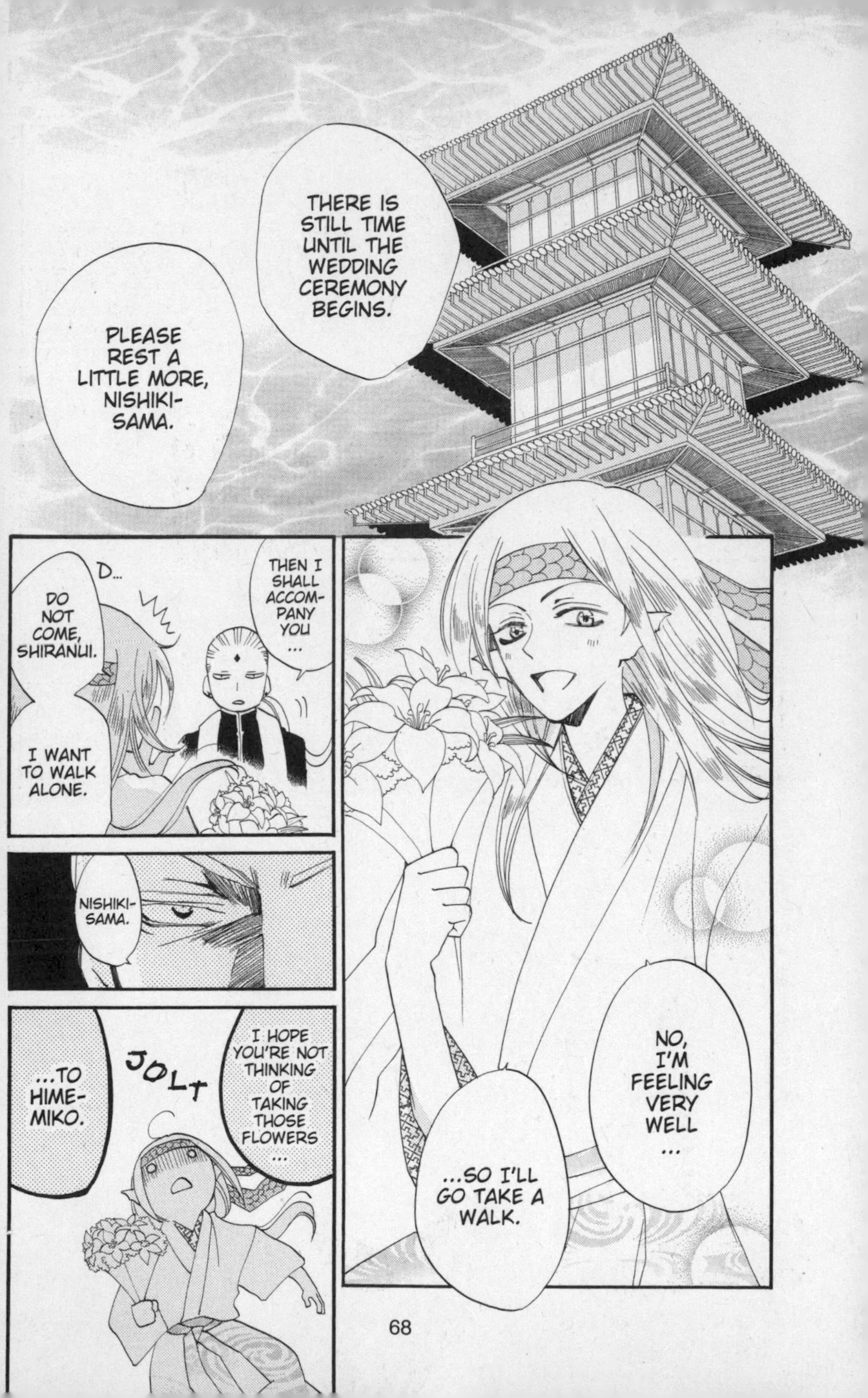
THERE IS STILL TIME UNTIL THE WEDDING CEREMONY BEGINS.
PLEASE REST A LITTLE MORE, NISHIKI-SAMA.
NO, I'M FEELING VERY WELL...
...SO I'LL GO TAKE A WALK.
THEN I SHALL ACCOMPANY YOU...
D...
DO NOT COME, SHIRANUI.
I WANT TO WALK ALONE.
NISHIKI-SAMA.
I HOPE YOU'RE NOT THINKING OF TAKING THOSE FLOWERS...
JOLT
...TO HIME-MIKO.

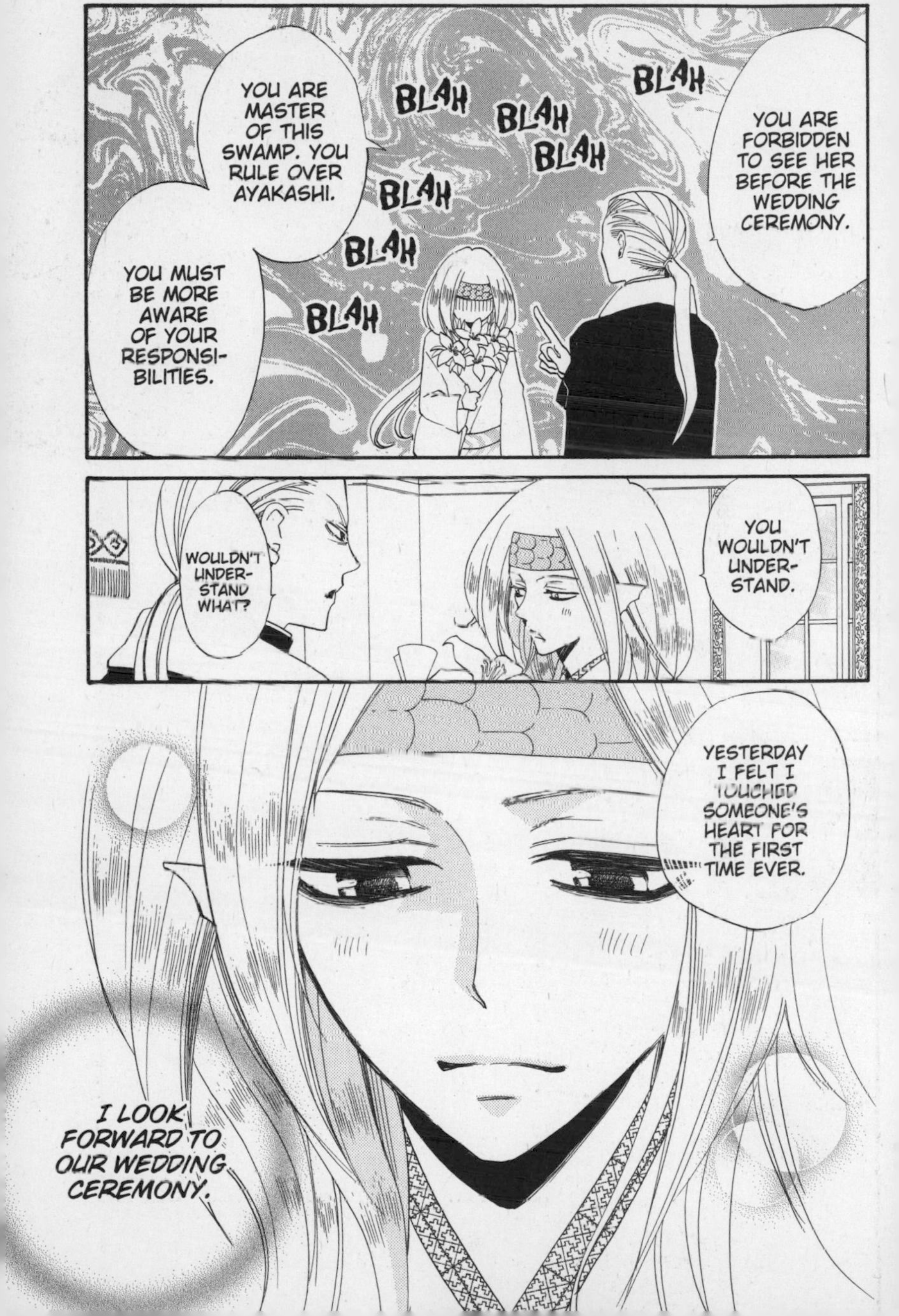
YOU ARE FORBIDDEN TO SEE HER BEFORE THE WEDDING CEREMONY.
BLAH
BLAH
BLAH
BLAH
BLAH
BLAH
BLAH
YOU ARE MASTER OF THIS SWAMP. YOU RULE OVER AYAKASHI.
YOU MUST BE MORE AWARE OF YOUR RESPONSI-BILITIES.
YOU WOULDN'T UNDER-STAND.
WOULDN'T UNDER-STAND WHAT?
YESTERDAY I FELT I TOUCHED SOMEONE'S HEART FOR THE FIRST TIME EVER.
I LOOK FORWARD TO OUR WEDDING CEREMONY.

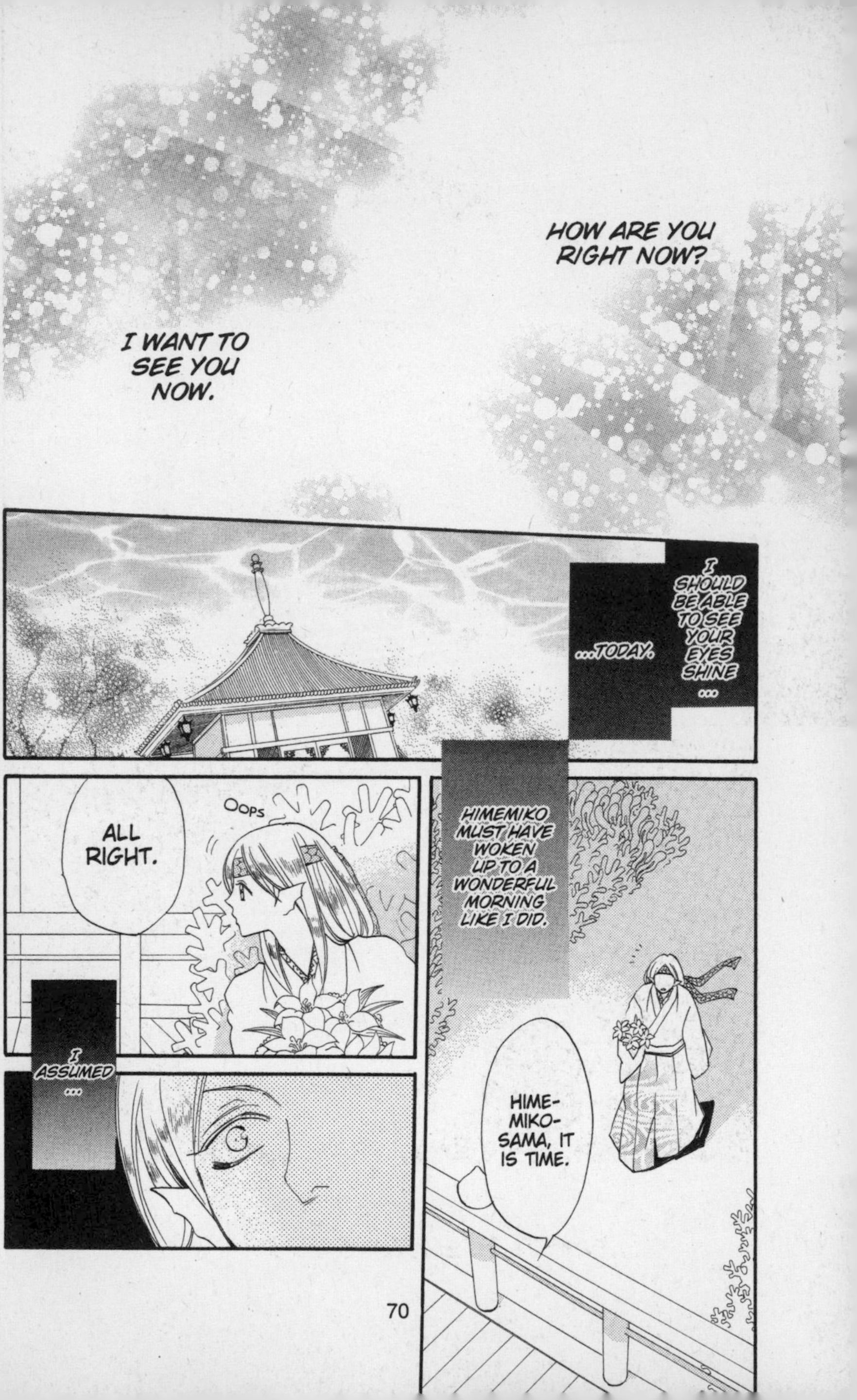
HOW ARE YOU RIGHT NOW?
I WANT TO SEE YOU NOW.
I SHOULD BE ABLE TO SEE YOUR EYES SHINE...
...TODAY.
HIMEMIKO MUST HAVE WOKEN UP TO A WONDERFUL MORNING LIKE I DID.
HIME-MIKO-SAMA, IT IS TIME.
ALL RIGHT.
OOPS
I ASSUMED...

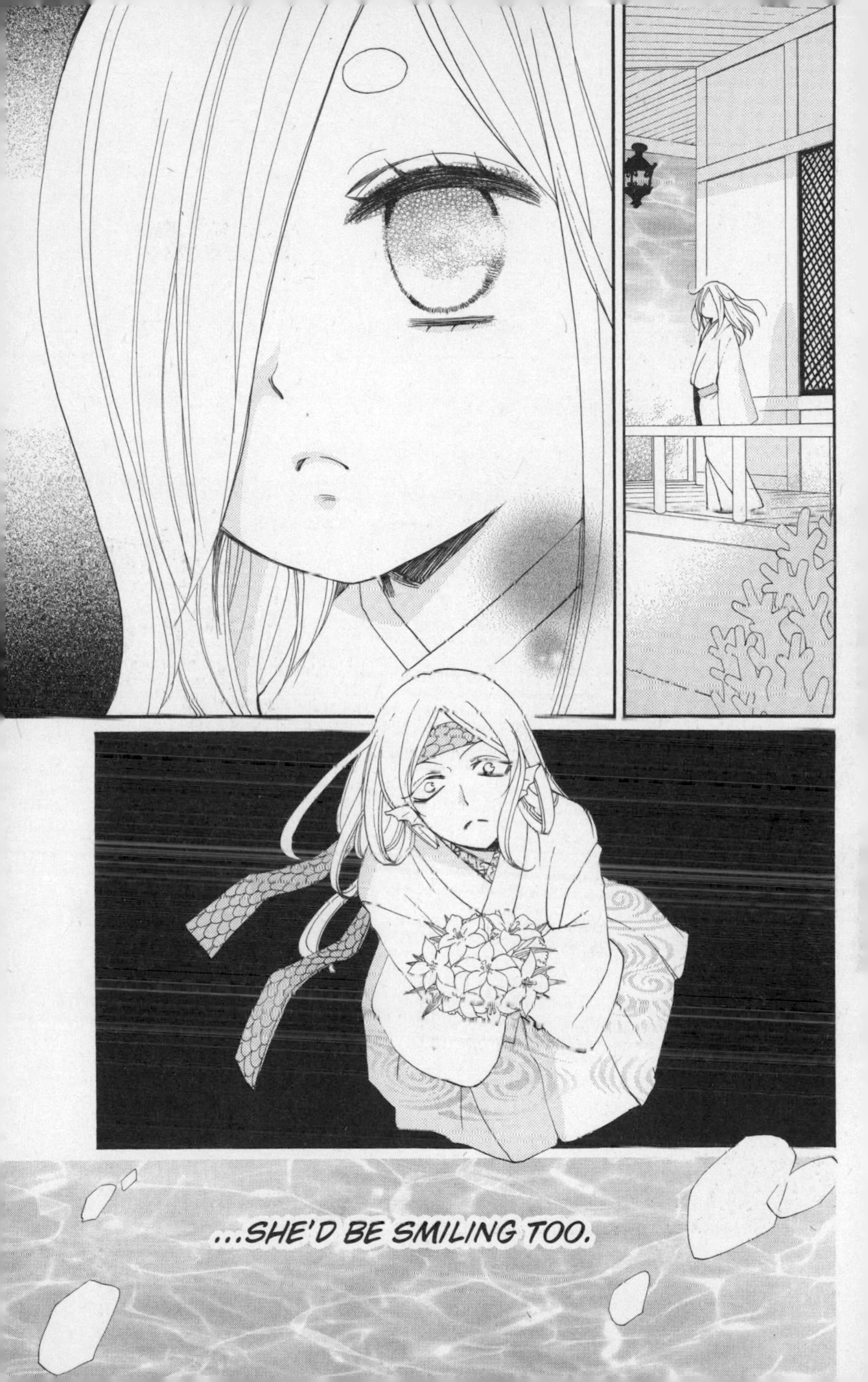
...SHE'D BE SMILING TOO.

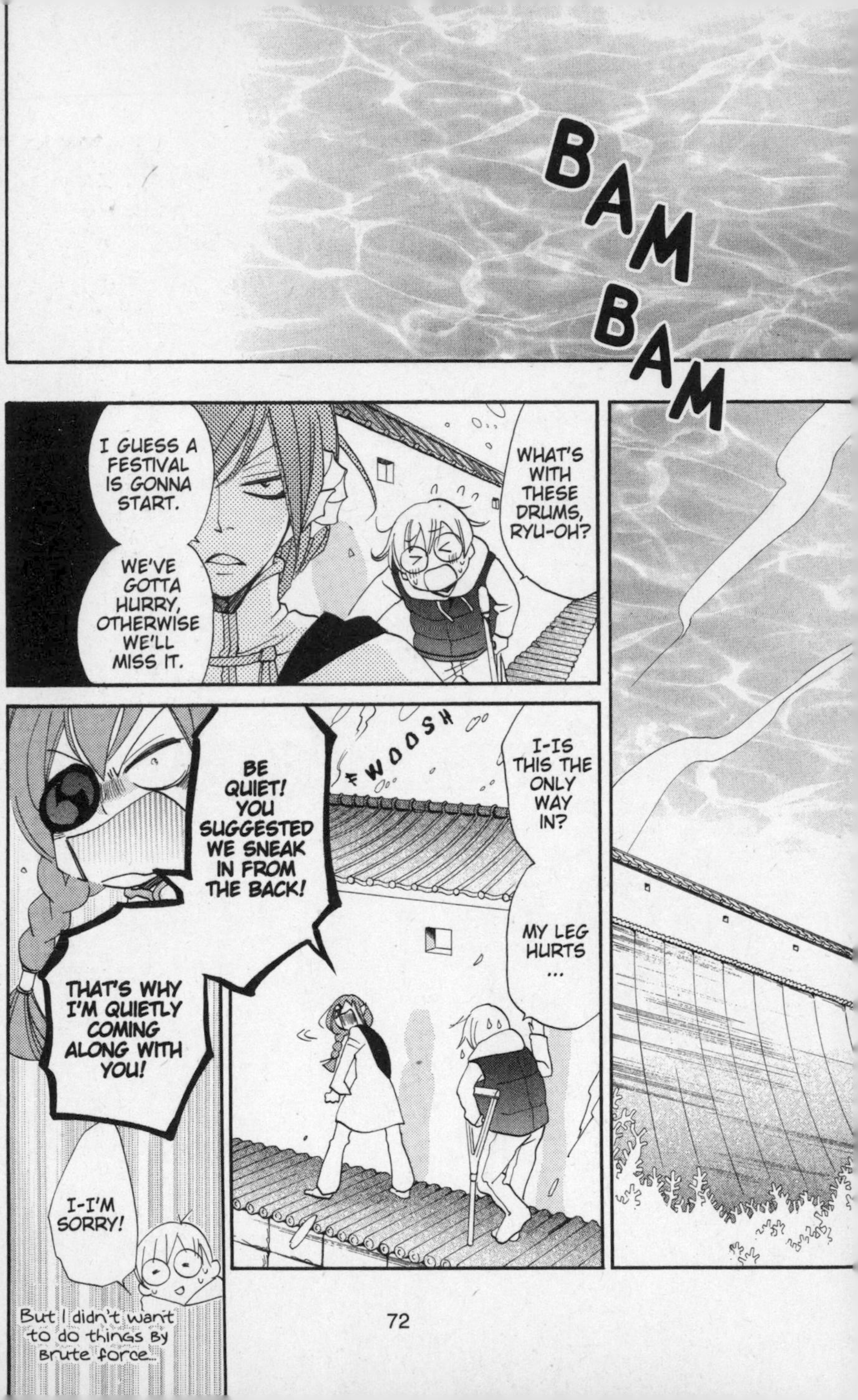
BAM BAM BAM BAM
WHAT'S WITH THESE DRUMS, RYU-OH?
I GUESS A FESTIVAL IS GONNA START.
WE'VE GOTTA HURRY, OTHERWISE WE'LL MISS IT.
I-IS THIS THE ONLY WAY IN?
MY LEG HURTS ...
WOOSH
BE QUIET! YOU SUGGESTED WE SNEAK IN FROM THE BACK!
THAT'S WHY I'M QUIETLY COMING ALONG WITH YOU!
I-I'M SORRY!
But I didn't want to do things by brute force...

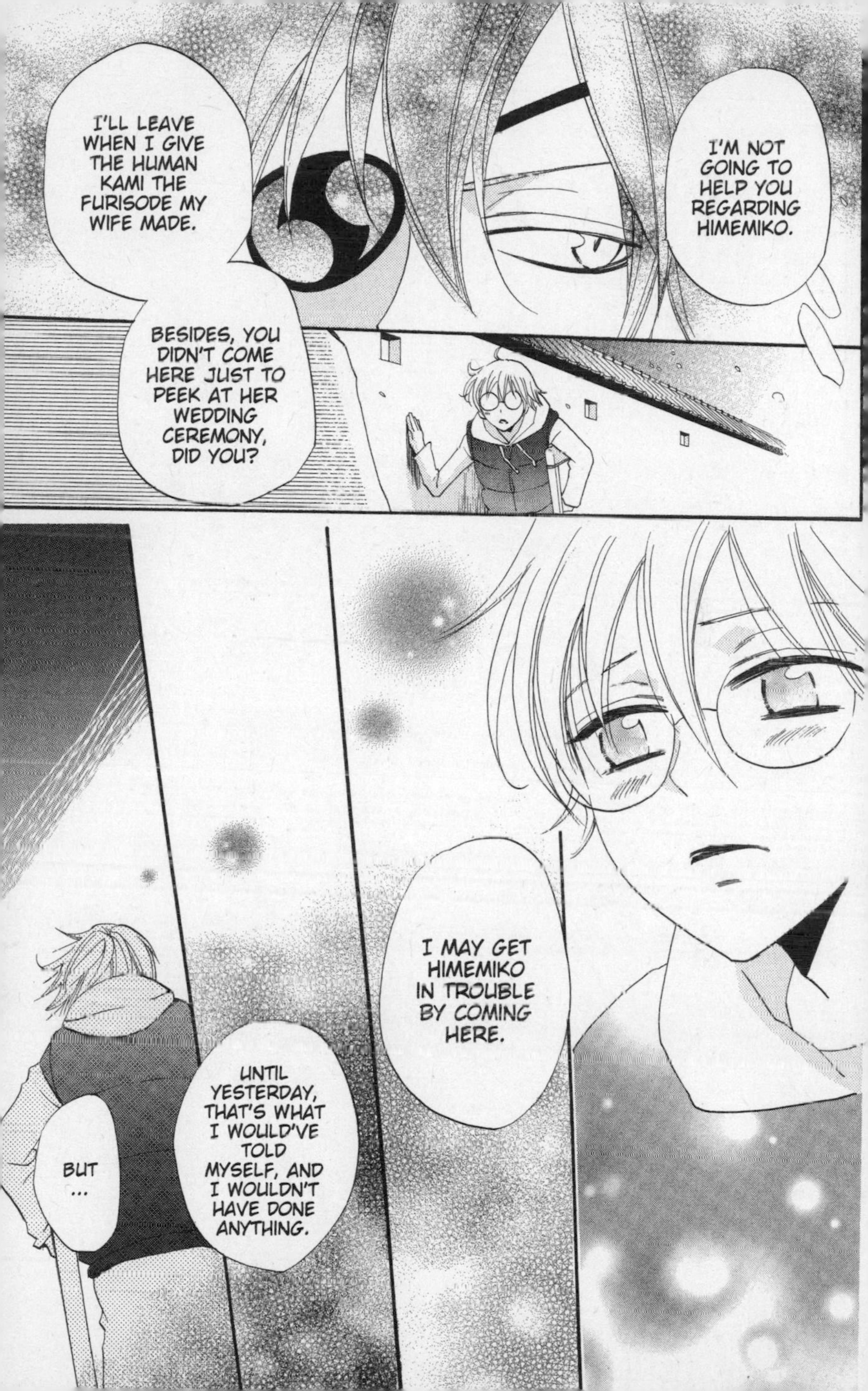
I'M NOT GOING TO HELP YOU REGARDING HIMEMIKO.
I'LL LEAVE WHEN I GIVE THE HUMAN KAMI THE FURISODE MY WIFE MADE.
BESIDES, YOU DIDN'T COME HERE JUST TO PEEK AT HER WEDDING CEREMONY, DID YOU?
I MAY GET HIMEMIKO IN TROUBLE BY COMING HERE.
UNTIL YESTERDAY, THAT'S WHAT I WOULD'VE TOLD MYSELF, AND I WOULDN'T HAVE DONE ANYTHING.
BUT ...

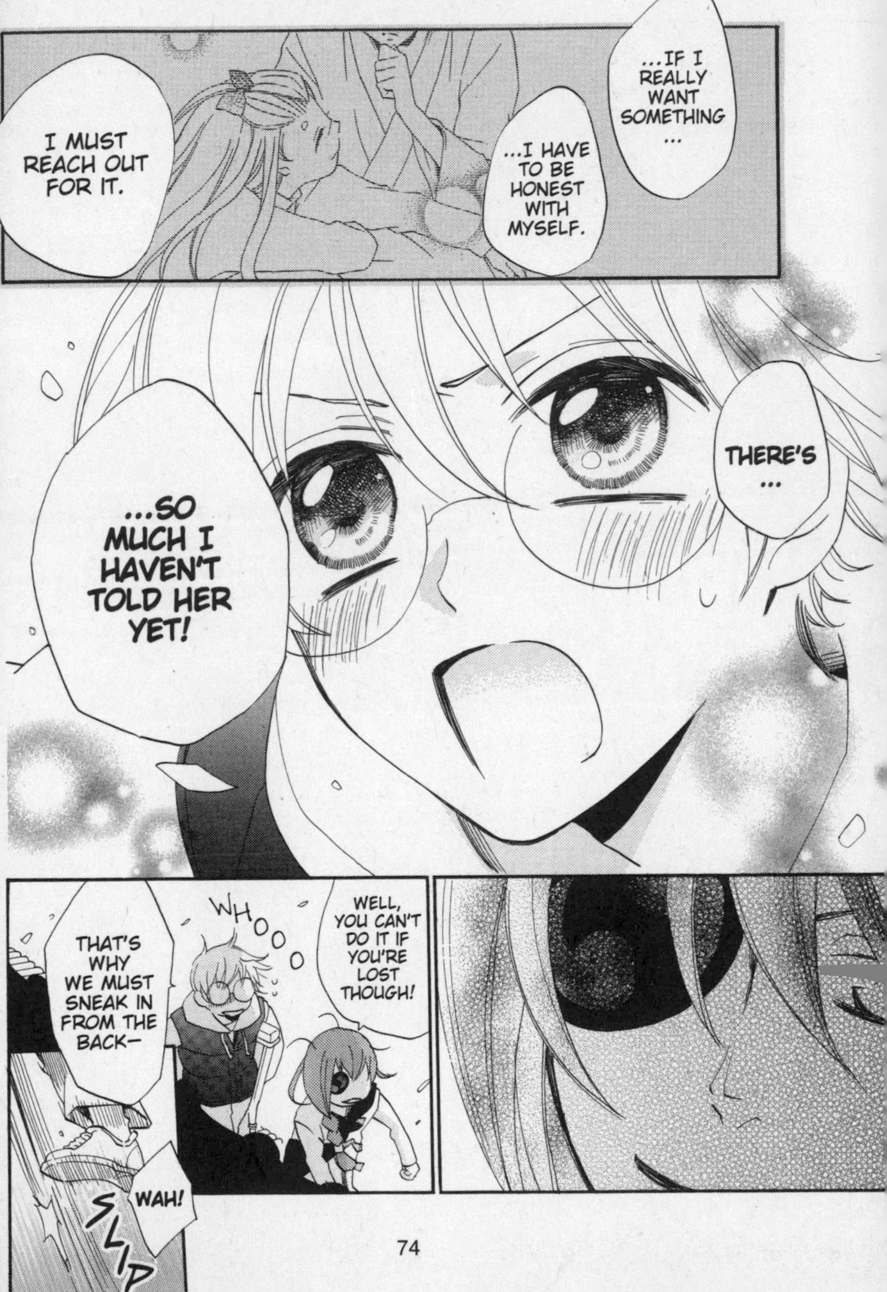
...IF I REALLY WANT SOMETHING ...
...I HAVE TO BE HONEST WITH MYSELF.
I MUST REACH OUT FOR IT.
THERE'S ...
...SO MUCH I HAVEN'T TOLD HER YET!
WELL, YOU CAN'T DO IT IF YOU'RE LOST THOUGH!
WHOOOO
THAT'S WHY WE MUST SNEAK IN FROM THE BACK—
WAH!
SLIP

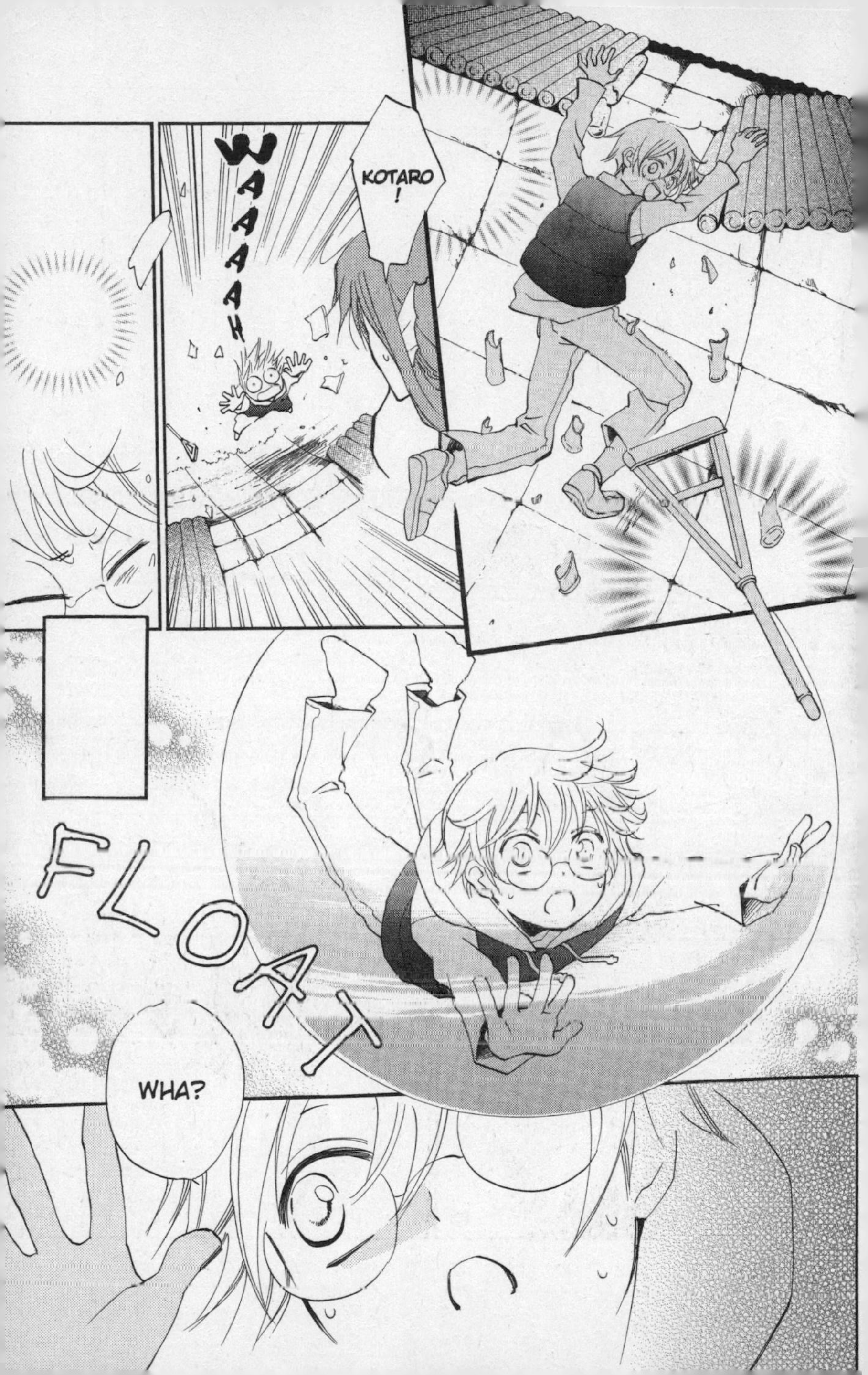
KOTARO!
WAAAAAH
FLOAT
WHA?

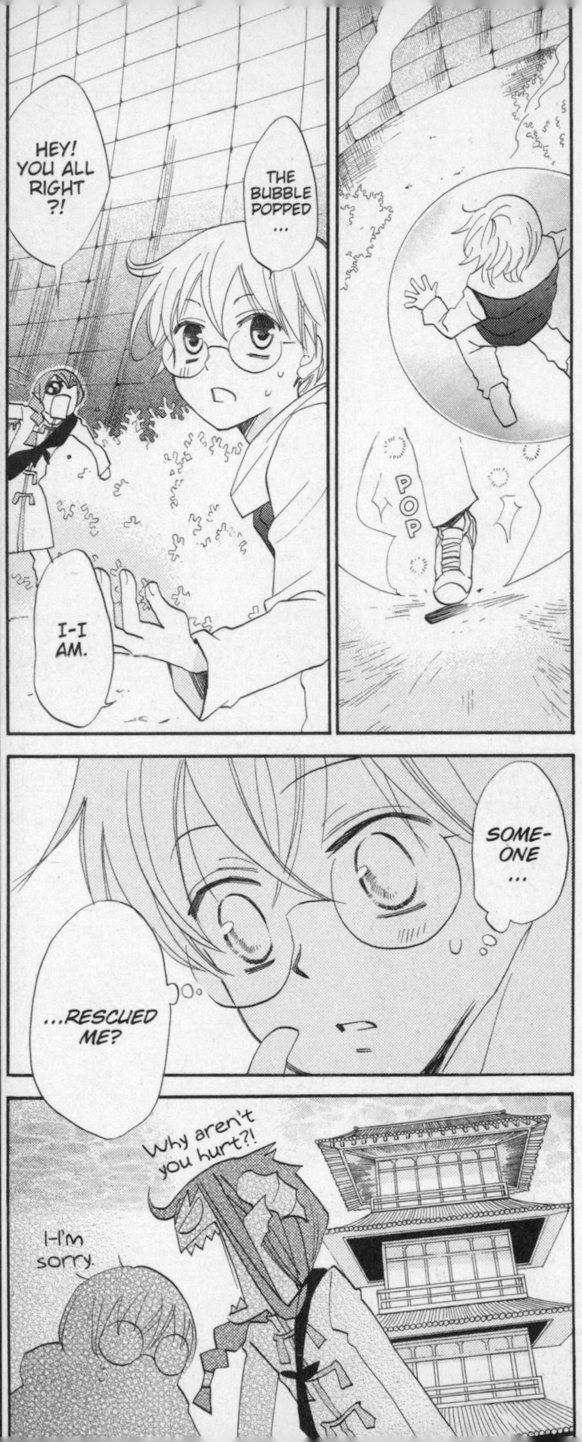
POP
THE BUBBLE POPPED...
HEY! YOU ALL RIGHT?!
I-I AM.
SOME-ONE...
...RESCUED ME?
Why aren't you hurt?!
I-I'm sorry.

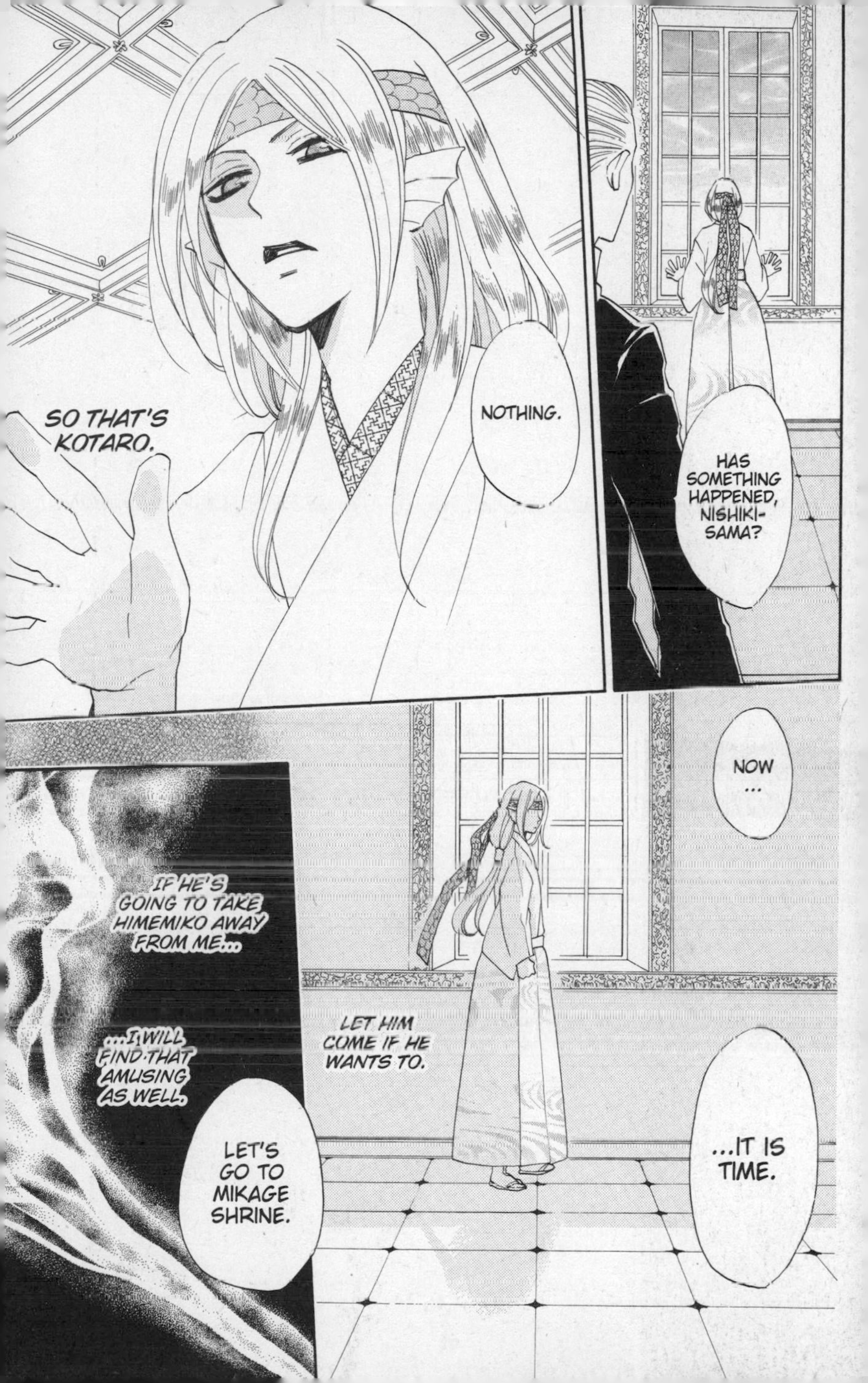
HAS SOMETHING HAPPENED, NISHIKI-SAMA?
NOTHING.
SO THAT'S KOTARO.
NOW...
...IT IS TIME.
LET HIM COME IF HE WANTS TO.
IF HE'S GOING TO TAKE HIMEMIKO AWAY FROM ME...
...I WILL FIND THAT AMUSING AS WELL.
LET'S GO TO MIKAGE SHRINE.

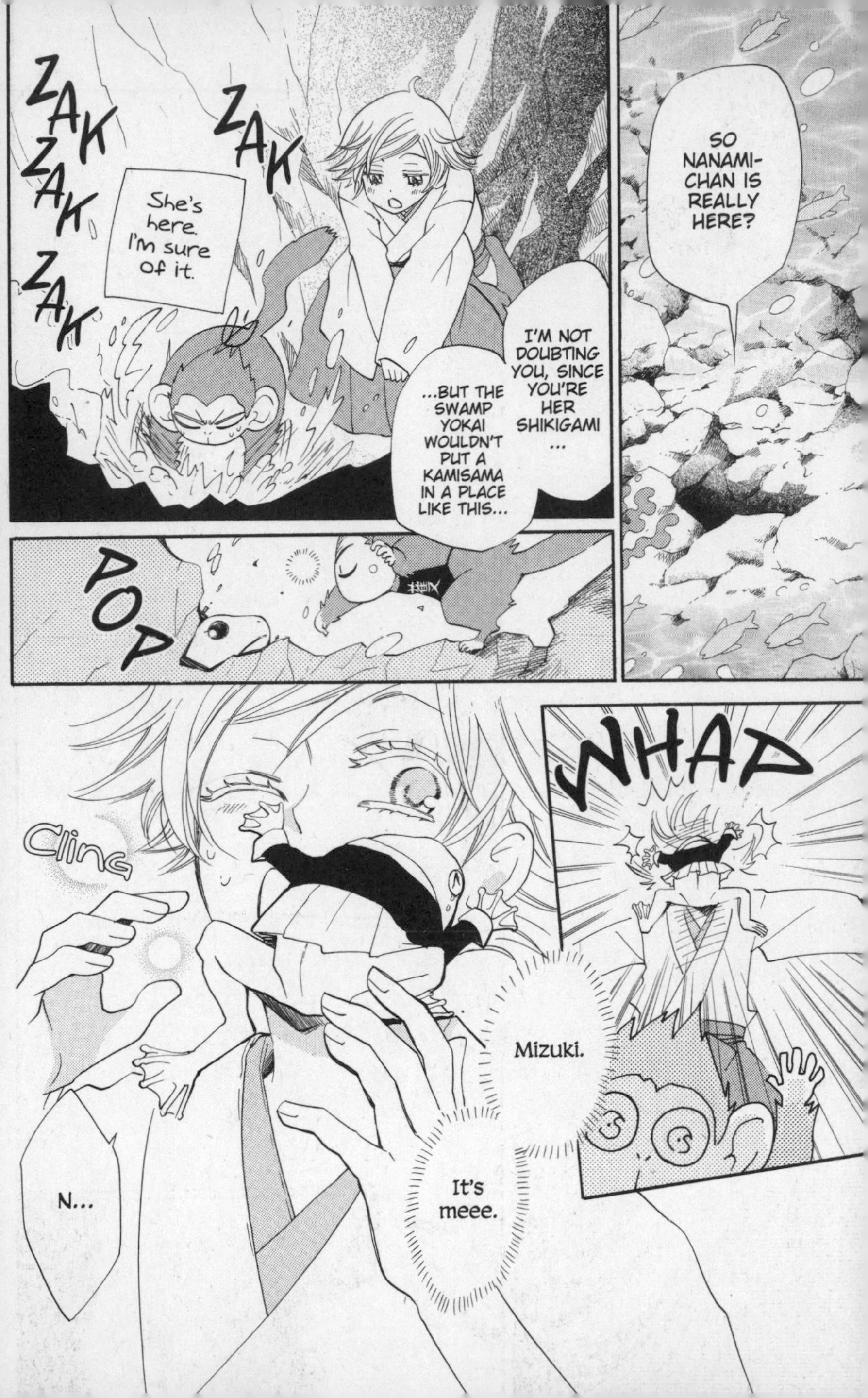
SO NANAMI-CHAN IS REALLY HERE?
ZAK
ZAK ZAK ZAK ZAK
She's here. I'm sure of it.
I'M NOT DOUBTING YOU, SINCE YOU'RE HER SHIKIGAMI...
...BUT THE SWAMP YOKAI WOULDN'T PUT A KAMISAMA IN A PLACE LIKE THIS...
POP
WHAP
Cling
Mizuki.
It's meee.
N...

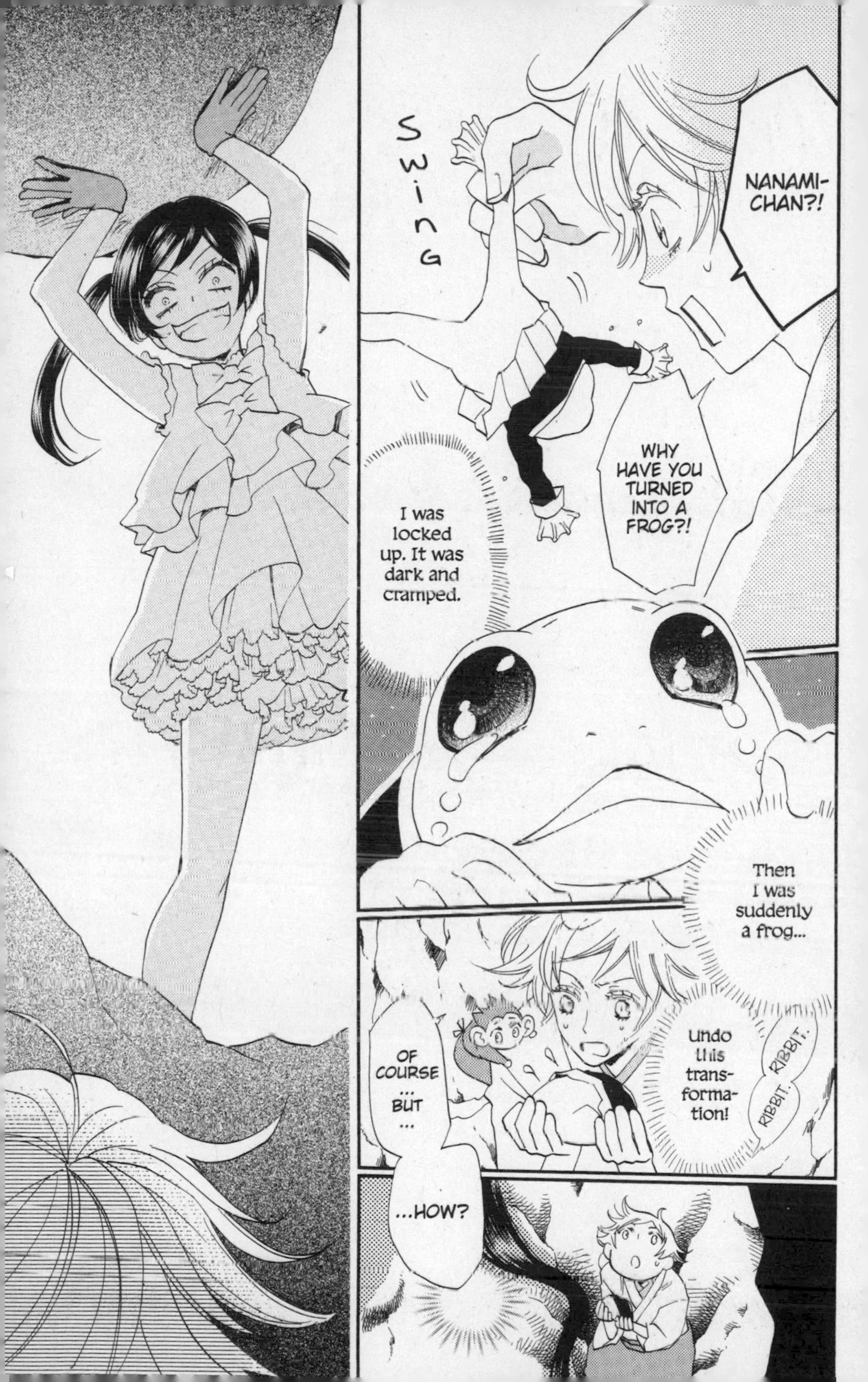
NANAMI-CHAN?!
WHY HAVE YOU TURNED INTO A FROG?!
SWING
I was locked up. It was dark and cramped.
Then I was suddenly a frog...
RIBBIT. RIBBIT.
Undo this transforma-tion!
OF COURSE ... BUT ...
...HOW?

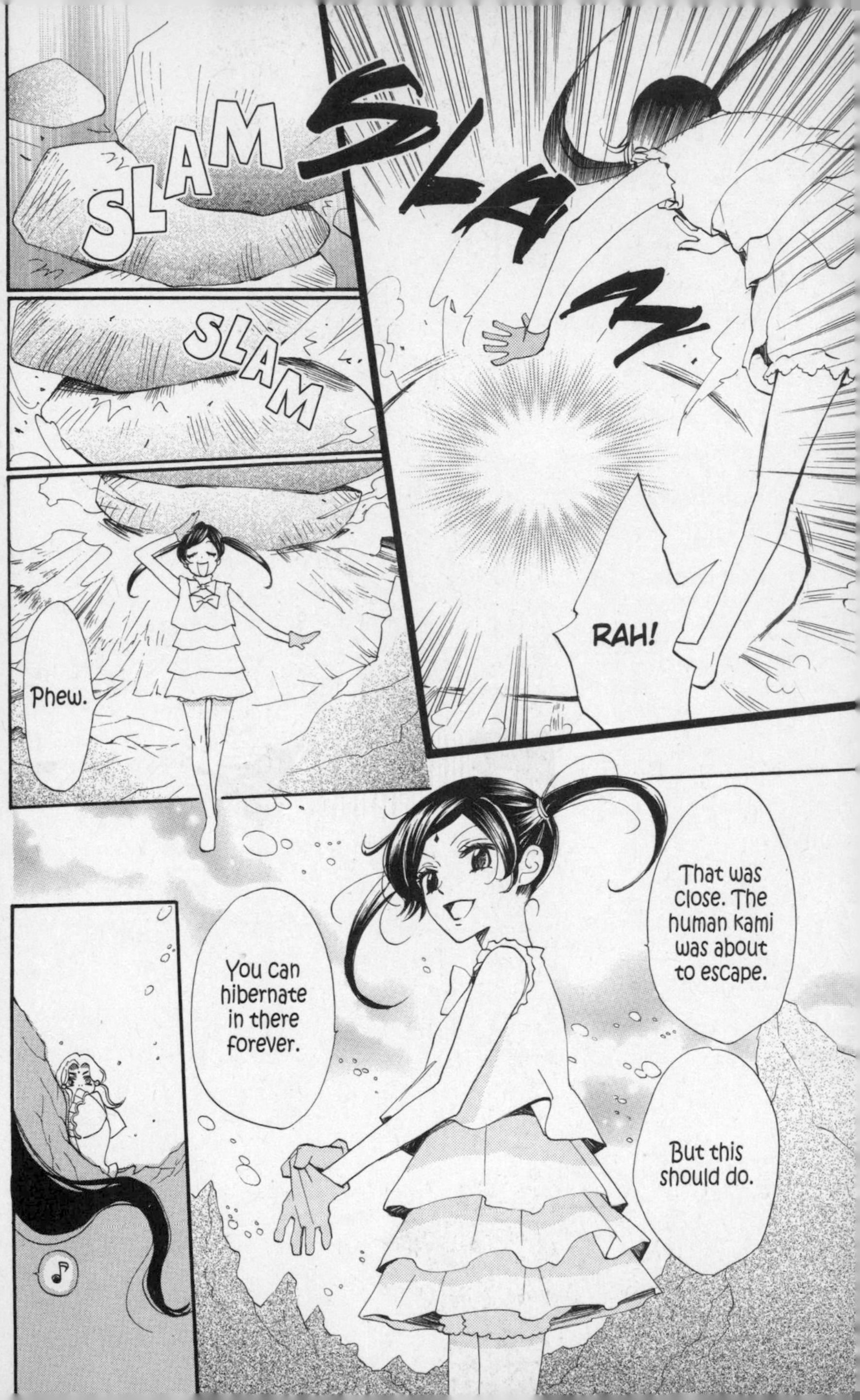
SLAM
RAH!
SLAM
SLAM
Phew.
That was close. The human kami was about to escape.
But this should do.
You can hibernate in there forever.

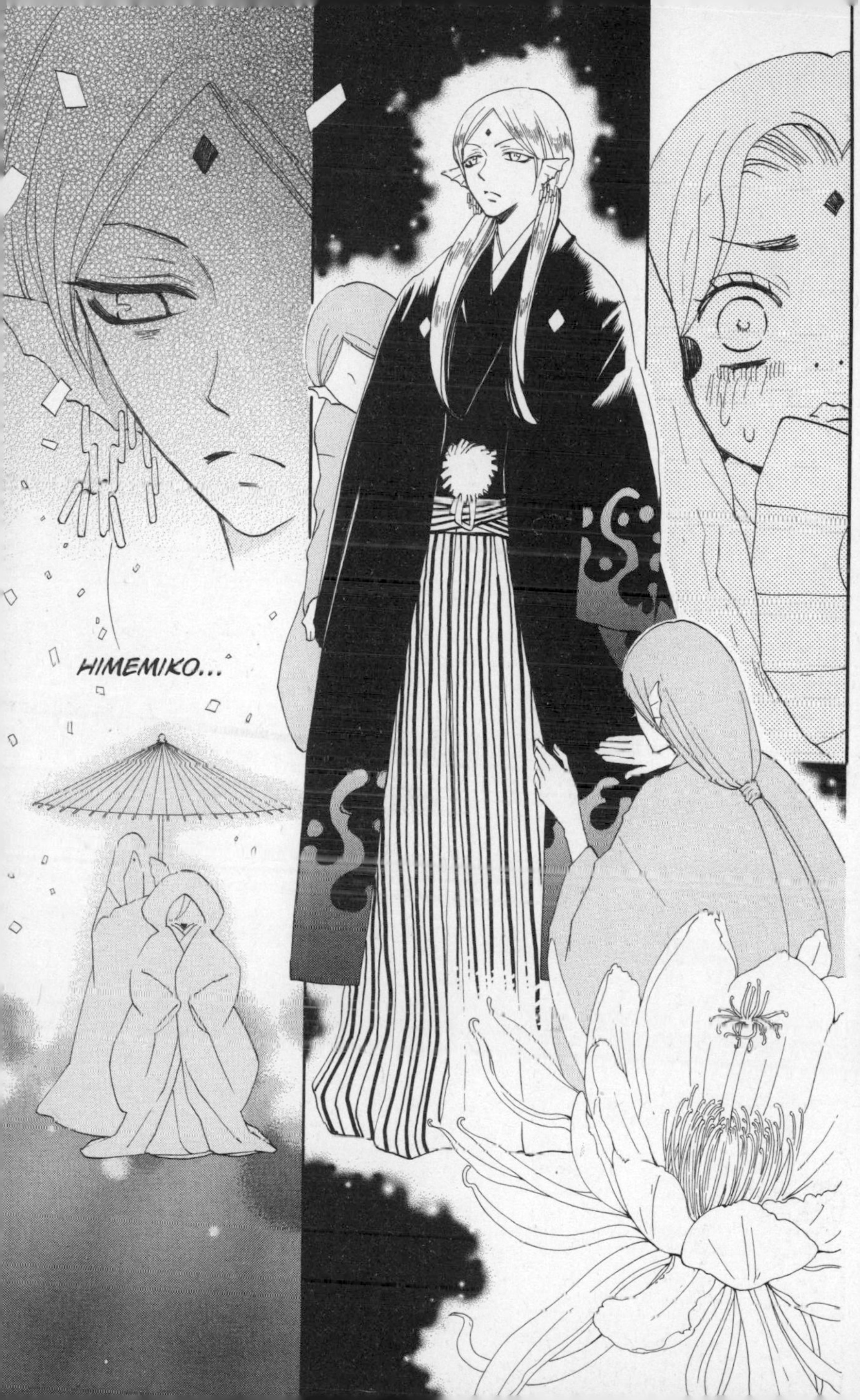
HIMEMIKO...

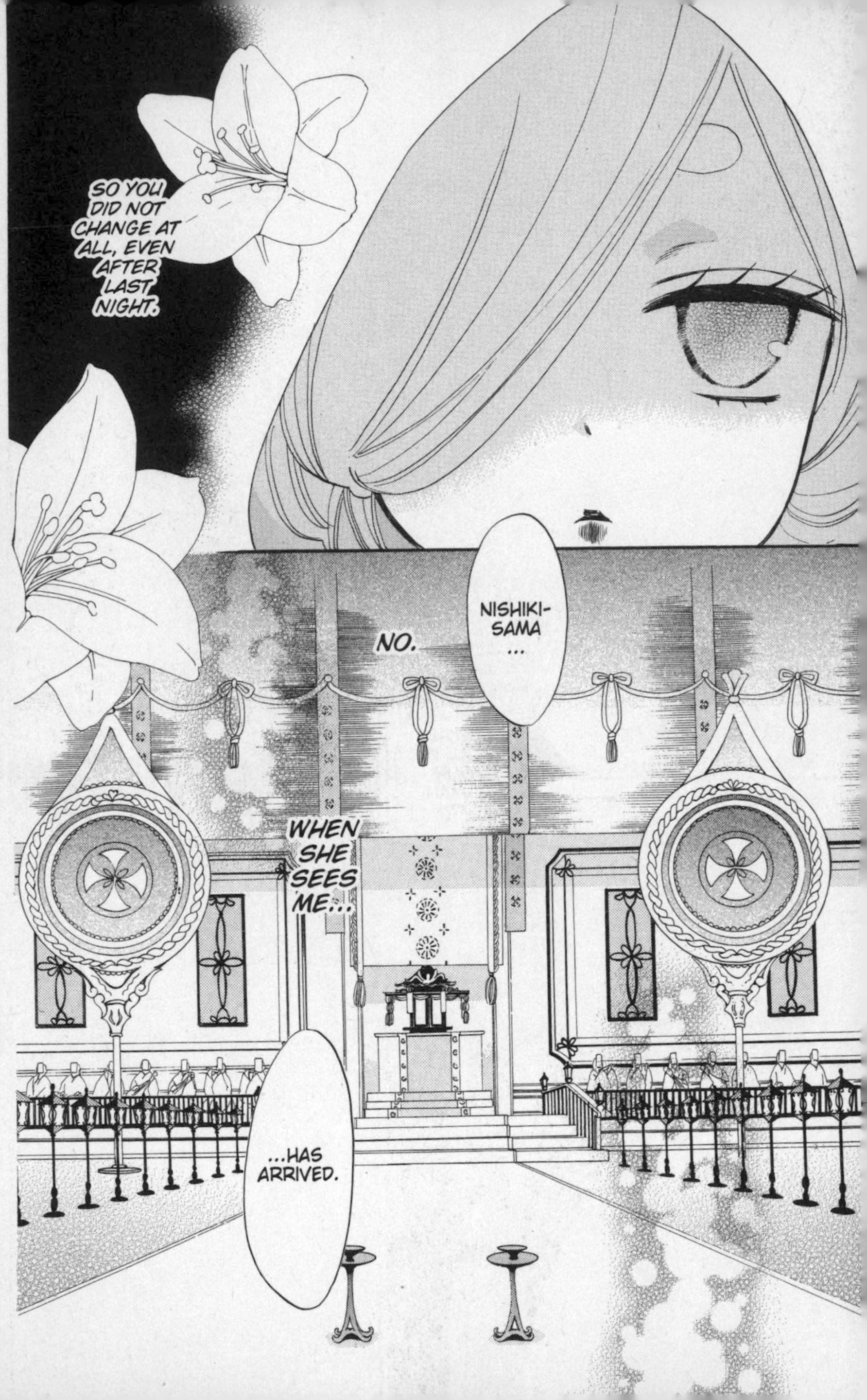
SO YOU DID NOT CHANGE AT ALL, EVEN AFTER LAST NIGHT.
NISHIKI-SAMA ...
NO.
WHEN SHE SEES ME...
...HAS ARRIVED.

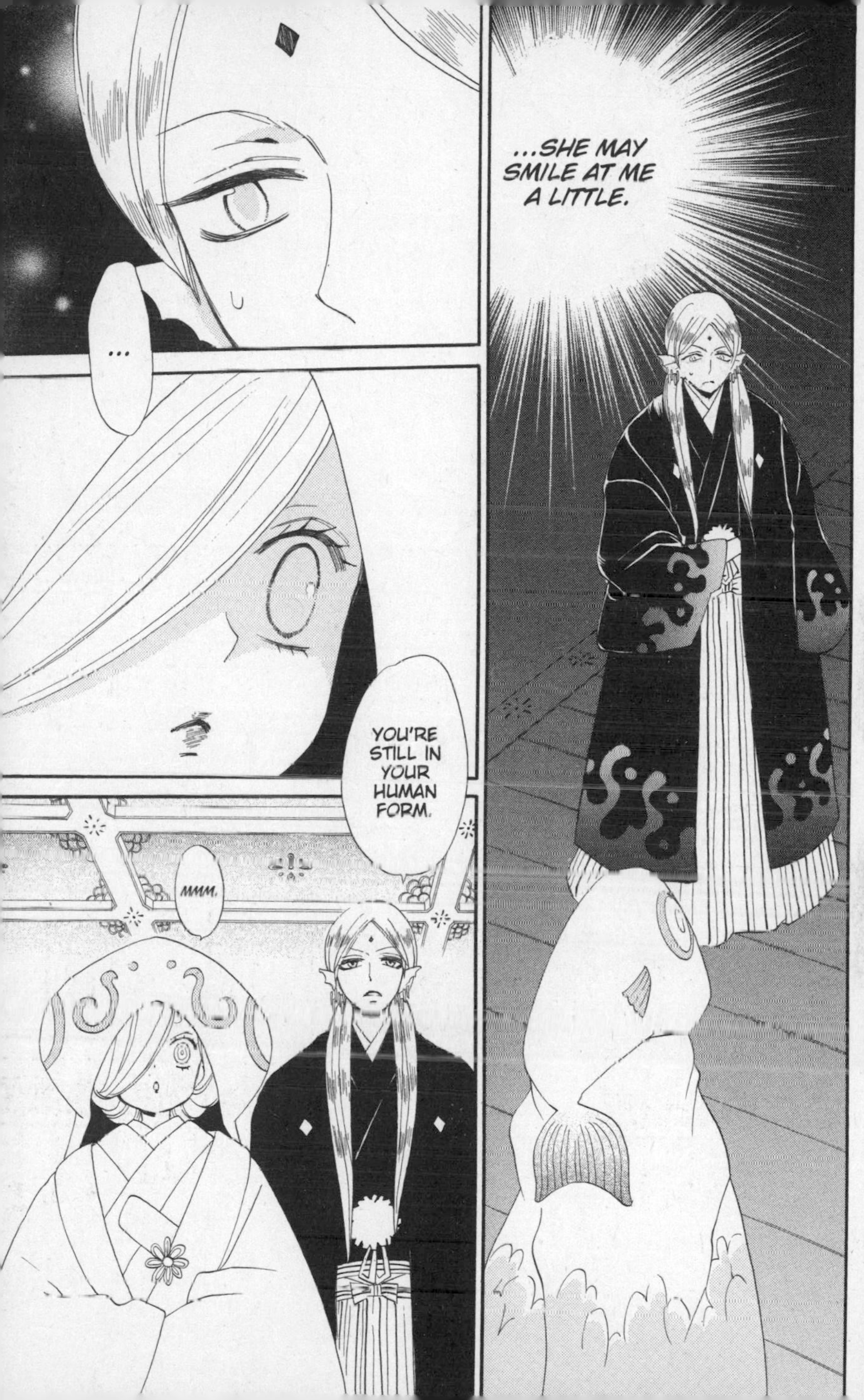
...SHE MAY SMILE AT ME A LITTLE.
...
YOU'RE STILL IN YOUR HUMAN FORM.
MMM.

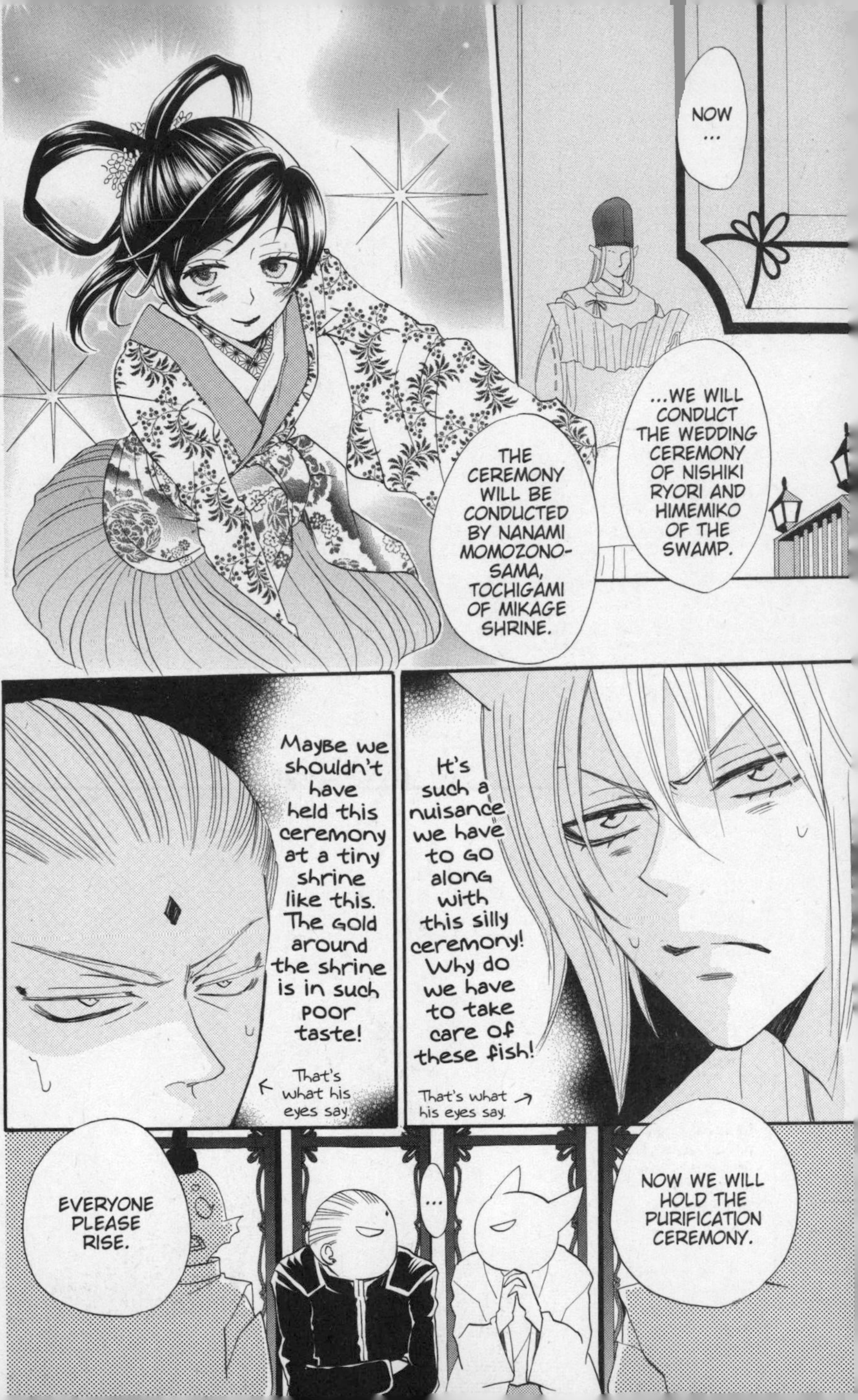
NOW ...
...WE WILL CONDUCT THE WEDDING CEREMONY OF NISHIKI RYORI AND HIMEMIKO OF THE SWAMP.
THE CEREMONY WILL BE CONDUCTED BY NANAMI MOMOZONO-SAMA, TOCHIGAMI OF MIKAGE SHRINE.
It's such a nuisance we have to go along with this silly ceremony! Why do we have to take care of these fish!
That's what his eyes say.
Maybe we shouldn't have held this ceremony at a tiny shrine like this. The gold around the shrine is in such poor taste!
That's what his eyes say.
NOW WE WILL HOLD THE PURIFICATION CEREMONY.
...
EVERYONE PLEASE RISE.

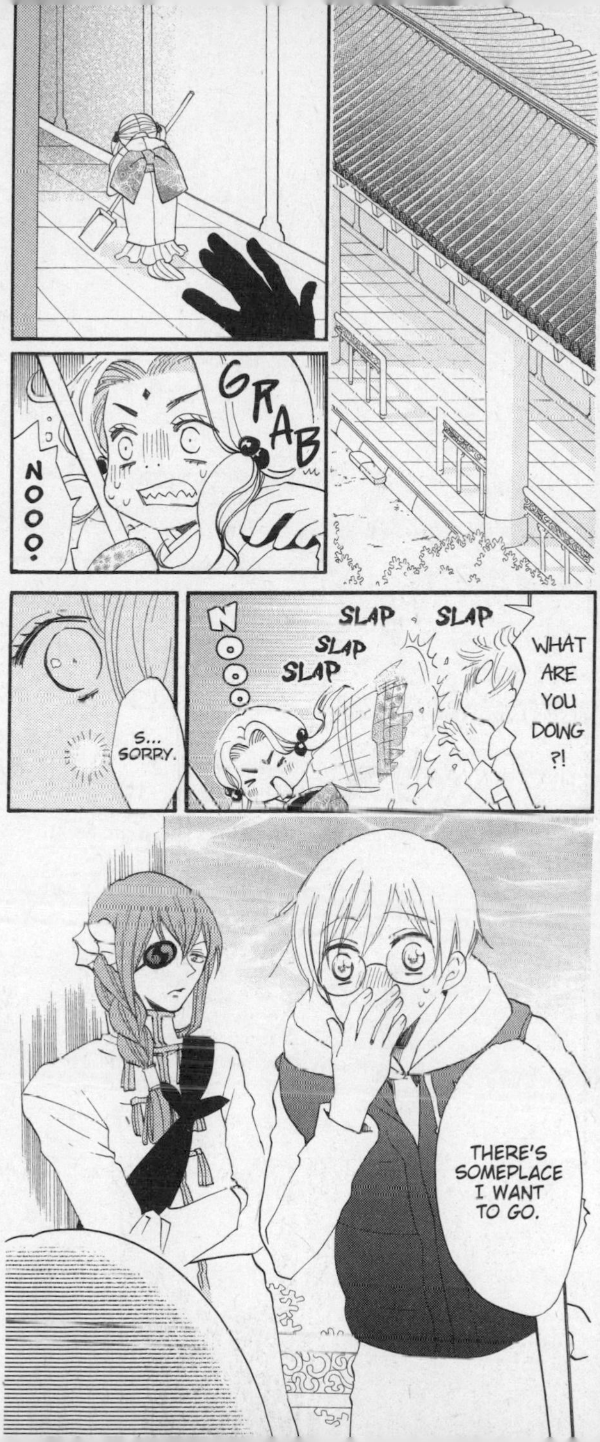
GRAB
NOOO.
NOOO
SLAP SLAP
SLAP SLAP
WHAT ARE YOU DOING?!
S... SORRY.
THERE'S SOMEPLACE I WANT TO GO.

→

(continued)

And so.

I moved to the new place, but it is very windy... and when I open the windows...

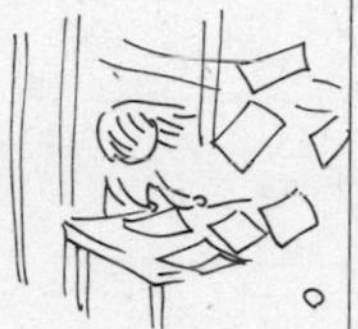

FWOOSH

...papers fly around, and my cat is so so scared, it hides underneath the sofa.

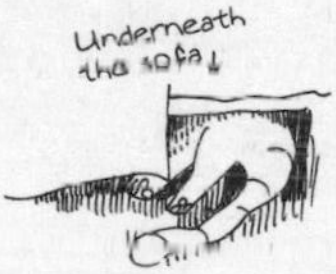
Underneath the sofa

So a paper-weight is unexpectedly very useful on my desk now.

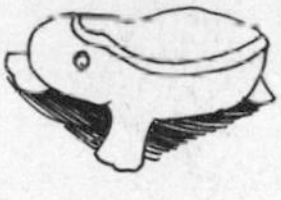

I bought the paperweight at Honnoji temple in Kyoto. It's cute.

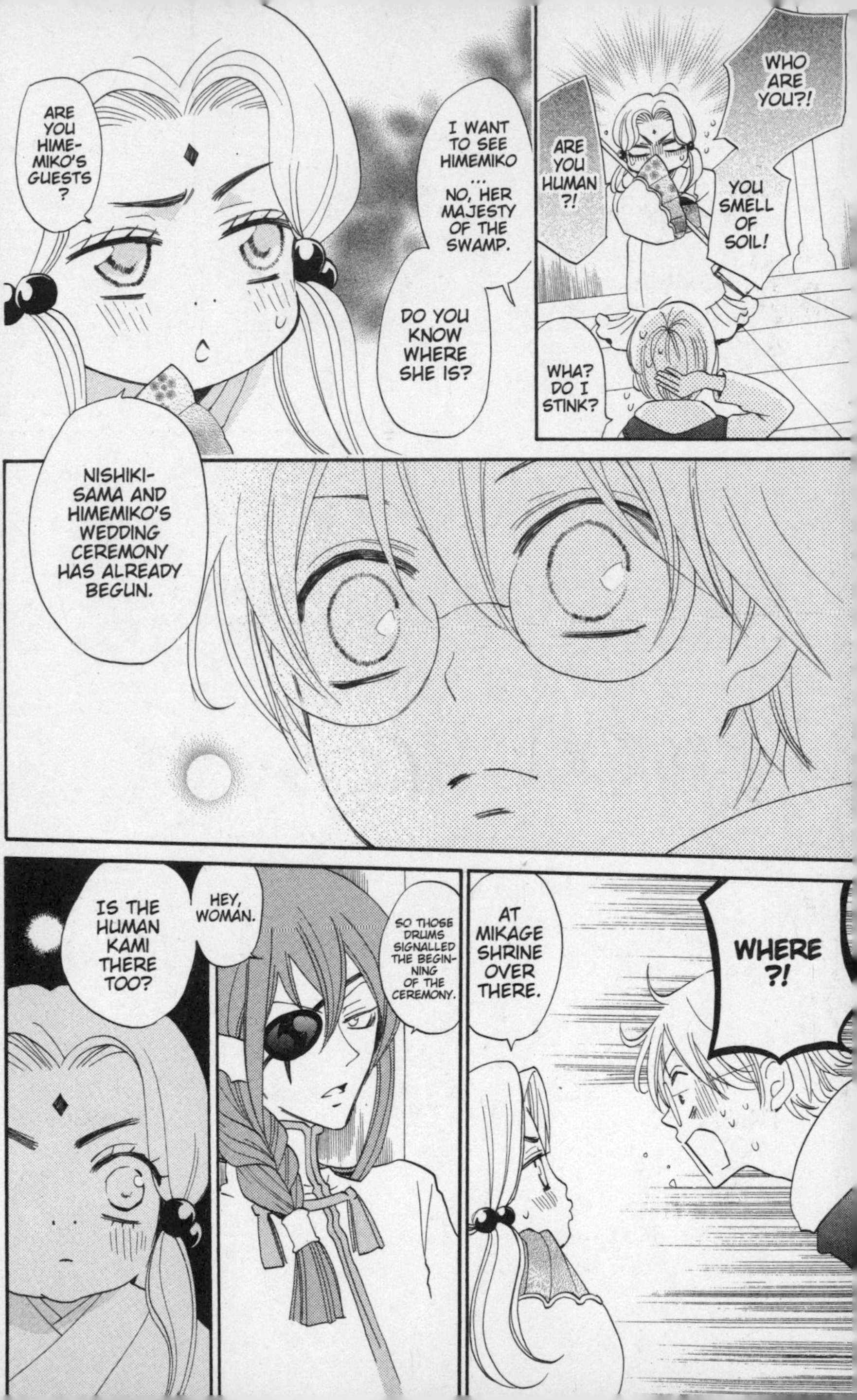
WHO ARE YOU?!
YOU SMELL OF SOIL!
ARE YOU HUMAN?!
WHA? DO I STINK?
I WANT TO SEE HIMEMIKO ... NO, HER MAJESTY OF THE SWAMP.
DO YOU KNOW WHERE SHE IS?
ARE YOU HIME-MIKO'S GUESTS?
NISHIKI-SAMA AND HIMEMIKO'S WEDDING CEREMONY HAS ALREADY BEGUN.
WHERE?!
AT MIKAGE SHRINE OVER THERE.
SO THOSE DRUMS SIGNALLED THE BEGIN-NING OF THE CEREMONY.
HEY, WOMAN.
IS THE HUMAN KAMI THERE TOO?

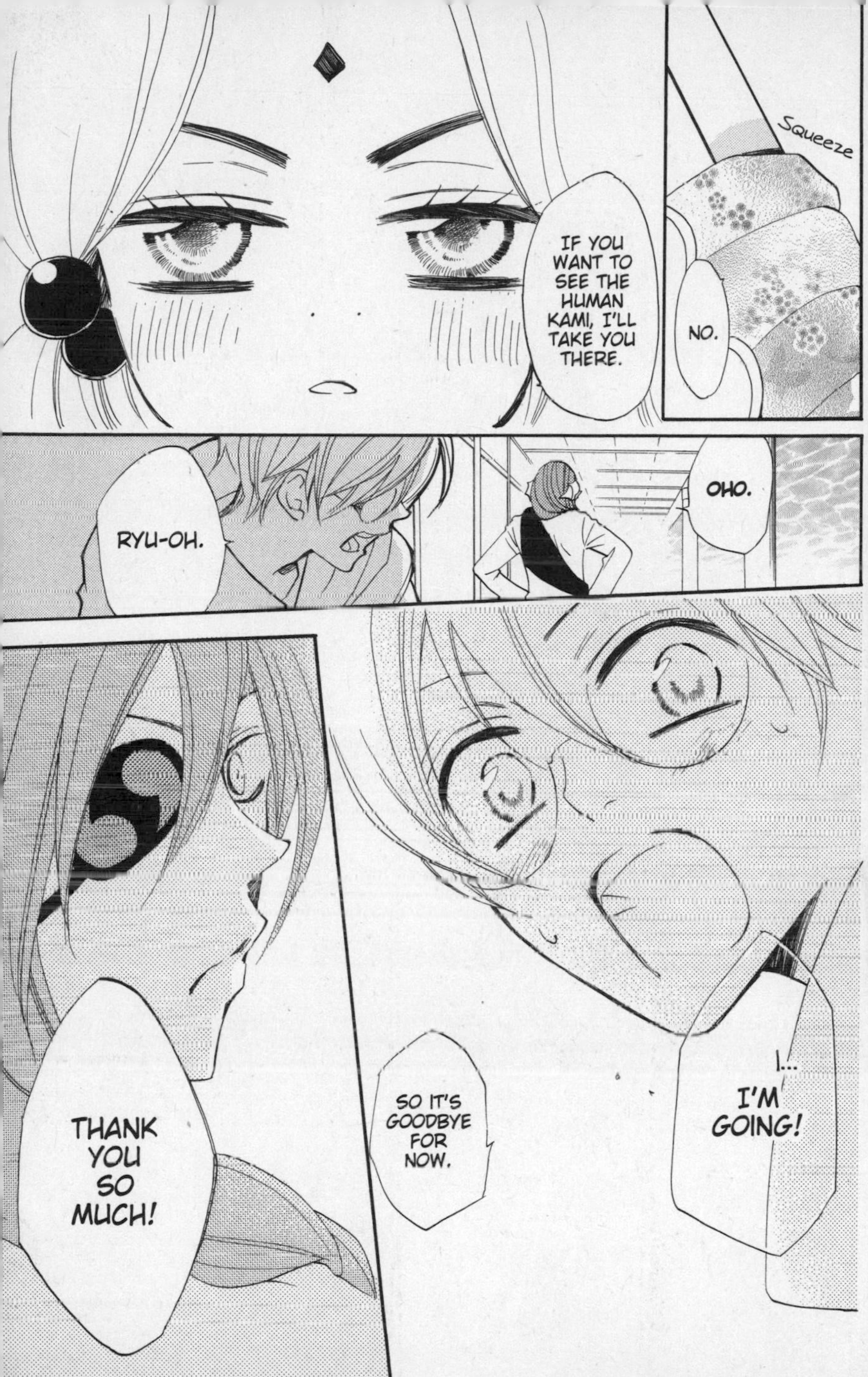
Squeeze
NO.
IF YOU WANT TO SEE THE HUMAN KAMI, I'LL TAKE YOU THERE.
OHO.
RYU-OH.
I... I'M GOING!
SO IT'S GOODBYE FOR NOW.
THANK YOU SO MUCH!

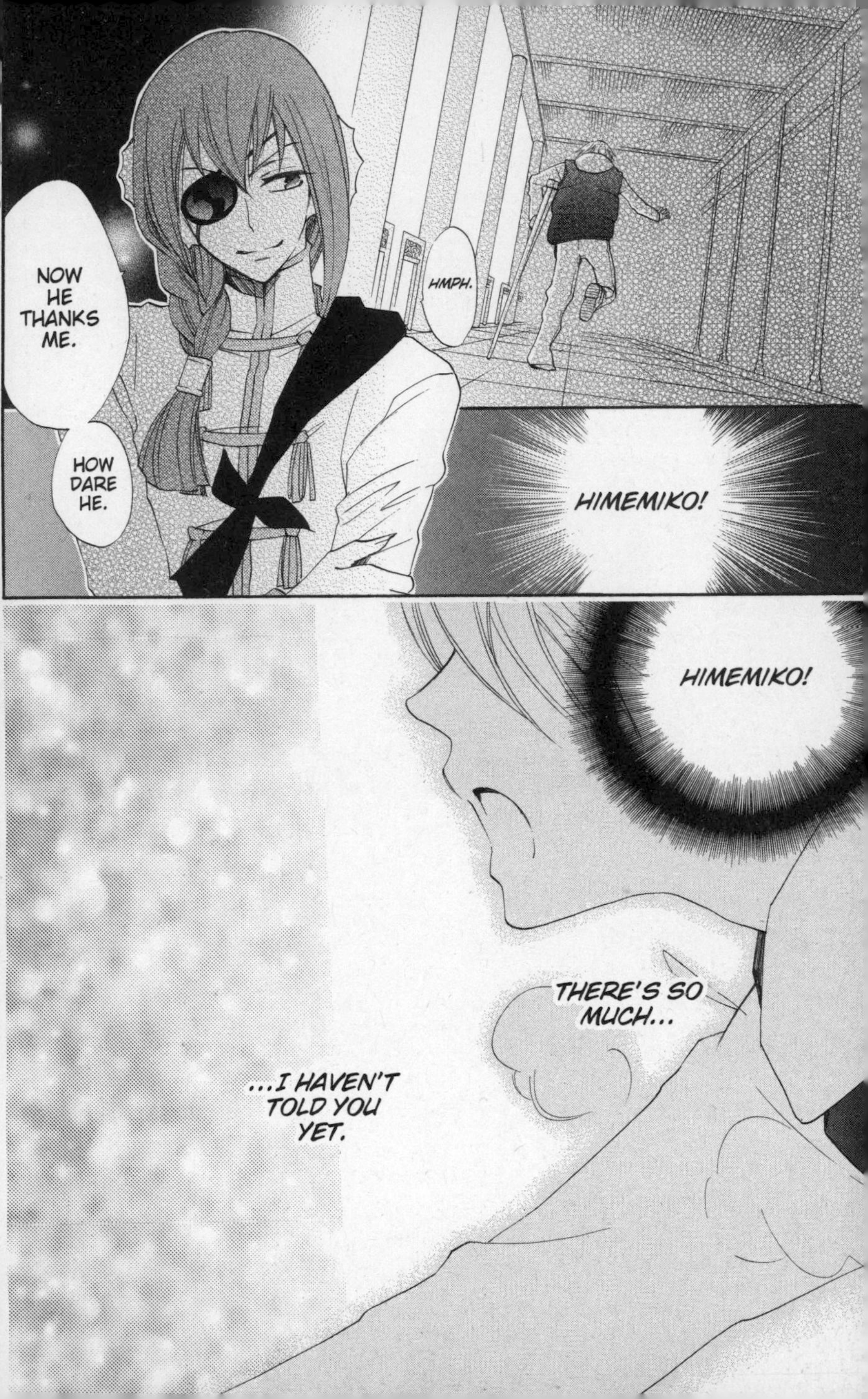
HMPH.
HIMEMIKO!
NOW HE THANKS ME.
HOW DARE HE.
HIMEMIKO!
THERE'S SO MUCH...
...I HAVEN'T TOLD YOU YET.

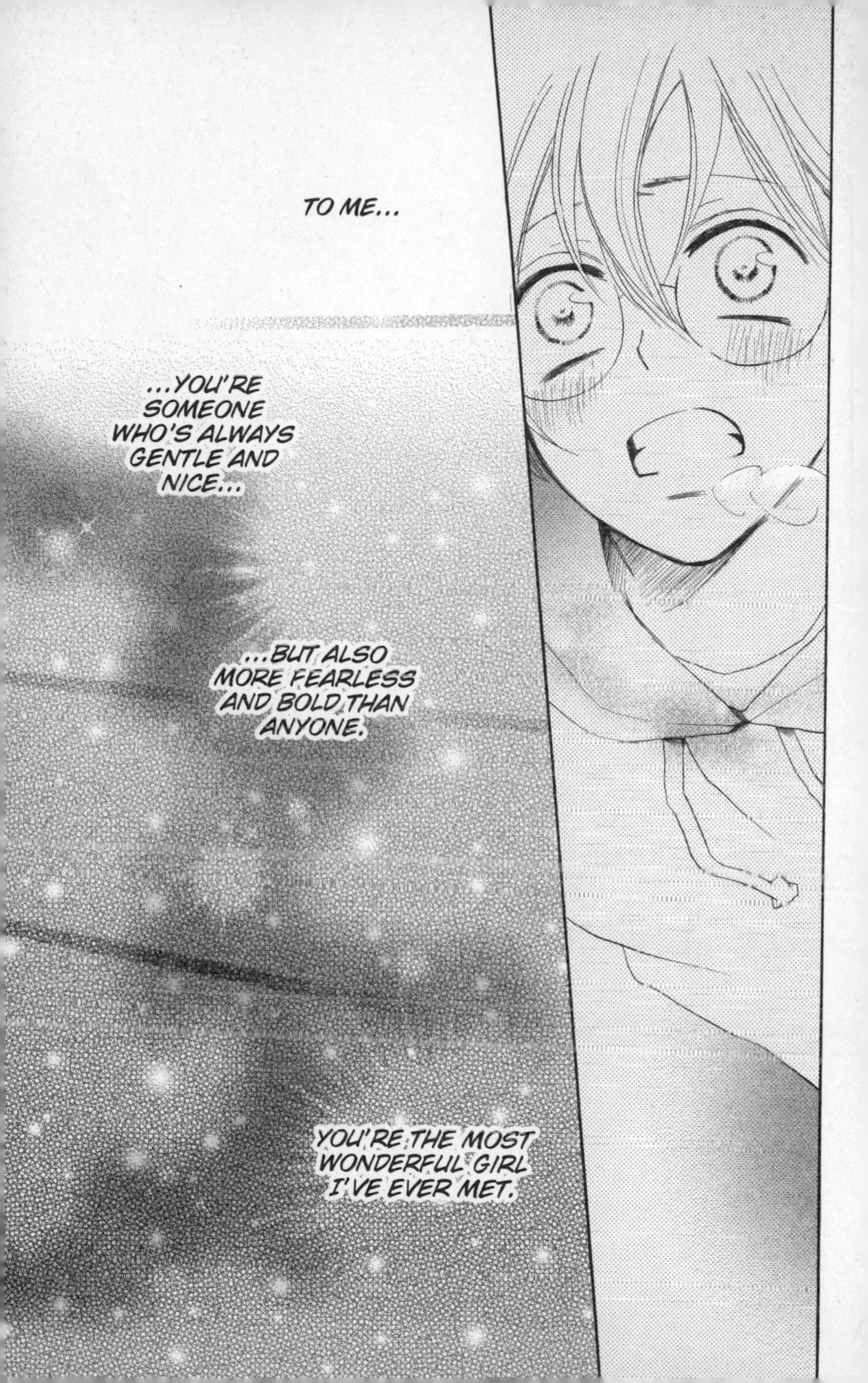
TO ME...
...YOU'RE SOMEONE WHO'S ALWAYS GENTLE AND NICE...
...BUT ALSO MORE FEARLESS AND BOLD THAN ANYONE.
YOU'RE THE MOST WONDERFUL GIRL I'VE EVER MET.

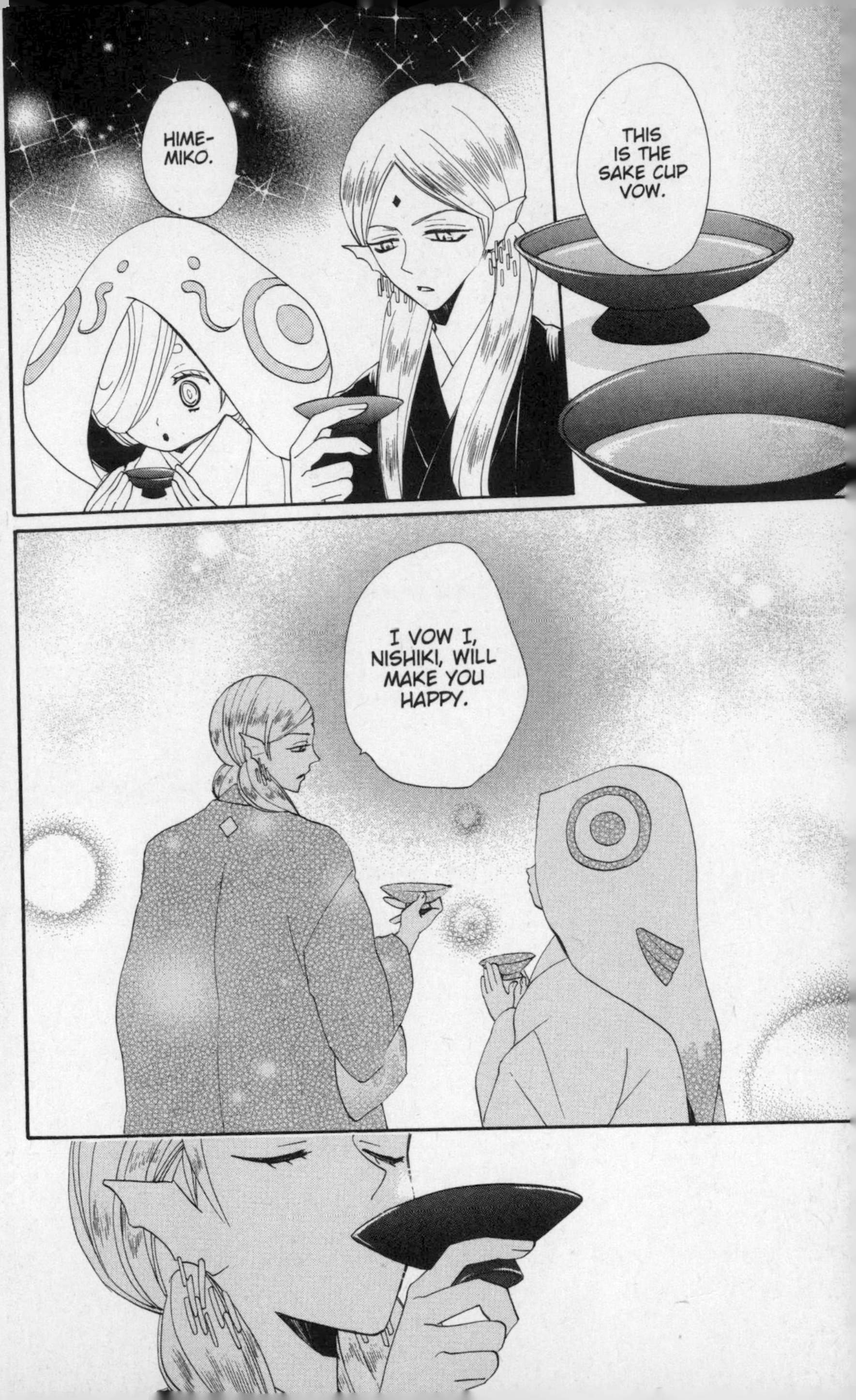
THIS IS THE SAKE CUP VOW.
HIME-MIKO.
I VOW I, NISHIKI, WILL MAKE YOU HAPPY.

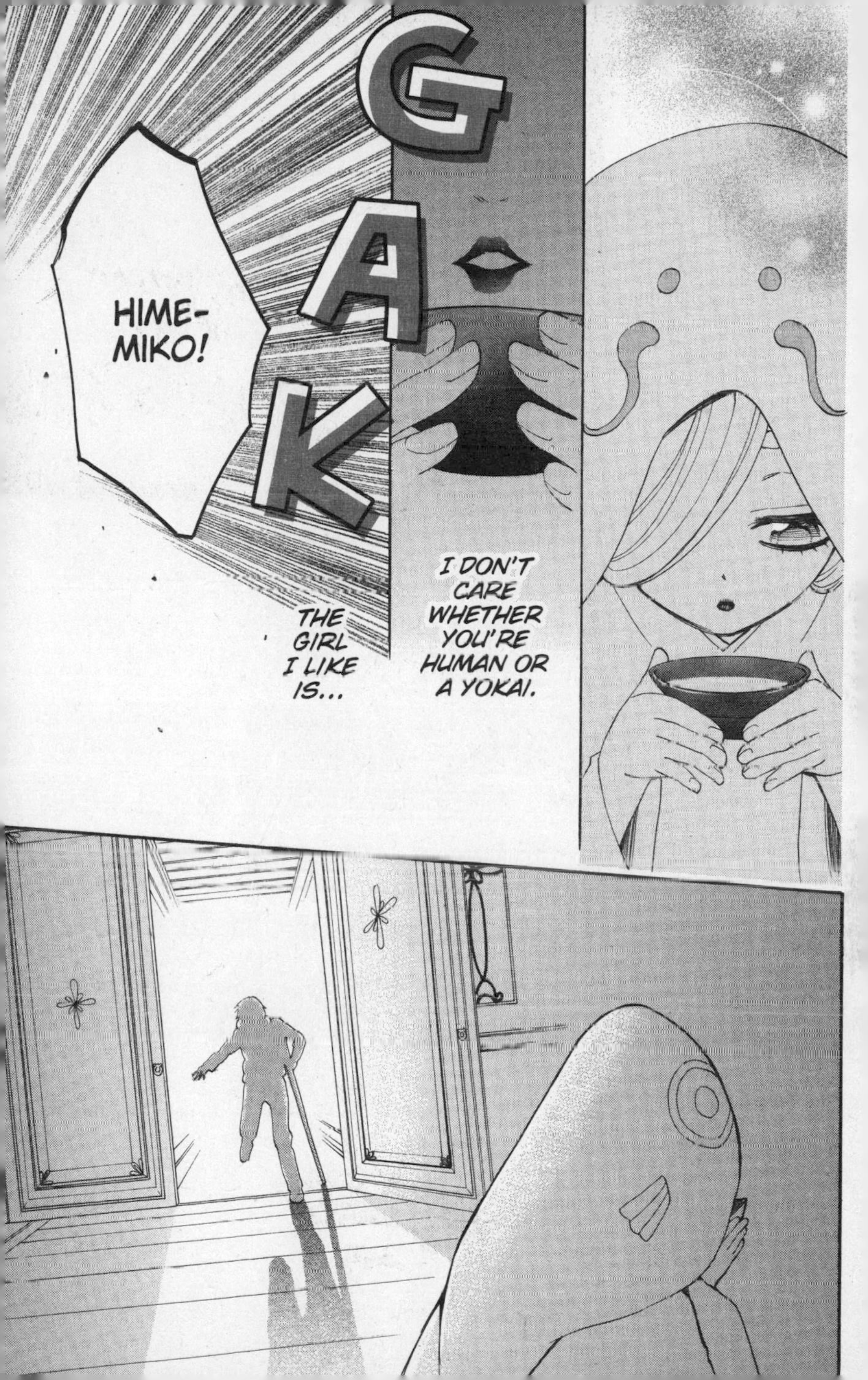
I DON'T CARE WHETHER YOU'RE HUMAN OR A YOKAI.
THE GIRL I LIKE IS...
GAK
HIME-MIKO!

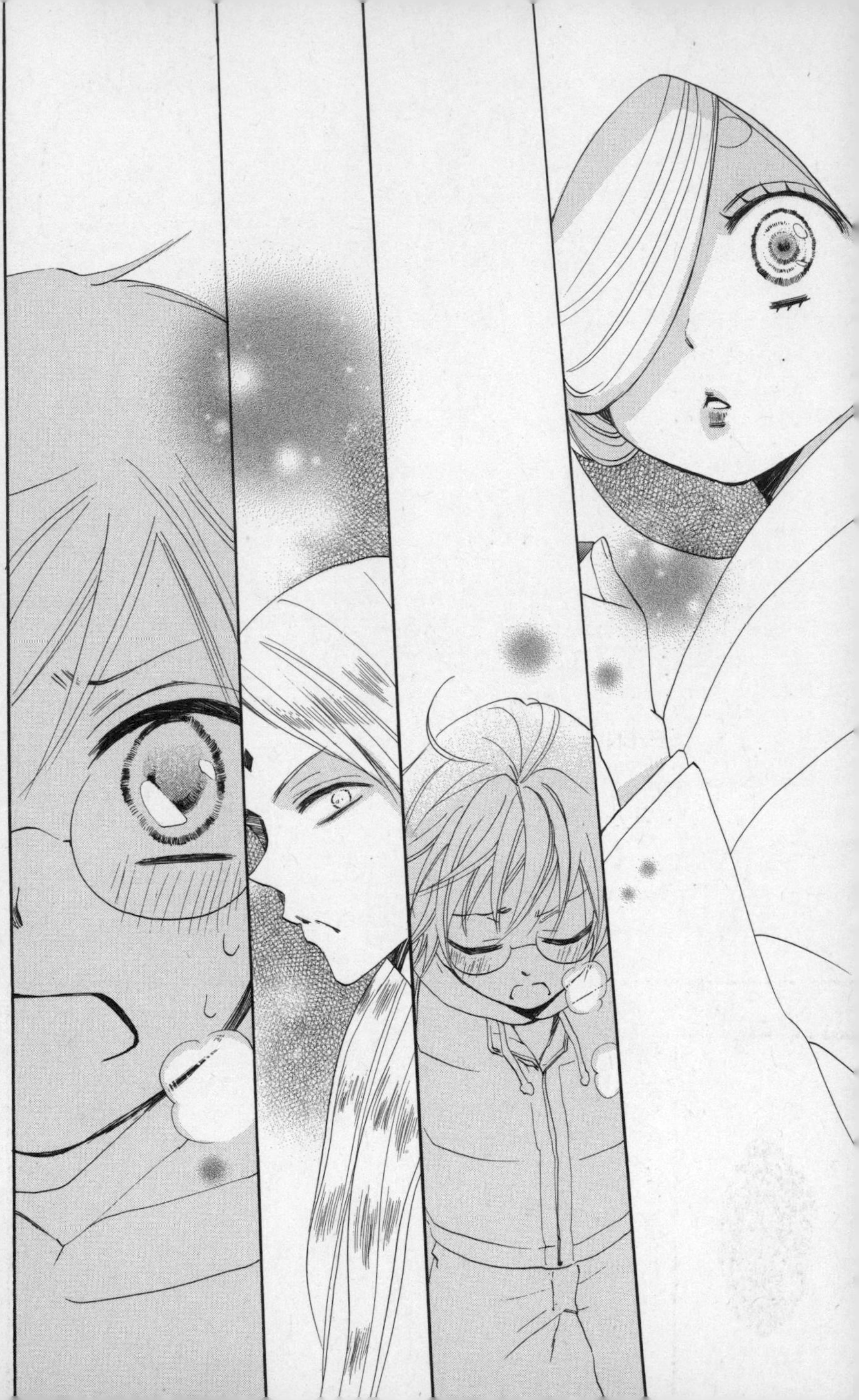

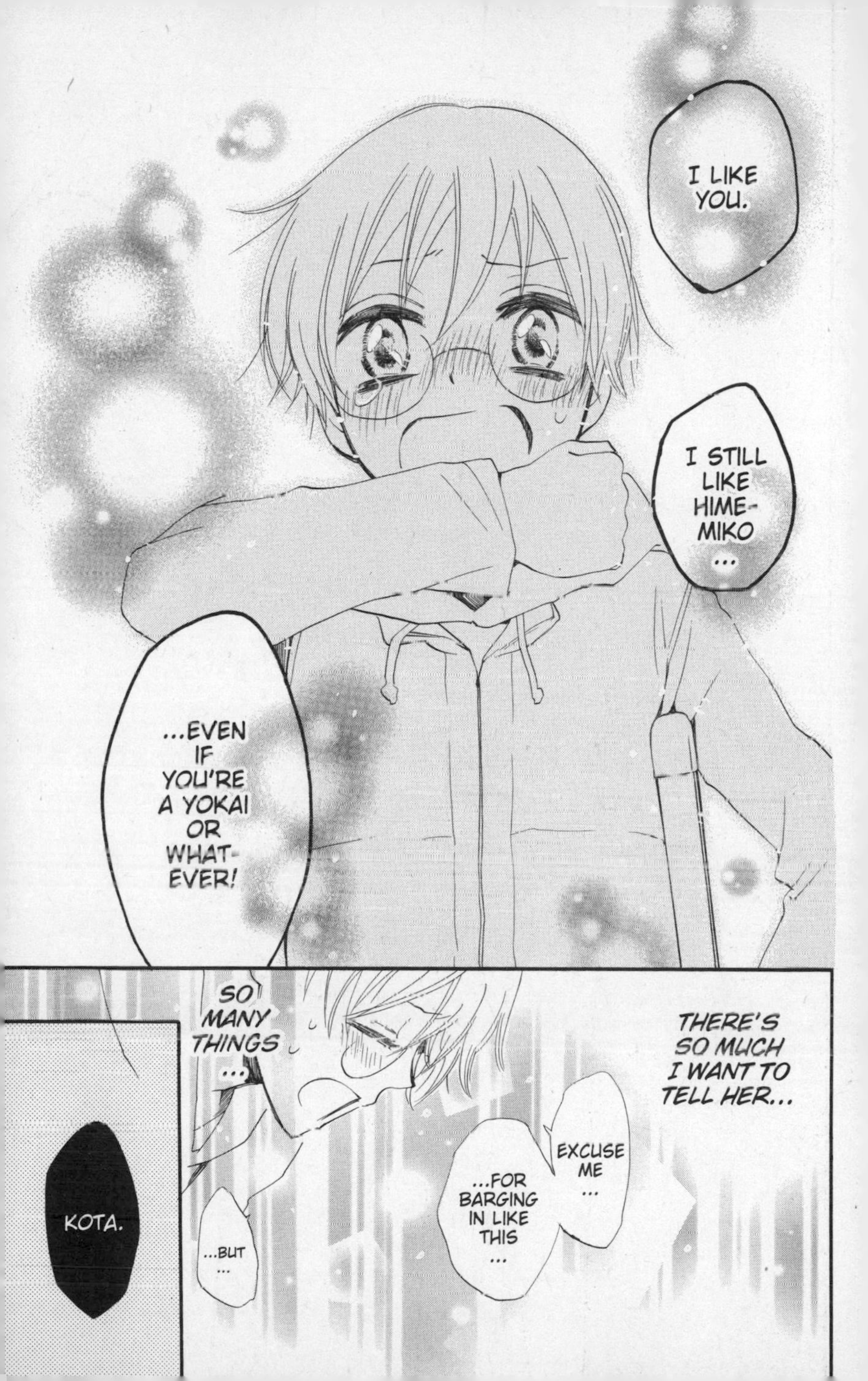
I LIKE YOU.
I STILL LIKE HIME-MIKO...
...EVEN IF YOU'RE A YOKAI OR WHATEVER!
THERE'S SO MUCH I WANT TO TELL HER...
SO MANY THINGS...
EXCUSE ME...
...FOR BARGING IN LIKE THIS...
...BUT...
KOTA.

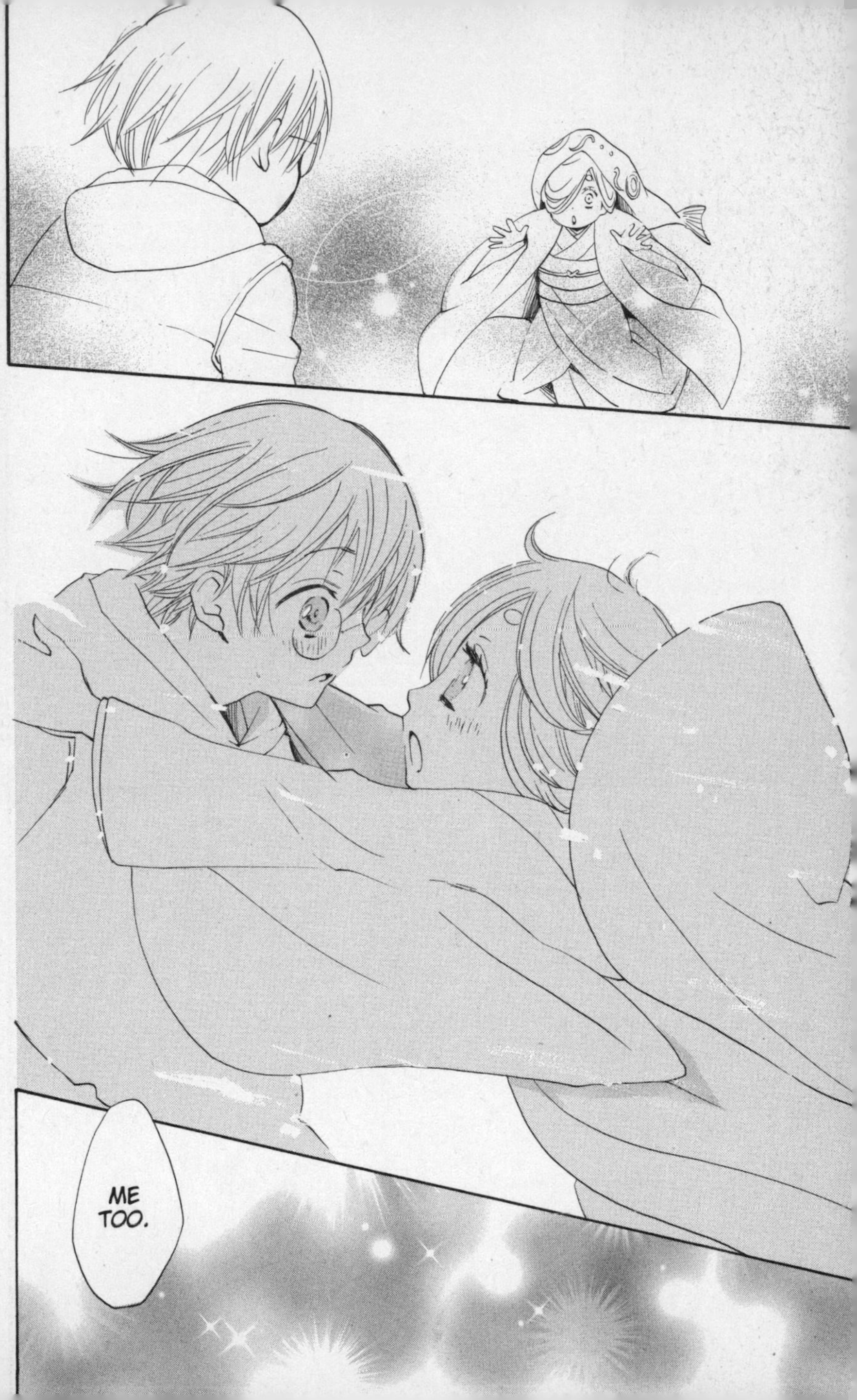
ME TOO.

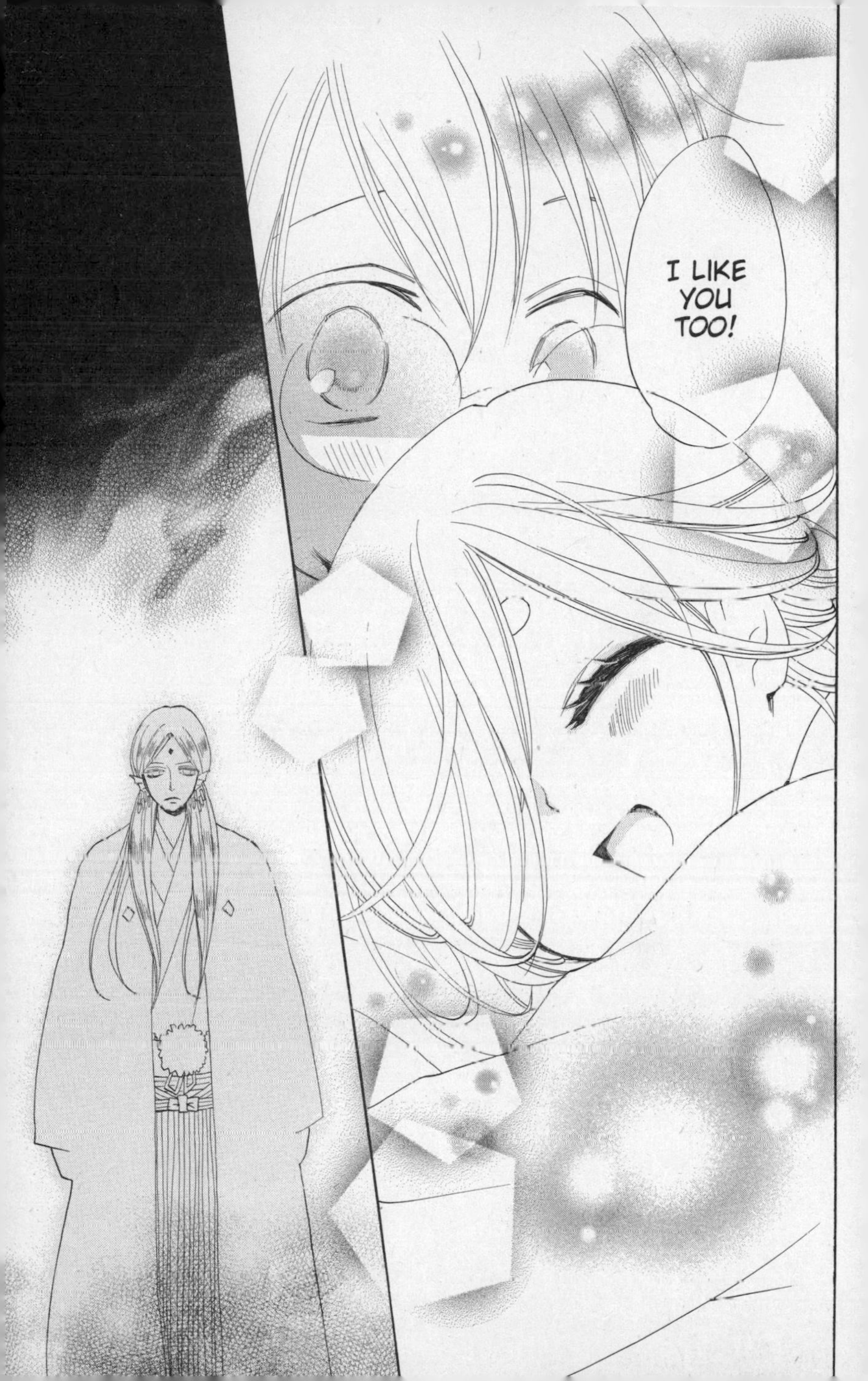
I LIKE YOU TOO!

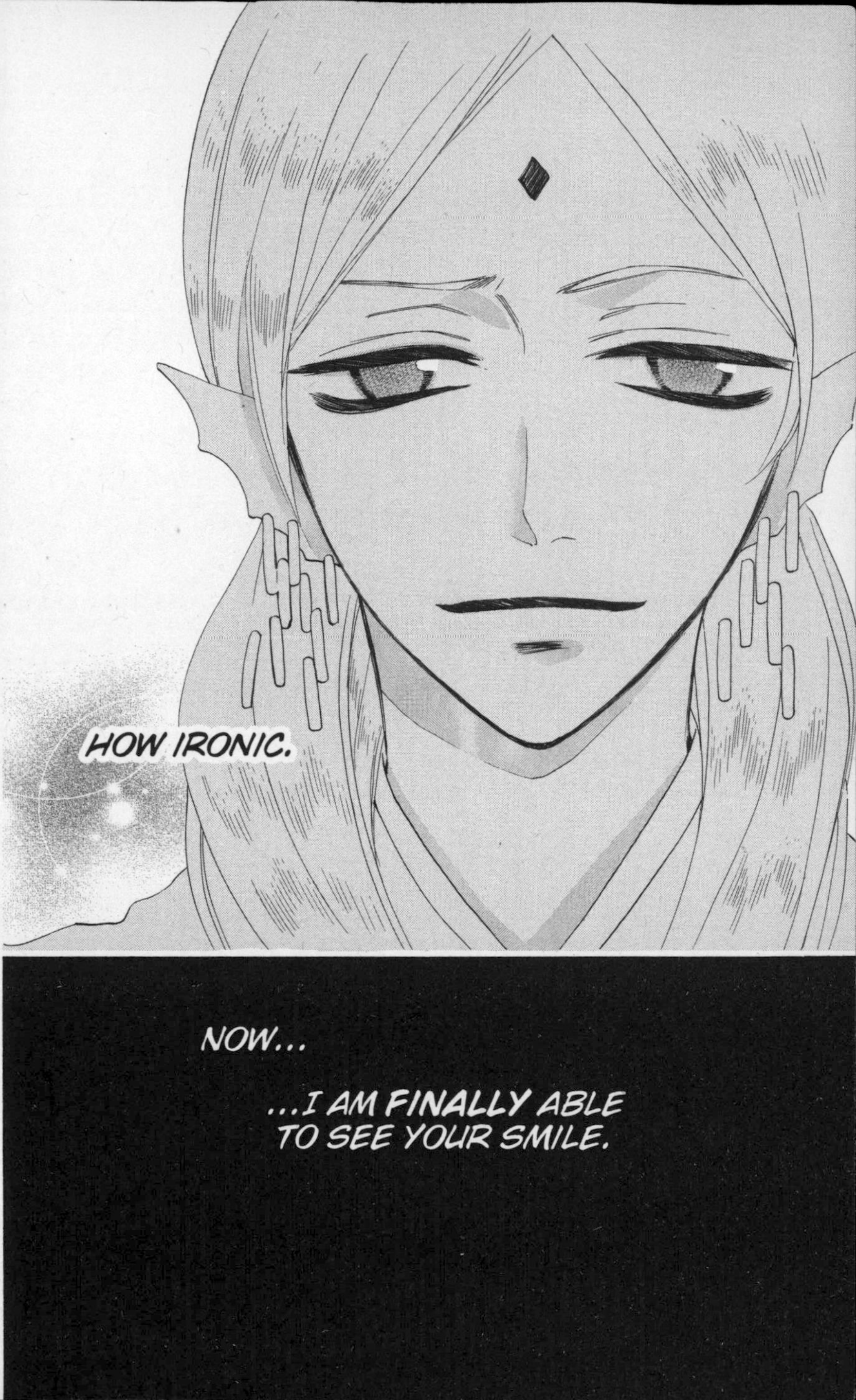
HOW IRONIC.
NOW...
...I AM FINALLY ABLE TO SEE YOUR SMILE.

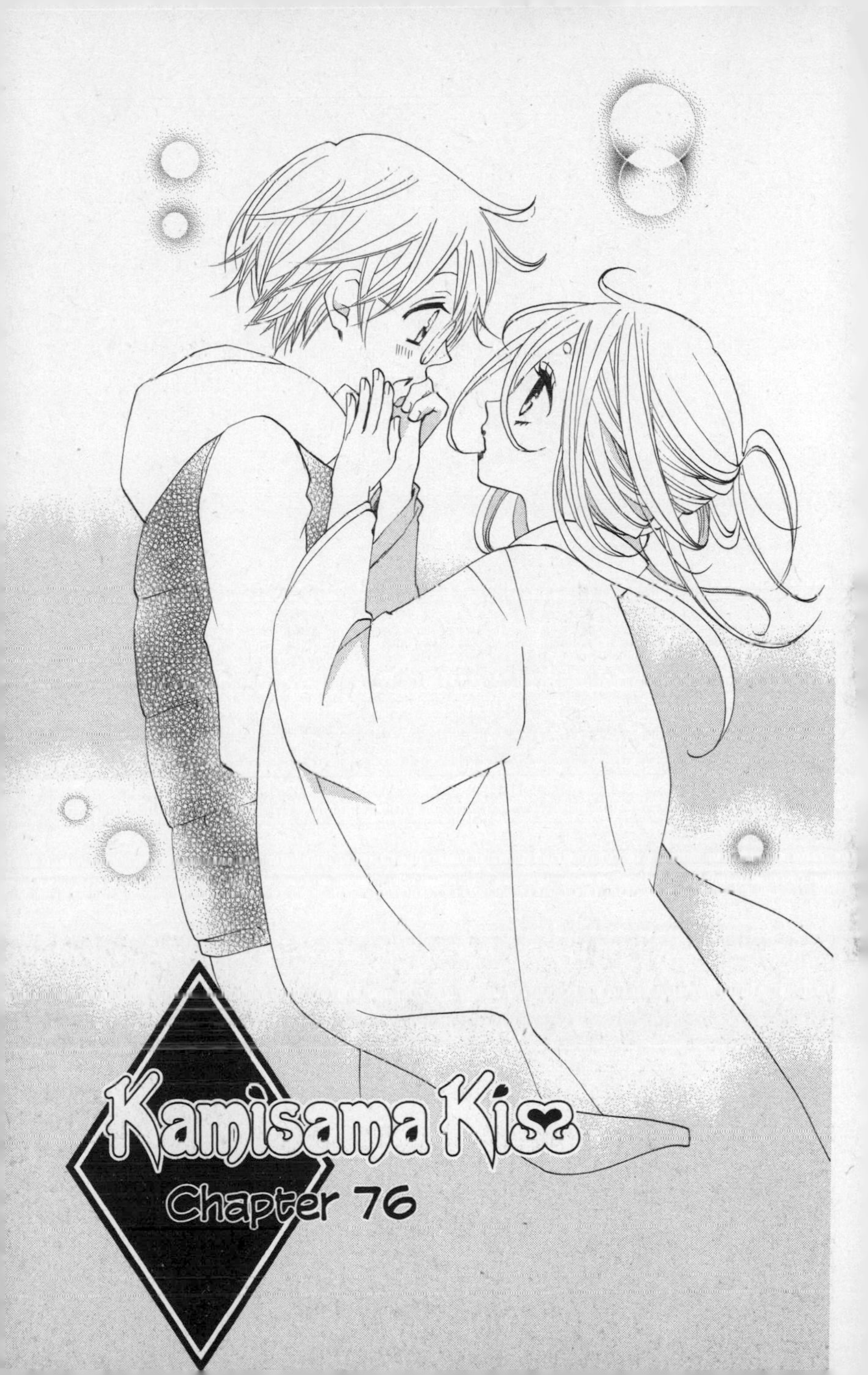
Kamisama Kiss
Chapter 76

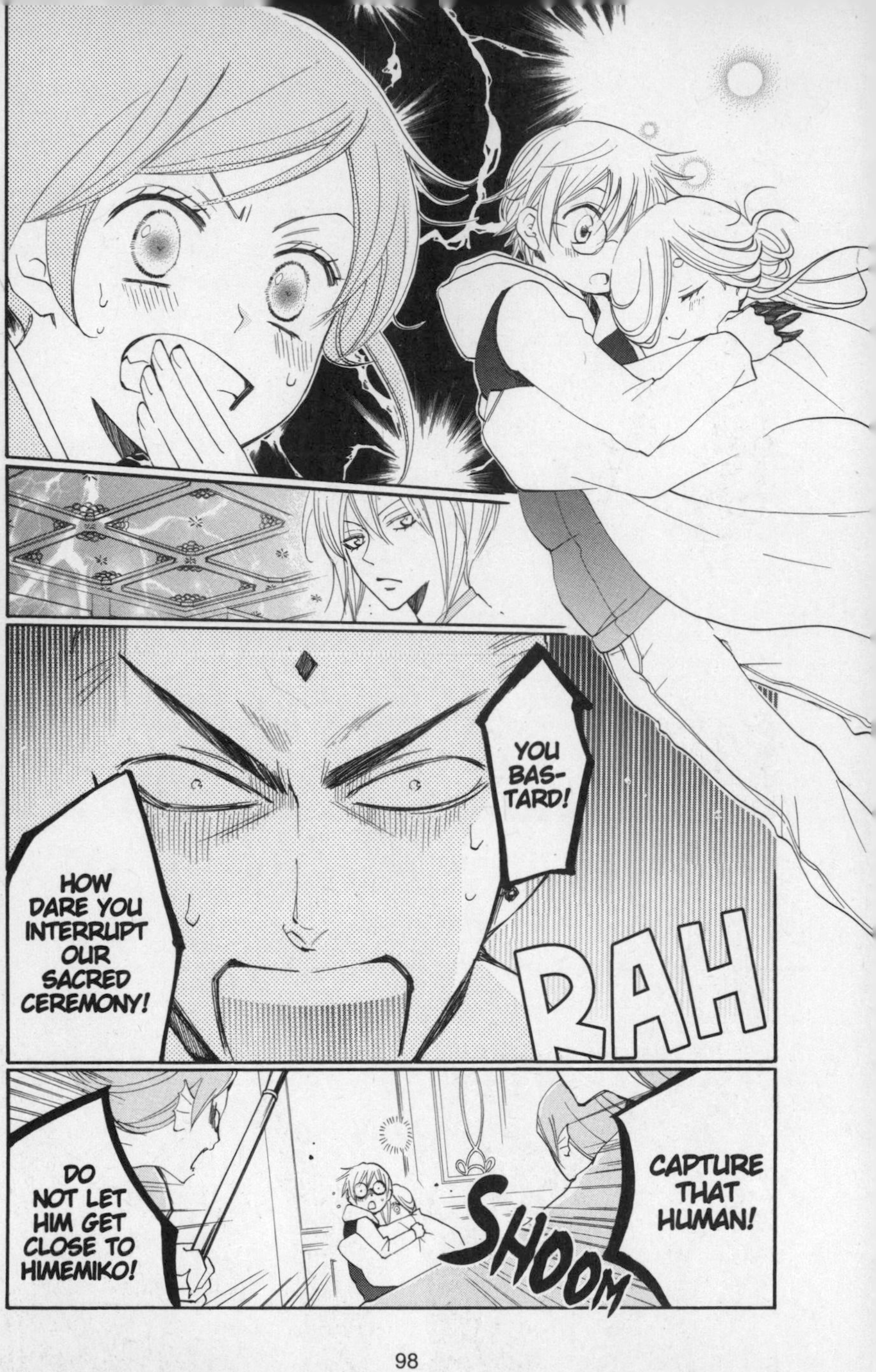
YOU BAS-TARD!
RAH
HOW DARE YOU INTERRUPT OUR SACRED CEREMONY!
CAPTURE THAT HUMAN!
SHOOM
DO NOT LET HIM GET CLOSE TO HIMEMIKO!

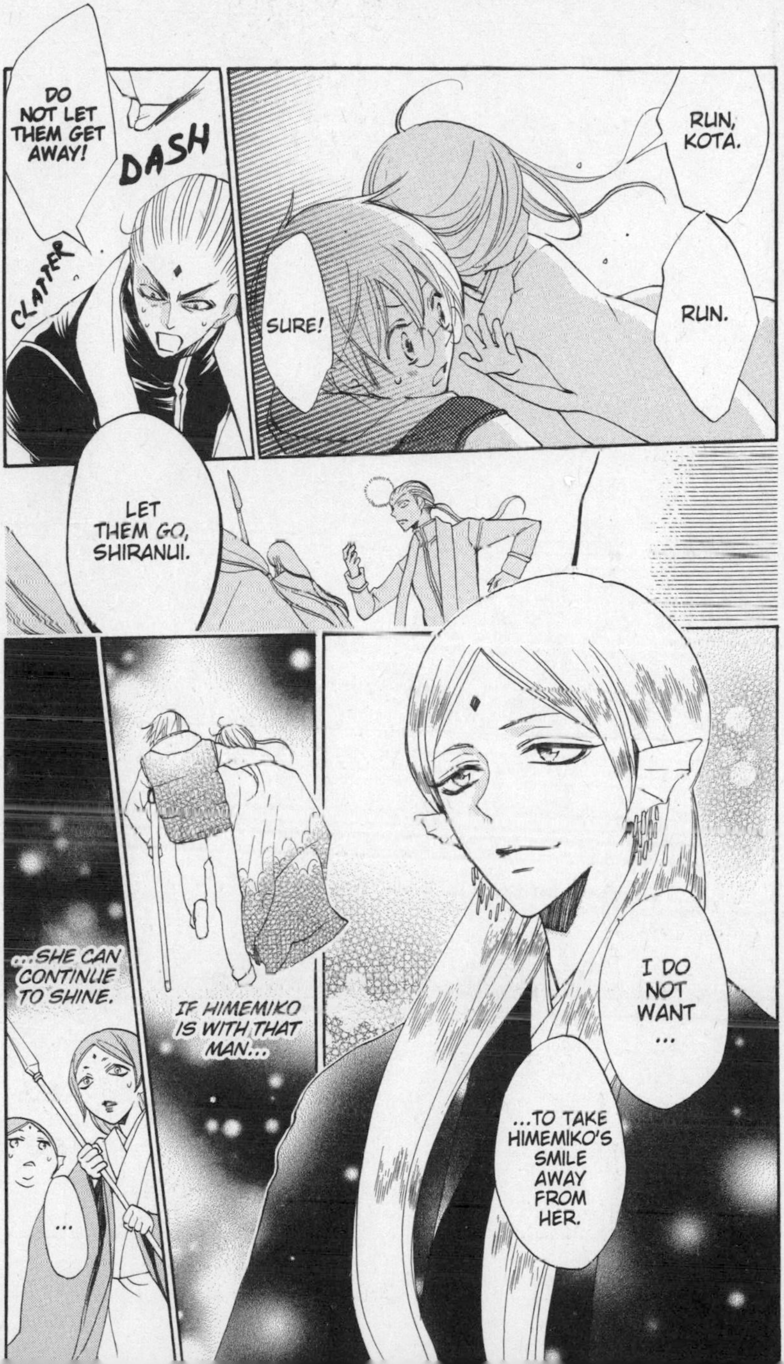
RUN, KOTA.
RUN.
SURE!
DO NOT LET THEM GET AWAY!
DASH
CLATTER
LET THEM GO, SHIRANUI.
I DO NOT WANT ...
...TO TAKE HIMEMIKO'S SMILE AWAY FROM HER.
IF HIMEMIKO IS WITH THAT MAN...
...SHE CAN CONTINUE TO SHINE.
...

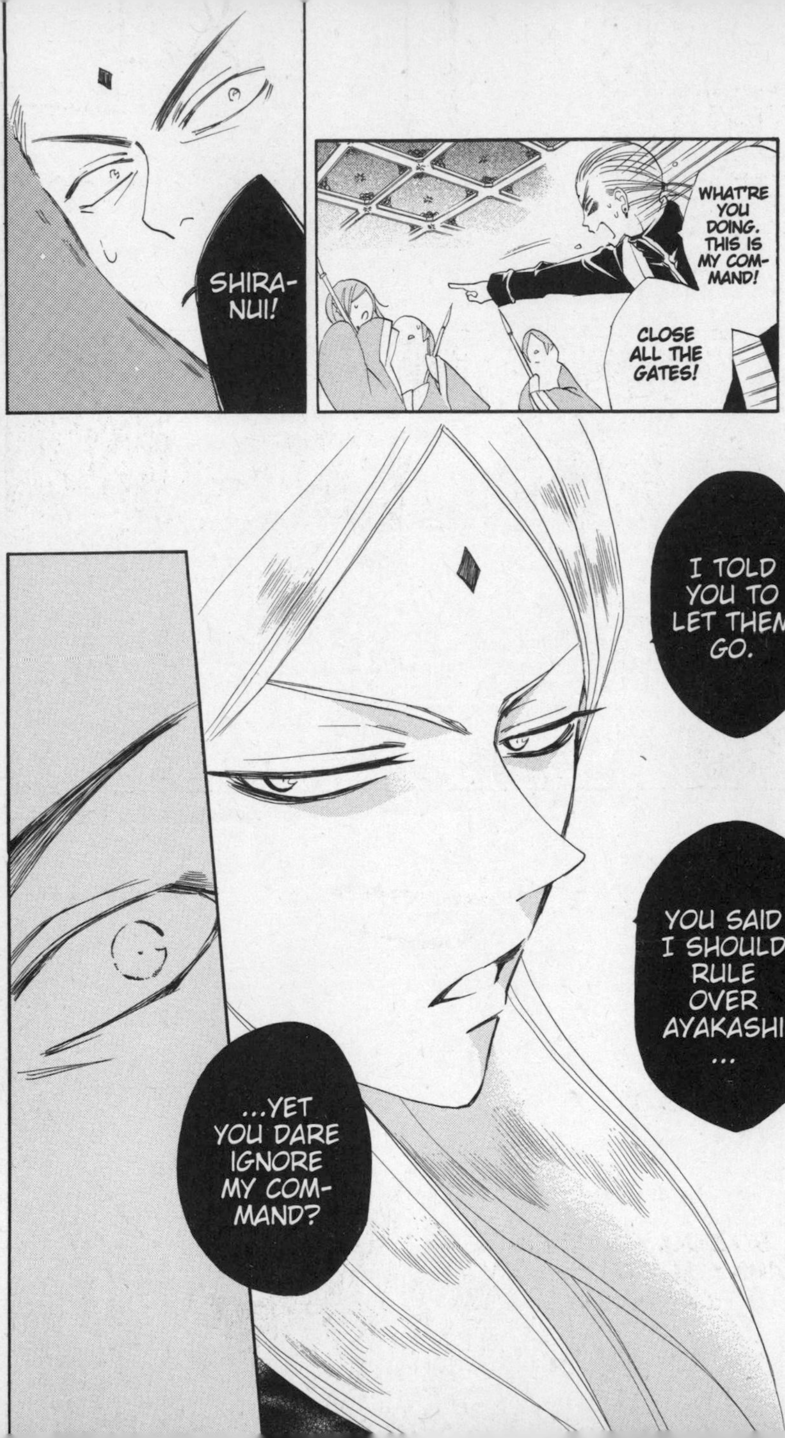
WHAT'RE YOU DOING. THIS IS MY COM-MAND!
CLOSE ALL THE GATES!
SHIRA-NUI!
I TOLD YOU TO LET THEM GO.
YOU SAID I SHOULD RULE OVER AYAKASHI...
...YET YOU DARE IGNORE MY COM-MAND?

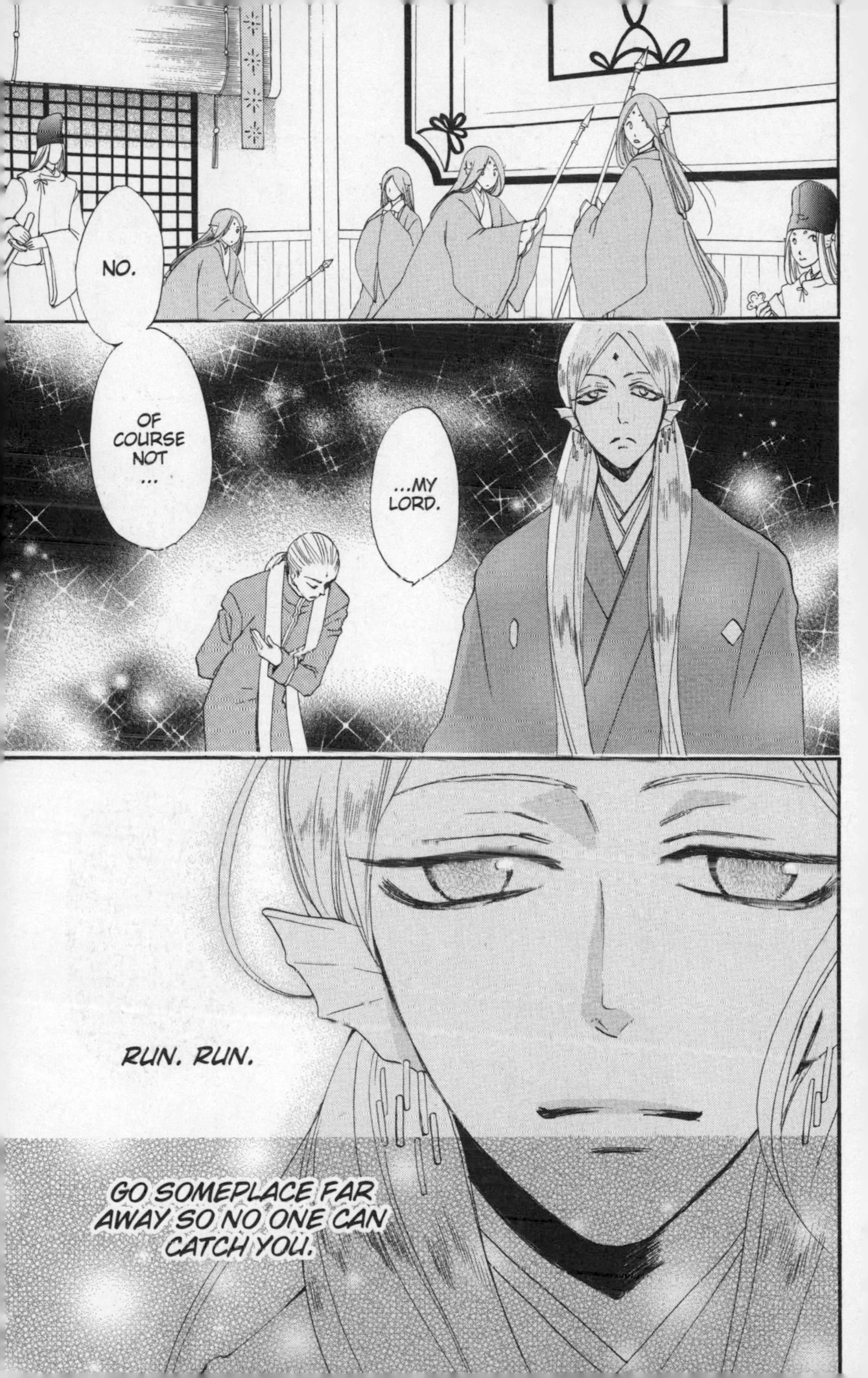
NO.
OF COURSE NOT ...
...MY LORD.
RUN. RUN.
GO SOMEPLACE FAR AWAY SO NO ONE CAN CATCH YOU.

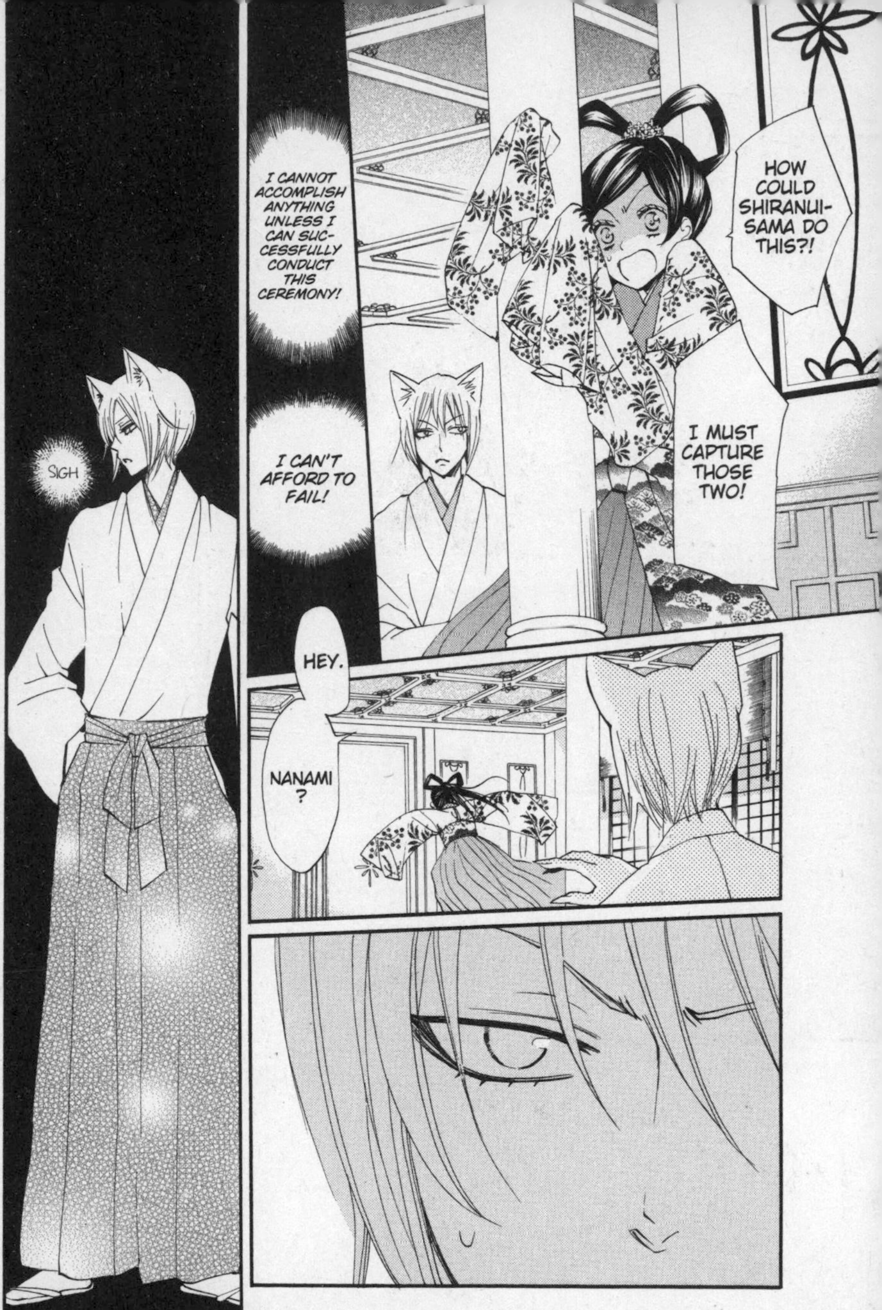
HOW COULD SHIRANUI-SAMA DO THIS?!
I CANNOT ACCOMPLISH ANYTHING UNLESS I CAN SUCCESSFULLY CONDUCT THIS CEREMONY!
I MUST CAPTURE THOSE TWO!
I CAN'T AFFORD TO FAIL!
HEY.
NANAMI?
SIGH

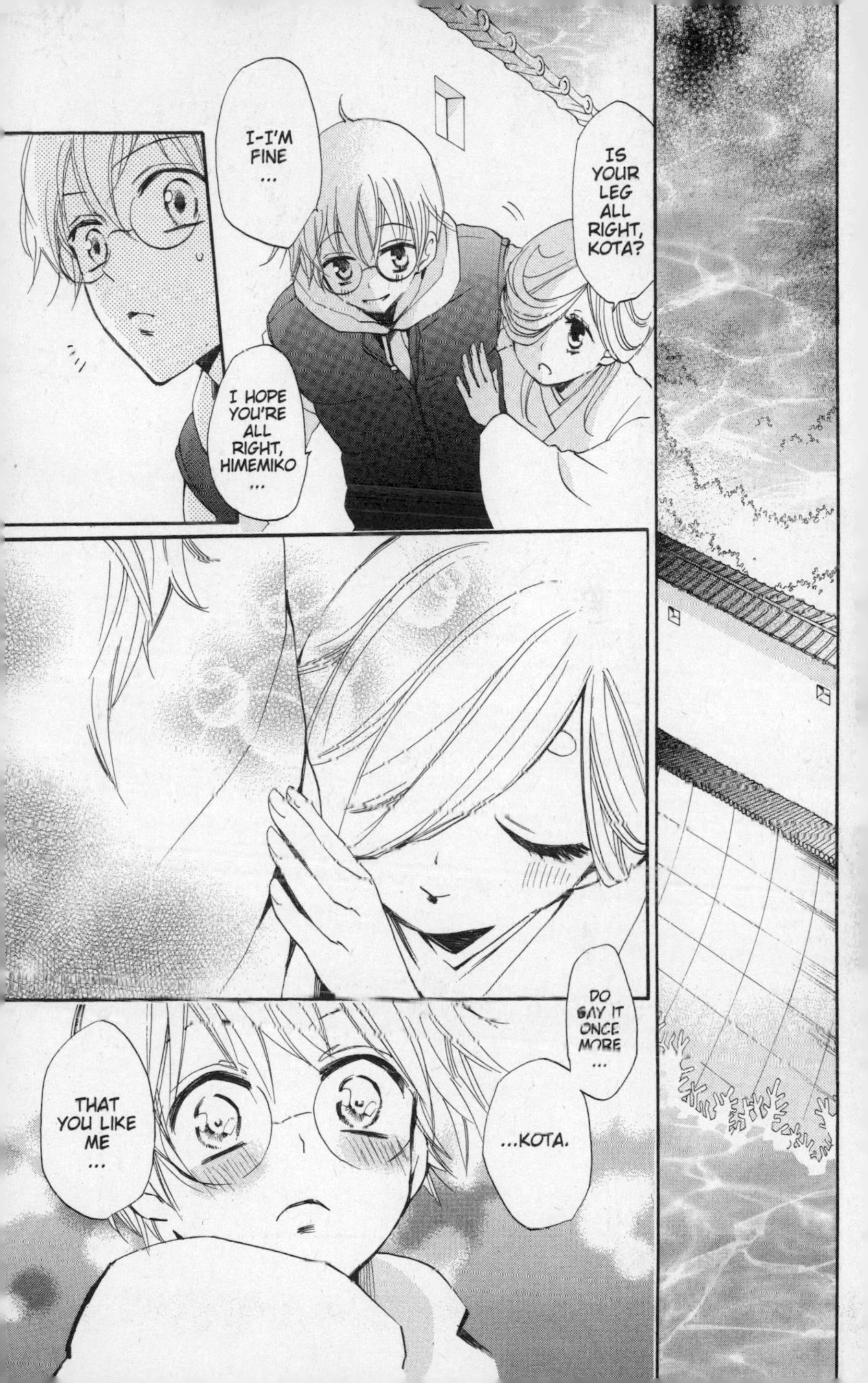
IS YOUR LEG ALL RIGHT, KOTA?
I-I'M FINE ...
I HOPE YOU'RE ALL RIGHT, HIMEMIKO ...
DO SAY IT ONCE MORE ...
...KOTA.
THAT YOU LIKE ME ...

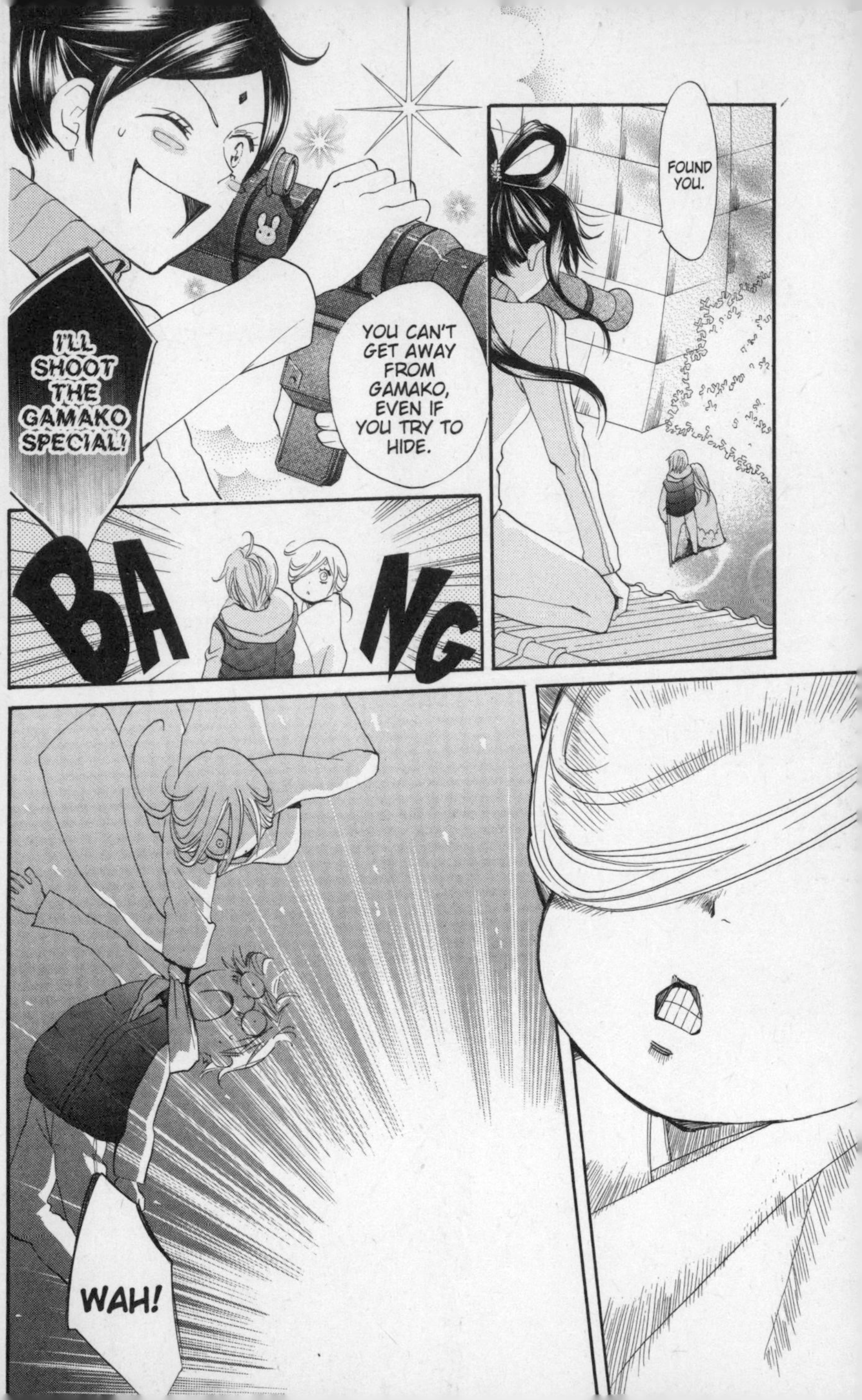
FOUND YOU.
YOU CAN'T GET AWAY FROM GAMAKO, EVEN IF YOU TRY TO HIDE.
I'LL SHOOT THE GAMAKO SPECIAL!
BANG
WAH!

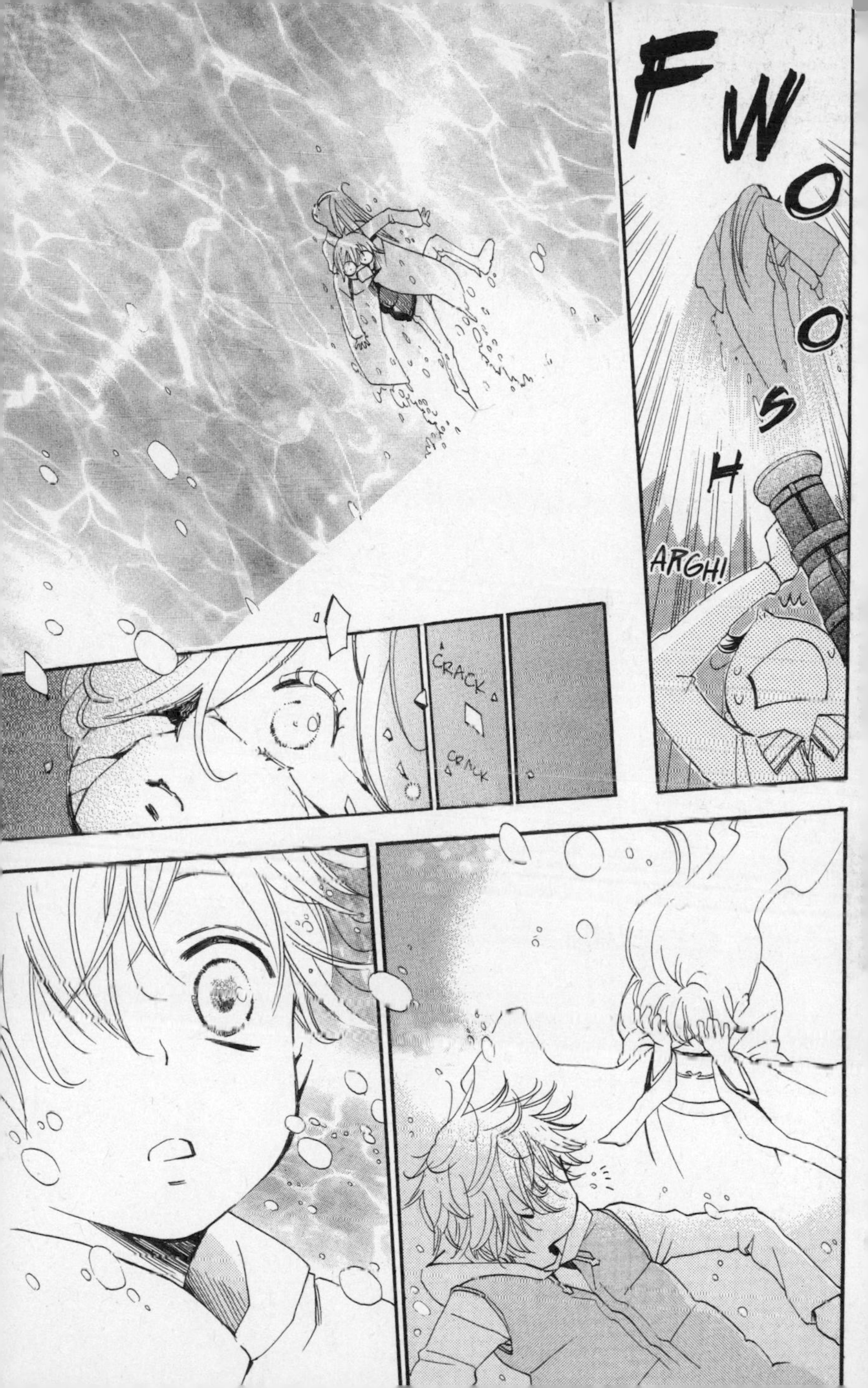
FWOOOSH
ARGH!
CRACK
CRACK

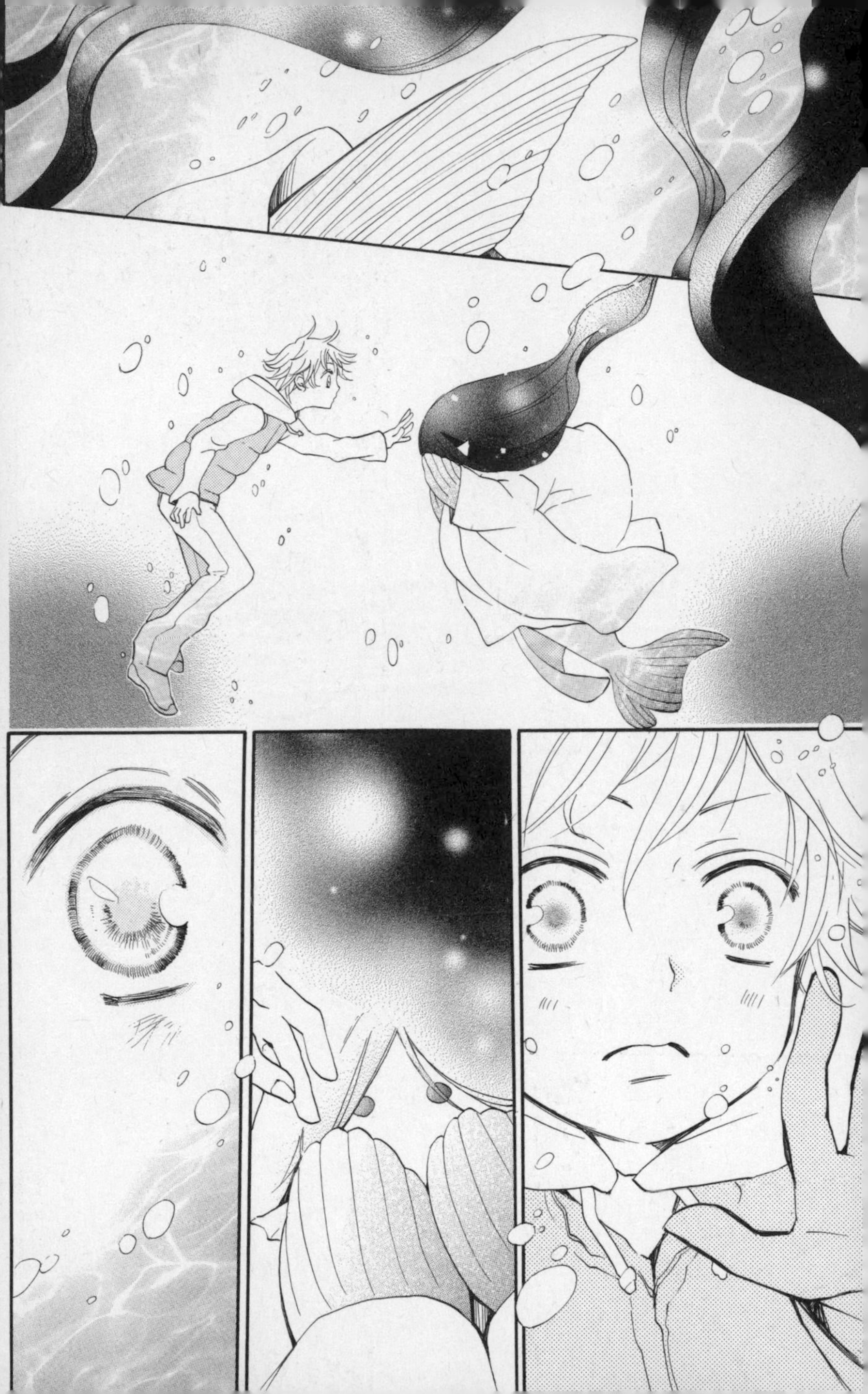

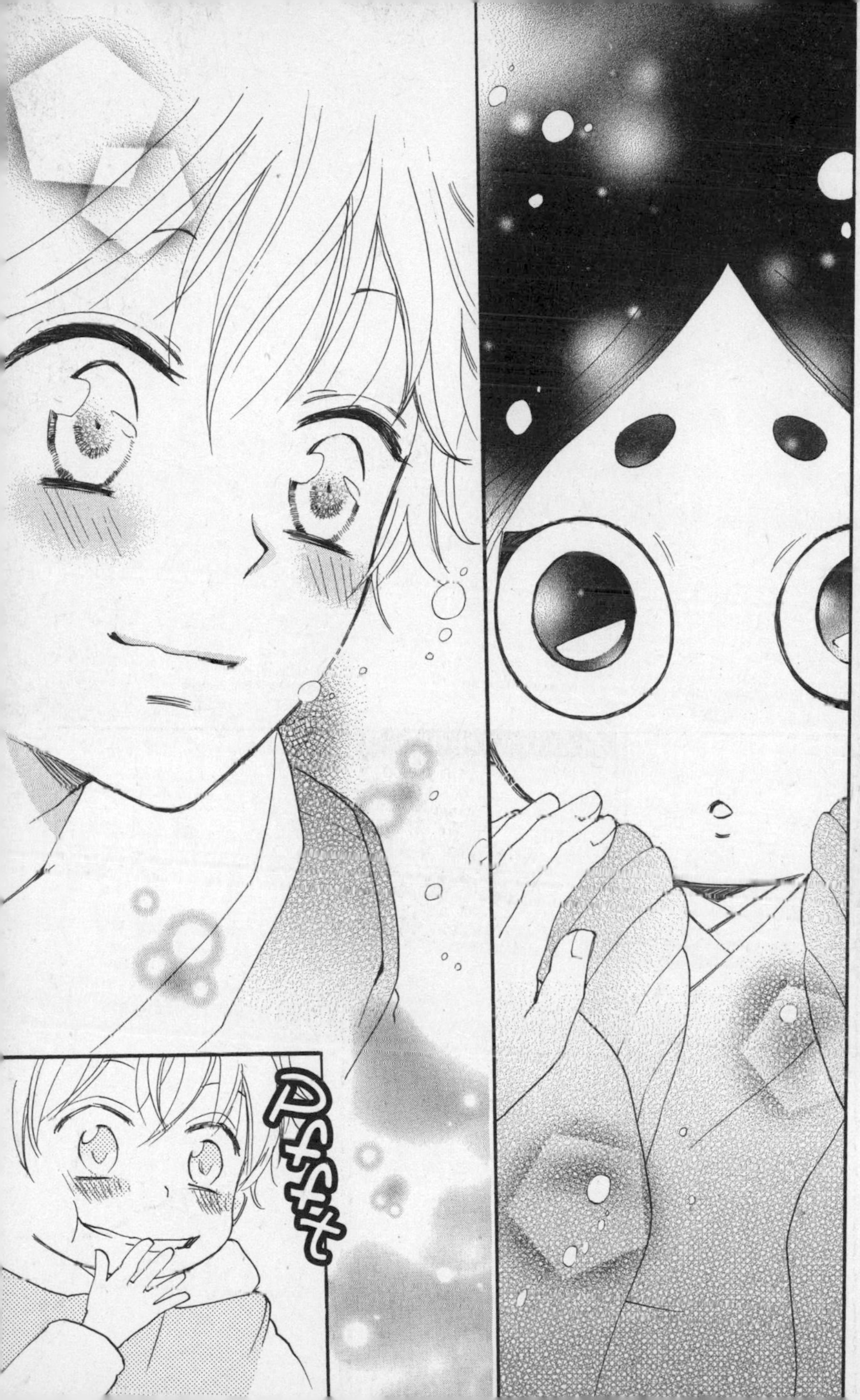
Pfft

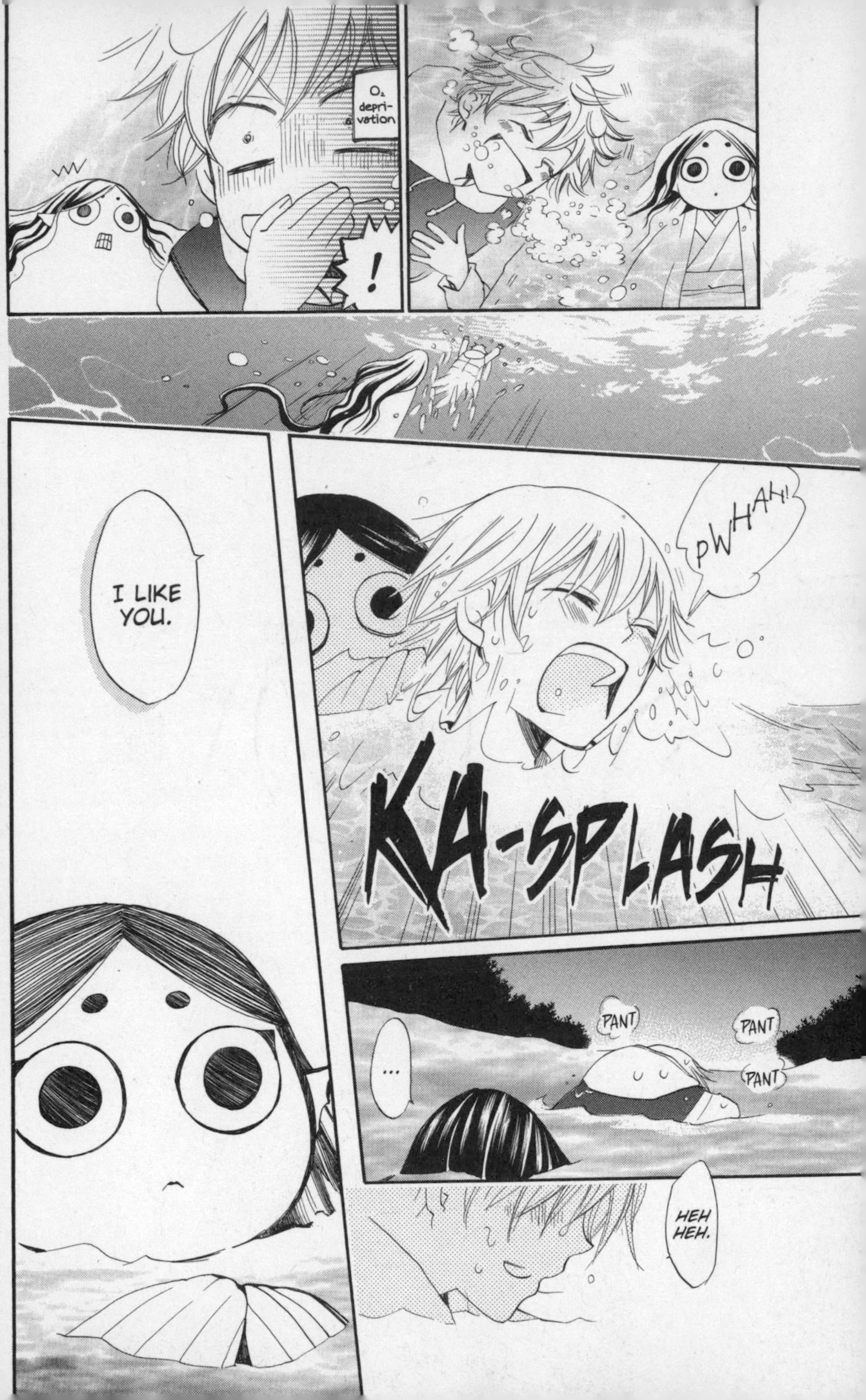
$O_2$ deprivation
!
PWHAH!
KA-SPLASH
PANT
PANT
PANT
...
HEH HEH.
I LIKE YOU.

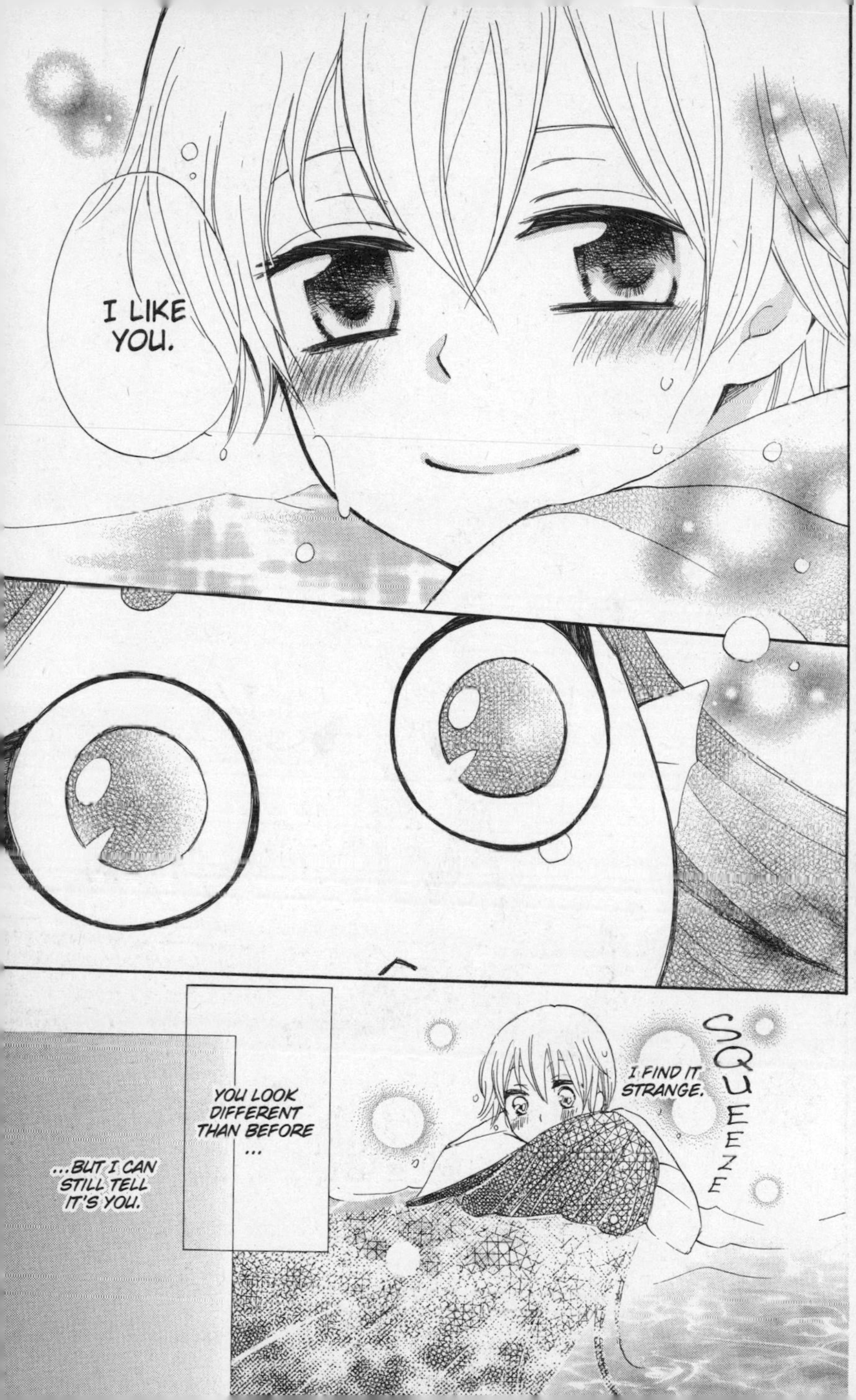
I LIKE YOU.
SQUEEZE
I FIND IT STRANGE.
YOU LOOK DIFFERENT THAN BEFORE...
...BUT I CAN STILL TELL IT'S YOU.

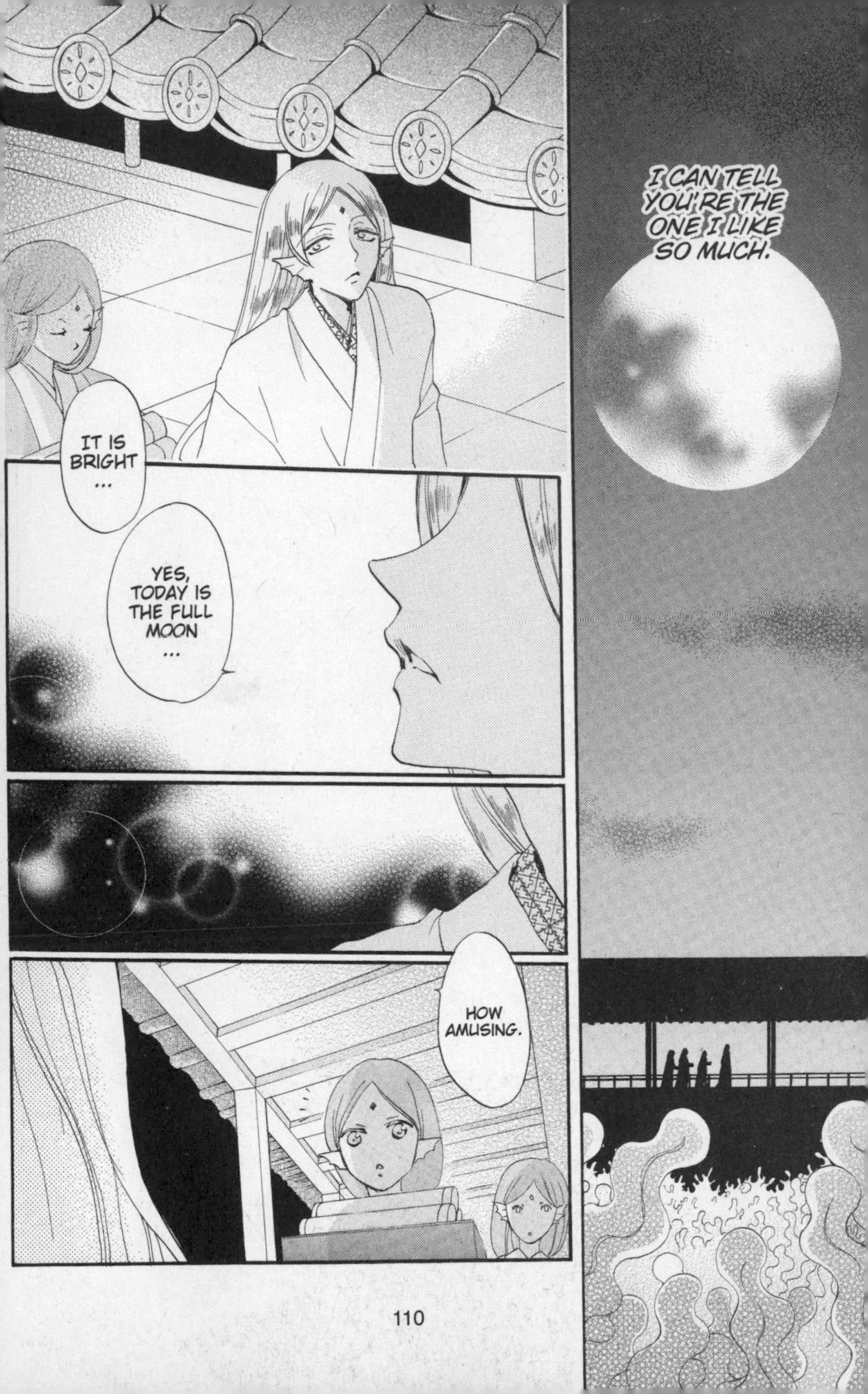
I CAN TELL YOU'RE THE ONE I LIKE SO MUCH.
IT IS BRIGHT ...
YES, TODAY IS THE FULL MOON ...
HOW AMUSING.

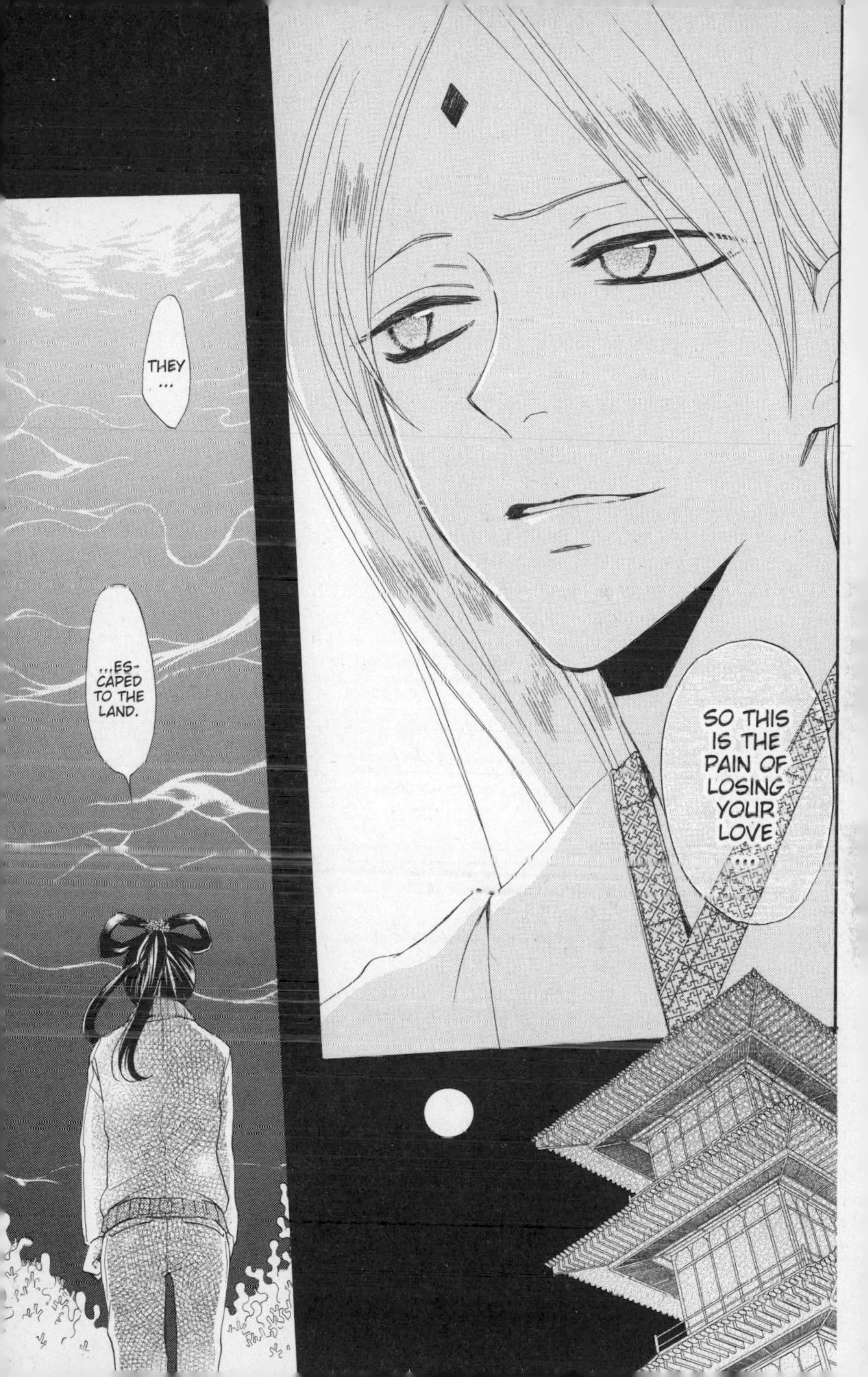
SO THIS IS THE PAIN OF LOSING YOUR LOVE ...
THEY ...
...ES-CAPED TO THE LAND.

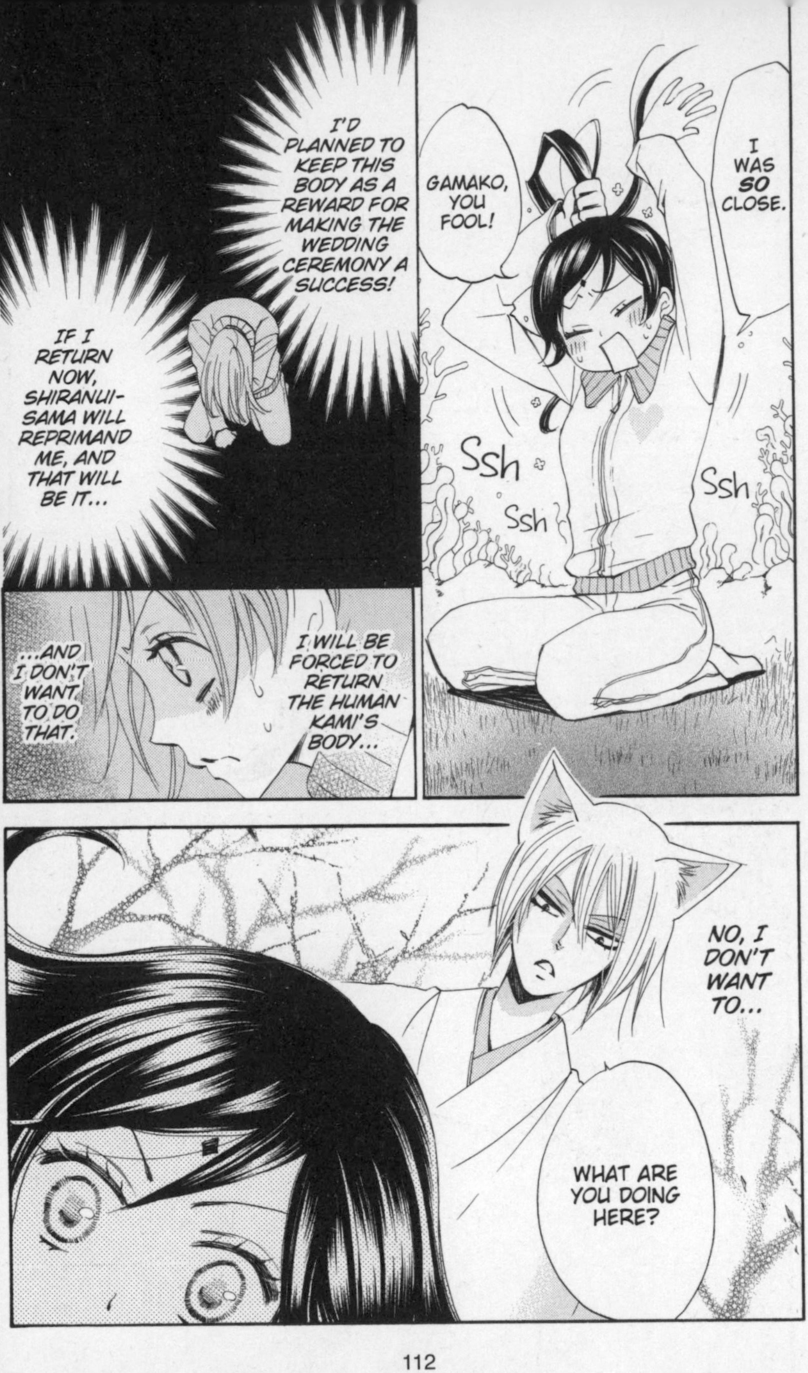
I WAS SO CLOSE.
GAMAKO, YOU FOOL!
Ssh
Ssh
Ssh
I'D PLANNED TO KEEP THIS BODY AS A REWARD FOR MAKING THE WEDDING CEREMONY A SUCCESS!
IF I RETURN NOW, SHIRANUI-SAMA WILL REPRIMAND ME, AND THAT WILL BE IT...
I WILL BE FORCED TO RETURN THE HUMAN KAMI'S BODY...
...AND I DON'T WANT TO DO THAT.
NO, I DON'T WANT TO...
WHAT ARE YOU DOING HERE?

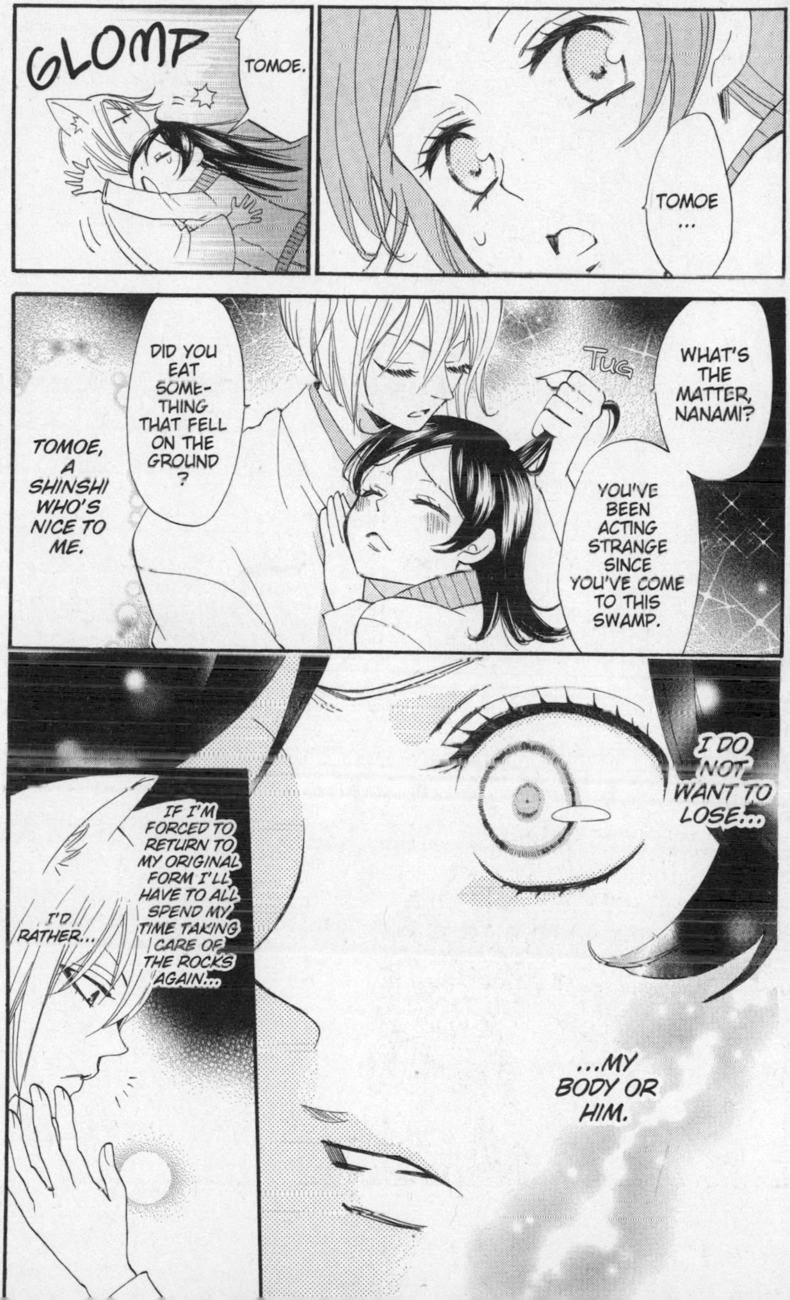
TOMOE ...
TOMOE.
GLOMP
WHAT'S THE MATTER, NANAMI?
TUG
YOU'VE BEEN ACTING STRANGE SINCE YOU'VE COME TO THIS SWAMP.
DID YOU EAT SOME-THING THAT FELL ON THE GROUND?
TOMOE, A SHINSHI WHO'S NICE TO ME.
I DO NOT WANT TO LOSE...
...MY BODY OR HIM.
IF I'M FORCED TO RETURN TO MY ORIGINAL FORM I'LL HAVE TO ALL SPEND MY TIME TAKING CARE OF THE ROCKS AGAIN...
I'D RATHER...

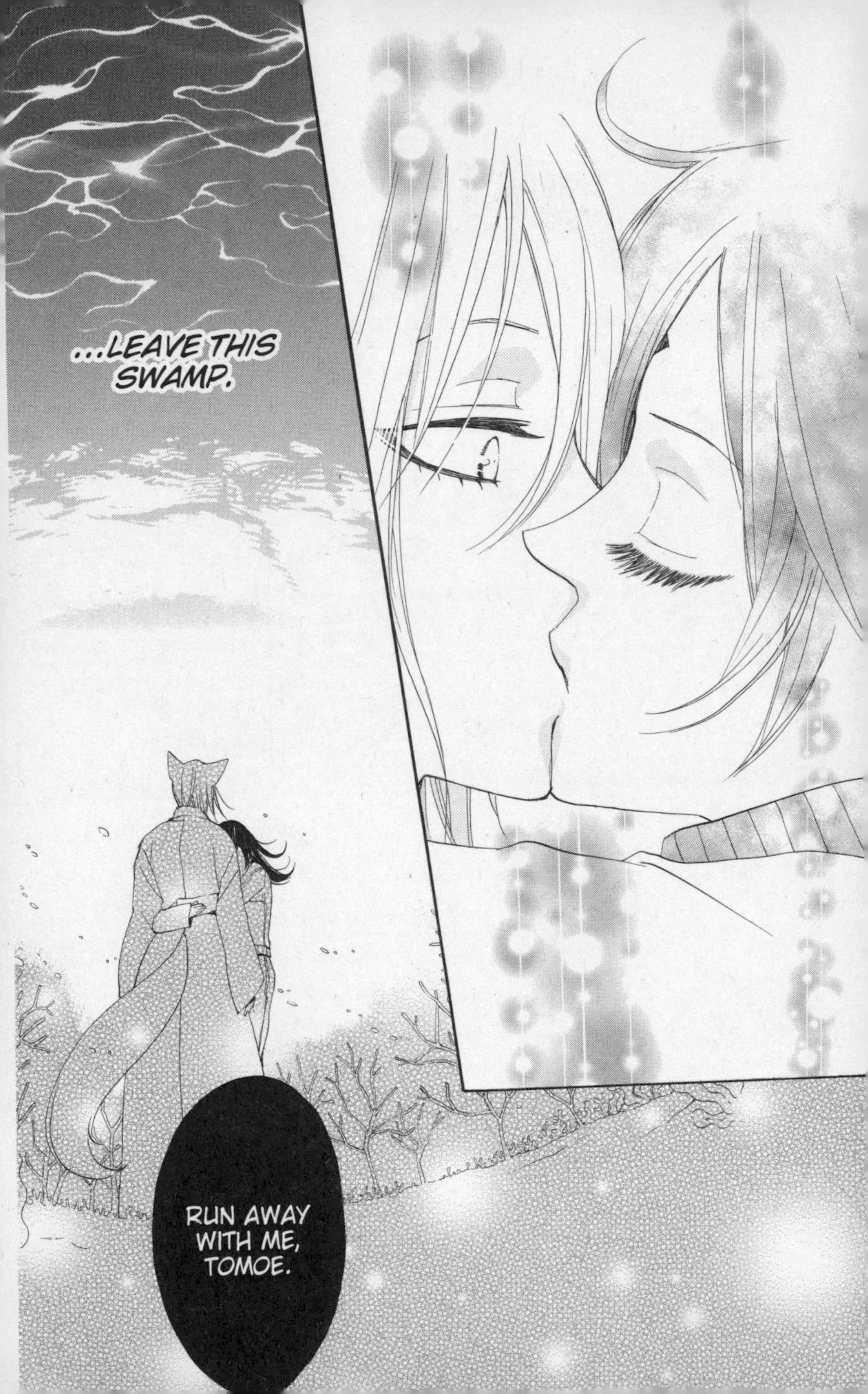
...LEAVE THIS SWAMP.
RUN AWAY WITH ME, TOMOE.

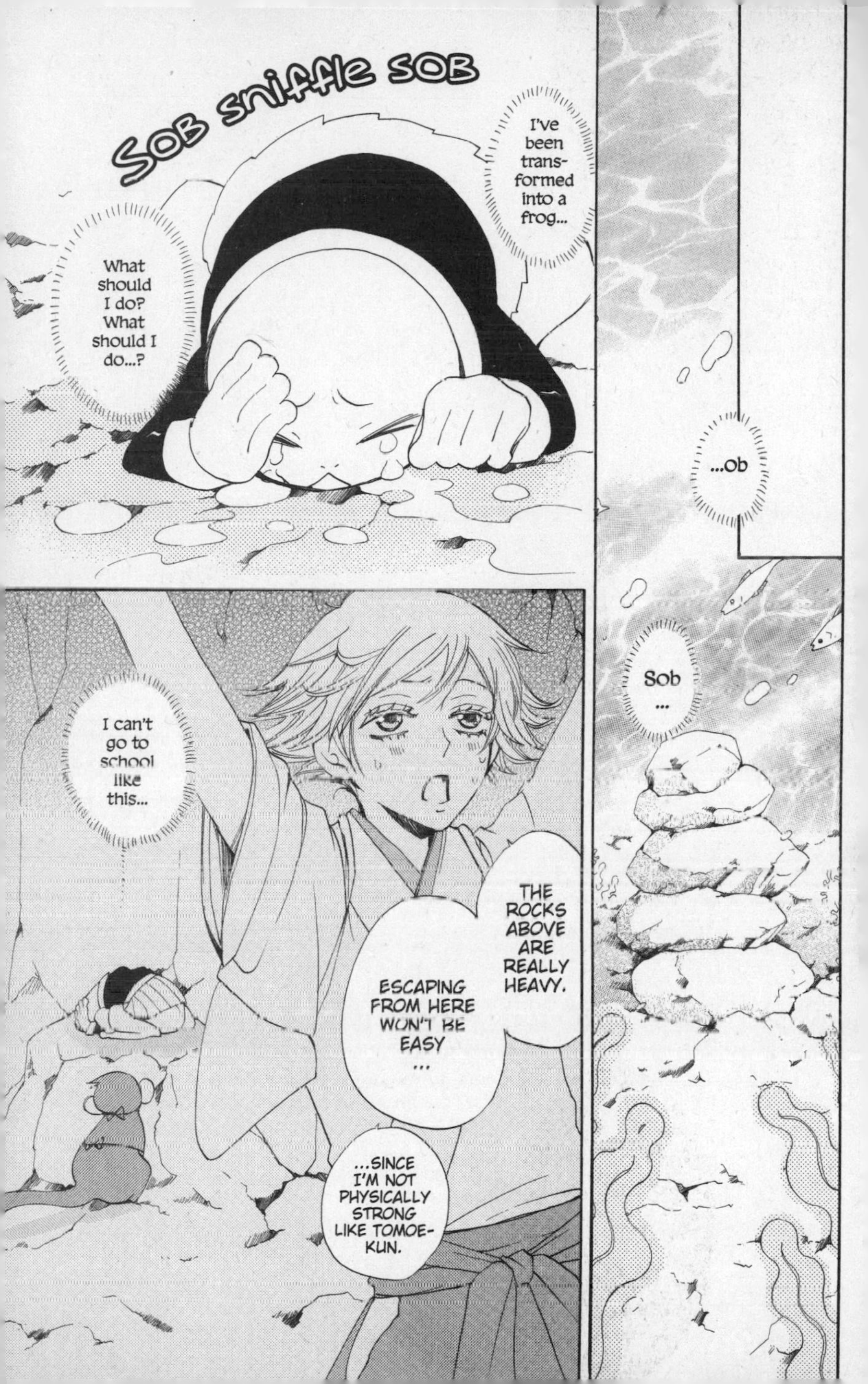
...Ob
Sob ...
SOB sniffle SOB
I've been transformed into a frog...
What should I do? What should I do...?
THE ROCKS ABOVE ARE REALLY HEAVY.
ESCAPING FROM HERE WON'T BE EASY ...
I can't go to school like this...
...SINCE I'M NOT PHYSICALLY STRONG LIKE TOMOE-KUN.

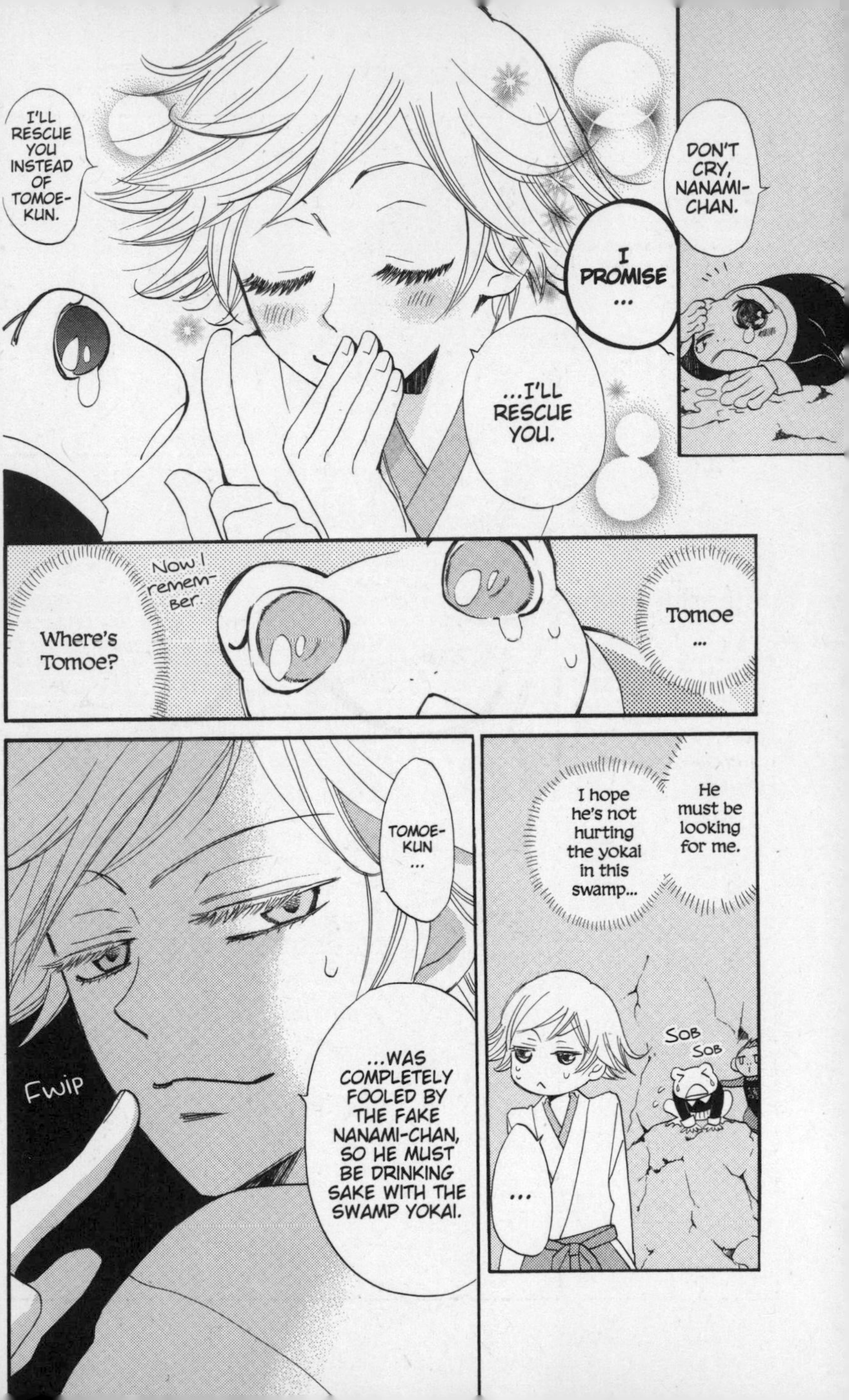
DON'T CRY, NANAMI-CHAN.
I'LL RESCUE YOU INSTEAD OF TOMOE-KUN.
I PROMISE...
...I'LL RESCUE YOU.
Tomoe...
Now I remember.
Where's Tomoe?
He must be looking for me.
I hope he's not hurting the yokai in this swamp...
SOB SOB
...
TOMOE-KUN...
...WAS COMPLETELY FOOLED BY THE FAKE NANAMI-CHAN, SO HE MUST BE DRINKING SAKE WITH THE SWAMP YOKAI.
Fwip

By the fake me?
HE ALWAYS PUTS ON AIRS, BUT HE'S ACTUALLY NO GOOD.
YES! AREN'T YOU SURPRISED?
HE IS HAPPY BEING ENTERTAINED BY THE BEAUTIES OF THIS SWAMP...
...WHILE HIS MASTER IS SUFFERING.
HE EVEN FLIRTED WITH THE CARPS AND CRUCIANS. HE'S SUCH A LECH.
SO...
...I'M USEFUL COMPARED TO HIM, RIGHT?
Crackle

Nowadays I love yoriyori, a sweet made in Nagasaki.

Yoriyori

They're twisted. They're Chinese sweets! And they're very tough. I can't eat a lot of them because I'm worried about my teeth, but I'd like to keep munching on them if possible.

Munch Munch

Ah, I gotta go to the dentist...

Take care of your teeth...!

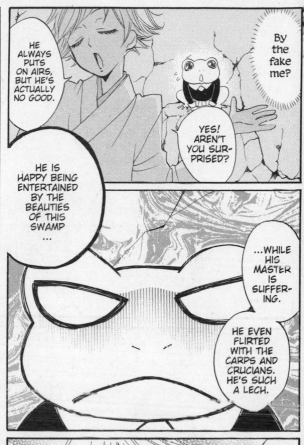

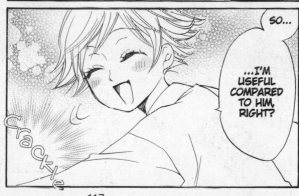

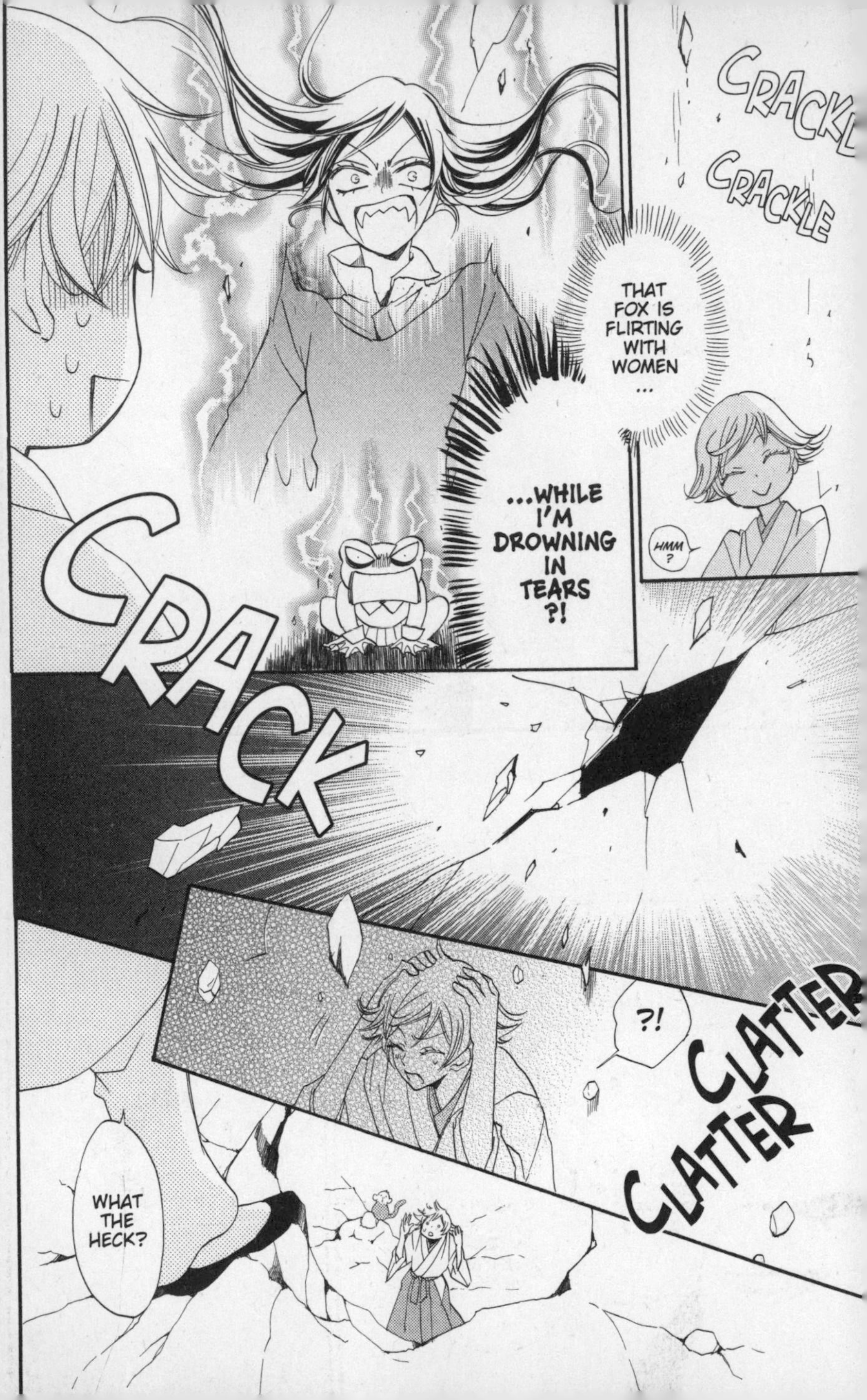
CRACKLE
CRACKLE
THAT FOX IS FLIRTING WITH WOMEN...
...WHILE I'M DROWNING IN TEARS?!
HMM?
CRACK
?!
CLATTER CLATTER
WHAT THE HECK?

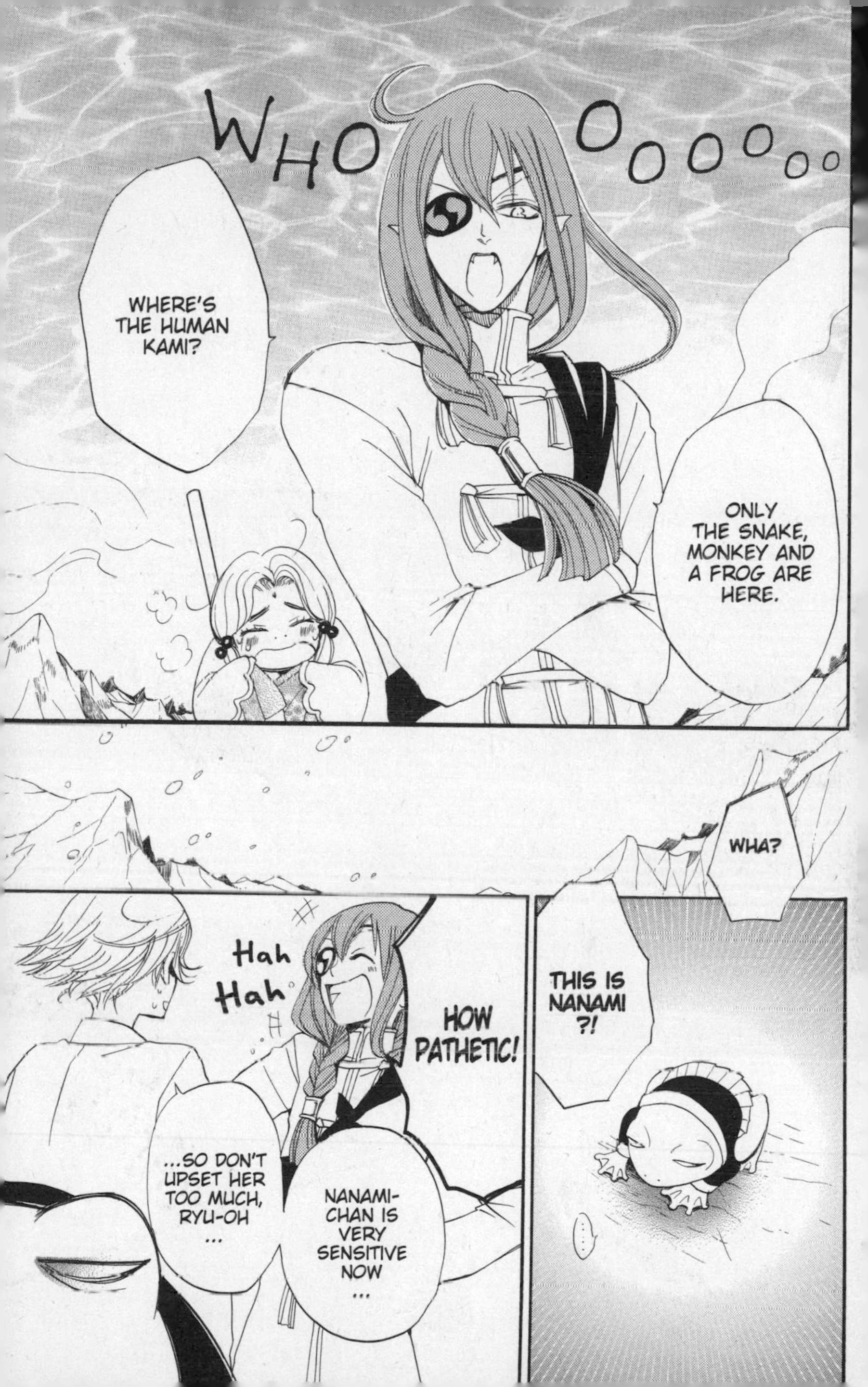
WHOOOOOOoo
ONLY THE SNAKE, MONKEY AND A FROG ARE HERE.
WHERE'S THE HUMAN KAMI?
WHA?
THIS IS NANAMI ?!
...
HOW PATHETIC!
Hah Hah
NANAMI-CHAN IS VERY SENSITIVE NOW ...
...SO DON'T UPSET HER TOO MUCH, RYU-OH ...

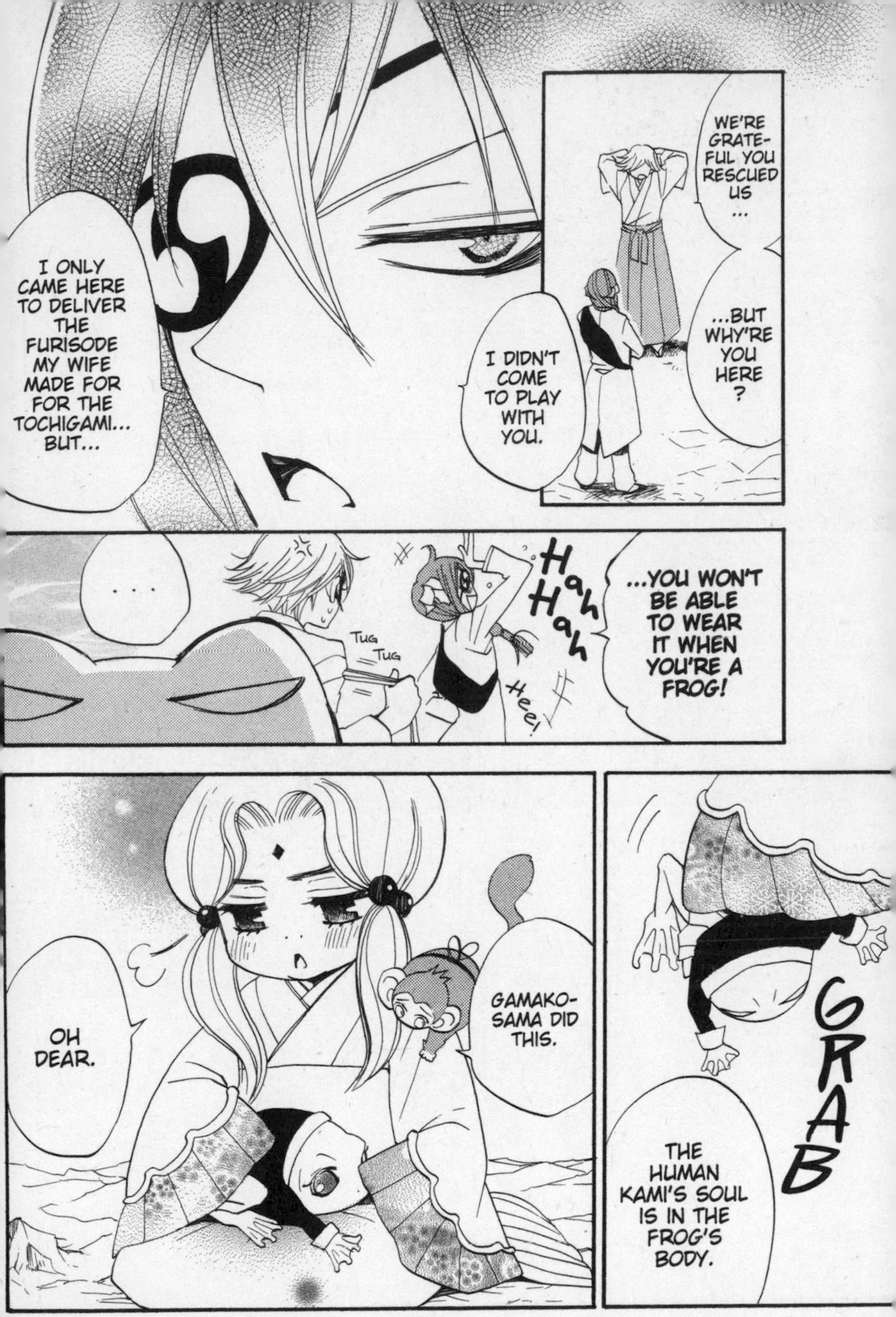
WE'RE GRATE-FUL YOU RESCUED US ...
...BUT WHY'RE YOU HERE ?
I DIDN'T COME TO PLAY WITH YOU.
I ONLY CAME HERE TO DELIVER THE FURISODE MY WIFE MADE FOR FOR THE TOCHIGAMI... BUT...
...YOU WON'T BE ABLE TO WEAR IT WHEN YOU'RE A FROG!
Hah Hah
Hee!
TUG TUG
...
GRAB
THE HUMAN KAMI'S SOUL IS IN THE FROG'S BODY.
GAMAKO-SAMA DID THIS.
OH DEAR.

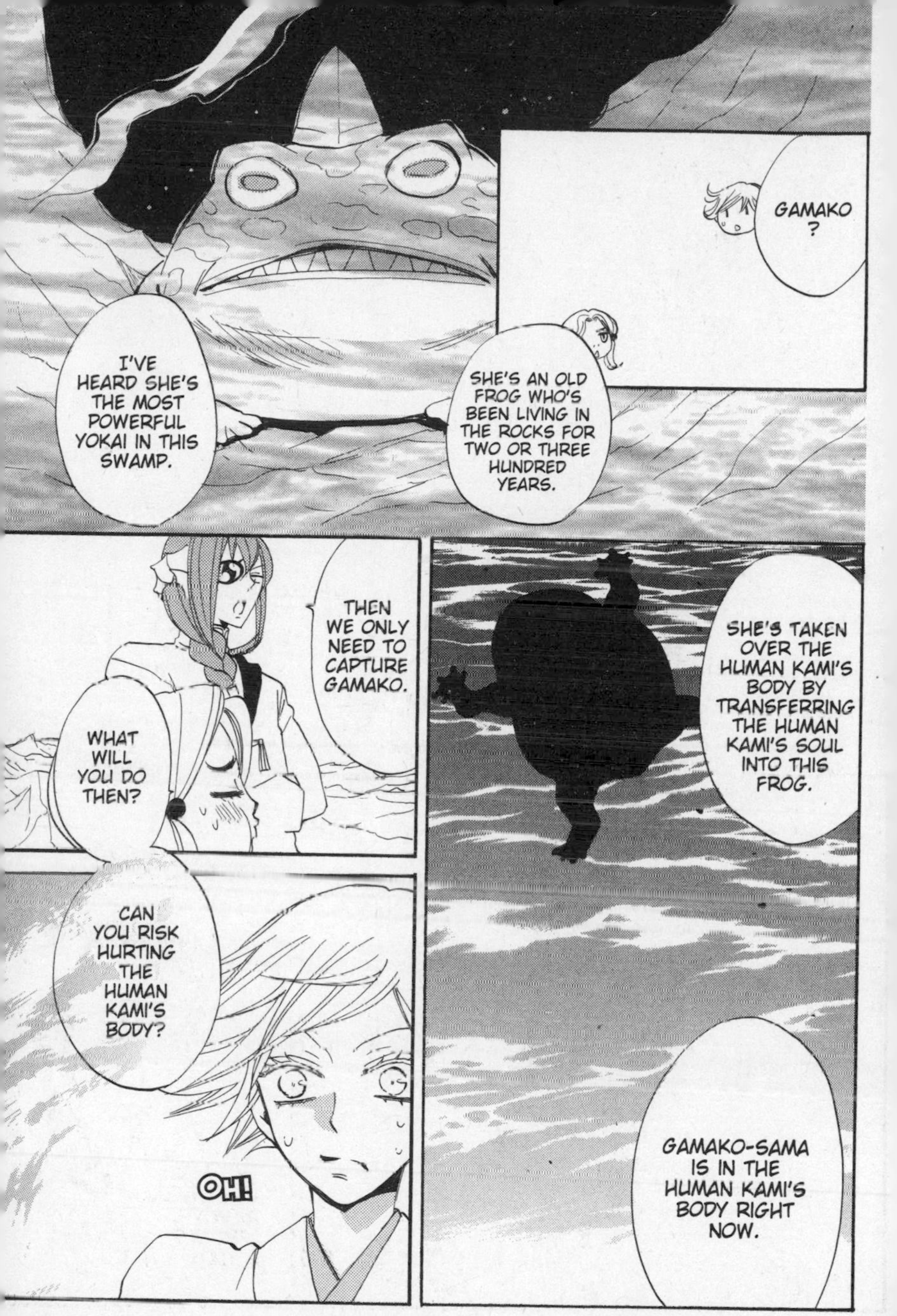
GAMAKO ?
SHE'S AN OLD FROG WHO'S BEEN LIVING IN THE ROCKS FOR TWO OR THREE HUNDRED YEARS.
I'VE HEARD SHE'S THE MOST POWERFUL YOKAI IN THIS SWAMP.
SHE'S TAKEN OVER THE HUMAN KAMI'S BODY BY TRANSFERRING THE HUMAN KAMI'S SOUL INTO THIS FROG.
GAMAKO-SAMA IS IN THE HUMAN KAMI'S BODY RIGHT NOW.
THEN WE ONLY NEED TO CAPTURE GAMAKO.
WHAT WILL YOU DO THEN?
CAN YOU RISK HURTING THE HUMAN KAMI'S BODY?
OH!

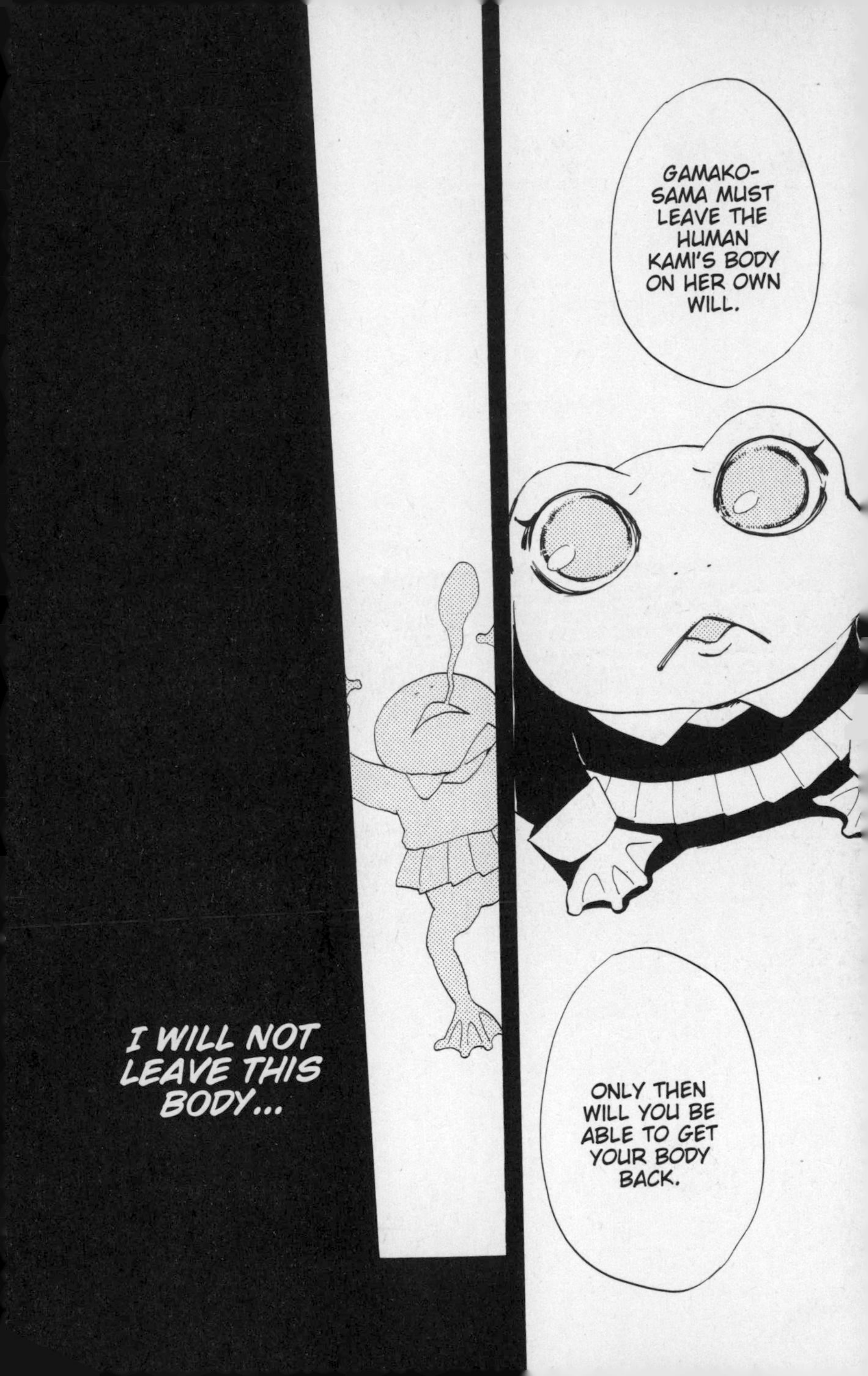
GAMAKO-SAMA MUST LEAVE THE HUMAN KAMI'S BODY ON HER OWN WILL.
ONLY THEN WILL YOU BE ABLE TO GET YOUR BODY BACK.
I WILL NOT LEAVE THIS BODY...

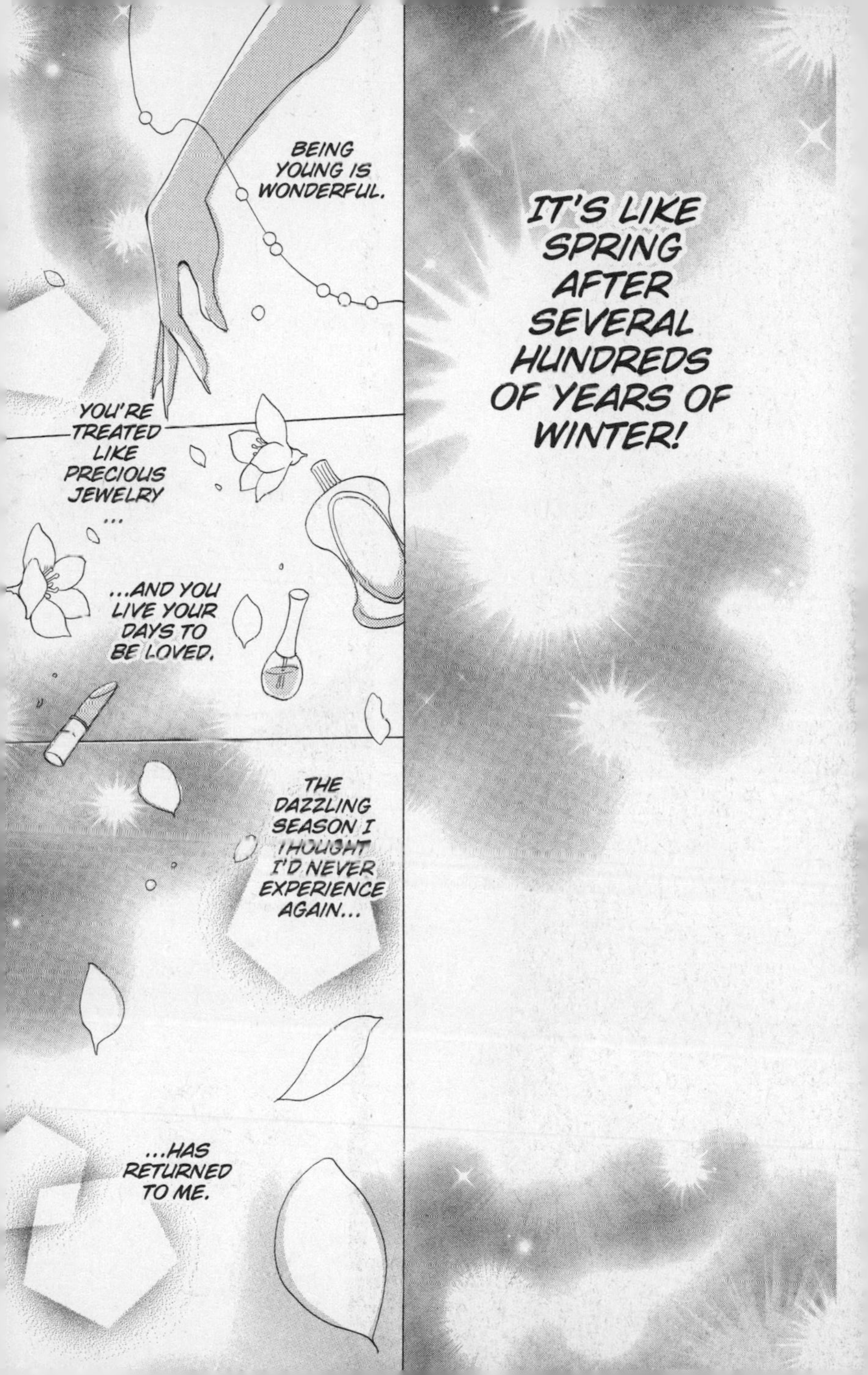
IT'S LIKE SPRING AFTER SEVERAL HUNDREDS OF YEARS OF WINTER!
BEING YOUNG IS WONDERFUL.
YOU'RE TREATED LIKE PRECIOUS JEWELRY ...
...AND YOU LIVE YOUR DAYS TO BE LOVED.
THE DAZZLING SEASON I THOUGHT I'D NEVER EXPERIENCE AGAIN...
...HAS RETURNED TO ME.

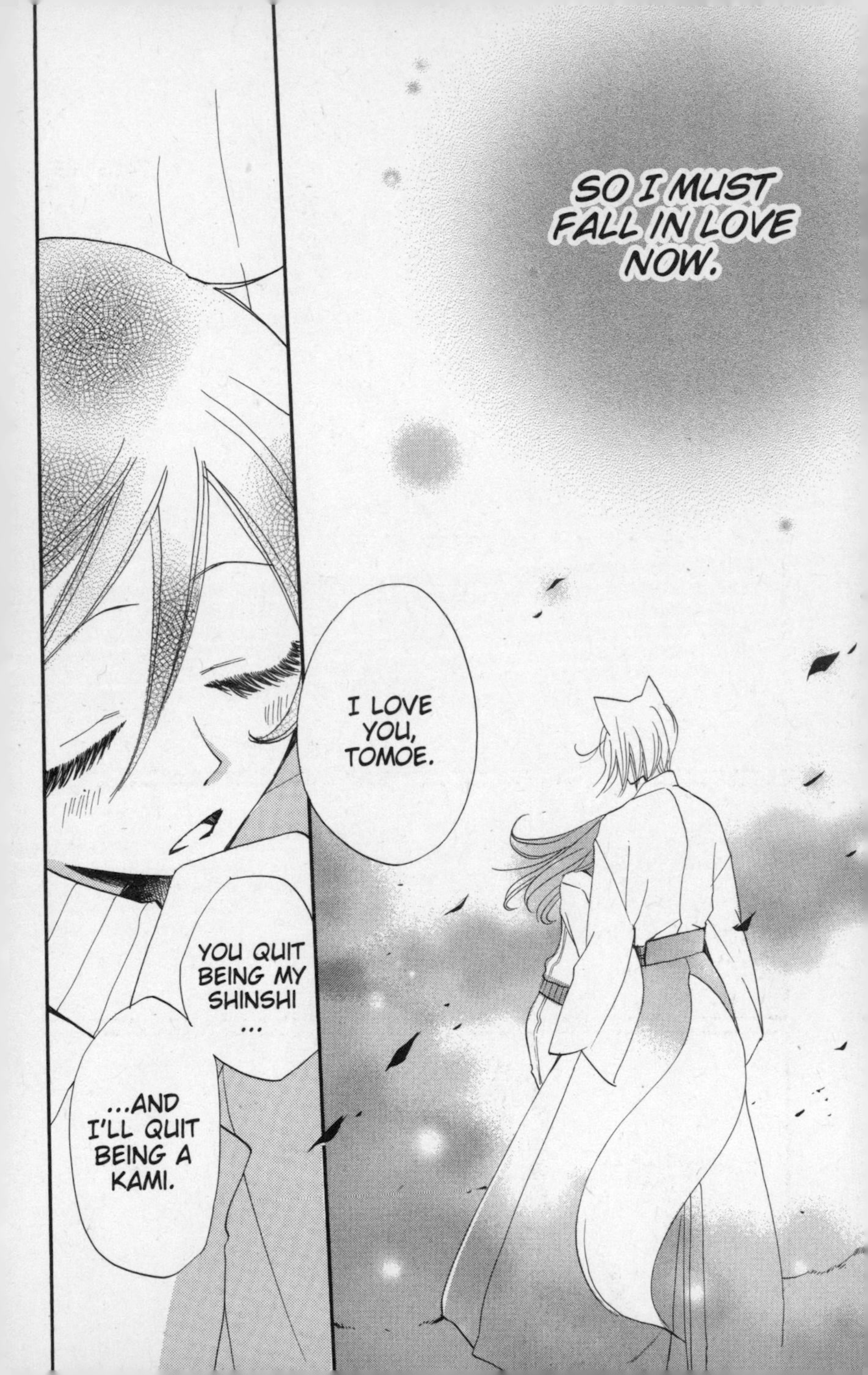
SO I MUST FALL IN LOVE NOW.
I LOVE YOU, TOMOE.
YOU QUIT BEING MY SHINSHI ...
...AND I'LL QUIT BEING A KAMI.

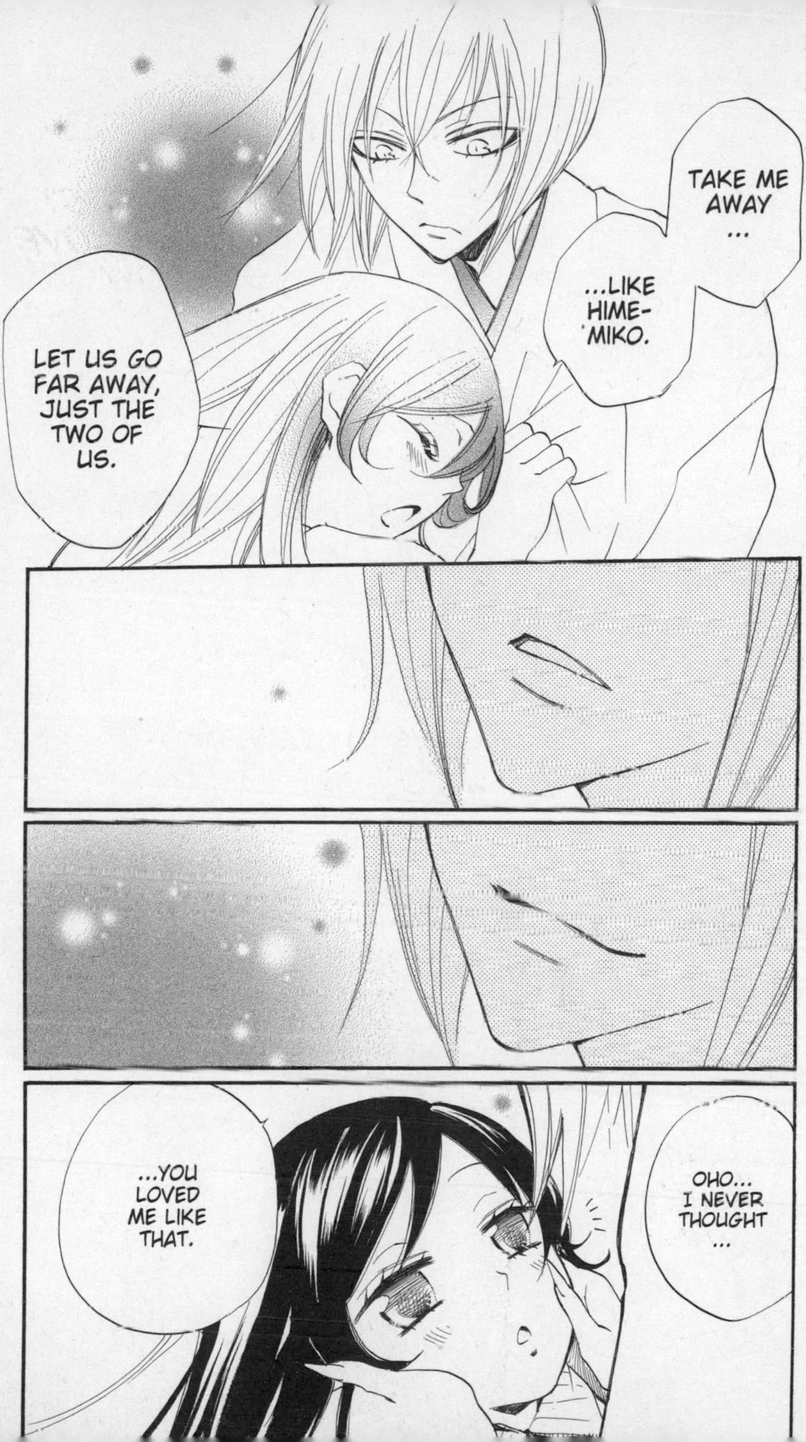
TAKE ME AWAY ...
...LIKE HIME-MIKO.
LET US GO FAR AWAY, JUST THE TWO OF US.
OHO... I NEVER THOUGHT ...
...YOU LOVED ME LIKE THAT.

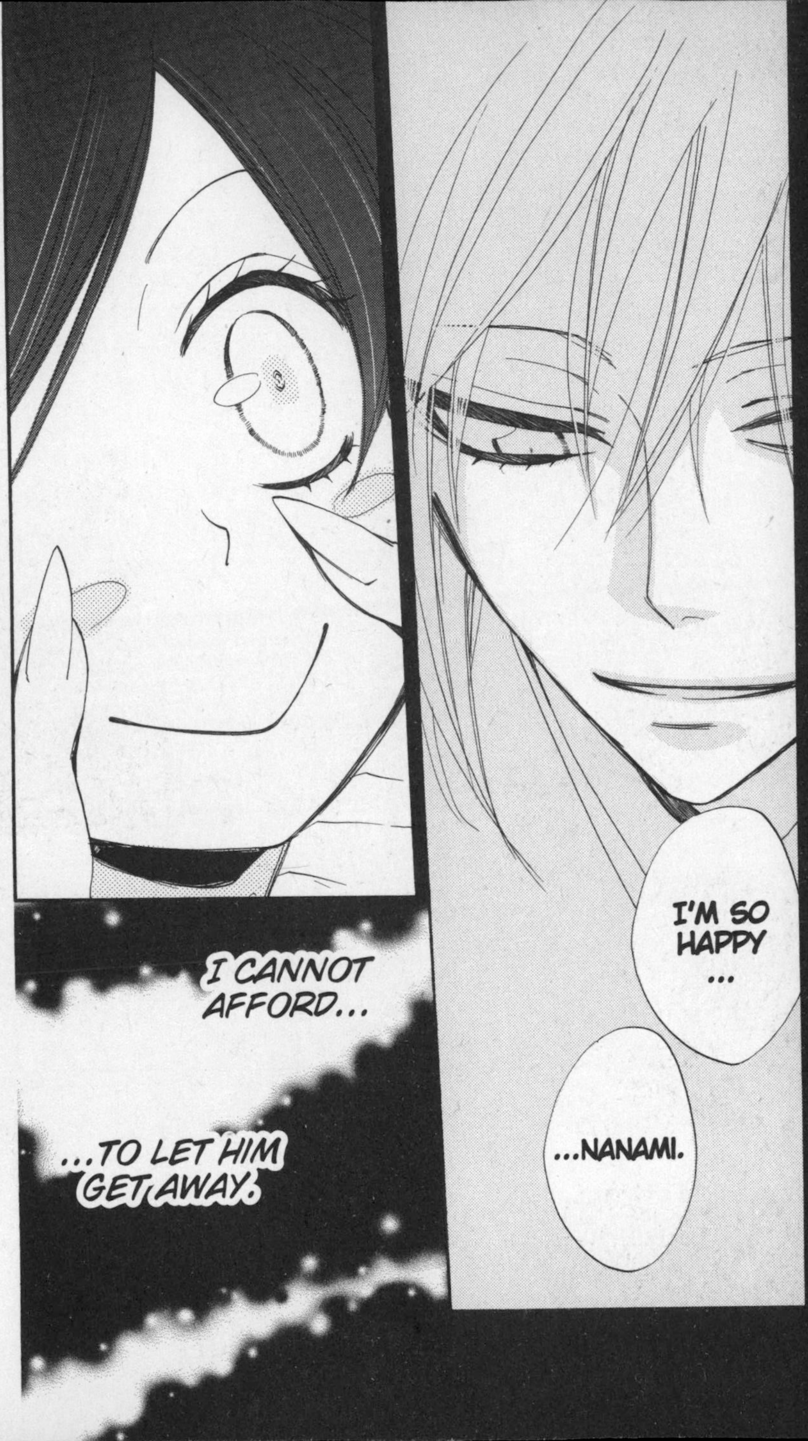
I'M SO HAPPY ...
...NANAMI.
I CANNOT AFFORD...
...TO LET HIM GET AWAY.

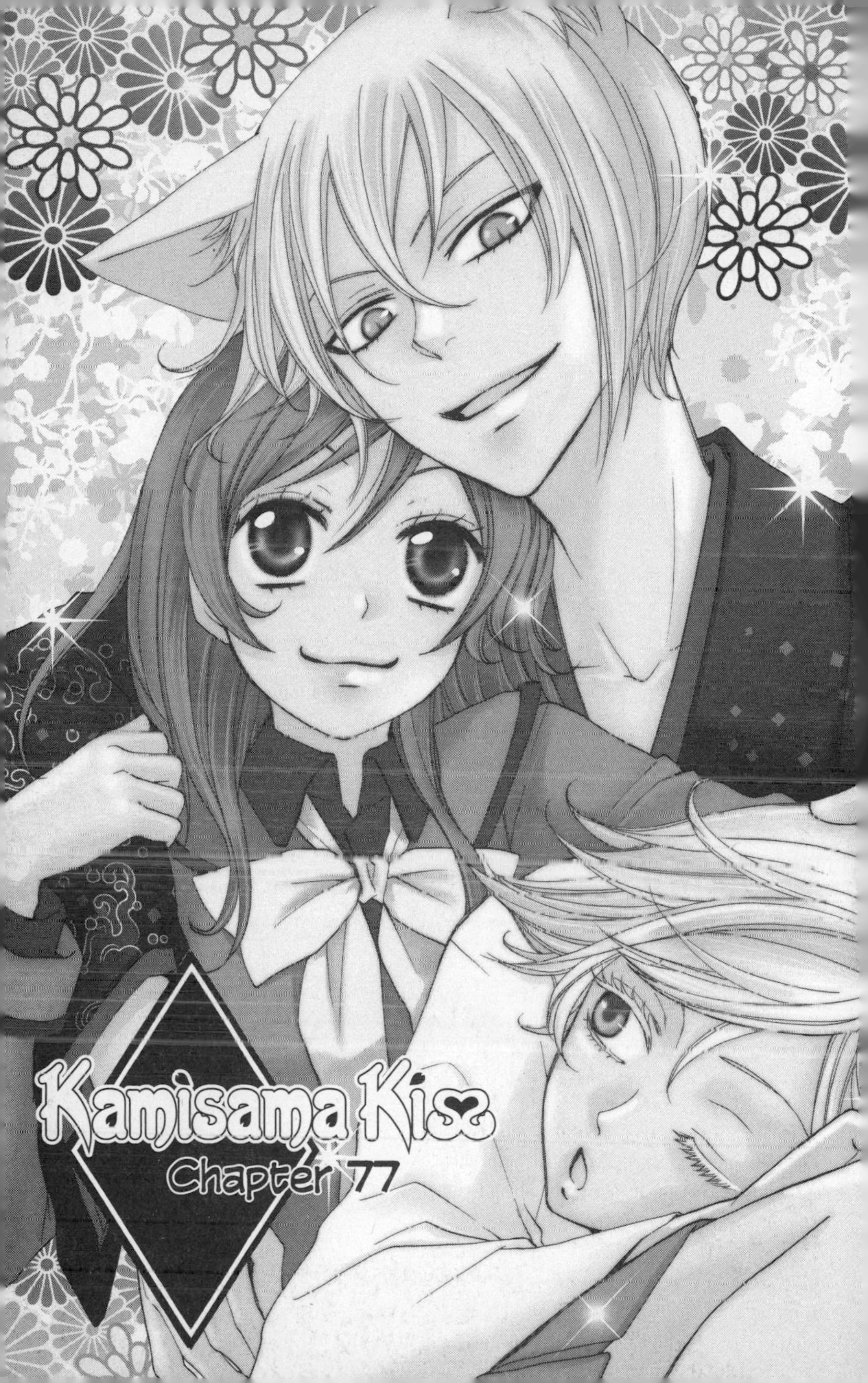
Kamisama Kiss
Chapter 77

# RESULT OF THE KAMISAMA KISS POPULARITY POLL!!

Fourth Anniversary!

**Here we announce the result of the popularity poll which was published in *Hana to Yume* 2012 issue 6 for those who only read the graphic novels!**

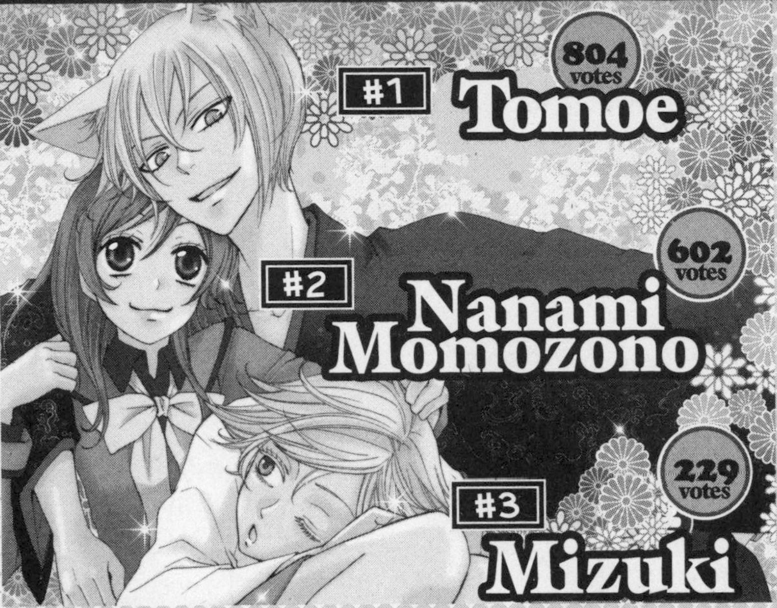

#1
Tomoe
804 votes
#2
Nanami Momozono
602 votes
#3
Mizuki
229 votes


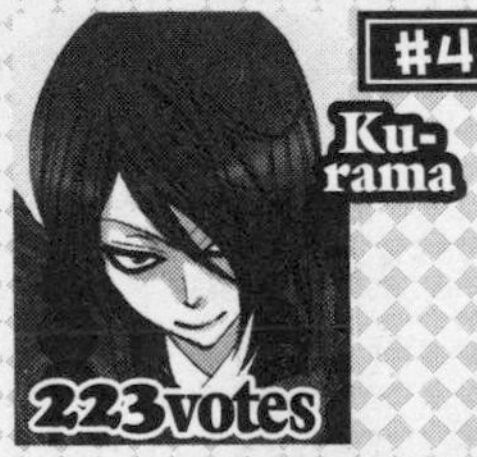

#4
Ku-rama
223 votes


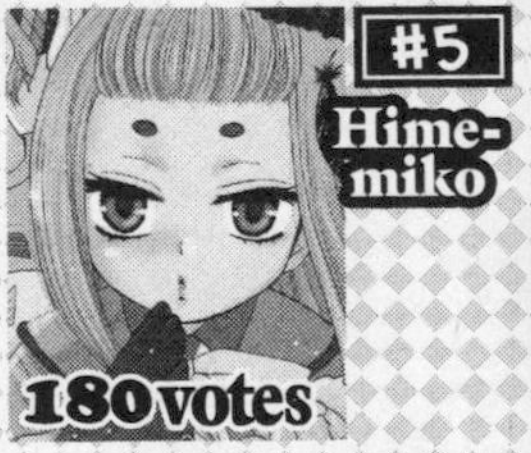

#5
Hime-miko
180 votes


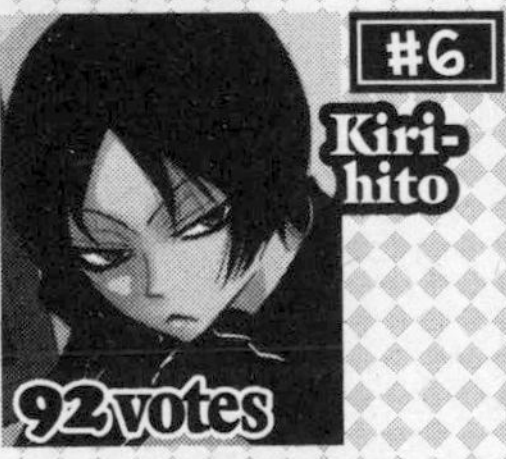

#6
Kiri-hito
92 votes


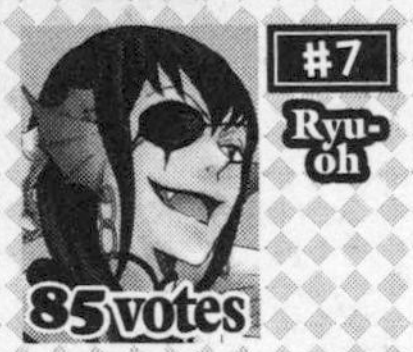

#7
Ryu-oh
85 votes


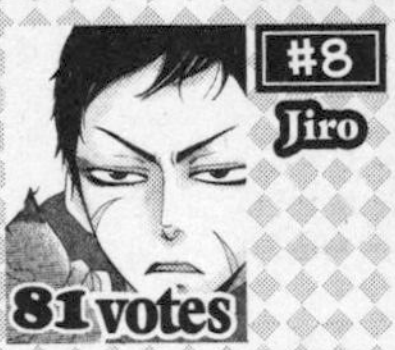

#8
Jiro
81 votes


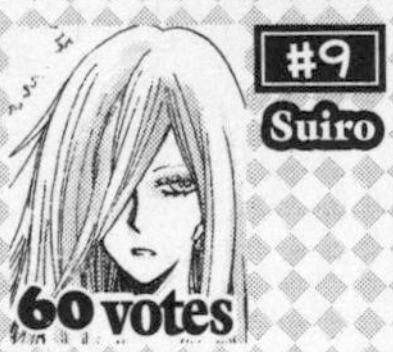

#9
Suiro
60 votes


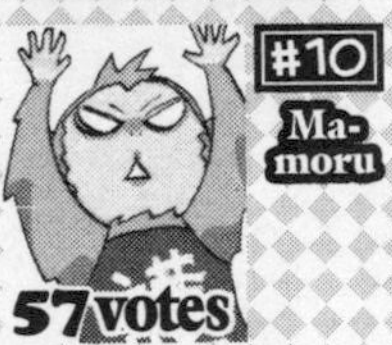

#10
Ma-moru
57 votes


- #11 Onikiri & Kotetsu...43 votes
- #12 Nishiki...39 votes
- #13 Kayako Hiiragi...39 votes
- #14 Mikage...36 votes
- #15 Otohiko...22 votes
- #16 Kotaro Urashima...20 votes
- #17 Botanmaru...9 votes
- #18 Julietta Suzuki-sensei...3 votes
- #19 Ami Nekota, Kamehime, Nanami's Mother...2 votes
- #20 Shiranui, Daidaimaru, Umiushi, Aoi, and others...1 vote

**Thank you for all your votes!**

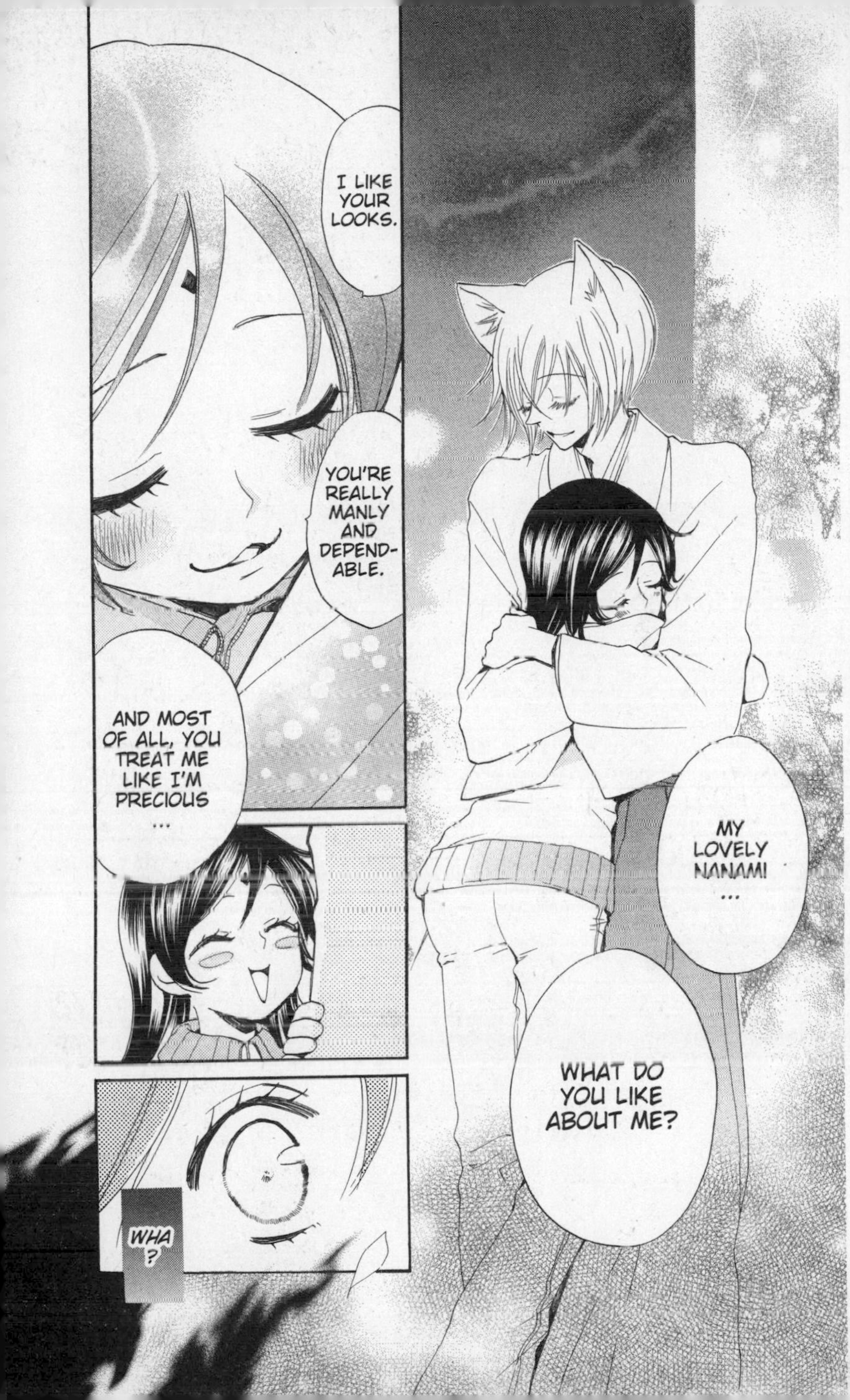
MY LOVELY NANAMI ...
WHAT DO YOU LIKE ABOUT ME?
I LIKE YOUR LOOKS.
YOU'RE REALLY MANLY AND DEPEND-ABLE.
AND MOST OF ALL, YOU TREAT ME LIKE I'M PRECIOUS ...
WHA ?

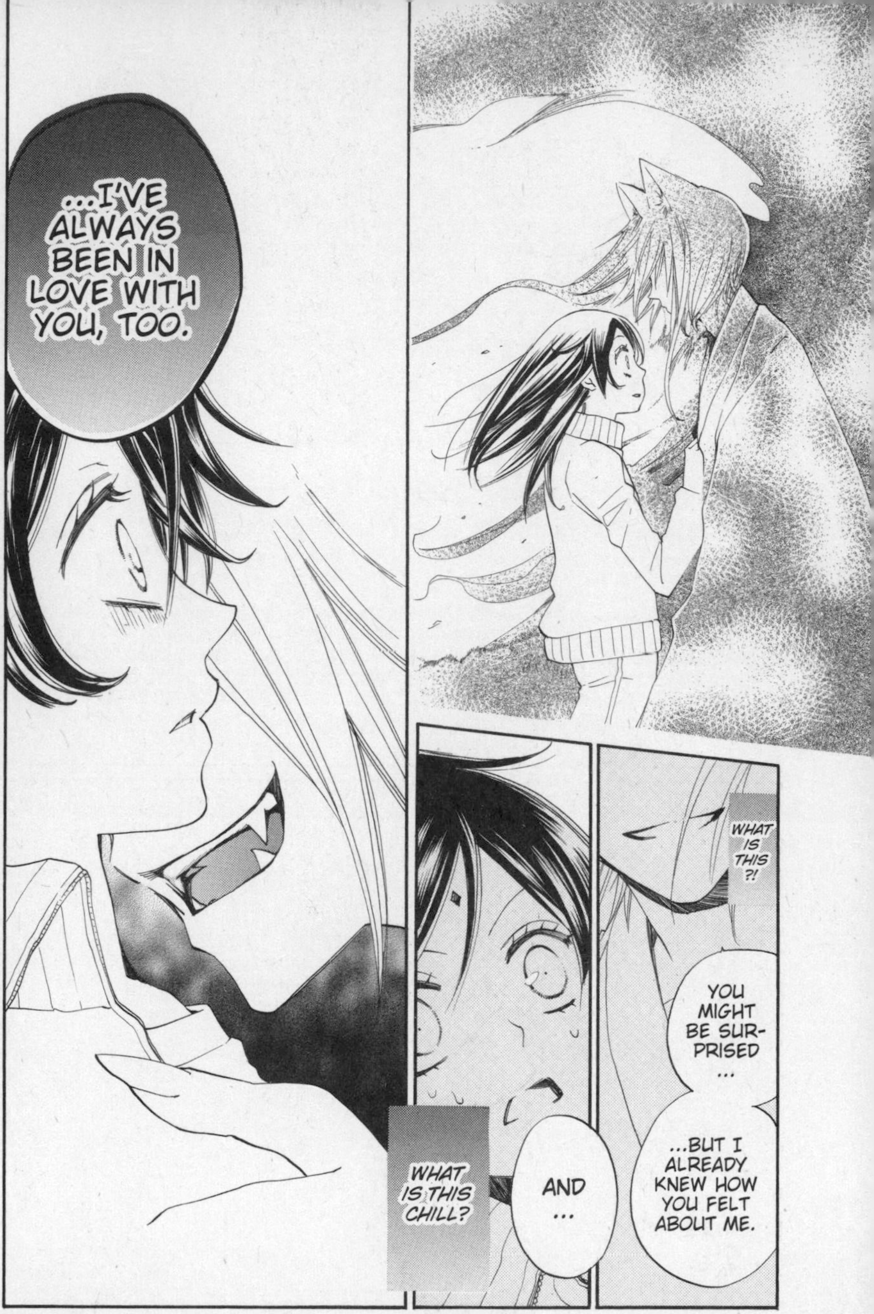
WHAT IS THIS ?!
YOU MIGHT BE SUR-PRISED ...
...BUT I ALREADY KNEW HOW YOU FELT ABOUT ME.
AND ...
WHAT IS THIS CHILL?
...I'VE ALWAYS BEEN IN LOVE WITH YOU, TOO.

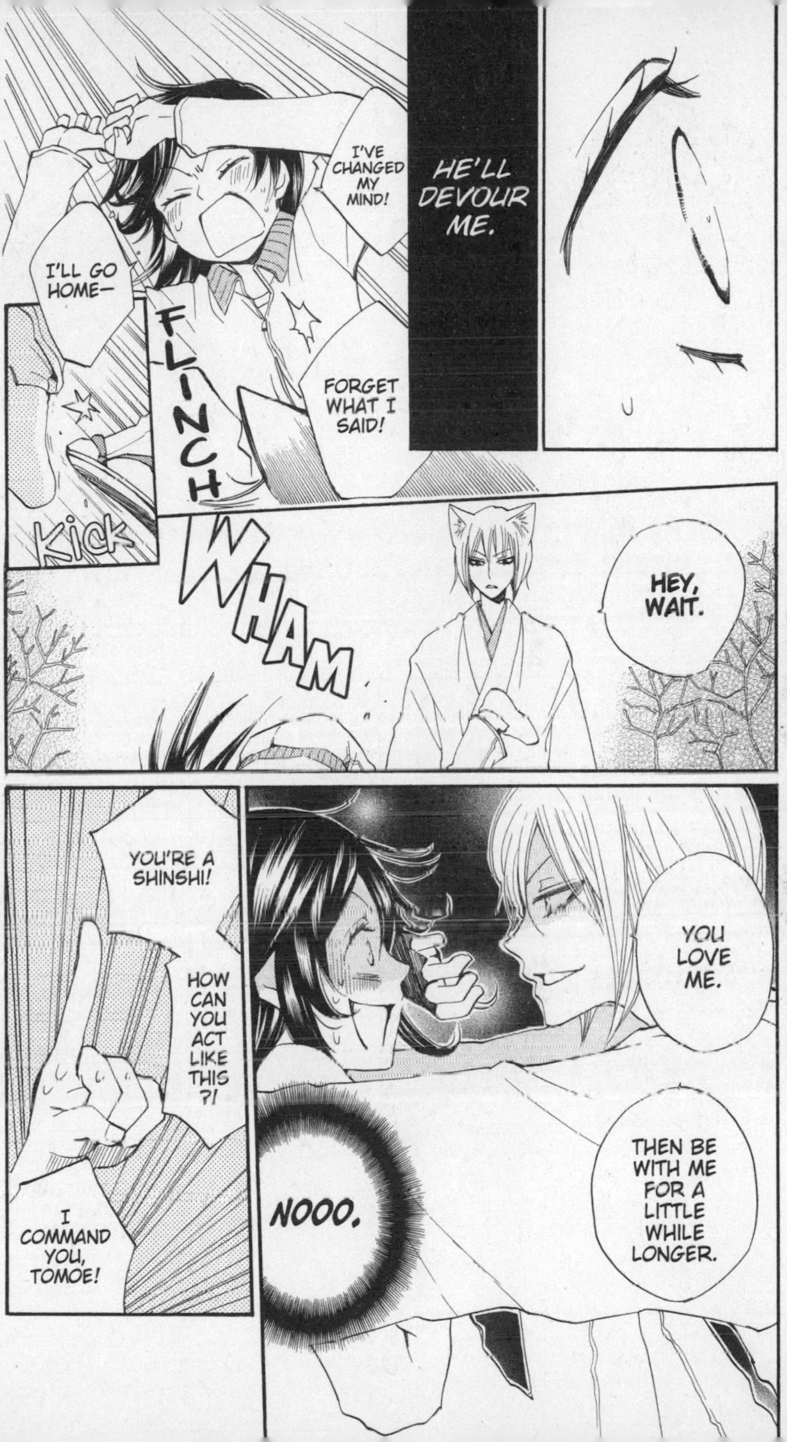
HE'LL DEVOUR ME.
I'VE CHANGED MY MIND!
I'LL GO HOME—
FORGET WHAT I SAID!
FLINCH
KICK
HEY, WAIT.
WHAM
YOU LOVE ME.
THEN BE WITH ME FOR A LITTLE WHILE LONGER.
NOOO.
YOU'RE A SHINSHI!
HOW CAN YOU ACT LIKE THIS?!
I COMMAND YOU, TOMOE!

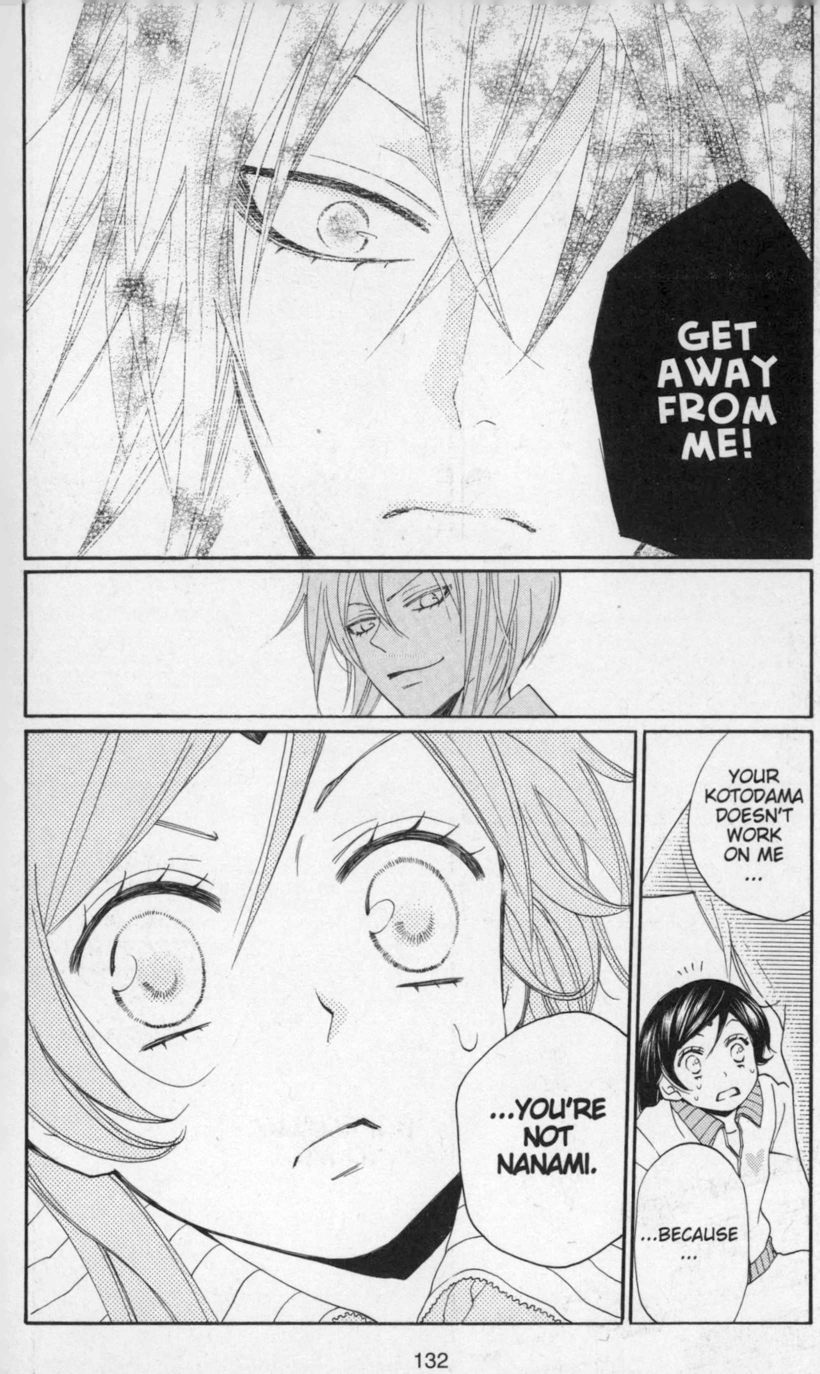
GET AWAY FROM ME!
YOUR KOTODAMA DOESN'T WORK ON ME ...
...BECAUSE ...
...YOU'RE NOT NANAMI.

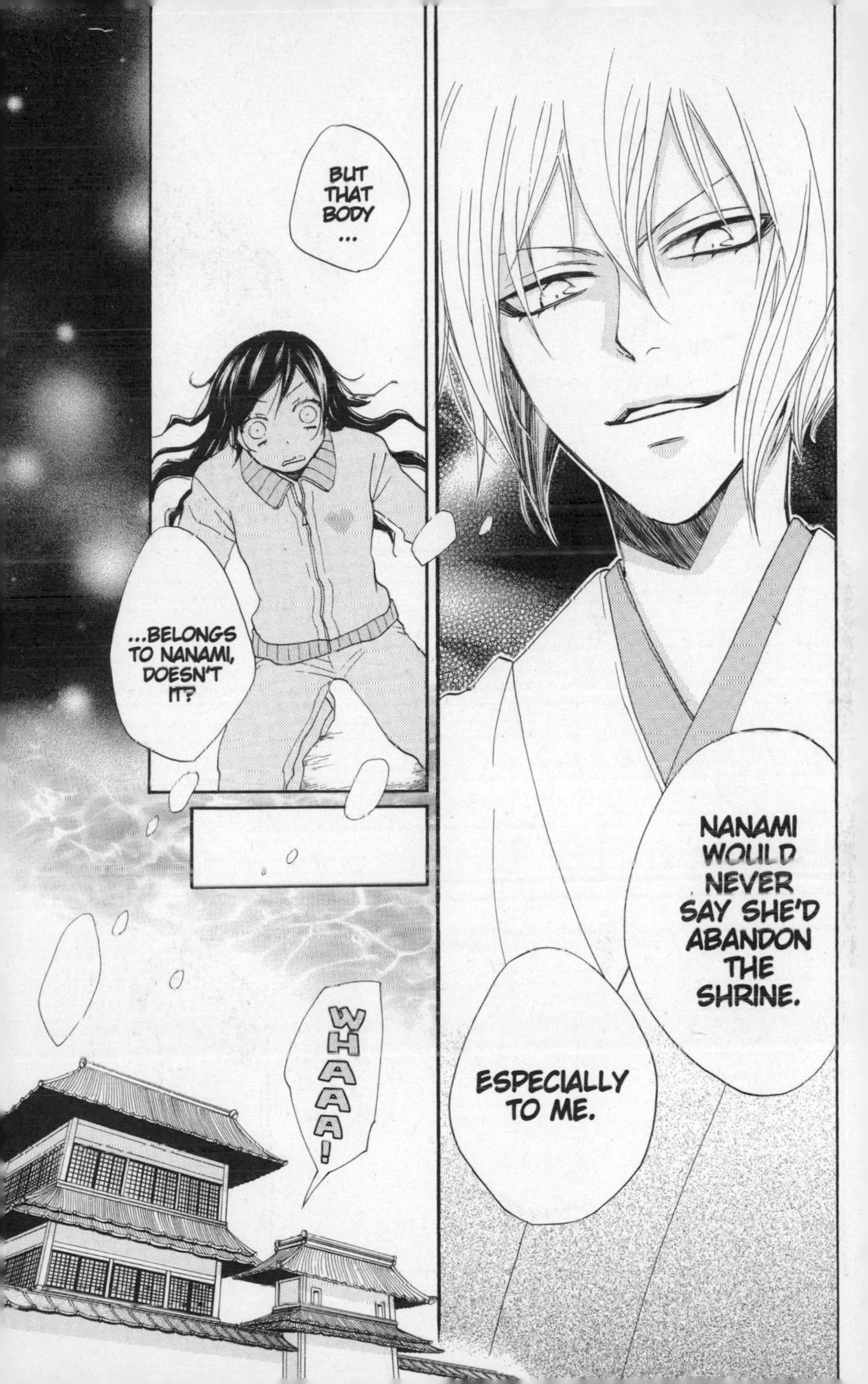
NANAMI WOULD NEVER SAY SHE'D ABANDON THE SHRINE.
ESPECIALLY TO ME.
BUT THAT BODY...
...BELONGS TO NANAMI, DOESN'T IT?
WHAAAA!

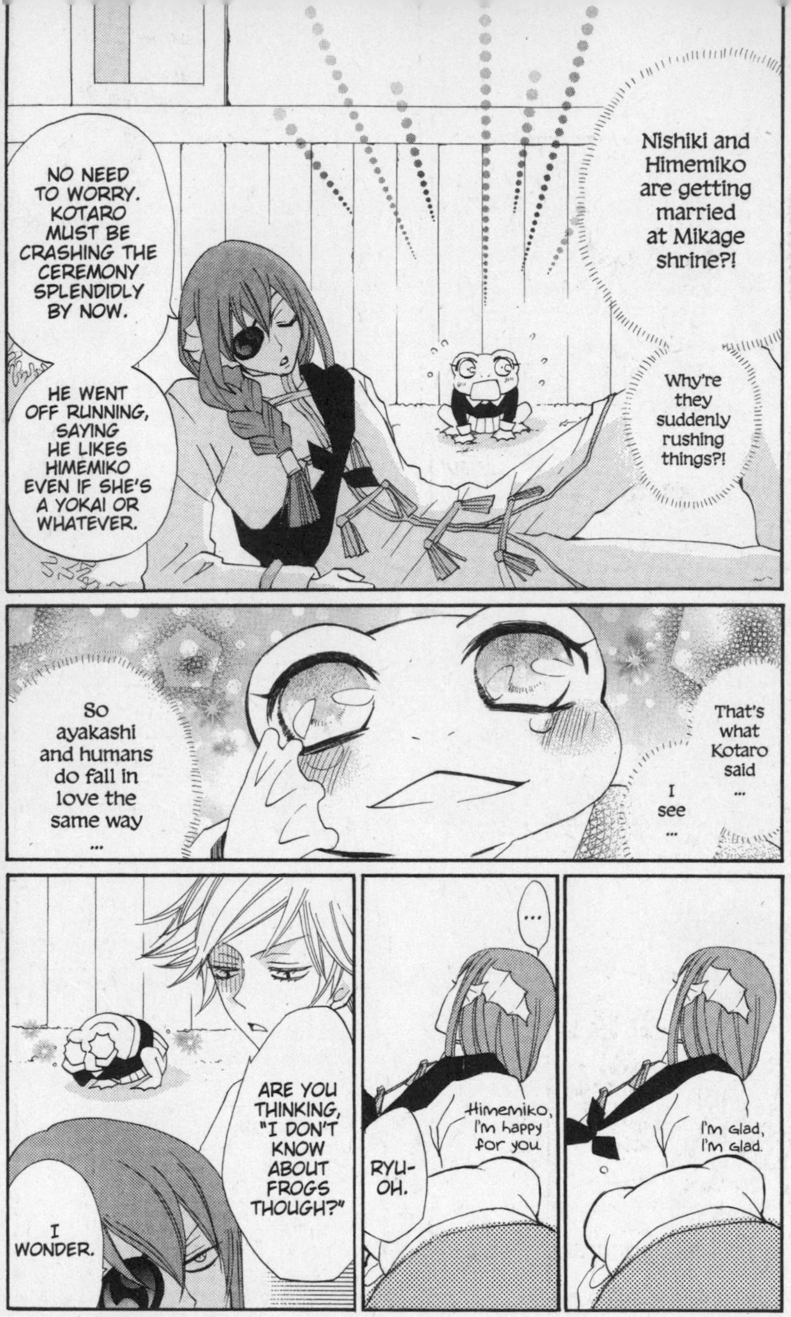
Nishiki and Himemiko are getting married at Mikage shrine?!
Why're they suddenly rushing things?!
NO NEED TO WORRY. KOTARO MUST BE CRASHING THE CEREMONY SPLENDIDLY BY NOW.
HE WENT OFF RUNNING, SAYING HE LIKES HIMEMIKO EVEN IF SHE'S A YOKAI OR WHATEVER.
That's what Kotaro said ...
I see ...
So ayakashi and humans do fall in love the same way ...
I'm Glad, I'm Glad.
...
Himemiko, I'm happy for you.
RYU-OH.
ARE YOU THINKING, "I DON'T KNOW ABOUT FROGS THOUGH?"
I WONDER.

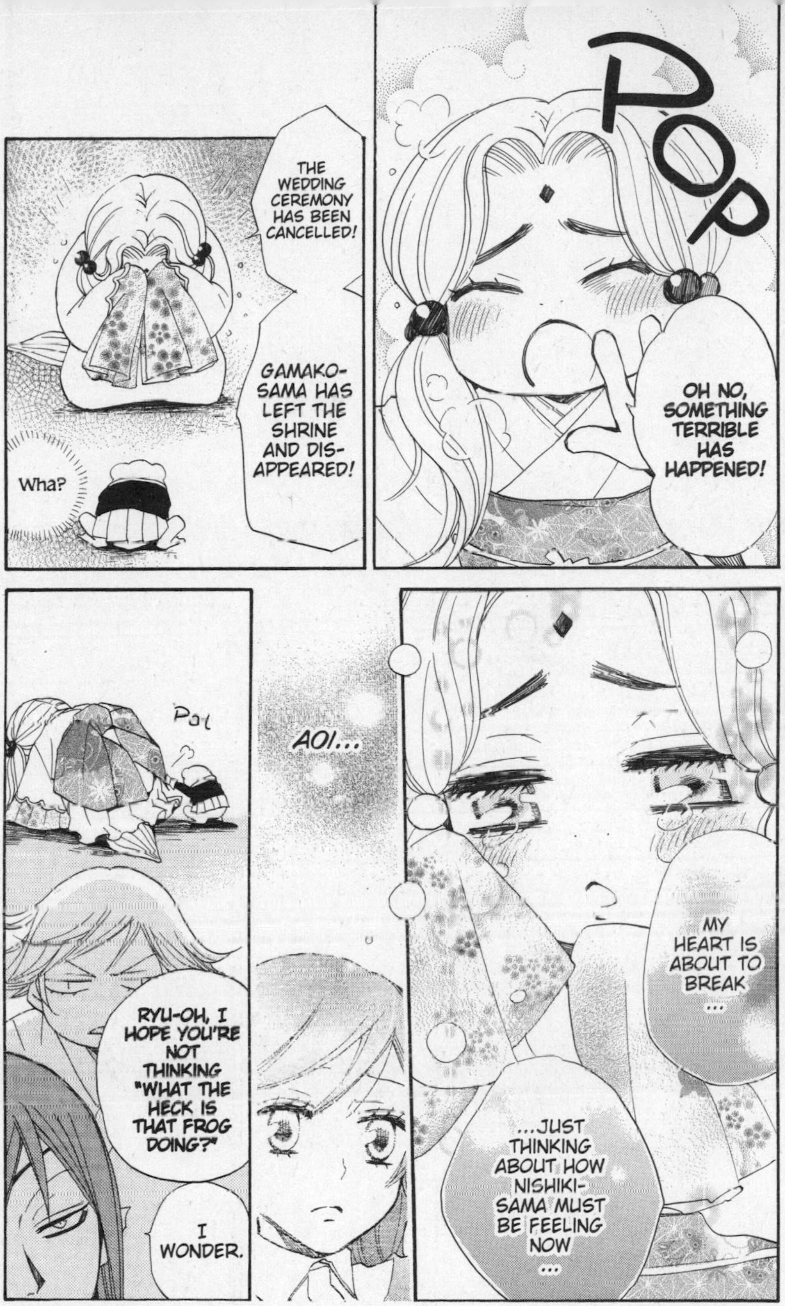
POP
OH NO, SOMETHING TERRIBLE HAS HAPPENED!
THE WEDDING CEREMONY HAS BEEN CANCELLED!
GAMAKO-SAMA HAS LEFT THE SHRINE AND DIS-APPEARED!
Wha?
AOI...
MY HEART IS ABOUT TO BREAK ...
...JUST THINKING ABOUT HOW NISHIKI-SAMA MUST BE FEELING NOW ...
Poi
RYU-OH, I HOPE YOU'RE NOT THINKING "WHAT THE HECK IS THAT FROG DOING?"
I WONDER.

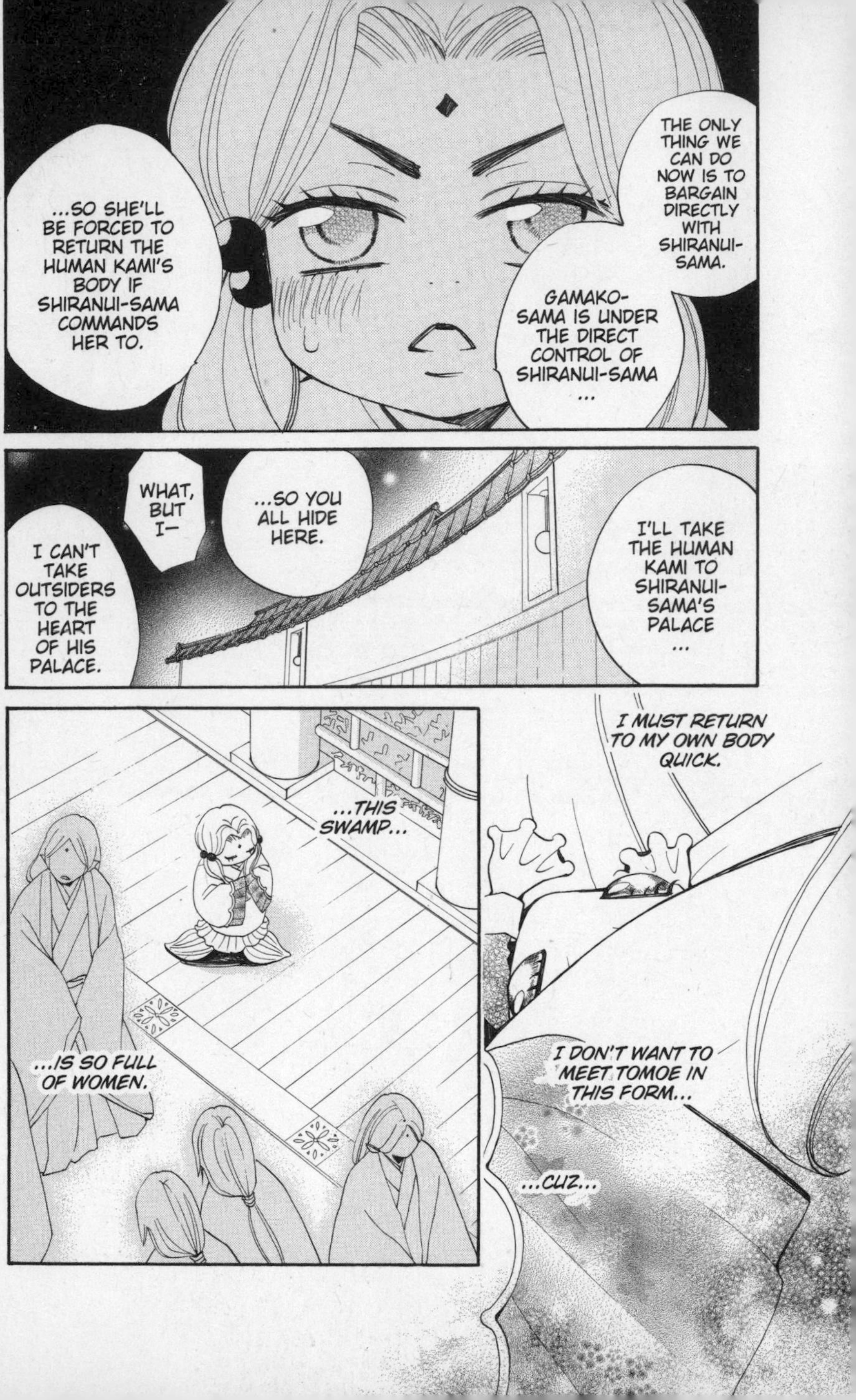
THE ONLY THING WE CAN DO NOW IS TO BARGAIN DIRECTLY WITH SHIRANUI-SAMA.
GAMAKO-SAMA IS UNDER THE DIRECT CONTROL OF SHIRANUI-SAMA ...
...SO SHE'LL BE FORCED TO RETURN THE HUMAN KAMI'S BODY IF SHIRANUI-SAMA COMMANDS HER TO.
I'LL TAKE THE HUMAN KAMI TO SHIRANUI-SAMA'S PALACE ...
...SO YOU ALL HIDE HERE.
WHAT, BUT I—
I CAN'T TAKE OUTSIDERS TO THE HEART OF HIS PALACE.
I MUST RETURN TO MY OWN BODY QUICK.
I DON'T WANT TO MEET TOMOE IN THIS FORM...
...CUZ...
...THIS SWAMP...
...IS SO FULL OF WOMEN.

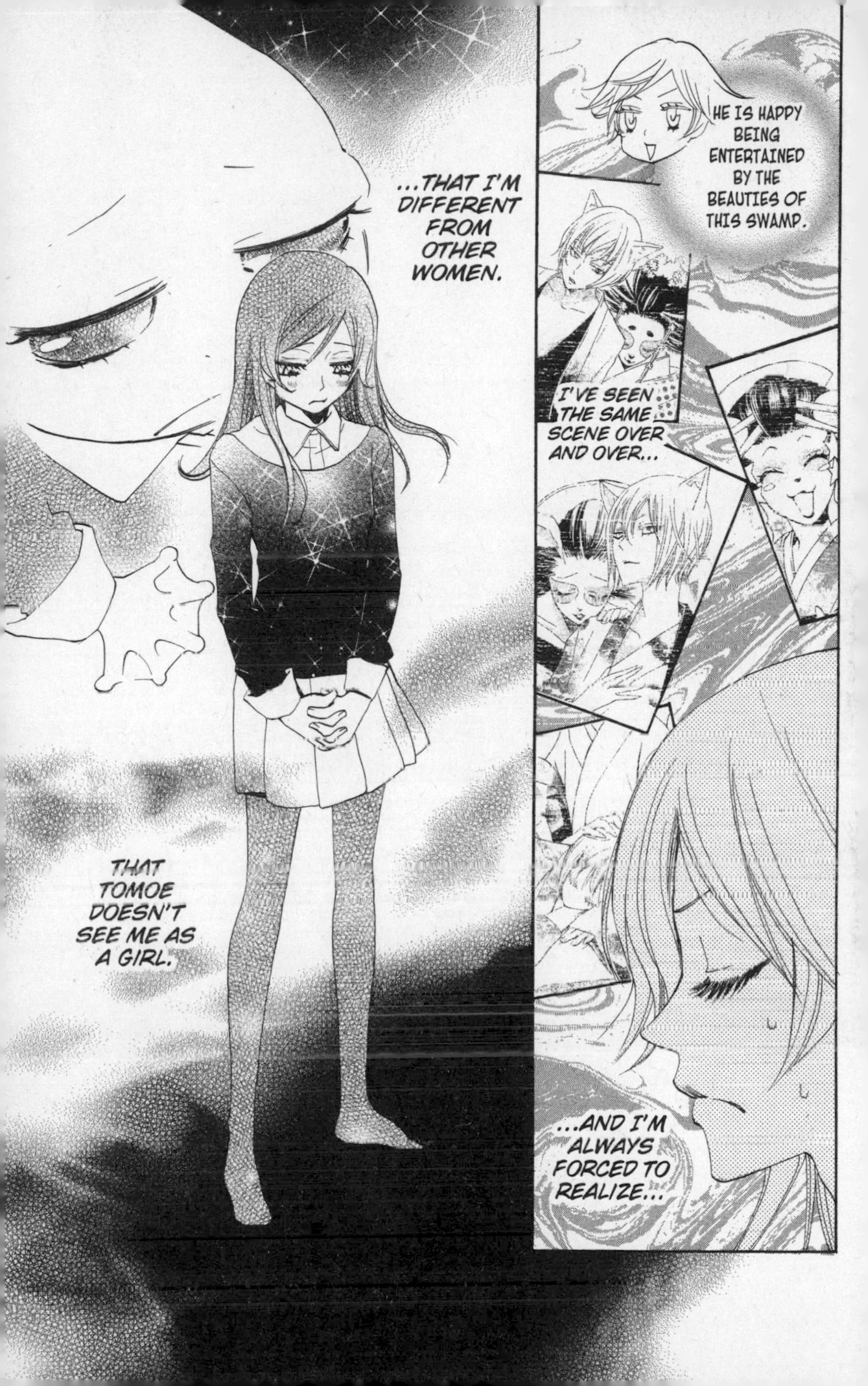
HE IS HAPPY BEING ENTERTAINED BY THE BEAUTIES OF THIS SWAMP.
I'VE SEEN THE SAME SCENE OVER AND OVER...
...AND I'M ALWAYS FORCED TO REALIZE...
...THAT I'M DIFFERENT FROM OTHER WOMEN.
THAT TOMOE DOESN'T SEE ME AS A GIRL.

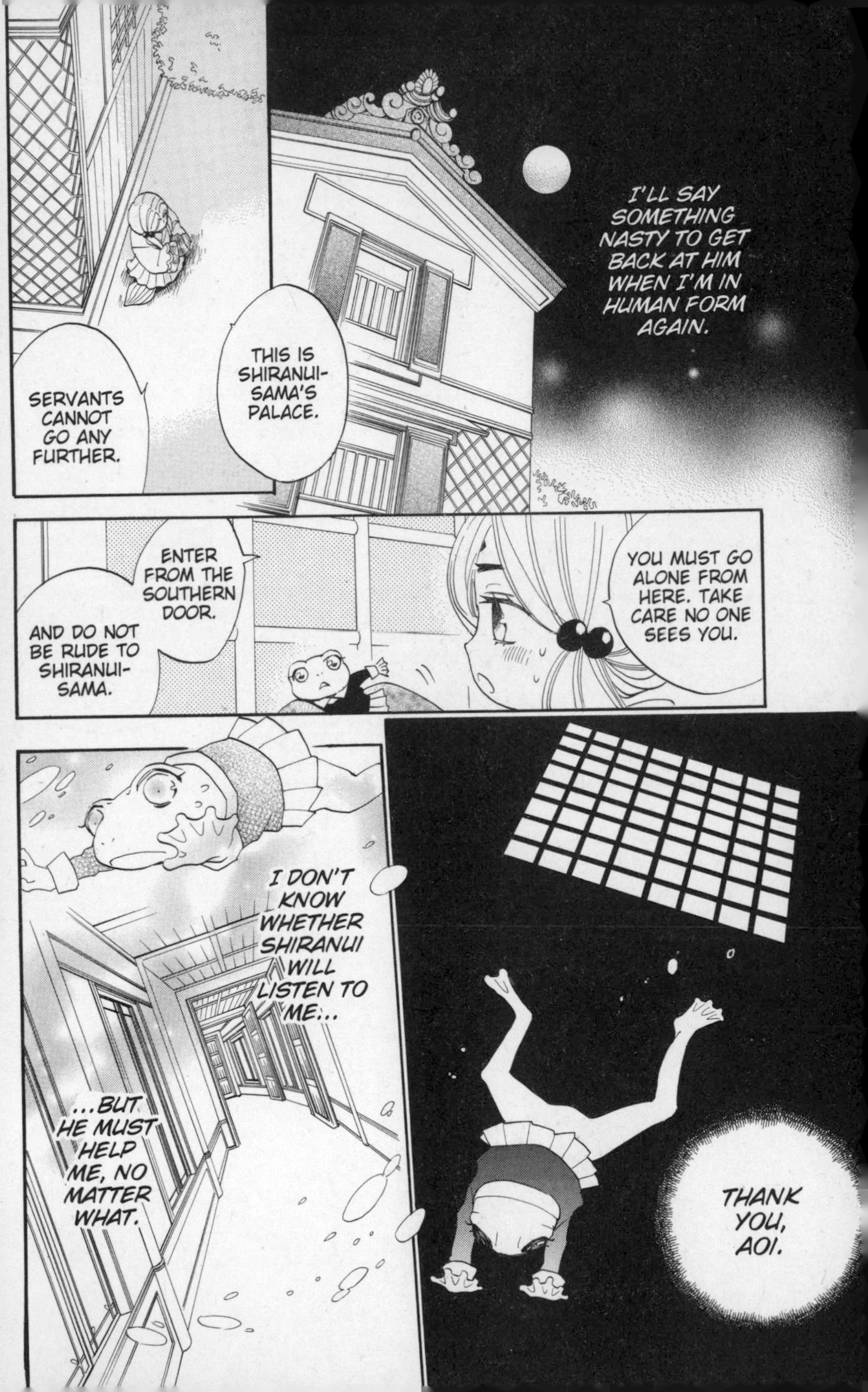
I'LL SAY SOMETHING NASTY TO GET BACK AT HIM WHEN I'M IN HUMAN FORM AGAIN.
THIS IS SHIRANUI-SAMA'S PALACE.
SERVANTS CANNOT GO ANY FURTHER.
YOU MUST GO ALONE FROM HERE. TAKE CARE NO ONE SEES YOU.
ENTER FROM THE SOUTHERN DOOR.
AND DO NOT BE RUDE TO SHIRANUI-SAMA.
THANK YOU, AOI.
I DON'T KNOW WHETHER SHIRANUI WILL LISTEN TO ME...
...BUT HE MUST HELP ME, NO MATTER WHAT.

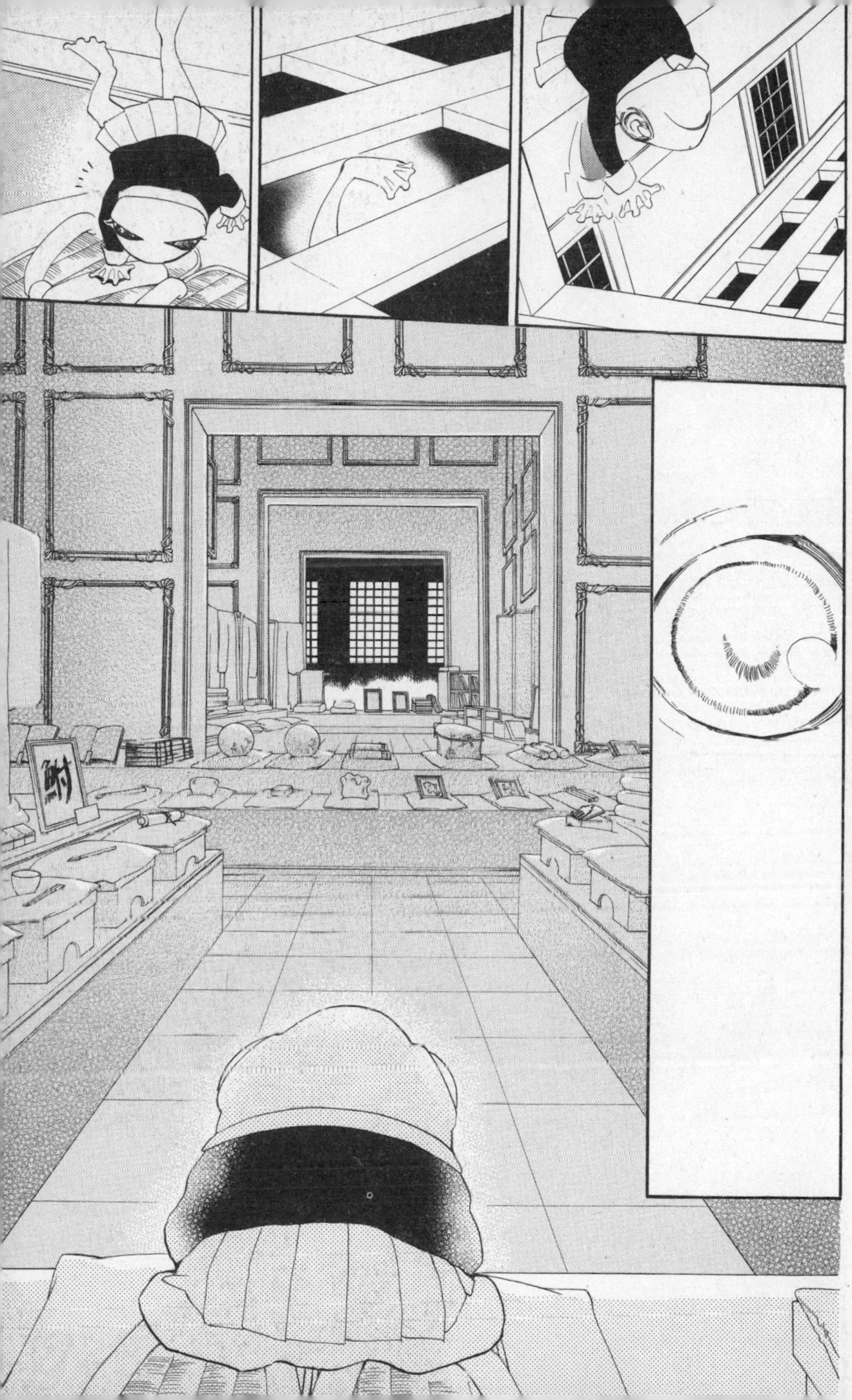

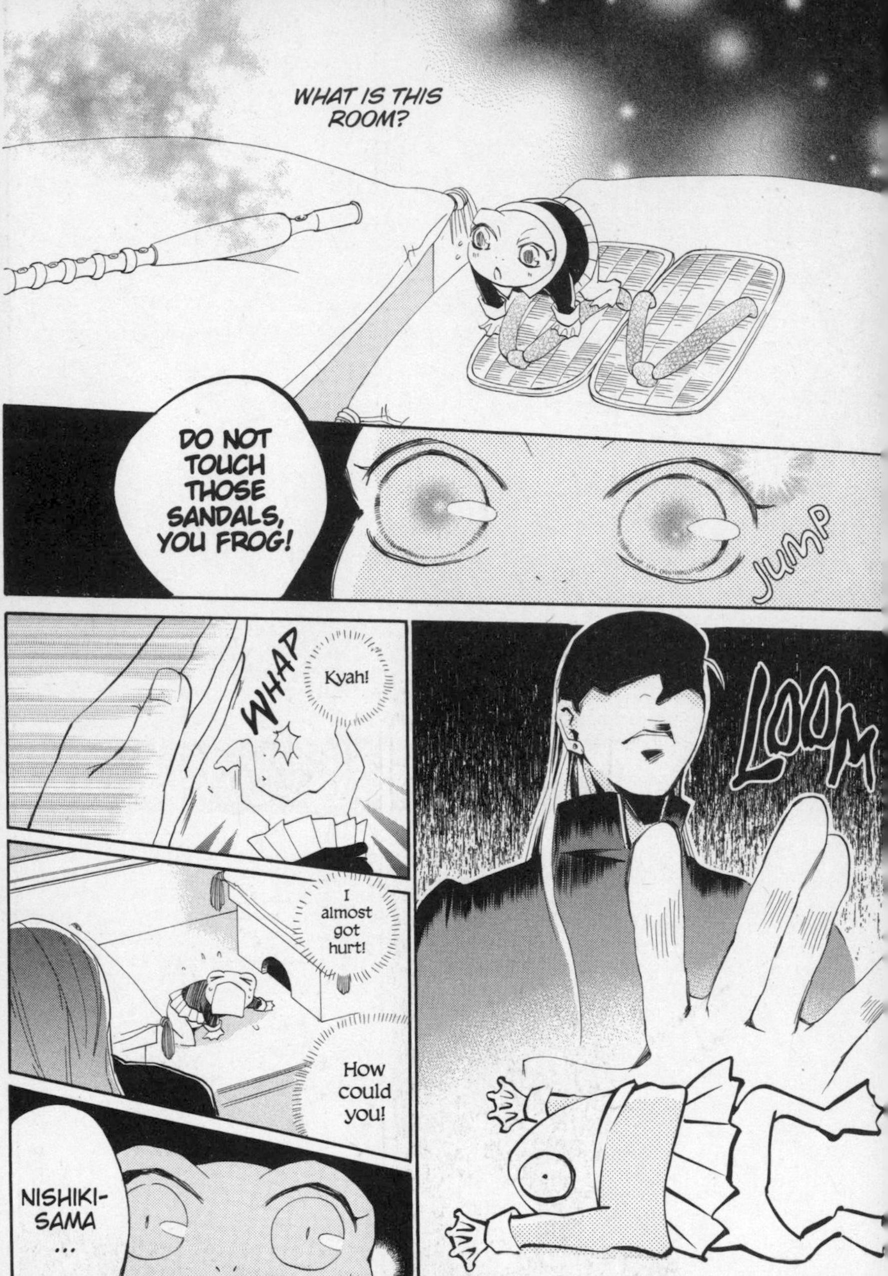
WHAT IS THIS ROOM?
DO NOT TOUCH THOSE SANDALS, YOU FROG!
JUMP
LOOM
WHAP
Kyah!
I almost got hurt!
How could you!
NISHIKI-SAMA ...

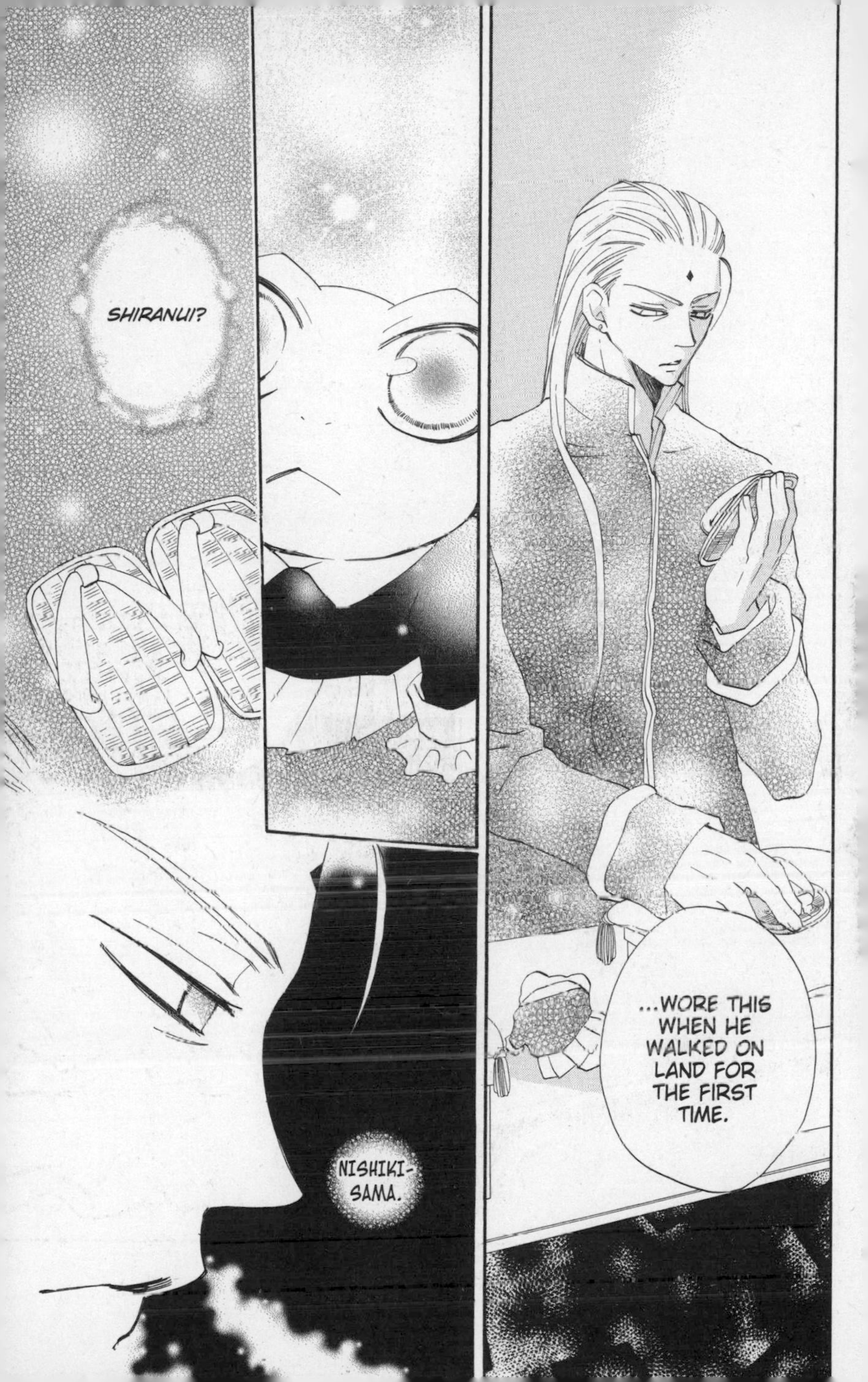
...WORE THIS WHEN HE WALKED ON LAND FOR THE FIRST TIME.
SHIRANUI?
NISHIKI-SAMA.

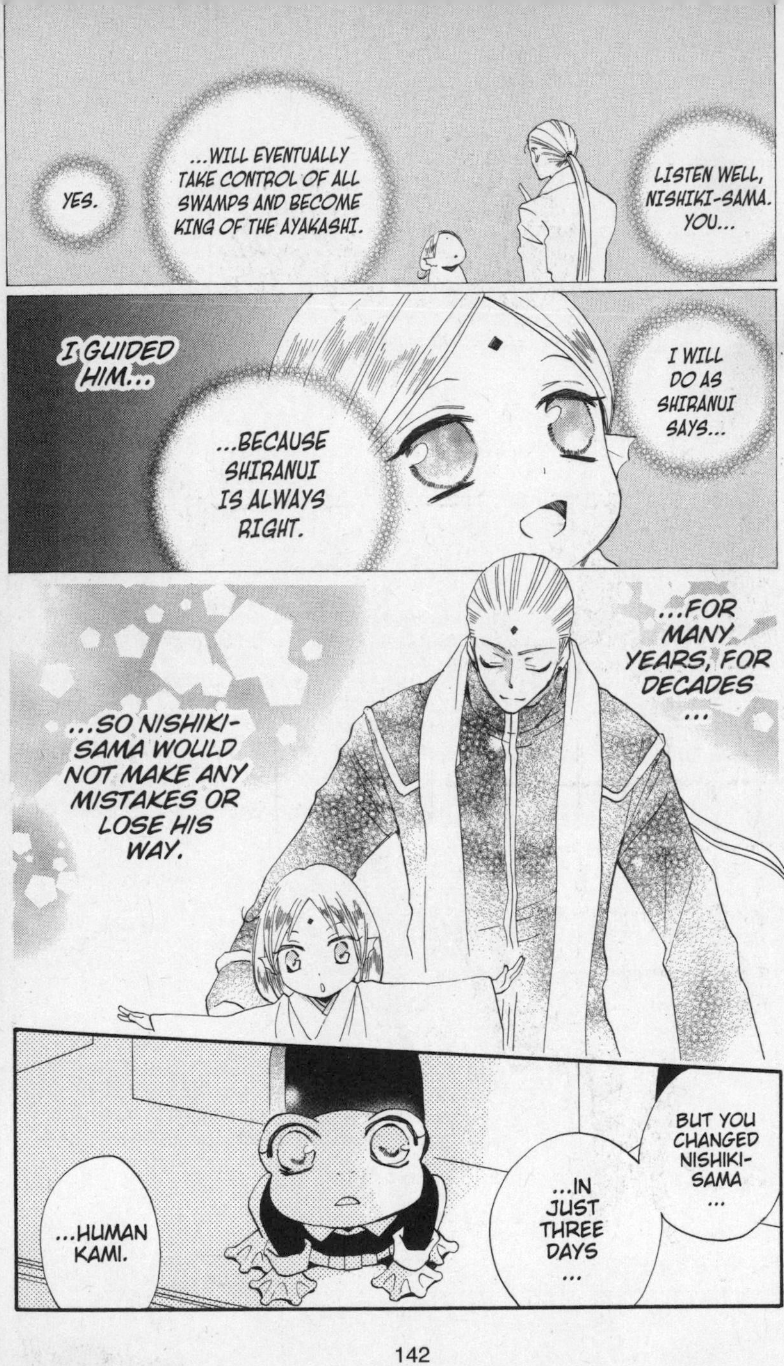
LISTEN WELL, NISHIKI-SAMA. YOU...
...WILL EVENTUALLY TAKE CONTROL OF ALL SWAMPS AND BECOME KING OF THE AYAKASHI.
YES.
I WILL DO AS SHIRANUI SAYS...
I GUIDED HIM...
...BECAUSE SHIRANUI IS ALWAYS RIGHT.
...FOR MANY YEARS, FOR DECADES...
...SO NISHIKI-SAMA WOULD NOT MAKE ANY MISTAKES OR LOSE HIS WAY.
BUT YOU CHANGED NISHIKI-SAMA...
...IN JUST THREE DAYS...
...HUMAN KAMI.

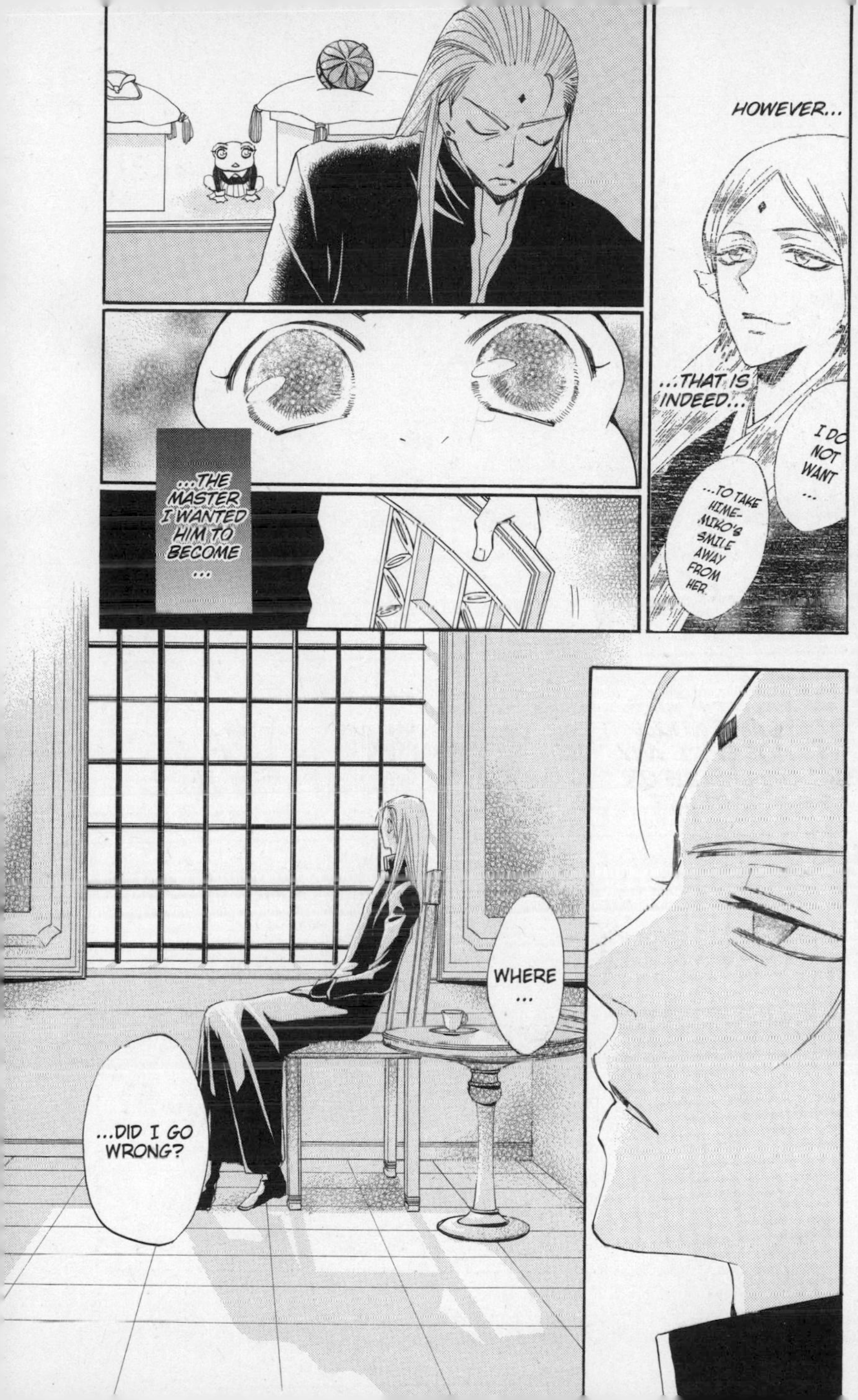
HOWEVER...
...THAT IS INDEED...
I DO NOT WANT ...
...TO TAKE HIME-MIKO'S SMILE AWAY FROM HER.
...THE MASTER I WANTED HIM TO BECOME ...
WHERE ...
...DID I GO WRONG?

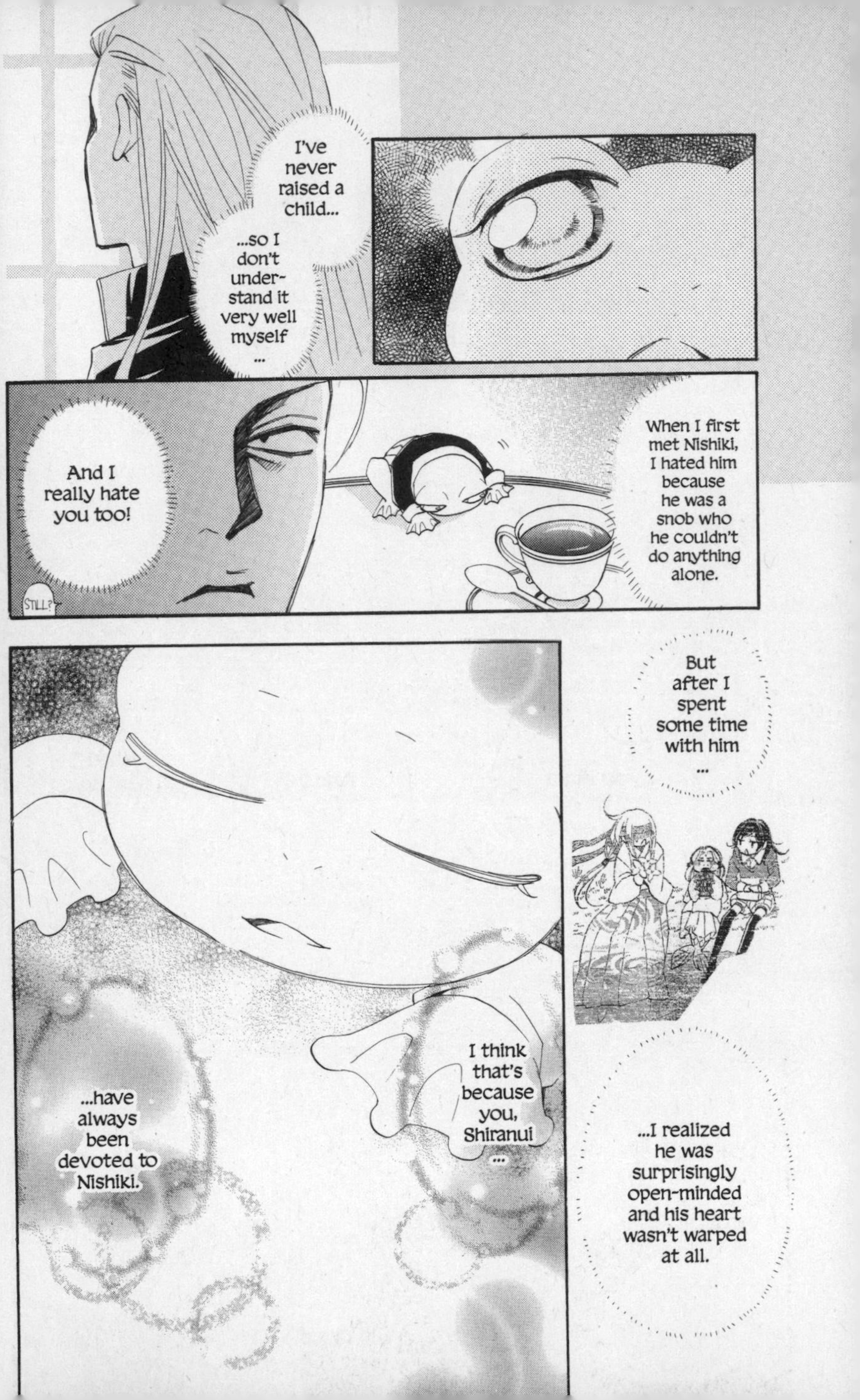
I've never raised a child...
...so I don't understand it very well myself...
When I first met Nishiki, I hated him because he was a snob who he couldn't do anything alone.
And I really hate you too!
STILL?
But after I spent some time with him...
...I realized he was surprisingly open-minded and his heart wasn't warped at all.
I think that's because you, Shiranui...
...have always been devoted to Nishiki.

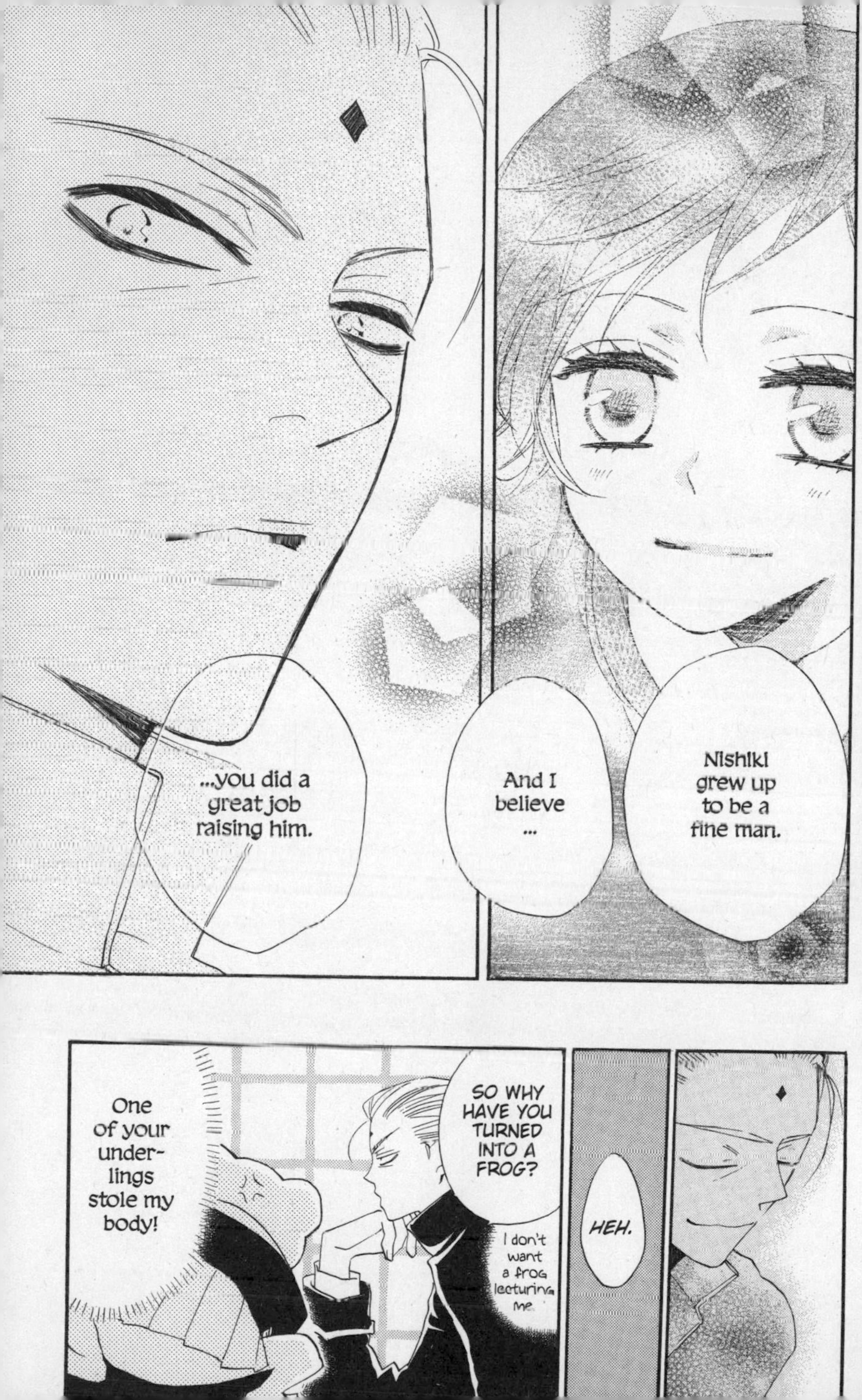
Nishiki grew up to be a fine man.
And I believe ...
...you did a great job raising him.
HEH.
SO WHY HAVE YOU TURNED INTO A FROG?
I don't want a frog lecturing me.
One of your under-lings stole my body!

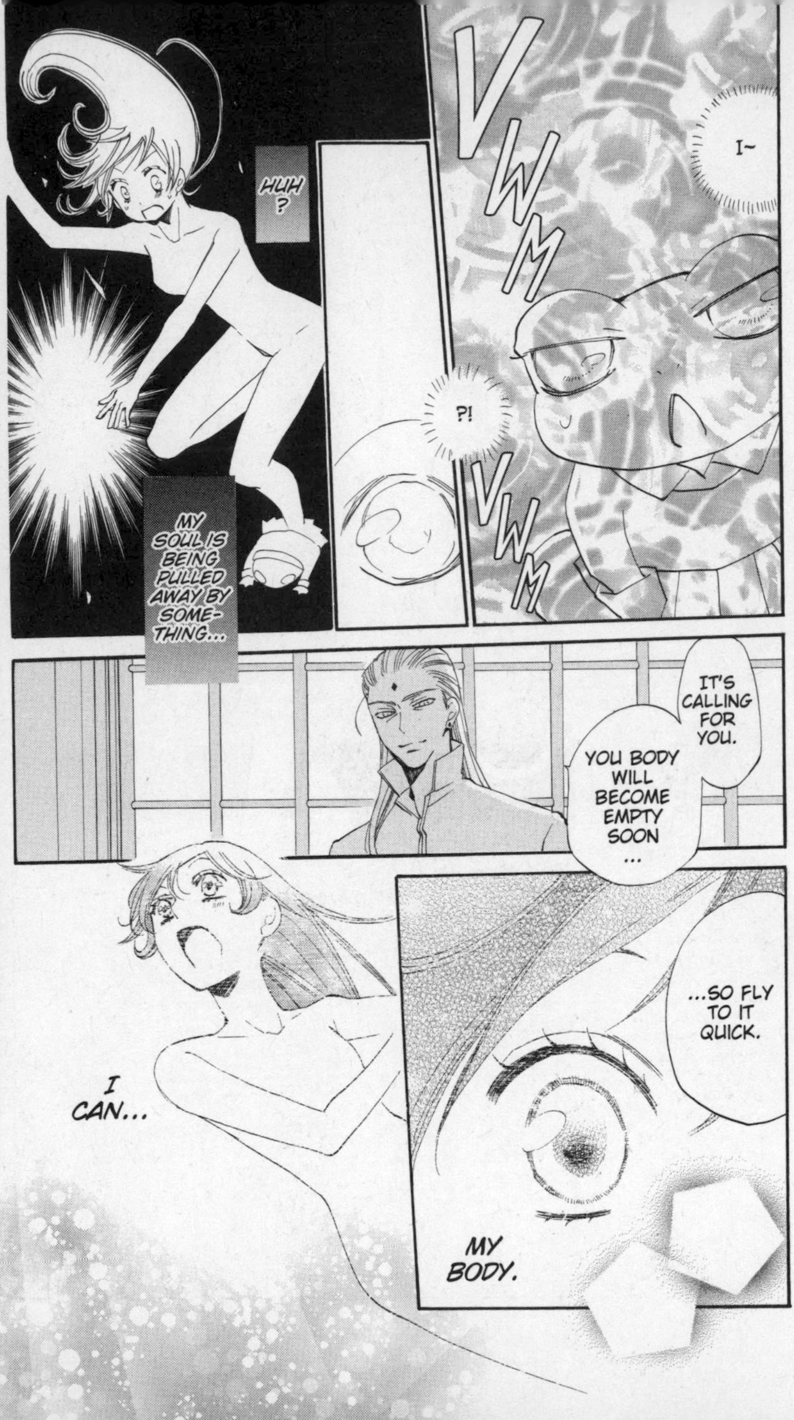
I~
VWM
?!
VWM
HUH?
MY SOUL IS BEING PULLED AWAY BY SOMETHING...
IT'S CALLING FOR YOU.
YOU BODY WILL BECOME EMPTY SOON...
...SO FLY TO IT QUICK.
MY BODY.
I CAN...

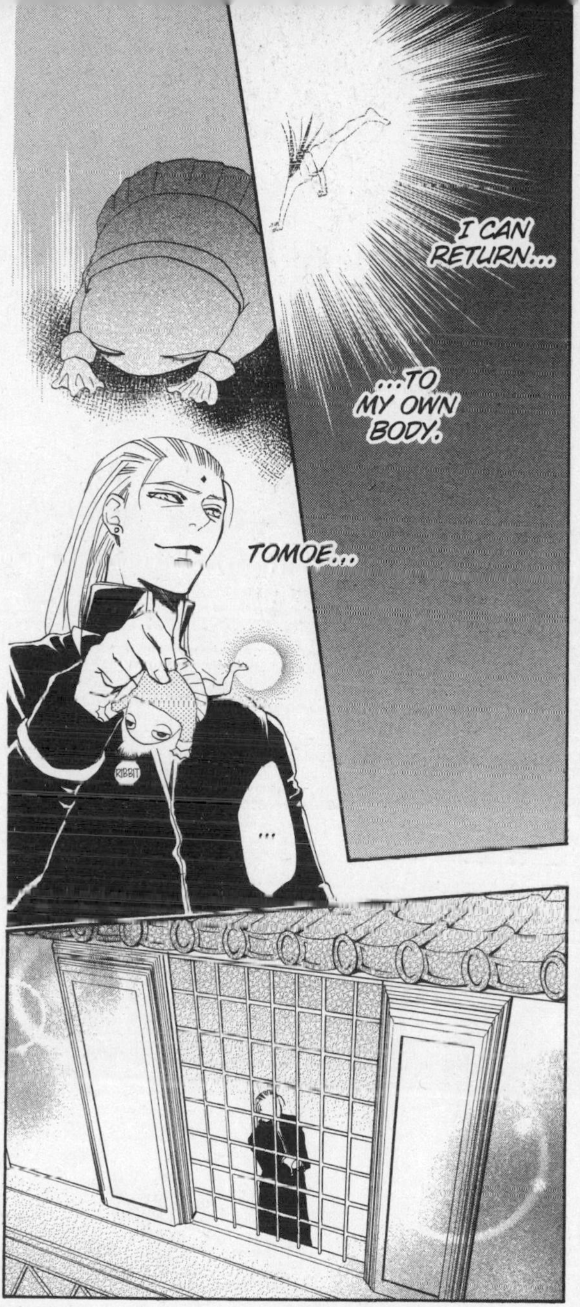
I CAN RETURN...
...TO MY OWN BODY.
TOMOE...
RIBBIT
...

I guess a lot of people know about it already, but Kamisama Kiss is going to be an anime!!

I actually got the offer quite some time ago. I was drawing the tengu arc then, so I was secretly thrilled alone for about two years.

And the anime is about to start broadcasting when this volume is on sale! Finally! I am such a lucky person for having all the wonderful staff create this anime...! This happened because all you readers supported the manga! Thank you so much!

Please do watch it!

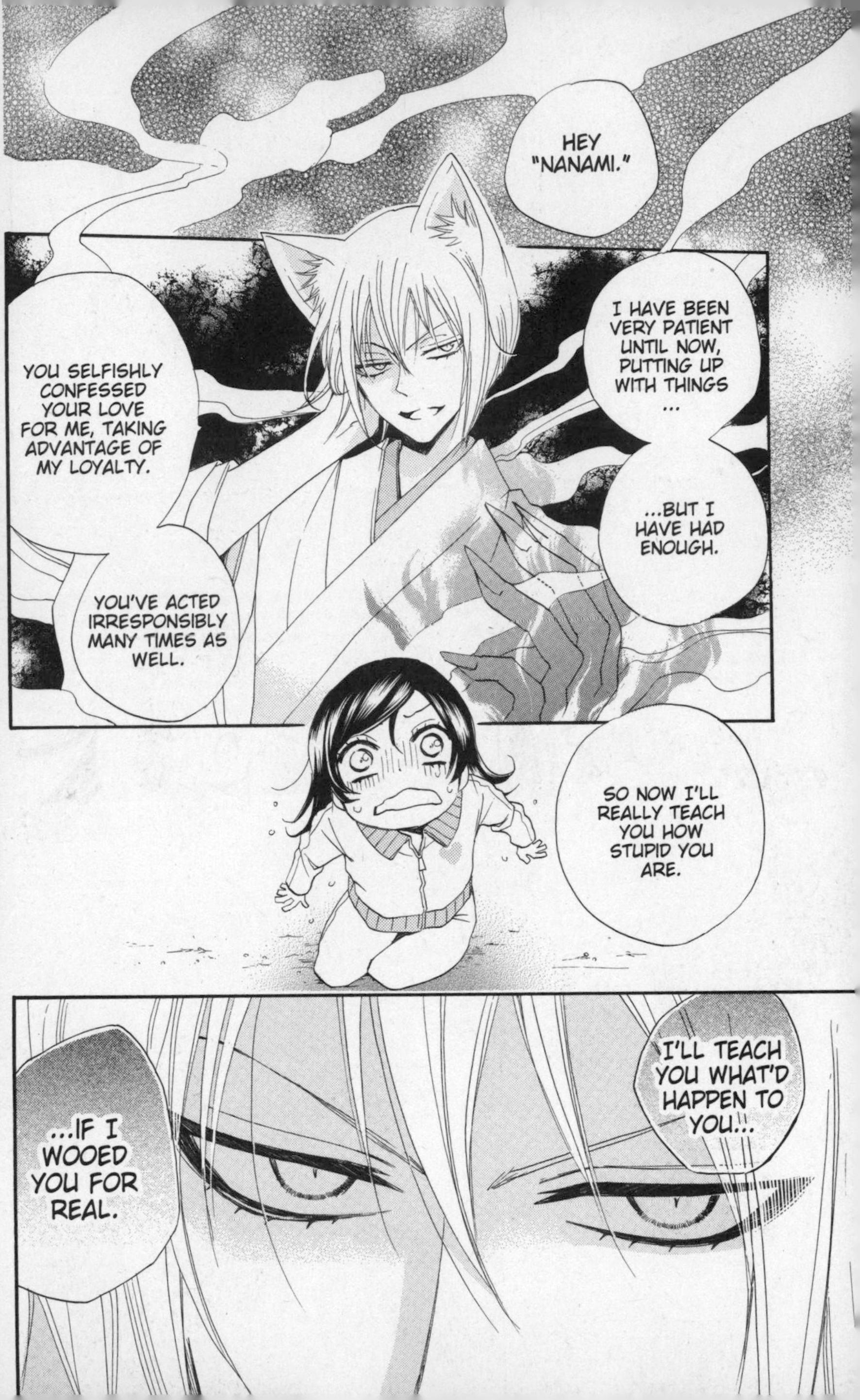
HEY "NANAMI."
I HAVE BEEN VERY PATIENT UNTIL NOW, PUTTING UP WITH THINGS ...
...BUT I HAVE HAD ENOUGH.
YOU SELFISHLY CONFESSED YOUR LOVE FOR ME, TAKING ADVANTAGE OF MY LOYALTY.
YOU'VE ACTED IRRESPONSIBLY MANY TIMES AS WELL.
SO NOW I'LL REALLY TEACH YOU HOW STUPID YOU ARE.
I'LL TEACH YOU WHAT'D HAPPEN TO YOU...
...IF I WOOED YOU FOR REAL.

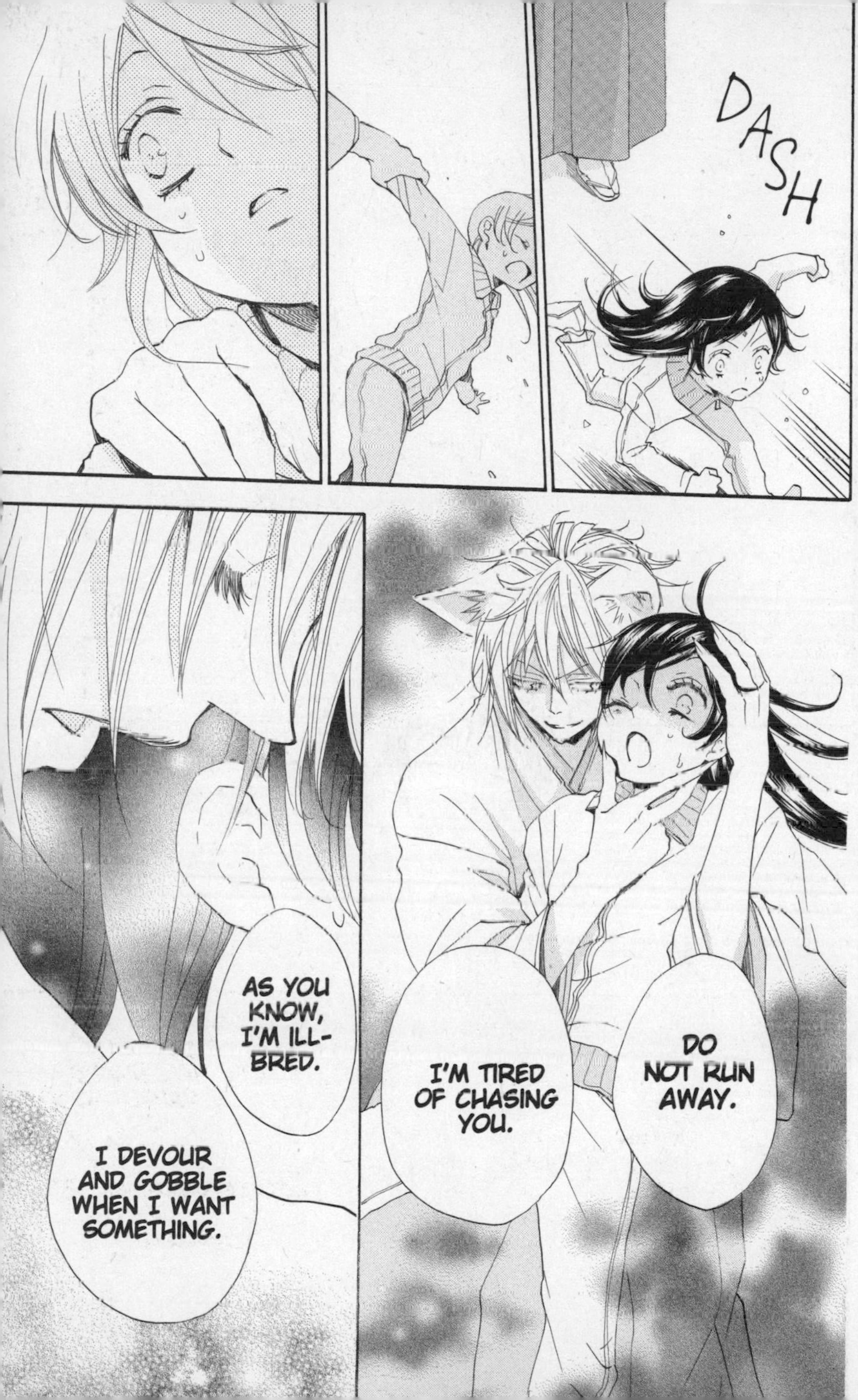
DASH
DO NOT RUN AWAY.
I'M TIRED OF CHASING YOU.
AS YOU KNOW, I'M ILL-BRED.
I DEVOUR AND GOBBLE WHEN I WANT SOMETHING.

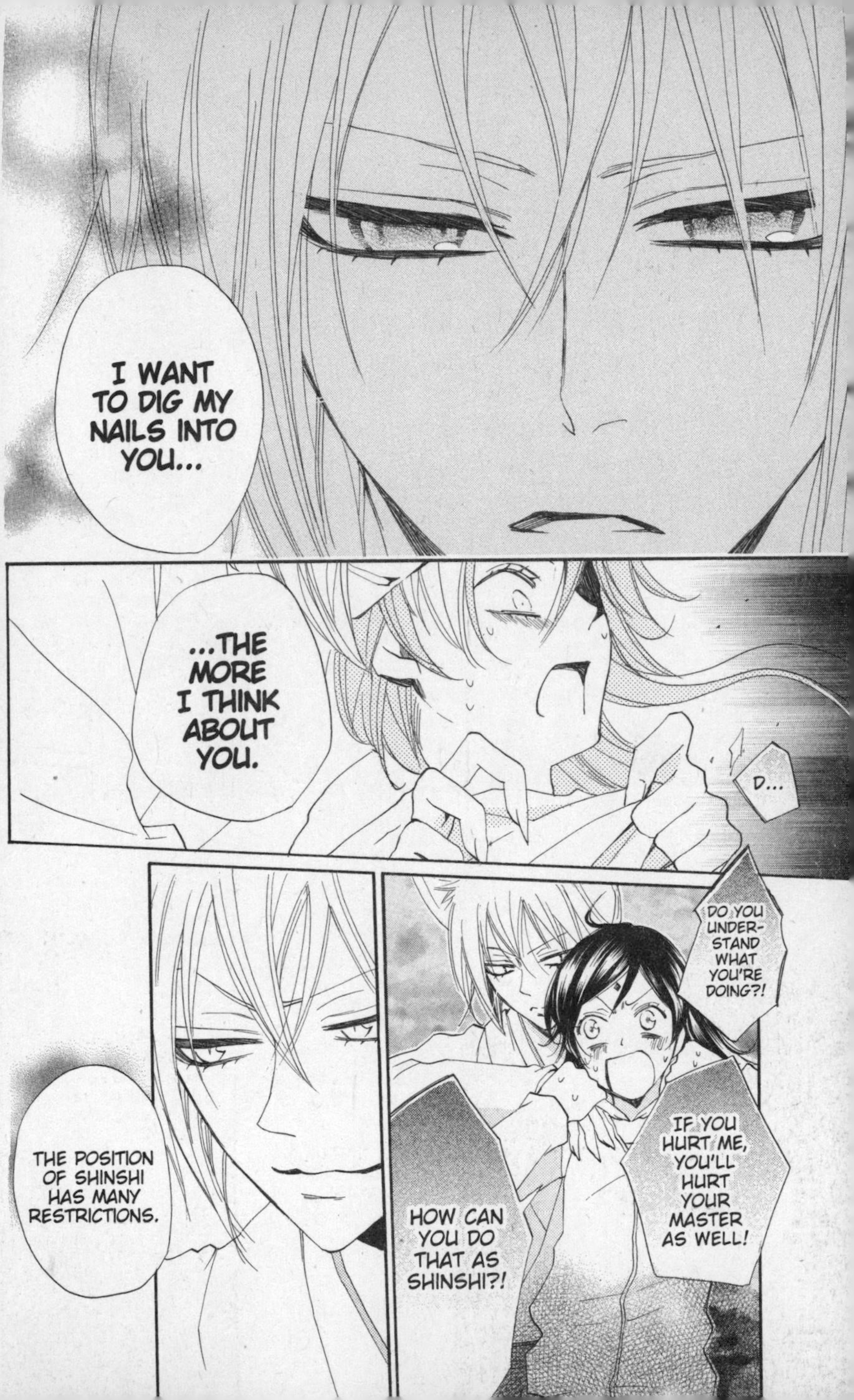
I WANT TO DIG MY NAILS INTO YOU...
...THE MORE I THINK ABOUT YOU.
D...
DO YOU UNDER-STAND WHAT YOU'RE DOING?!
IF YOU HURT ME, YOU'LL HURT YOUR MASTER AS WELL!
HOW CAN YOU DO THAT AS SHINSHI?!
THE POSITION OF SHINSHI HAS MANY RESTRICTIONS.

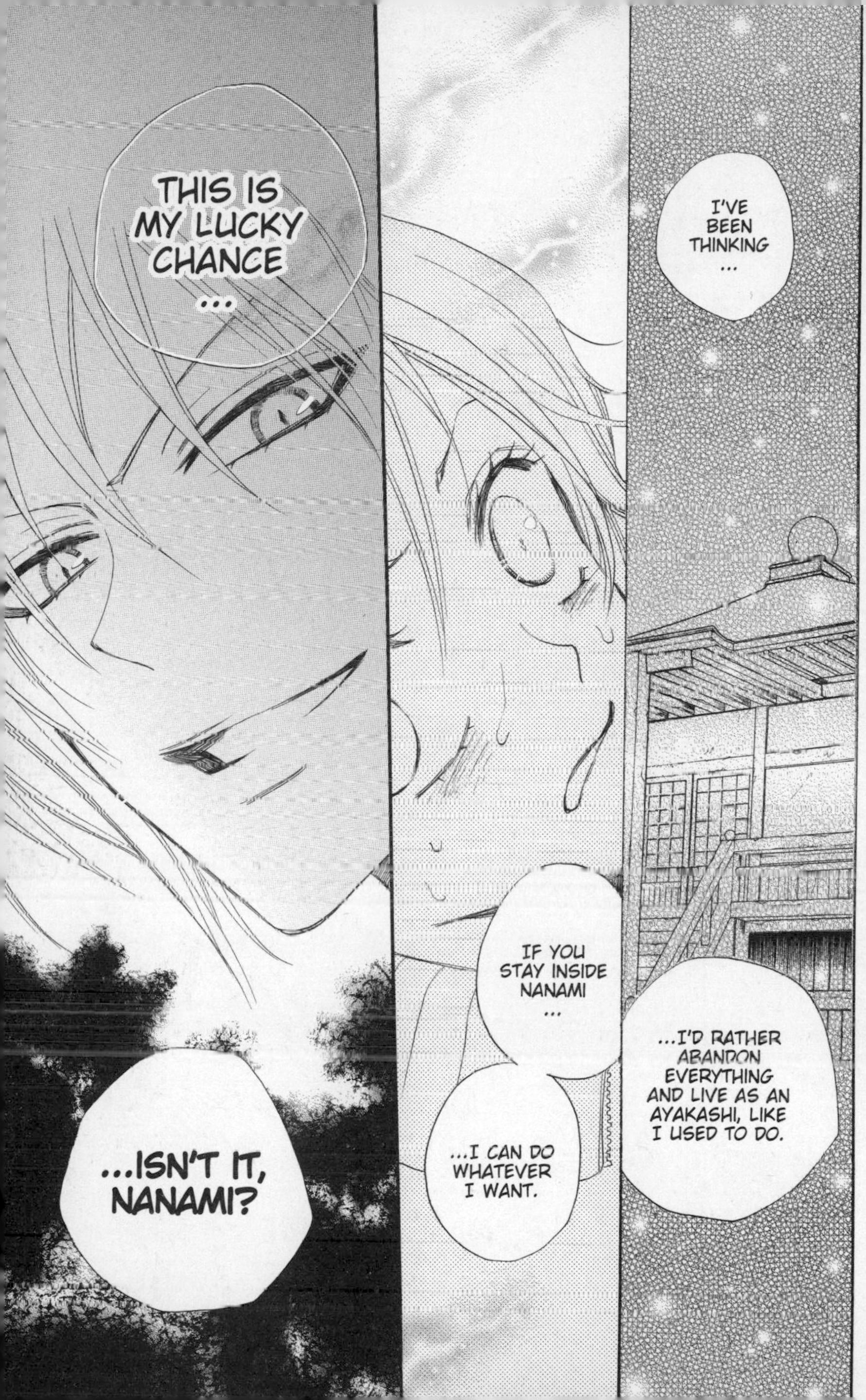
I'VE BEEN THINKING ...
...I'D RATHER ABANDON EVERYTHING AND LIVE AS AN AYAKASHI, LIKE I USED TO DO.
IF YOU STAY INSIDE NANAMI ...
...I CAN DO WHATEVER I WANT.
THIS IS MY LUCKY CHANCE ...
...ISN'T IT, NANAMI?

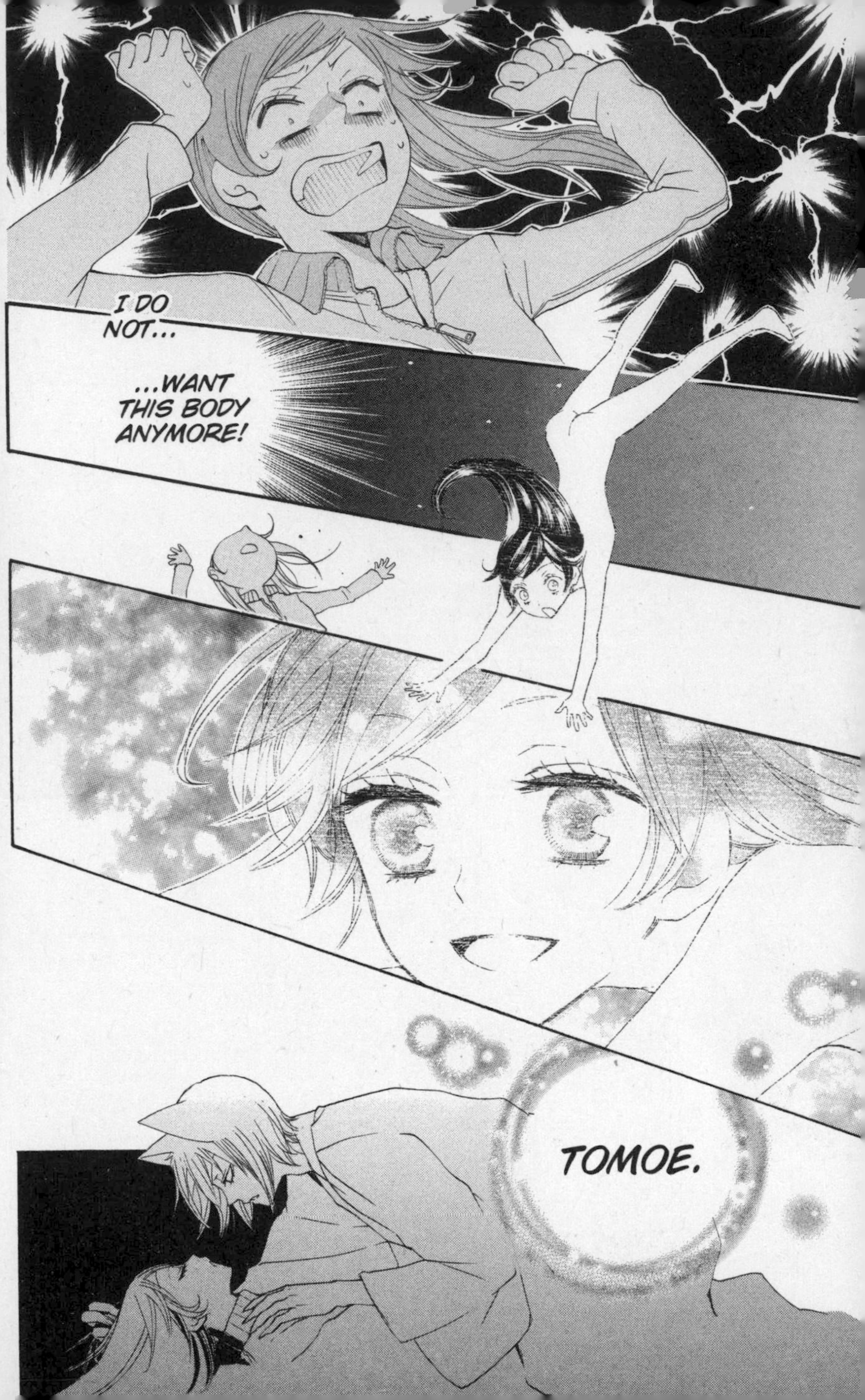
I DO NOT...
...WANT THIS BODY ANYMORE!
TOMOE.

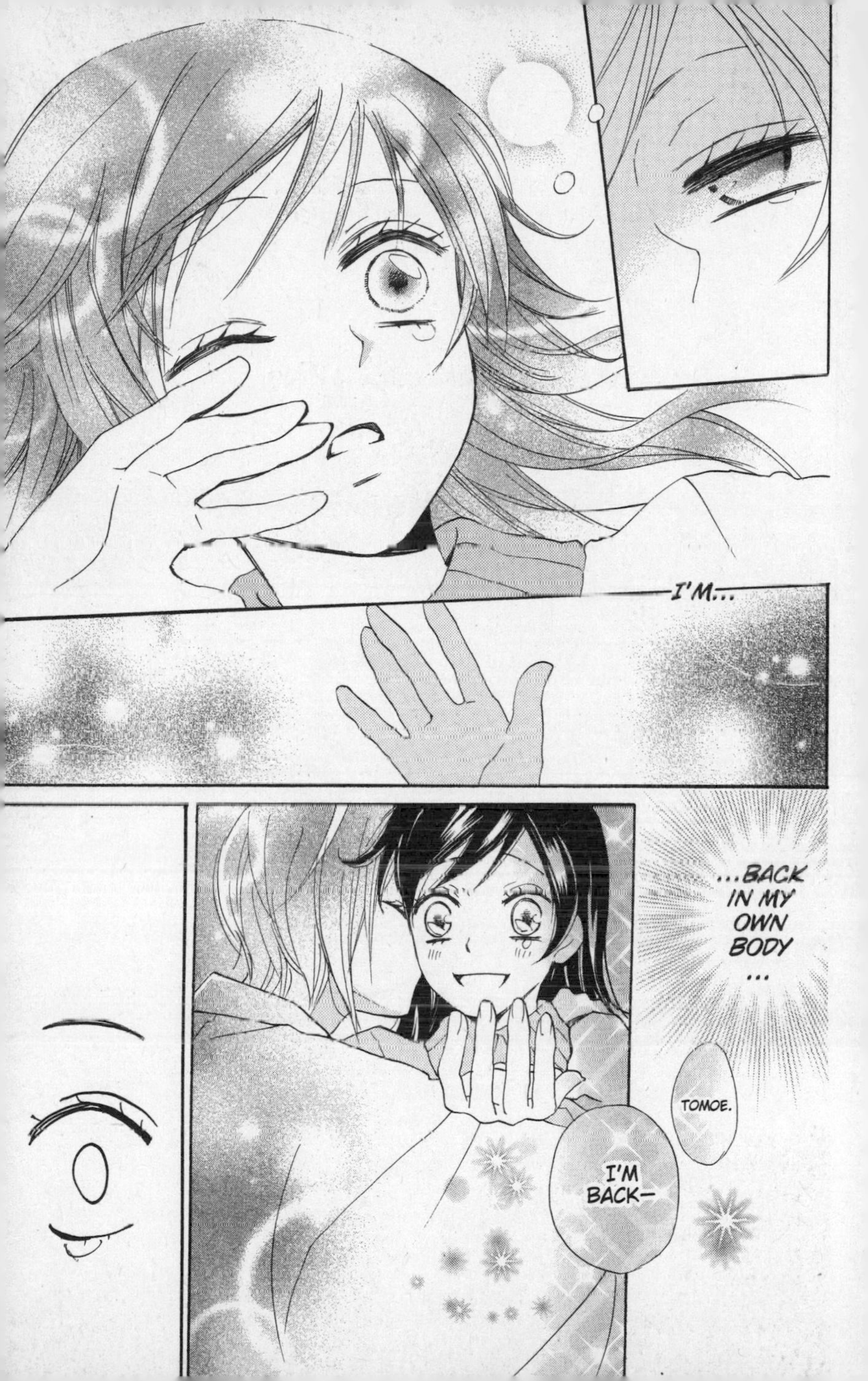
I'M...
...BACK IN MY OWN BODY ...
TOMOE.
I'M BACK—

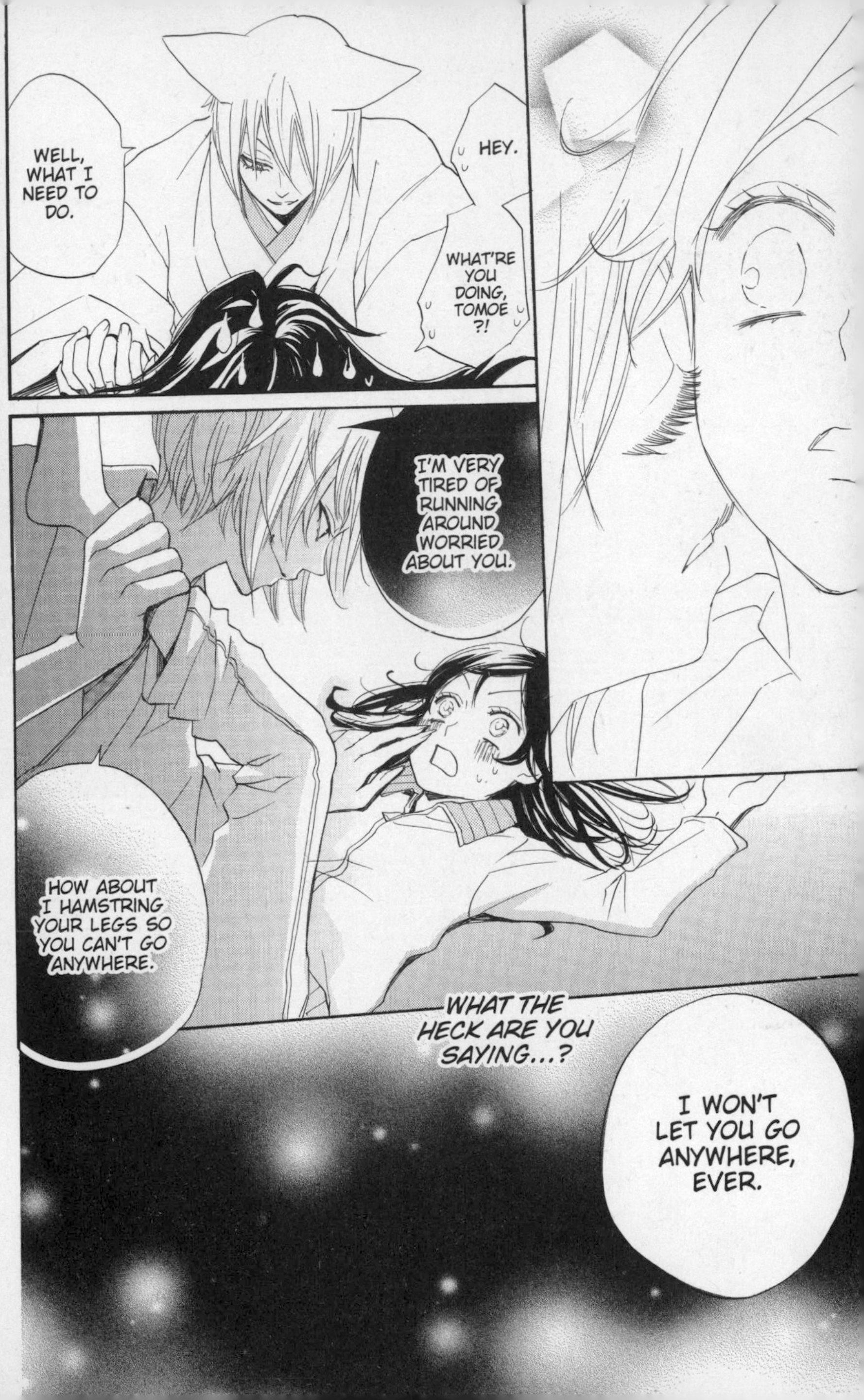
HEY.
WHAT'RE YOU DOING, TOMOE ?!
WELL, WHAT I NEED TO DO.
I'M VERY TIRED OF RUNNING AROUND WORRIED ABOUT YOU.
HOW ABOUT I HAMSTRING YOUR LEGS SO YOU CAN'T GO ANYWHERE.
WHAT THE HECK ARE YOU SAYING...?
I WON'T LET YOU GO ANYWHERE, EVER.

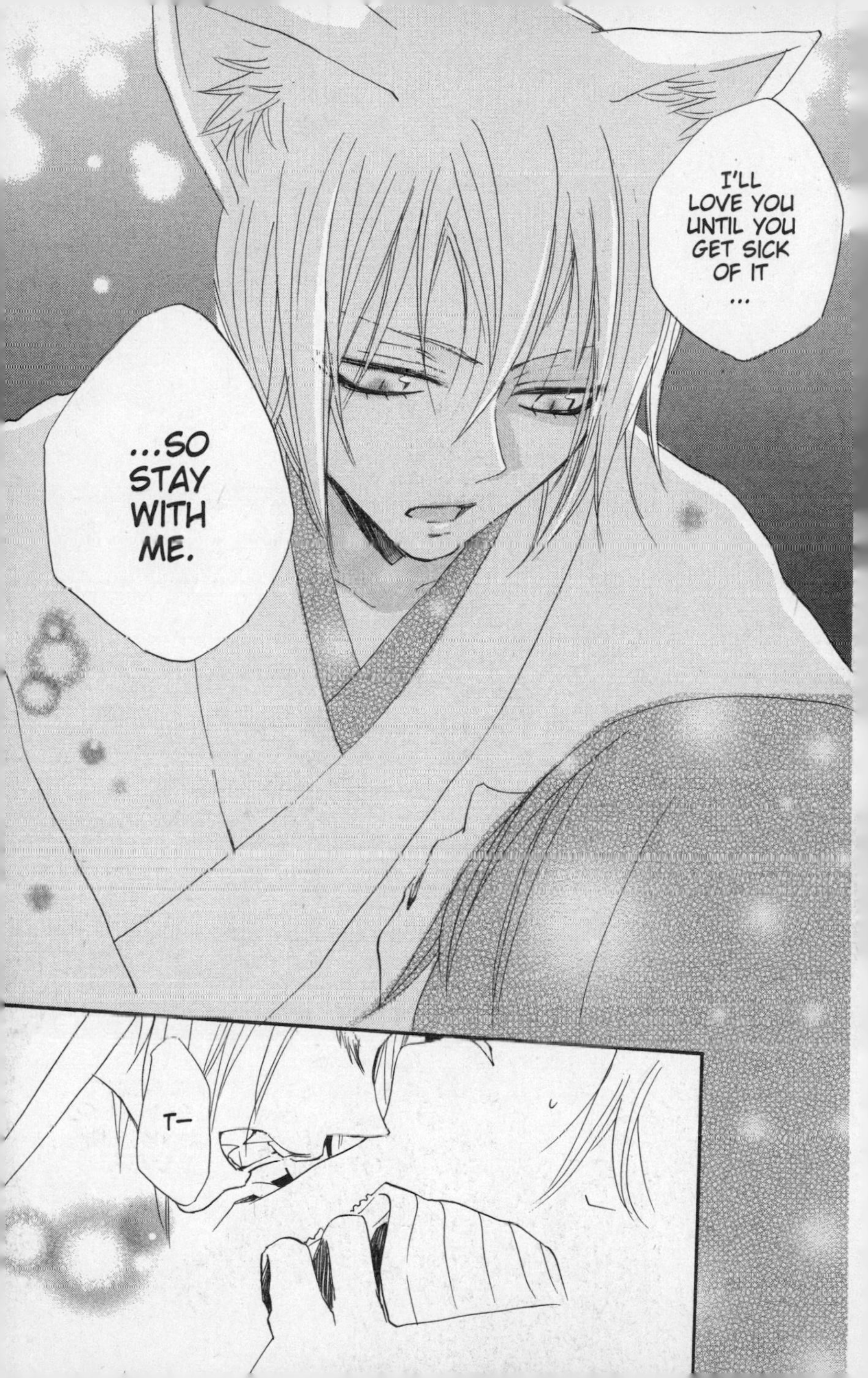
I'LL LOVE YOU UNTIL YOU GET SICK OF IT ...
...SO STAY WITH ME.
T—

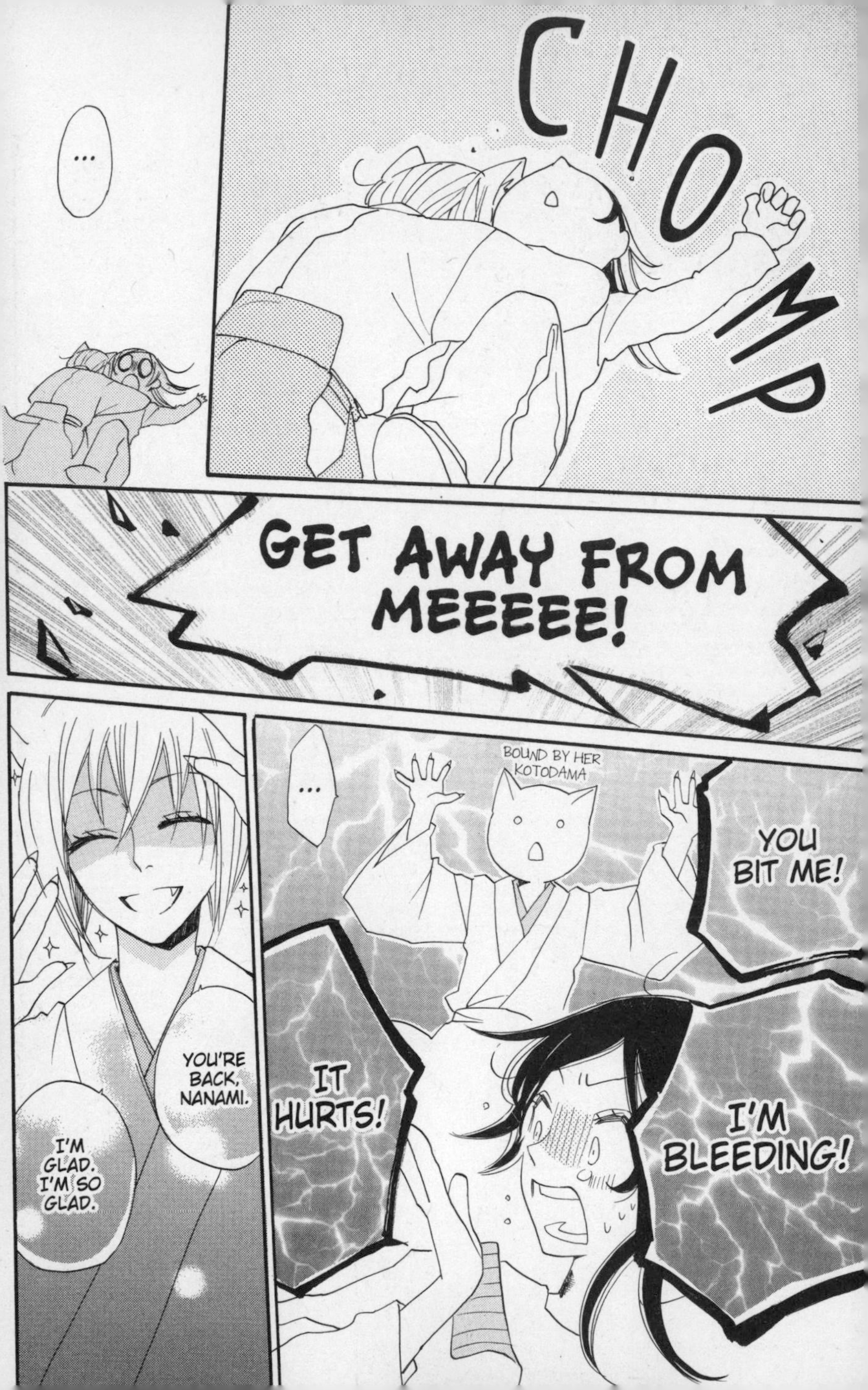
CHOMP
...
GET AWAY FROM MEEEEEE!
BOUND BY HER KOTODAMA
...
YOU BIT ME!
I'M BLEEDING!
IT HURTS!
YOU'RE BACK, NANAMI.
I'M GLAD. I'M SO GLAD.

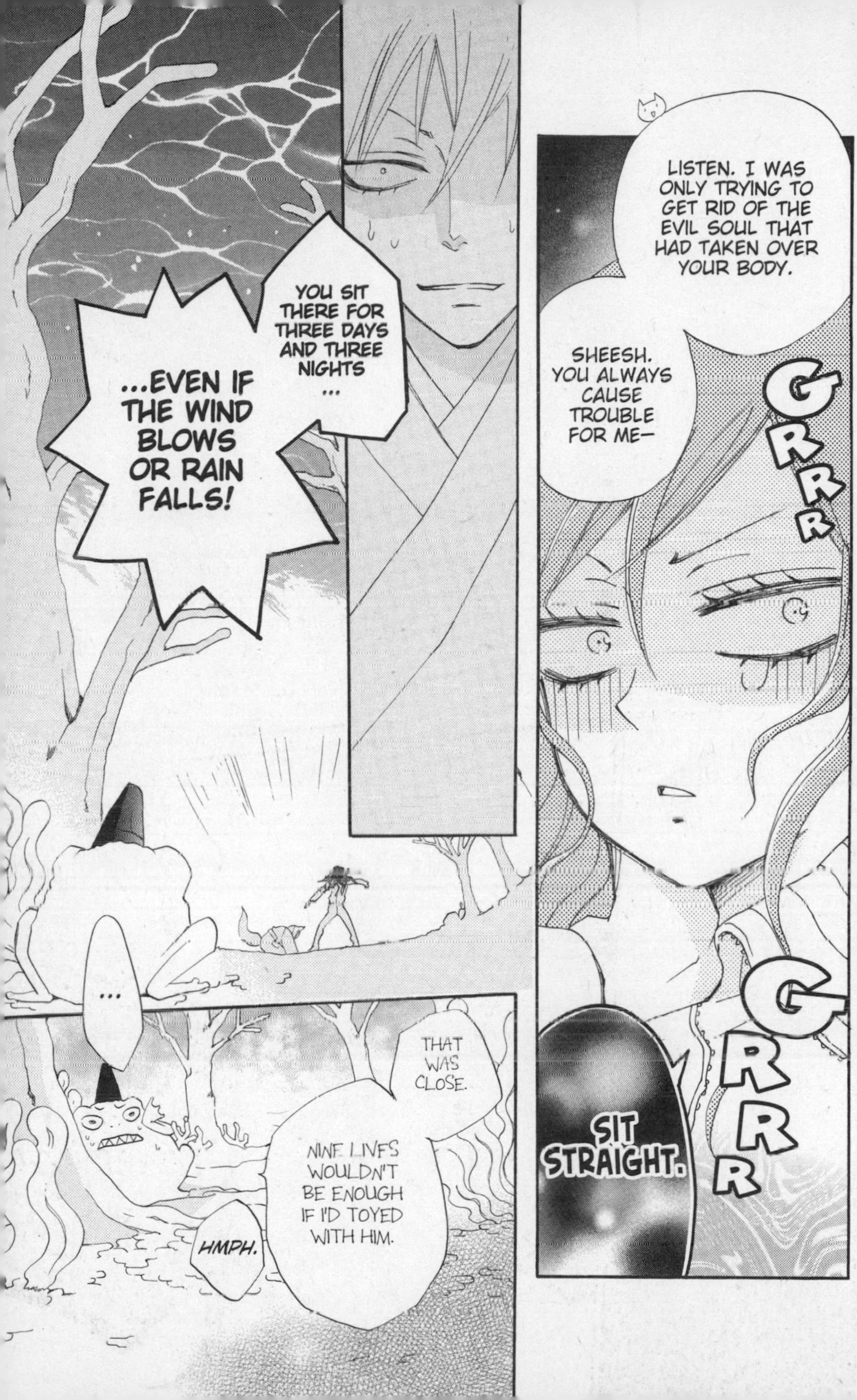
LISTEN. I WAS ONLY TRYING TO GET RID OF THE EVIL SOUL THAT HAD TAKEN OVER YOUR BODY.
SHEESH. YOU ALWAYS CAUSE TROUBLE FOR ME—
GRRR
SIT STRAIGHT.
GRRR
YOU SIT THERE FOR THREE DAYS AND THREE NIGHTS ...
...EVEN IF THE WIND BLOWS OR RAIN FALLS!
...
THAT WAS CLOSE.
NINE LIVES WOULDN'T BE ENOUGH IF I'D TOYED WITH HIM.
HMPH.

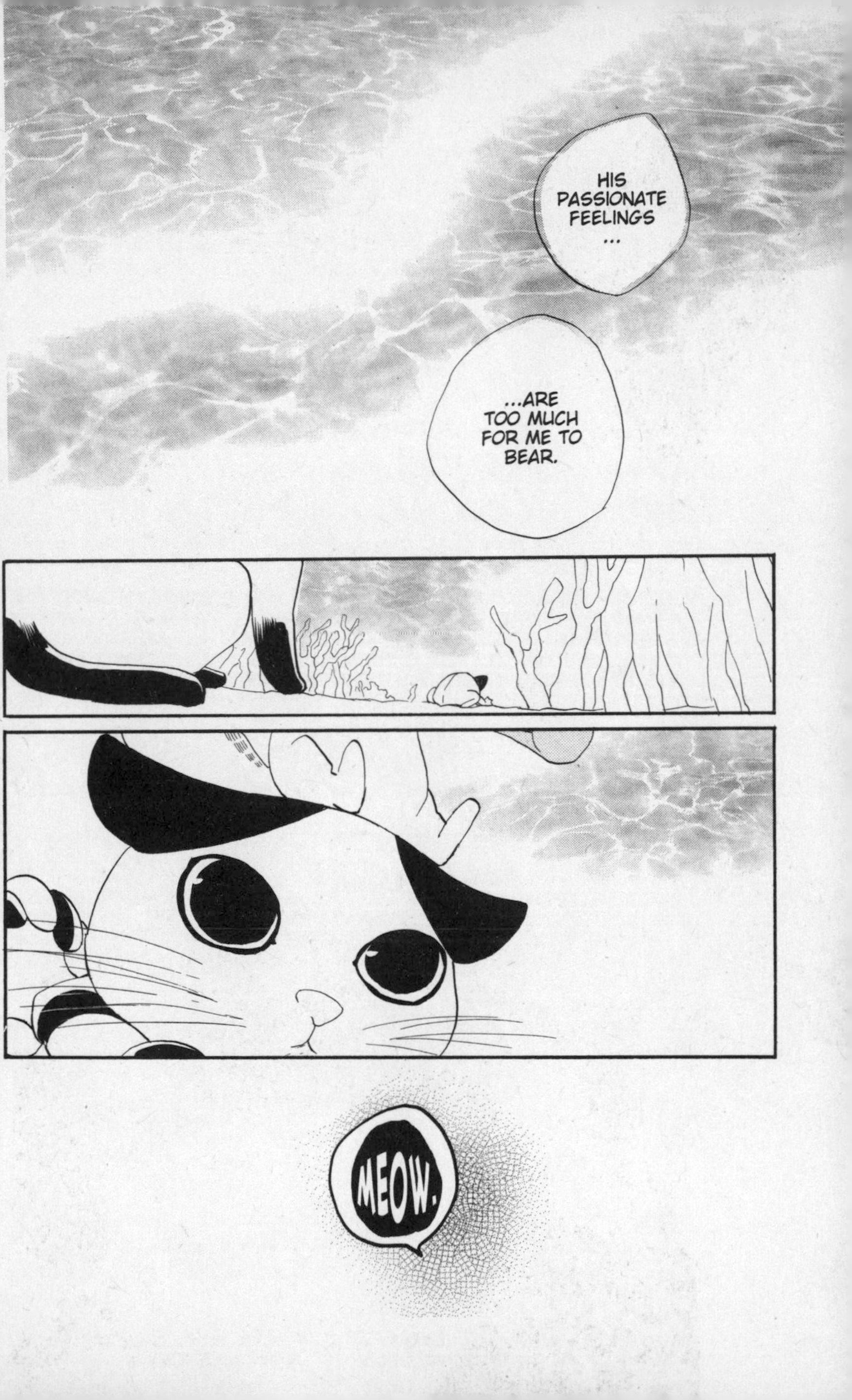
HIS PASSIONATE FEELINGS ...
...ARE TOO MUCH FOR ME TO BEAR.
MEOW.

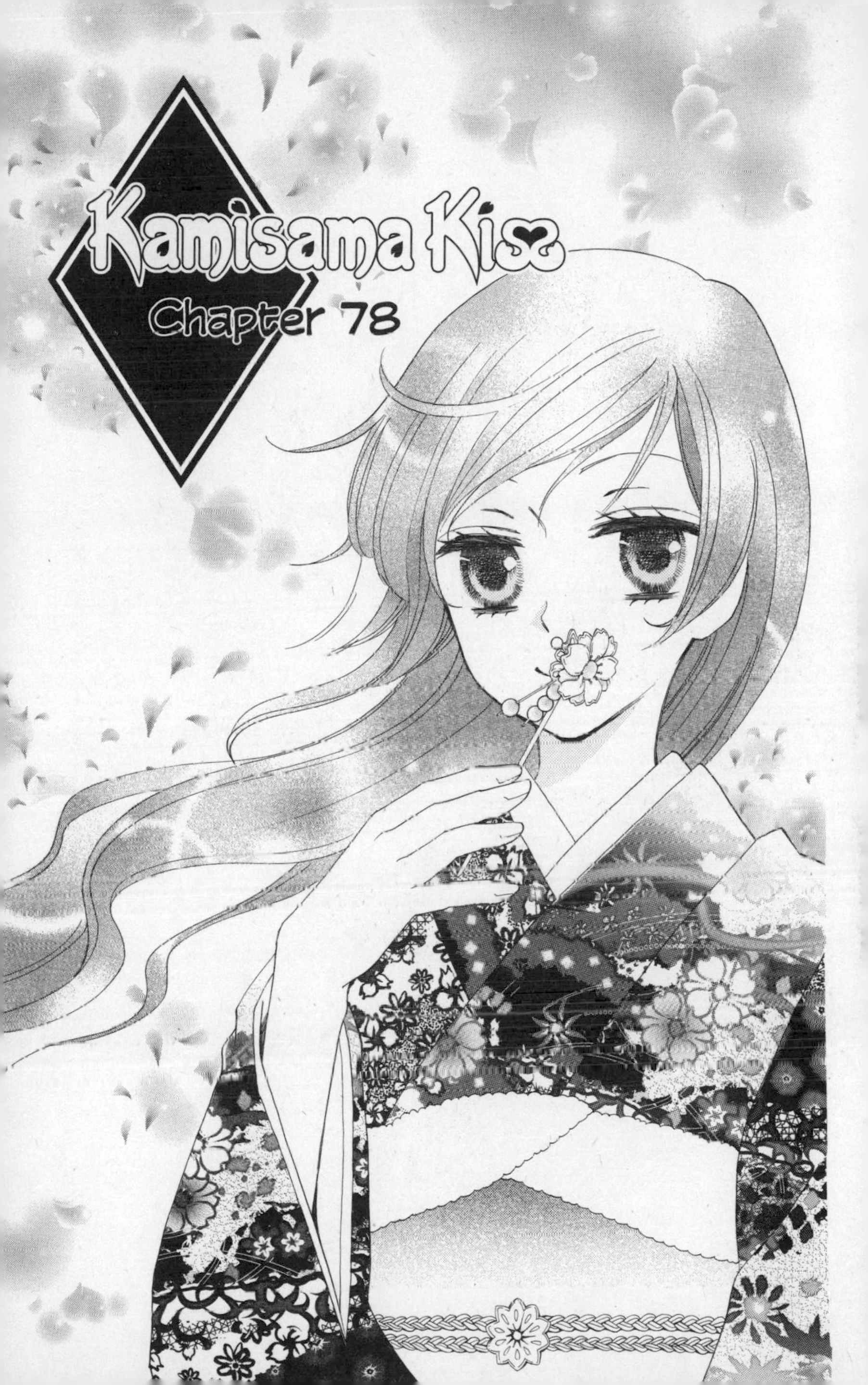
Kamisama Kiss
Chapter 78

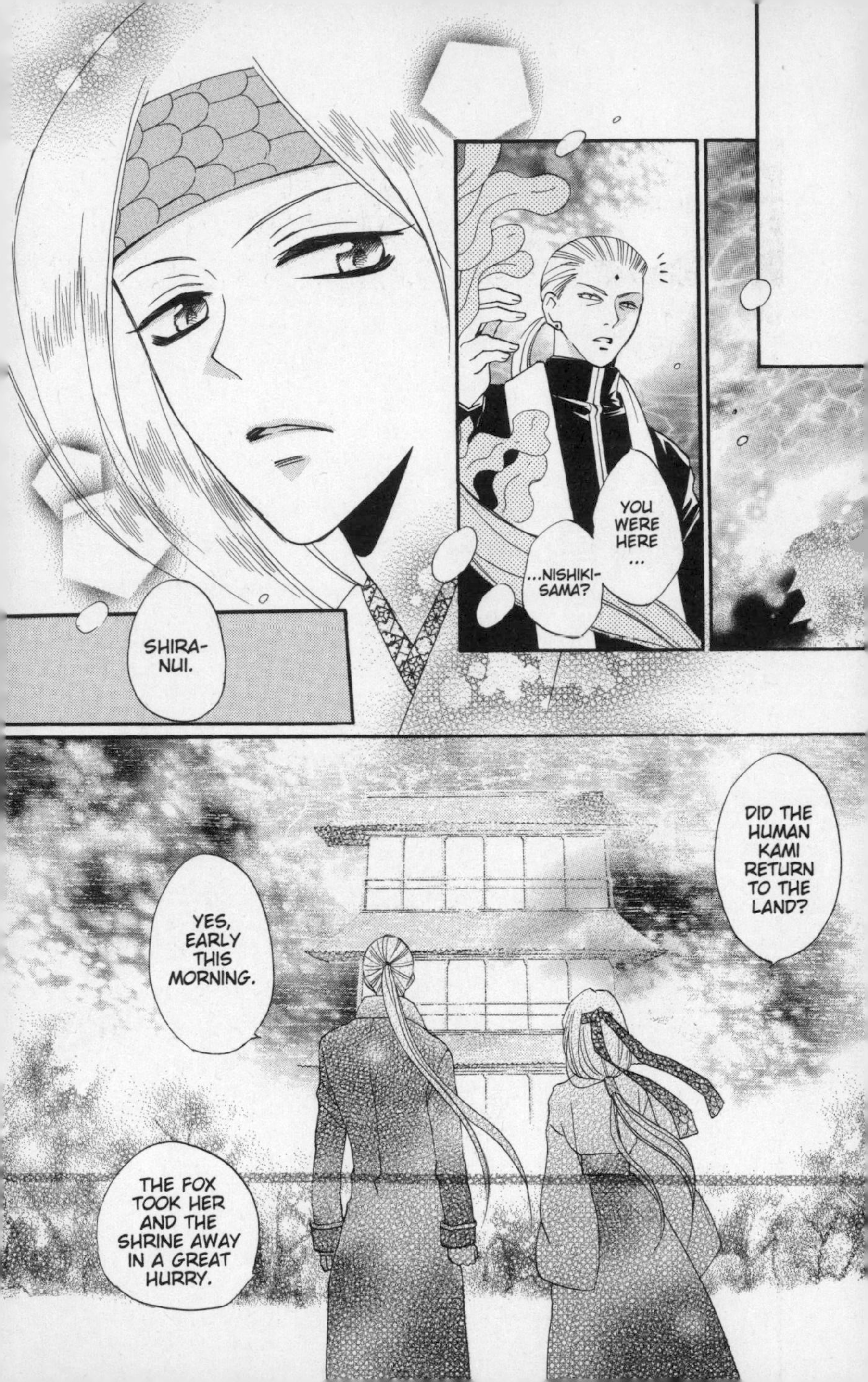
YOU WERE HERE ...
...NISHIKI-SAMA?
SHIRA-NUI.
DID THE HUMAN KAMI RETURN TO THE LAND?
YES, EARLY THIS MORNING.
THE FOX TOOK HER AND THE SHRINE AWAY IN A GREAT HURRY.

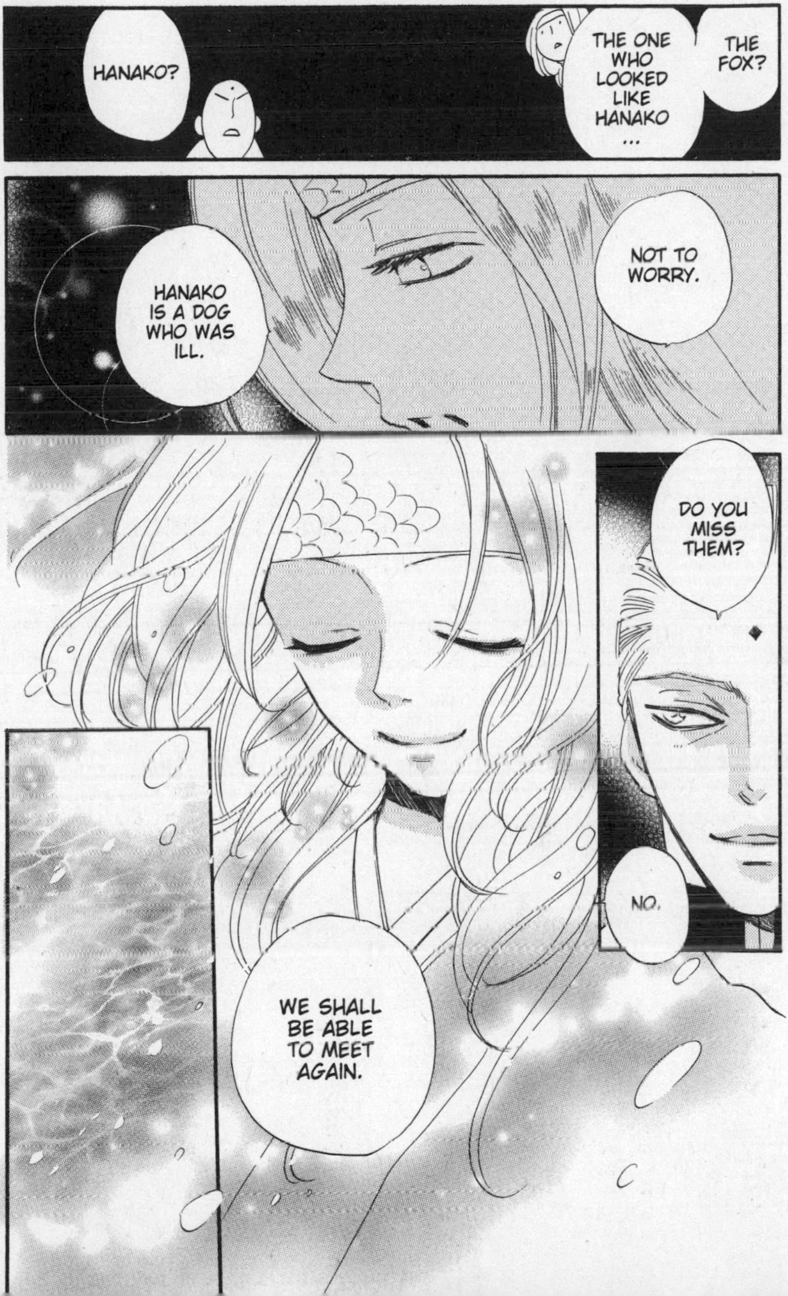
THE FOX?
THE ONE WHO LOOKED LIKE HANAKO ...
HANAKO?
NOT TO WORRY.
HANAKO IS A DOG WHO WAS ILL.
DO YOU MISS THEM?
NO.
WE SHALL BE ABLE TO MEET AGAIN.

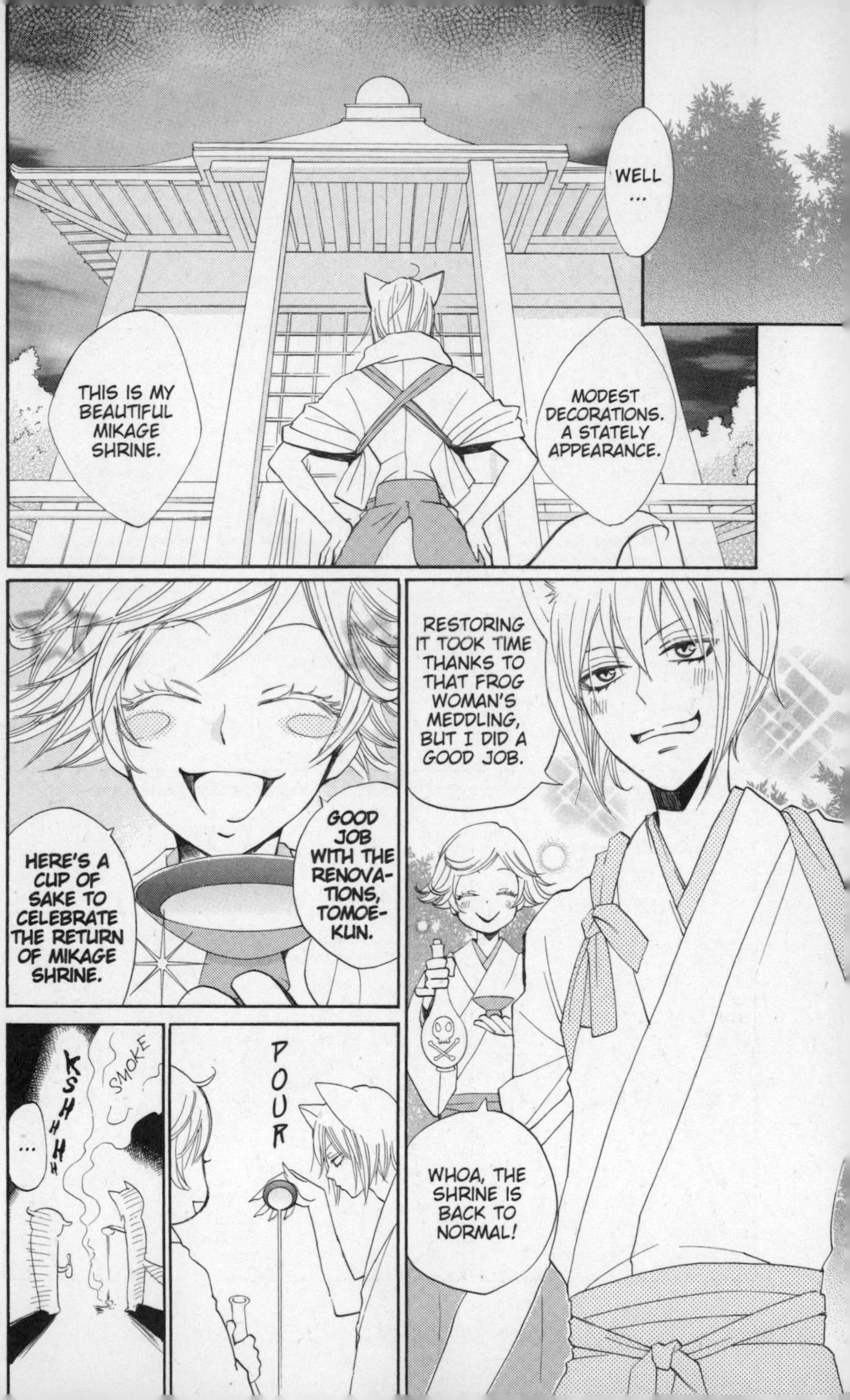
WELL ...
MODEST DECORATIONS. A STATELY APPEARANCE.
THIS IS MY BEAUTIFUL MIKAGE SHRINE.
RESTORING IT TOOK TIME THANKS TO THAT FROG WOMAN'S MEDDLING, BUT I DID A GOOD JOB.
WHOA, THE SHRINE IS BACK TO NORMAL!
GOOD JOB WITH THE RENOVATIONS, TOMOE-KUN.
HERE'S A CUP OF SAKE TO CELEBRATE THE RETURN OF MIKAGE SHRINE.
POUR
SMOKE
KSHHHHH
...

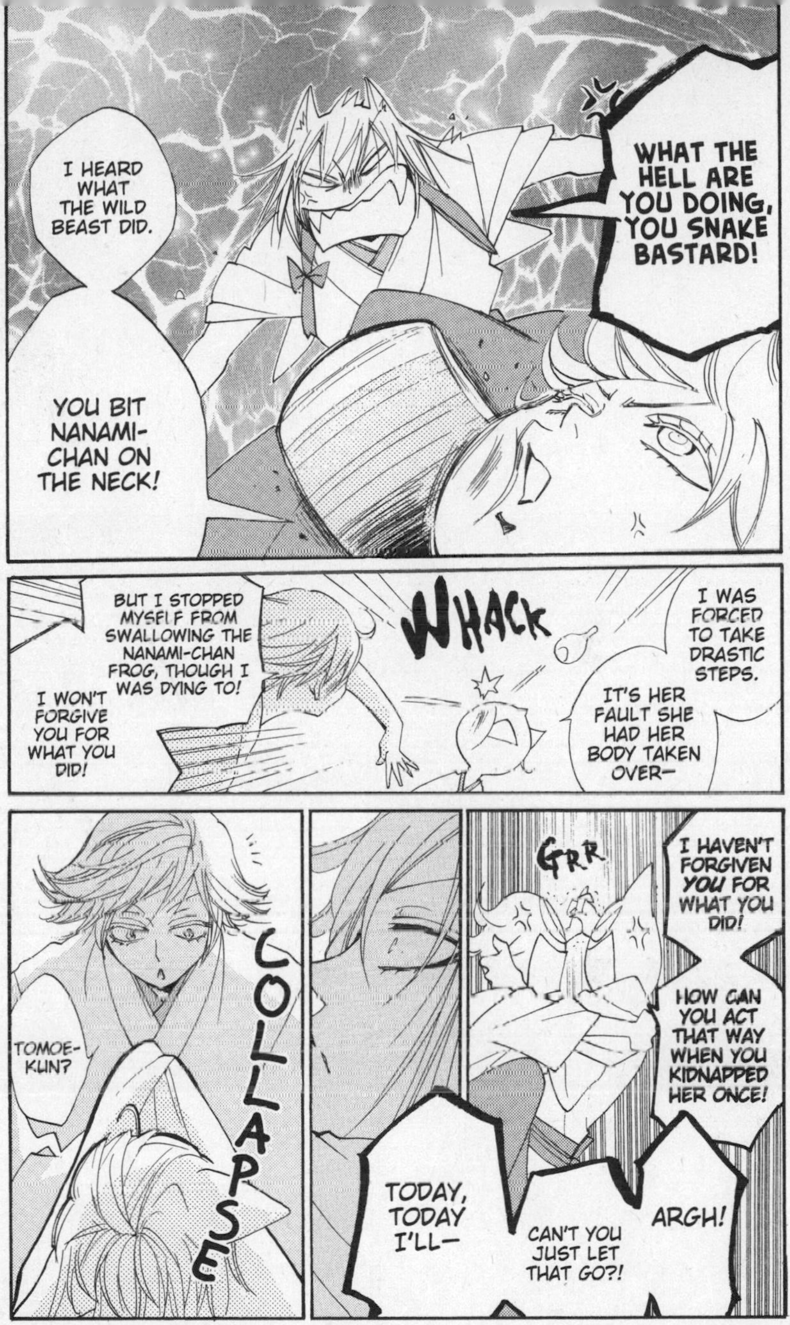
WHAT THE HELL ARE YOU DOING, YOU SNAKE BASTARD!
I HEARD WHAT THE WILD BEAST DID.
YOU BIT NANAMI-CHAN ON THE NECK!
I WAS FORCED TO TAKE DRASTIC STEPS.
IT'S HER FAULT SHE HAD HER BODY TAKEN OVER—
WHACK
BUT I STOPPED MYSELF FROM SWALLOWING THE NANAMI-CHAN FROG, THOUGH I WAS DYING TO!
I WON'T FORGIVE YOU FOR WHAT YOU DID!
GRR
I HAVEN'T FORGIVEN *YOU* FOR WHAT YOU DID!
HOW CAN YOU ACT THAT WAY WHEN YOU KIDNAPPED HER ONCE!
ARGH!
CAN'T YOU JUST LET THAT GO?!
TODAY, TODAY I'LL—
COLLAPSE
TOMOE-KUN?

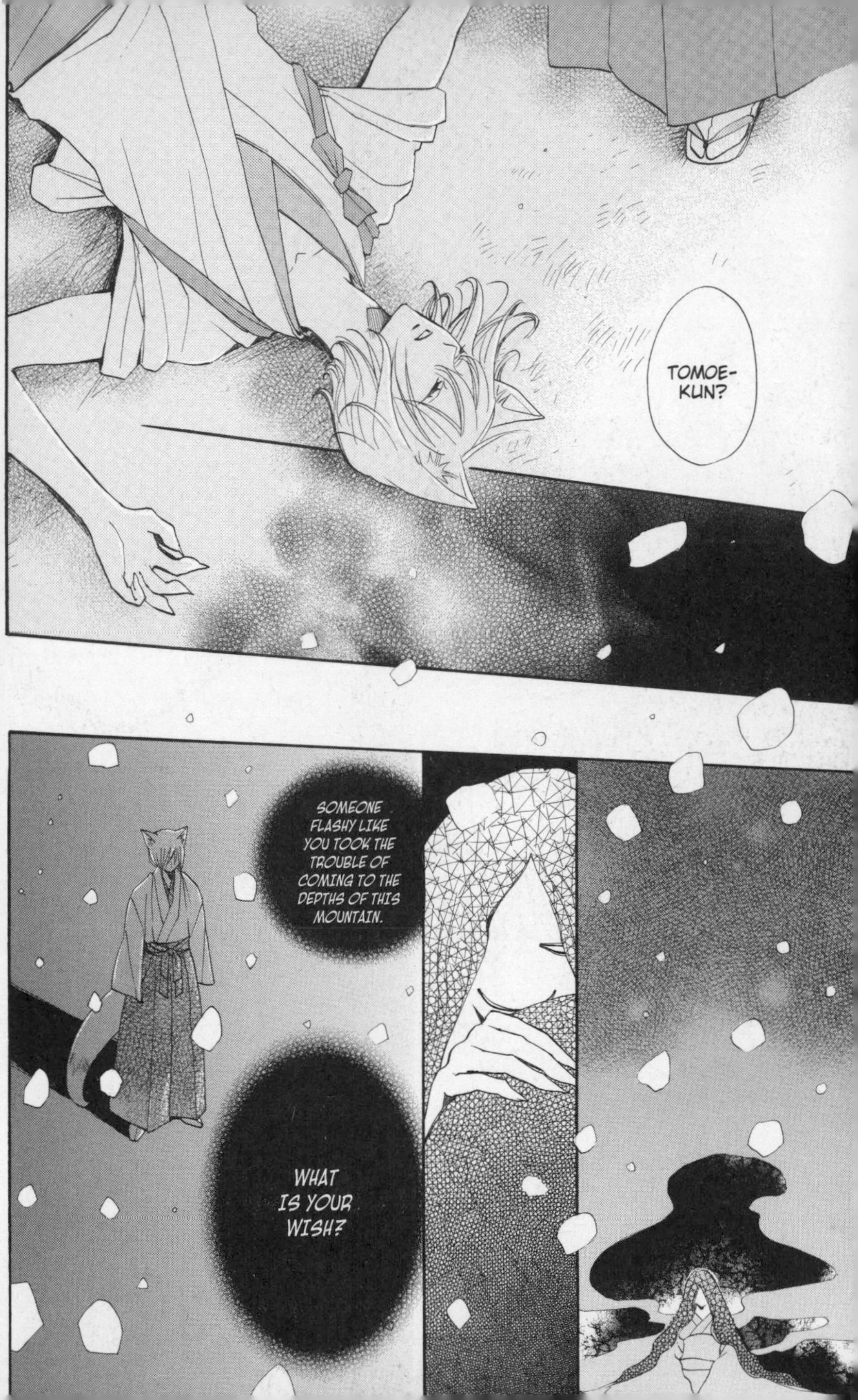
TOMOE-KUN?
SOMEONE FLASHY LIKE YOU TOOK THE TROUBLE OF COMING TO THE DEPTHS OF THIS MOUNTAIN.
WHAT IS YOUR WISH?

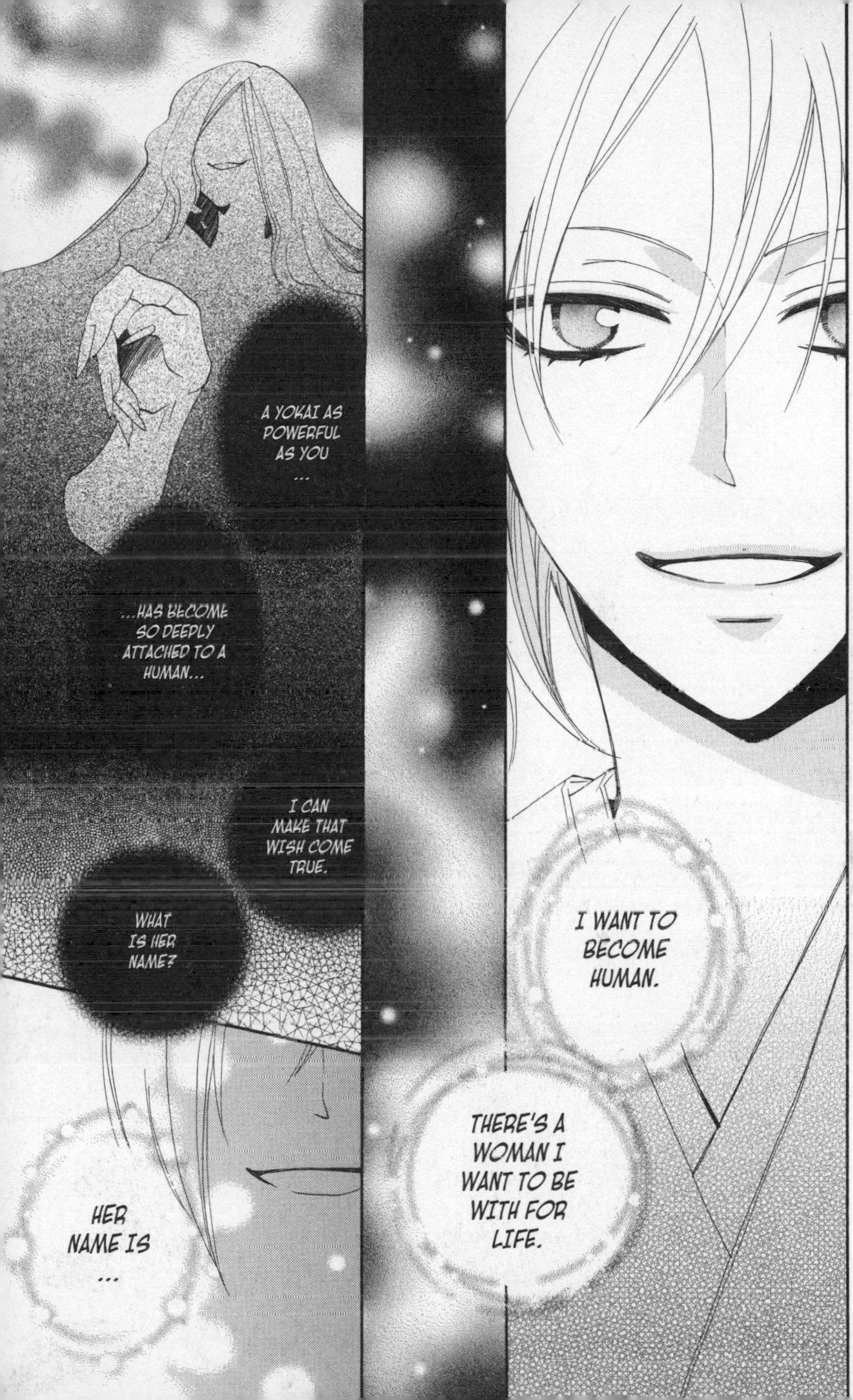
I WANT TO BECOME HUMAN.
THERE'S A WOMAN I WANT TO BE WITH FOR LIFE.
A YOKAI AS POWERFUL AS YOU ...
...HAS BECOME SO DEEPLY ATTACHED TO A HUMAN...
I CAN MAKE THAT WISH COME TRUE.
WHAT IS HER NAME?
HER NAME IS ...

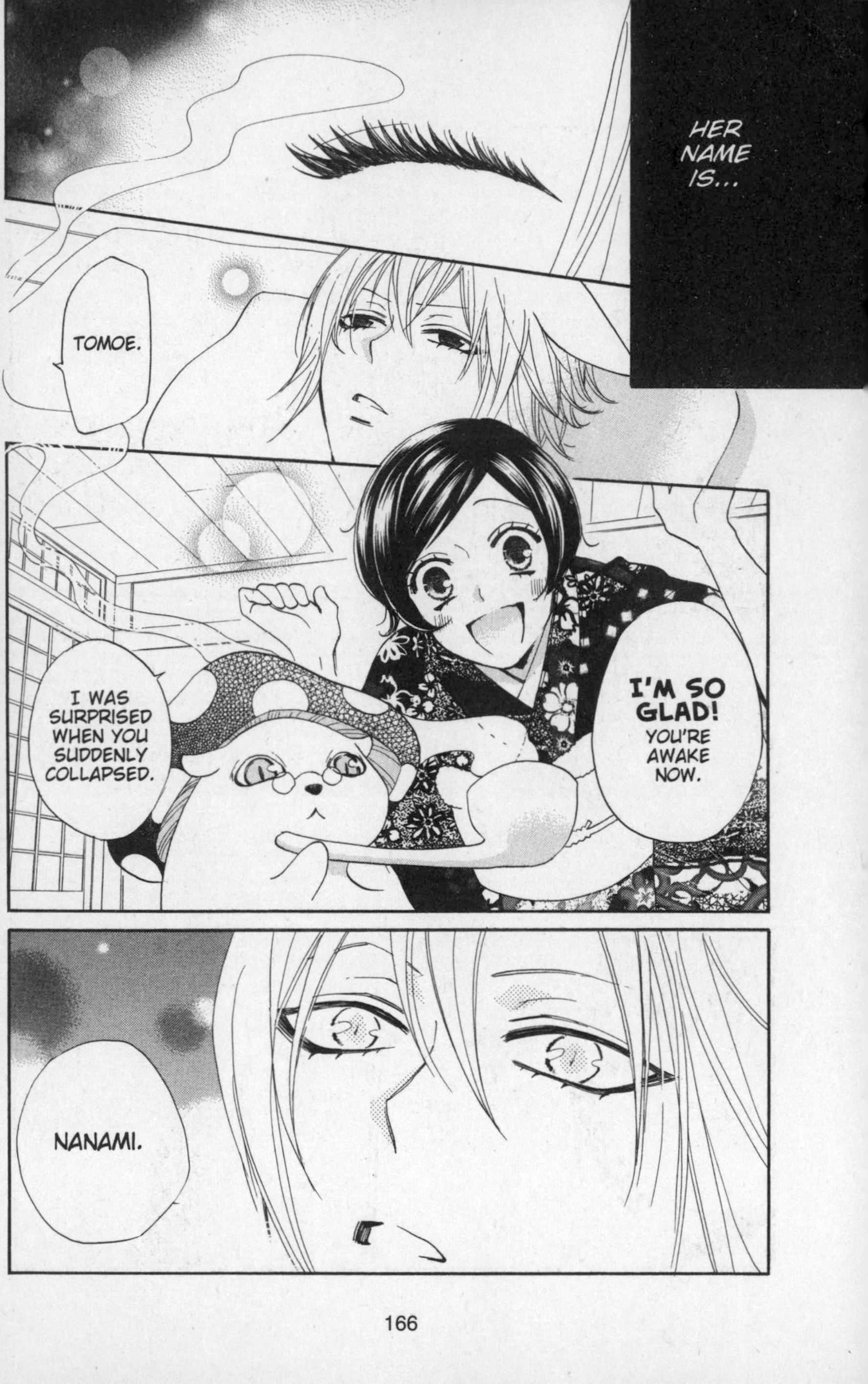
HER NAME IS...
TOMOE.
I'M SO GLAD! YOU'RE AWAKE NOW.
I WAS SURPRISED WHEN YOU SUDDENLY COLLAPSED.
NANAMI.

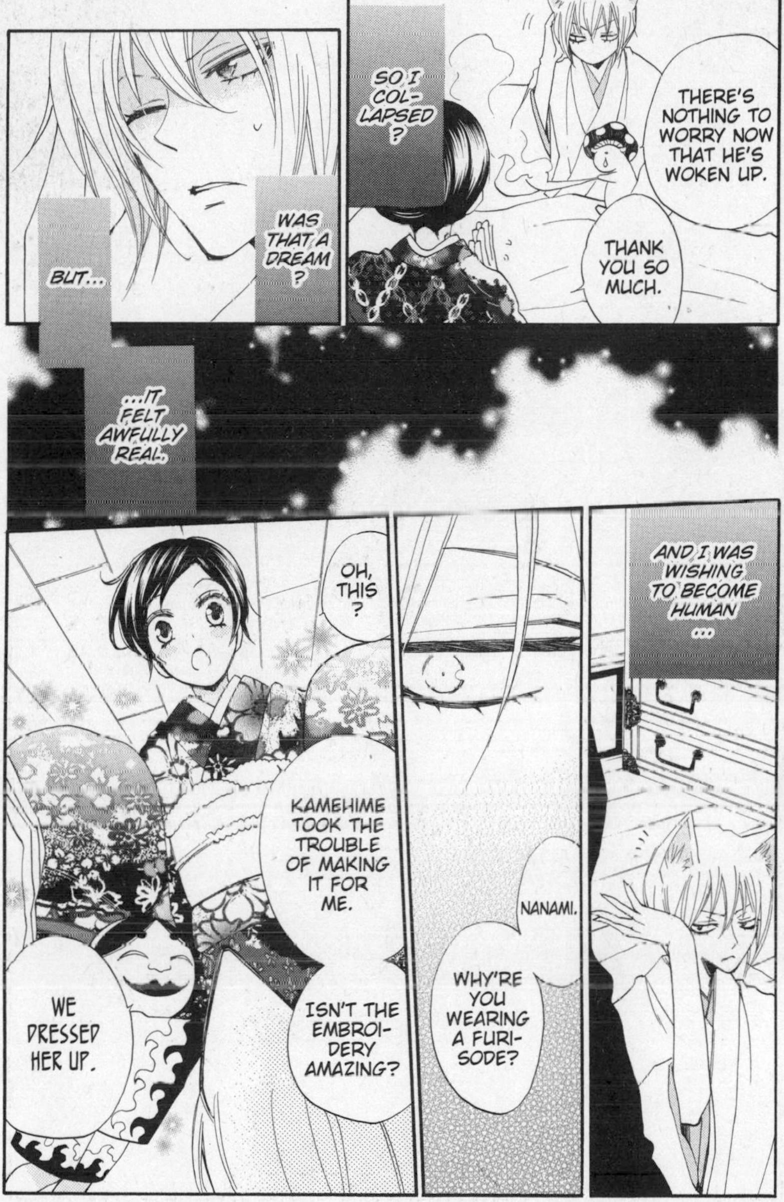
THERE'S NOTHING TO WORRY NOW THAT HE'S WOKEN UP.
THANK YOU SO MUCH.
SO I COL-LAPSED?
WAS THAT A DREAM?
BUT...
...IT FELT AWFULLY REAL.
AND I WAS WISHING TO BECOME HUMAN...
NANAMI.
WHY'RE YOU WEARING A FURI-SODE?
OH, THIS?
KAMEHIME TOOK THE TROUBLE OF MAKING IT FOR ME.
ISN'T THE EMBROI-DERY AMAZING?
WE DRESSED HER UP.

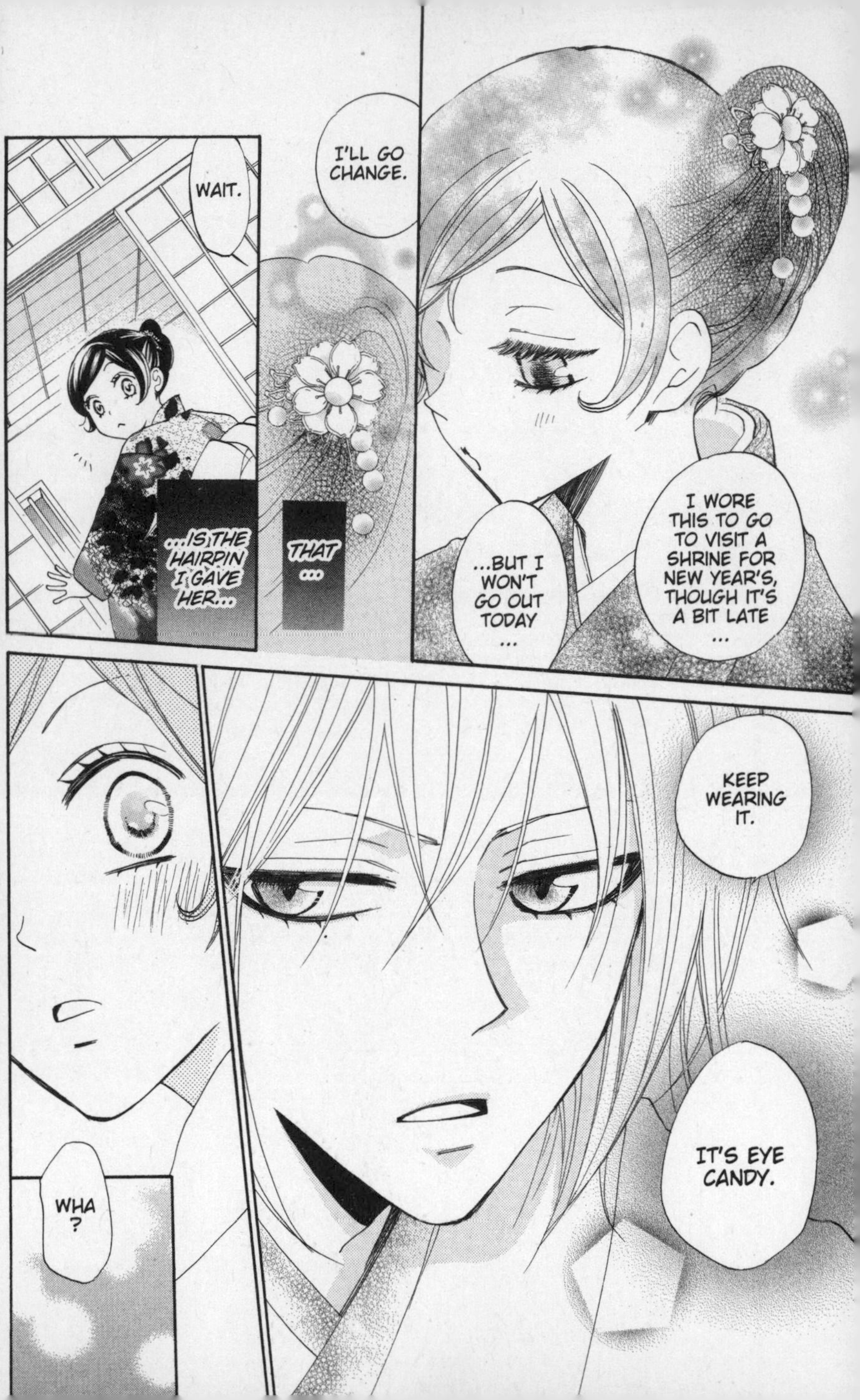
I WORE THIS TO GO TO VISIT A SHRINE FOR NEW YEAR'S, THOUGH IT'S A BIT LATE ...
...BUT I WON'T GO OUT TODAY ...
I'LL GO CHANGE.
THAT ...
WAIT.
...IS THE HAIRPIN I GAVE HER...
KEEP WEARING IT.
IT'S EYE CANDY.
WHA ?

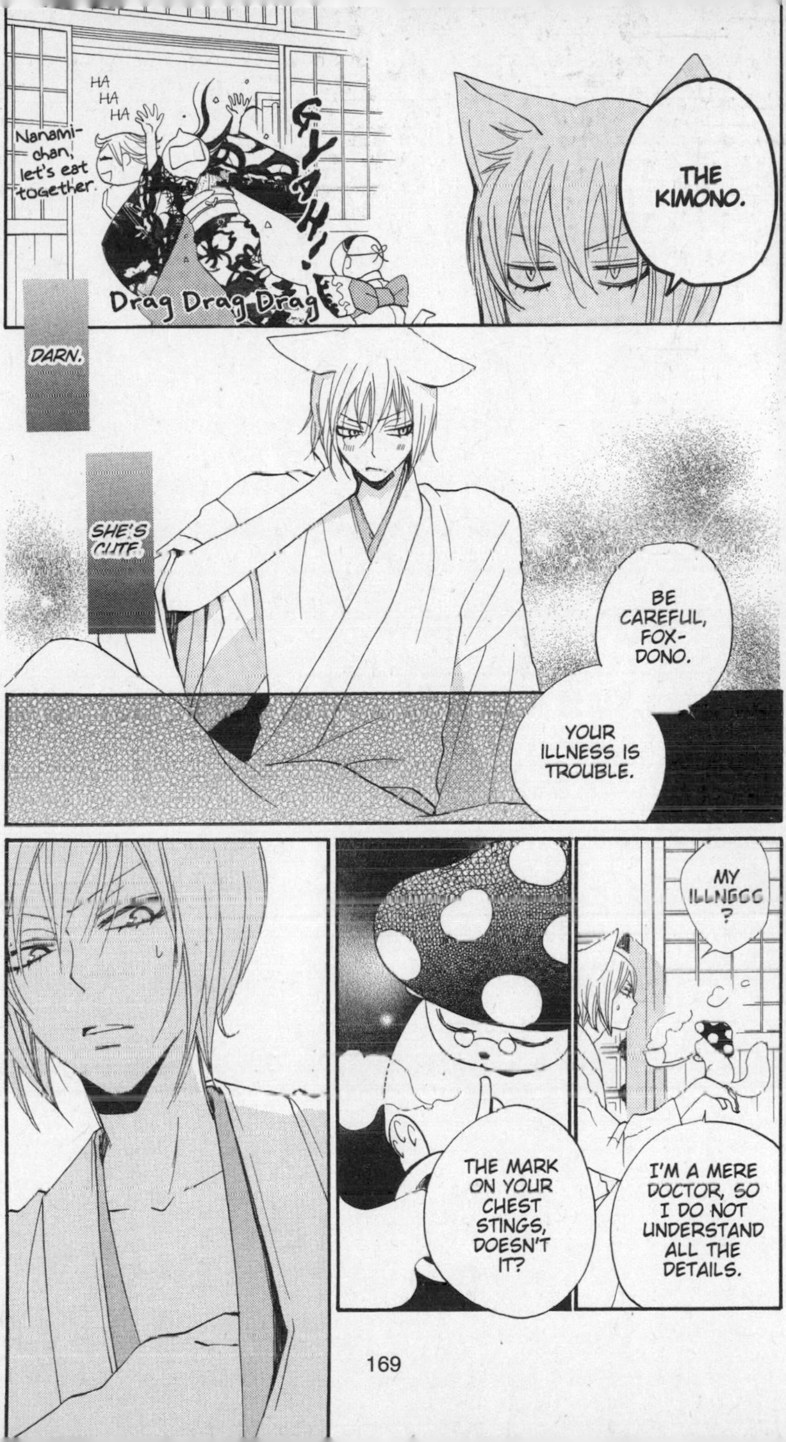
THE KIMONO.
Nanami-chan, let's eat together.
HA HA HA
GYAAH!
Drag Drag Drag
DARN.
SHE'S CUTE.
BE CAREFUL, FOX-DONO.
YOUR ILLNESS IS TROUBLE.
MY ILLNESS?
I'M A MERE DOCTOR, SO I DO NOT UNDERSTAND ALL THE DETAILS.
THE MARK ON YOUR CHEST STINGS, DOESN'T IT?

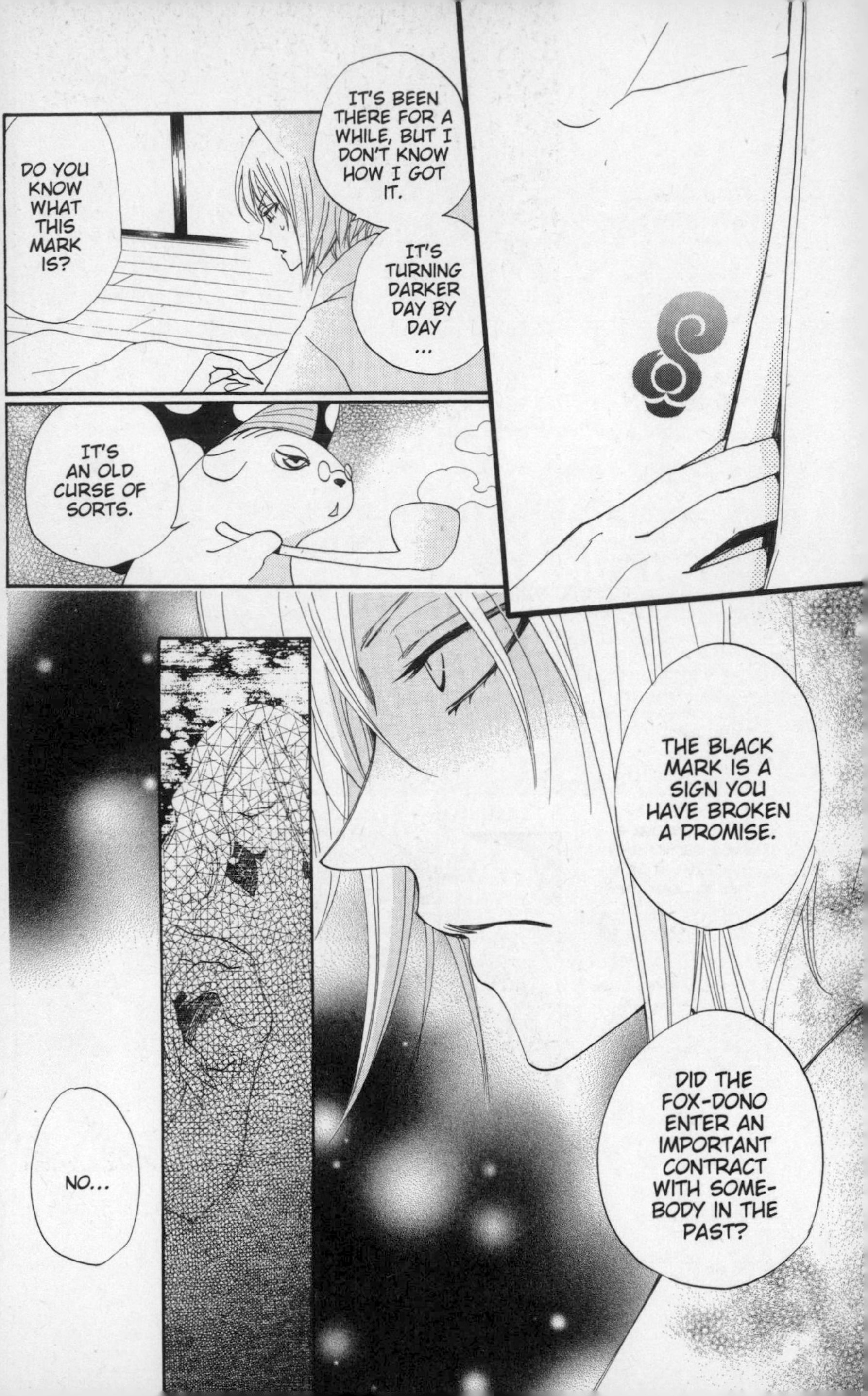
IT'S BEEN THERE FOR A WHILE, BUT I DON'T KNOW HOW I GOT IT.
IT'S TURNING DARKER DAY BY DAY ...
DO YOU KNOW WHAT THIS MARK IS?
IT'S AN OLD CURSE OF SORTS.
THE BLACK MARK IS A SIGN YOU HAVE BROKEN A PROMISE.
DID THE FOX-DONO ENTER AN IMPORTANT CONTRACT WITH SOME-BODY IN THE PAST?
NO...

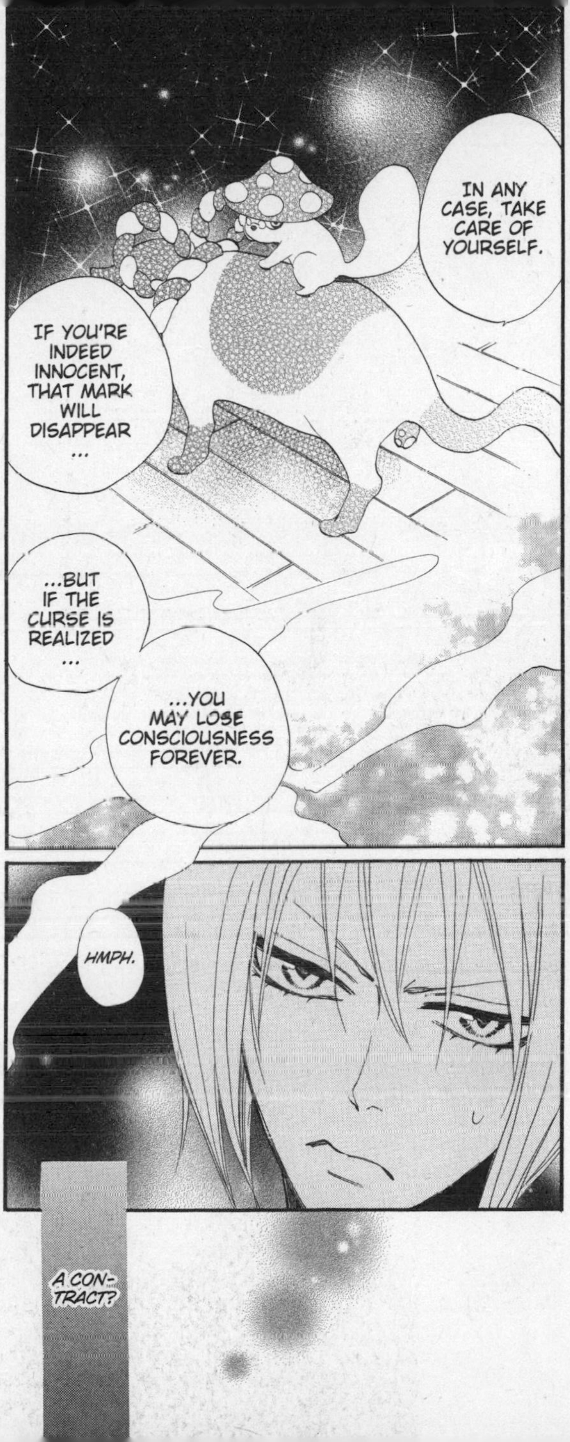
IN ANY CASE, TAKE CARE OF YOURSELF.
IF YOU'RE INDEED INNOCENT, THAT MARK WILL DISAPPEAR...
...BUT IF THE CURSE IS REALIZED...
...YOU MAY LOSE CONSCIOUSNESS FOREVER.
HMPH.
A CON-TRACT?

This is the last sidebar!

Thank you for reading this far.

The Nishiki arc ends here, and a new arc will begin in the next volume.

The series is continuing in *Hana to Yume*, so please take a look at the magazine as well.

The magazine made Kamisama Kiss freebies as well. Thank you so much!

The next volume will come out a little earlier than usual. It will be on sale in Japan next month. I hope you read it as well.

I hope we'll be able to meet again.

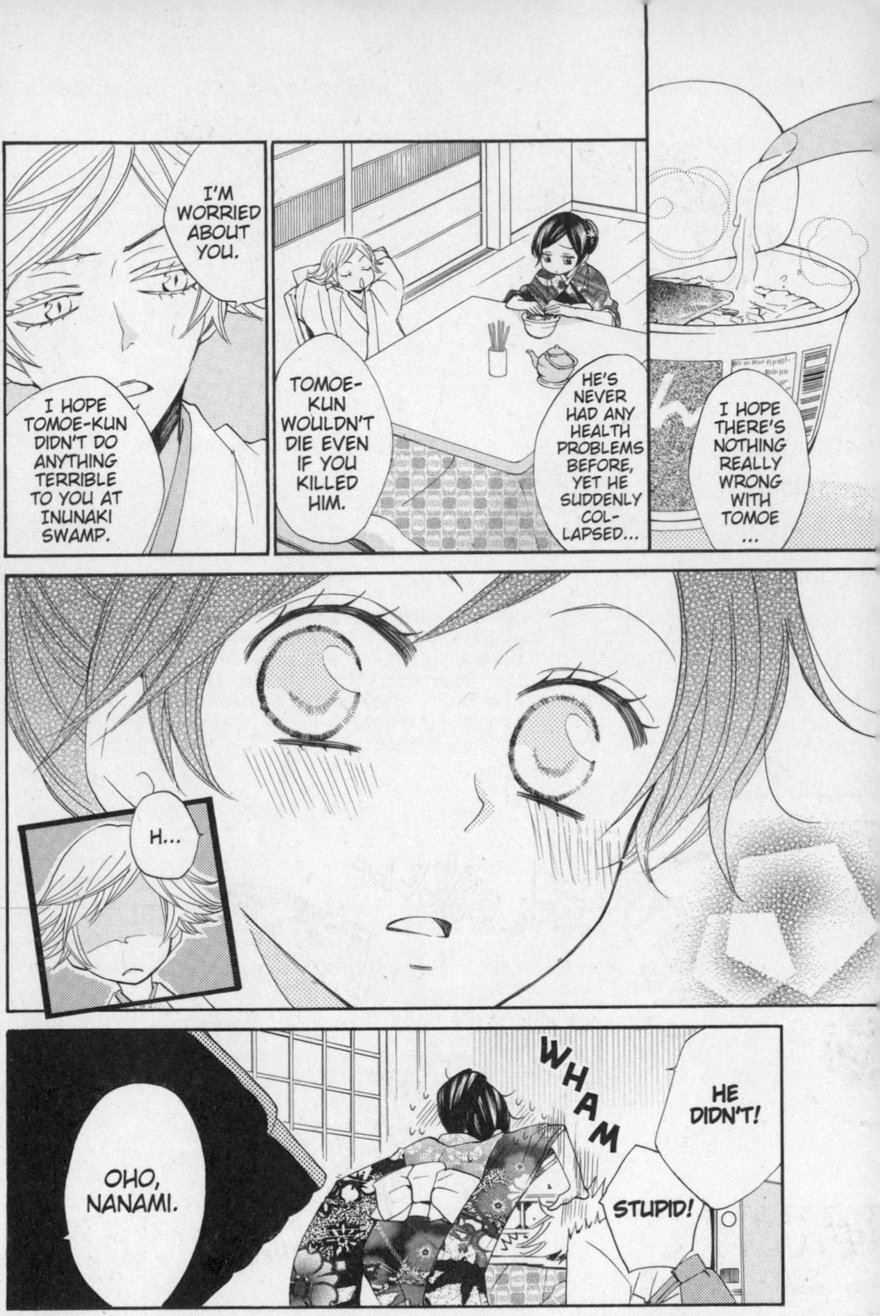

I HOPE THERE'S NOTHING REALLY WRONG WITH TOMOE ...
HE'S NEVER HAD ANY HEALTH PROBLEMS BEFORE, YET HE SUDDENLY COL-LAPSED...
TOMOE-KUN WOULDN'T DIE EVEN IF YOU KILLED HIM.
I'M WORRIED ABOUT YOU.
I HOPE TOMOE-KUN DIDN'T DO ANYTHING TERRIBLE TO YOU AT INUNAKI SWAMP.
H...
HE DIDN'T!
WHAM
STUPID!
OHO, NANAMI.

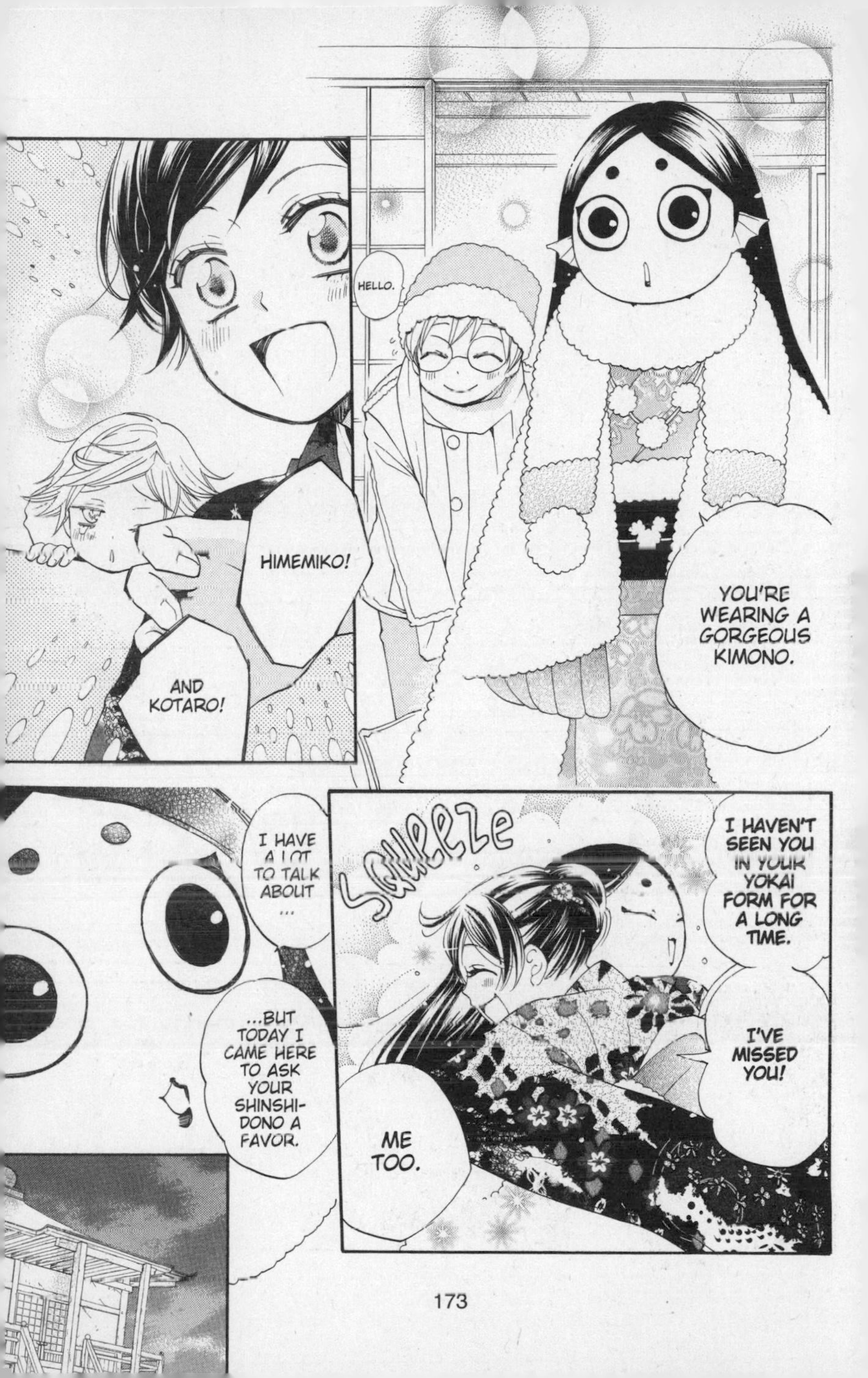
HELLO.
YOU'RE WEARING A GORGEOUS KIMONO.
HIMEMIKO!
AND KOTARO!
SQUEEZE
I HAVEN'T SEEN YOU IN YOUR YOKAI FORM FOR A LONG TIME.
I'VE MISSED YOU!
ME TOO.
I HAVE A LOT TO TALK ABOUT ...
...BUT TODAY I CAME HERE TO ASK YOUR SHINSHI-DONO A FAVOR.

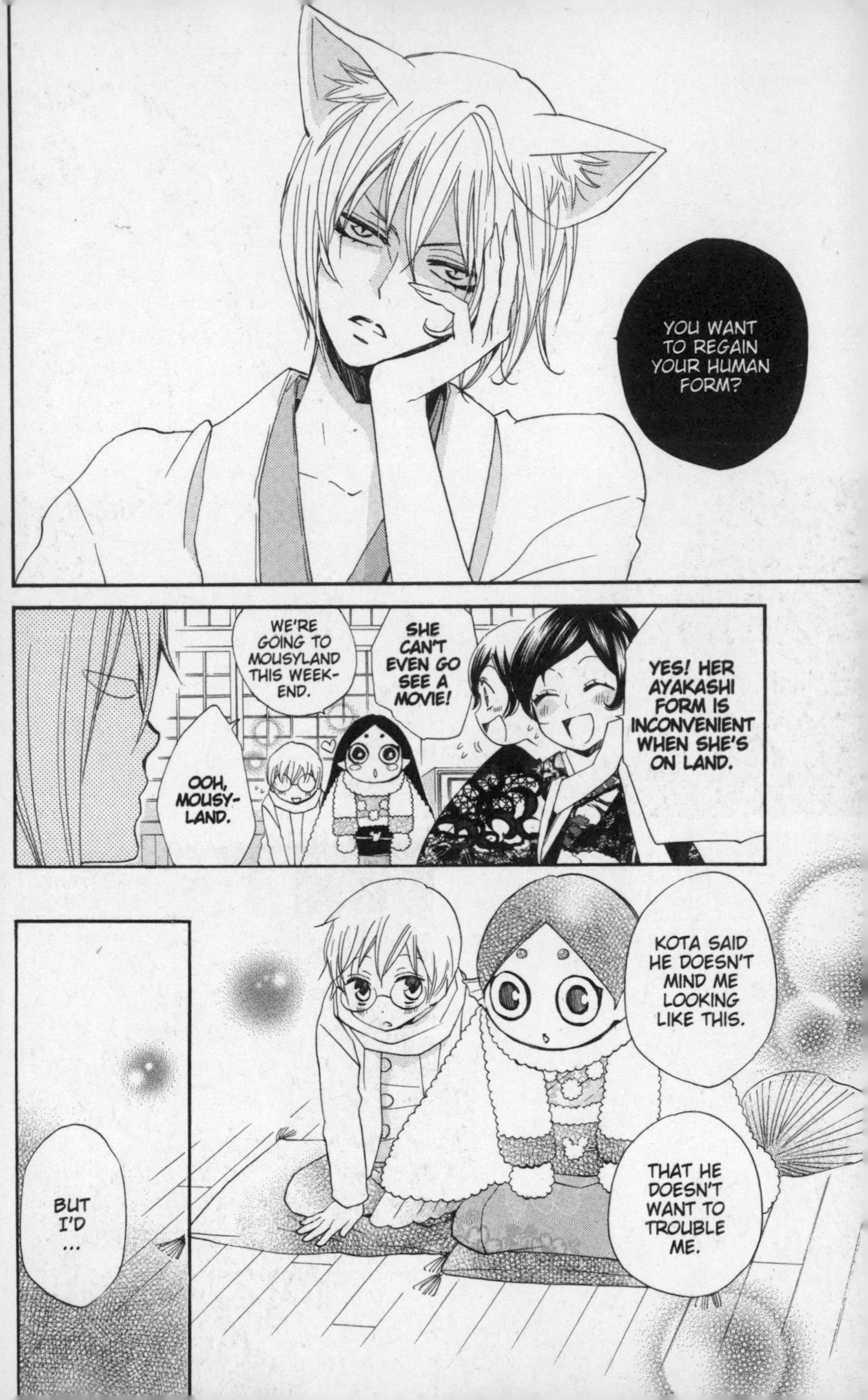
YOU WANT TO REGAIN YOUR HUMAN FORM?
YES! HER AYAKASHI FORM IS INCONVENIENT WHEN SHE'S ON LAND.
SHE CAN'T EVEN GO SEE A MOVIE!
WE'RE GOING TO MOUSYLAND THIS WEEK-END.
OOH, MOUSY-LAND.
KOTA SAID HE DOESN'T MIND ME LOOKING LIKE THIS.
THAT HE DOESN'T WANT TO TROUBLE ME.
BUT I'D ...

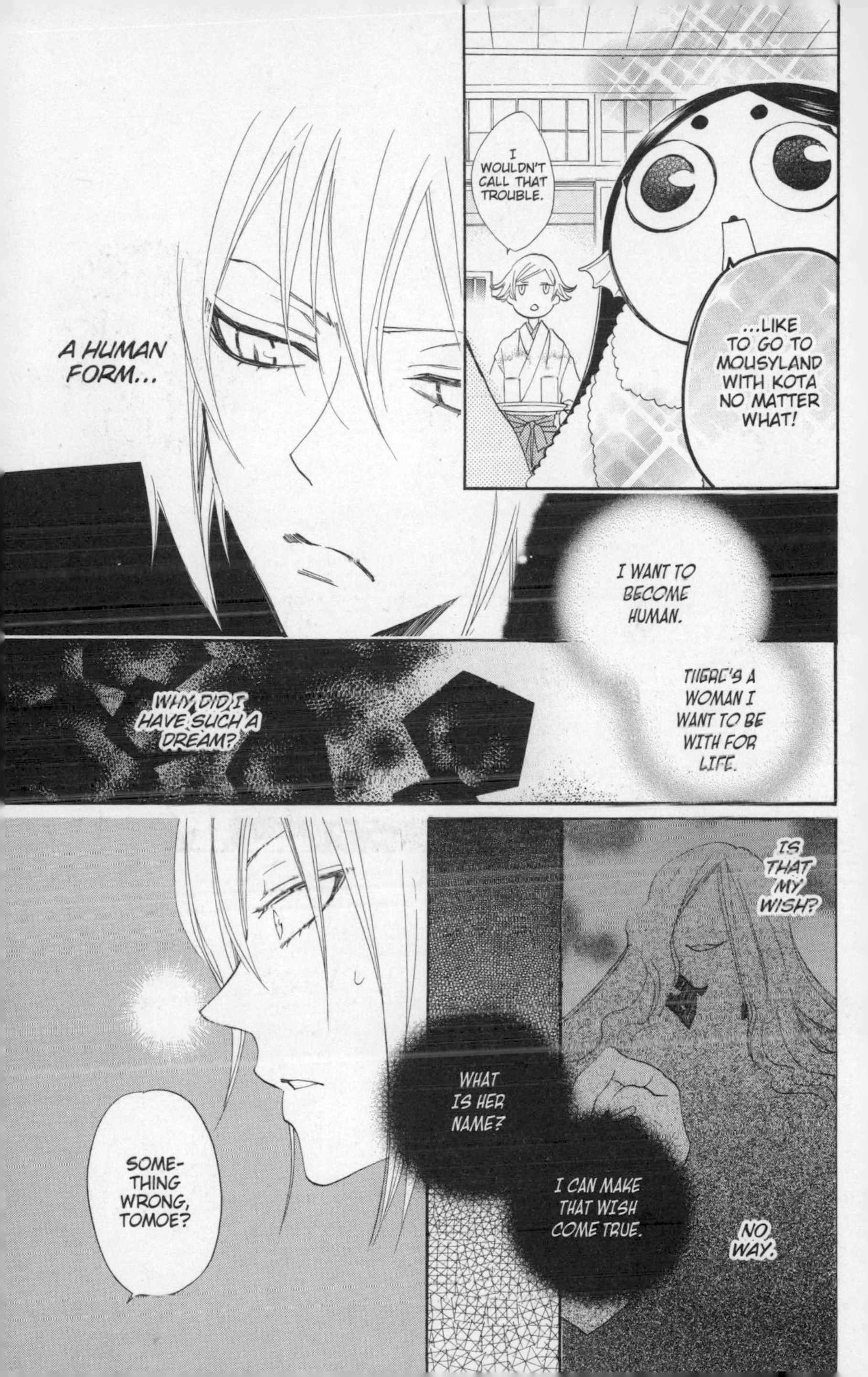
...LIKE TO GO TO MOUSYLAND WITH KOTA NO MATTER WHAT!
I WOULDN'T CALL THAT TROUBLE.
A HUMAN FORM...
I WANT TO BECOME HUMAN.
THERE'S A WOMAN I WANT TO BE WITH FOR LIFE.
WHY DID I HAVE SUCH A DREAM?
IS THAT MY WISH?
NO WAY.
WHAT IS HER NAME?
I CAN MAKE THAT WISH COME TRUE.
SOME-THING WRONG, TOMOE?

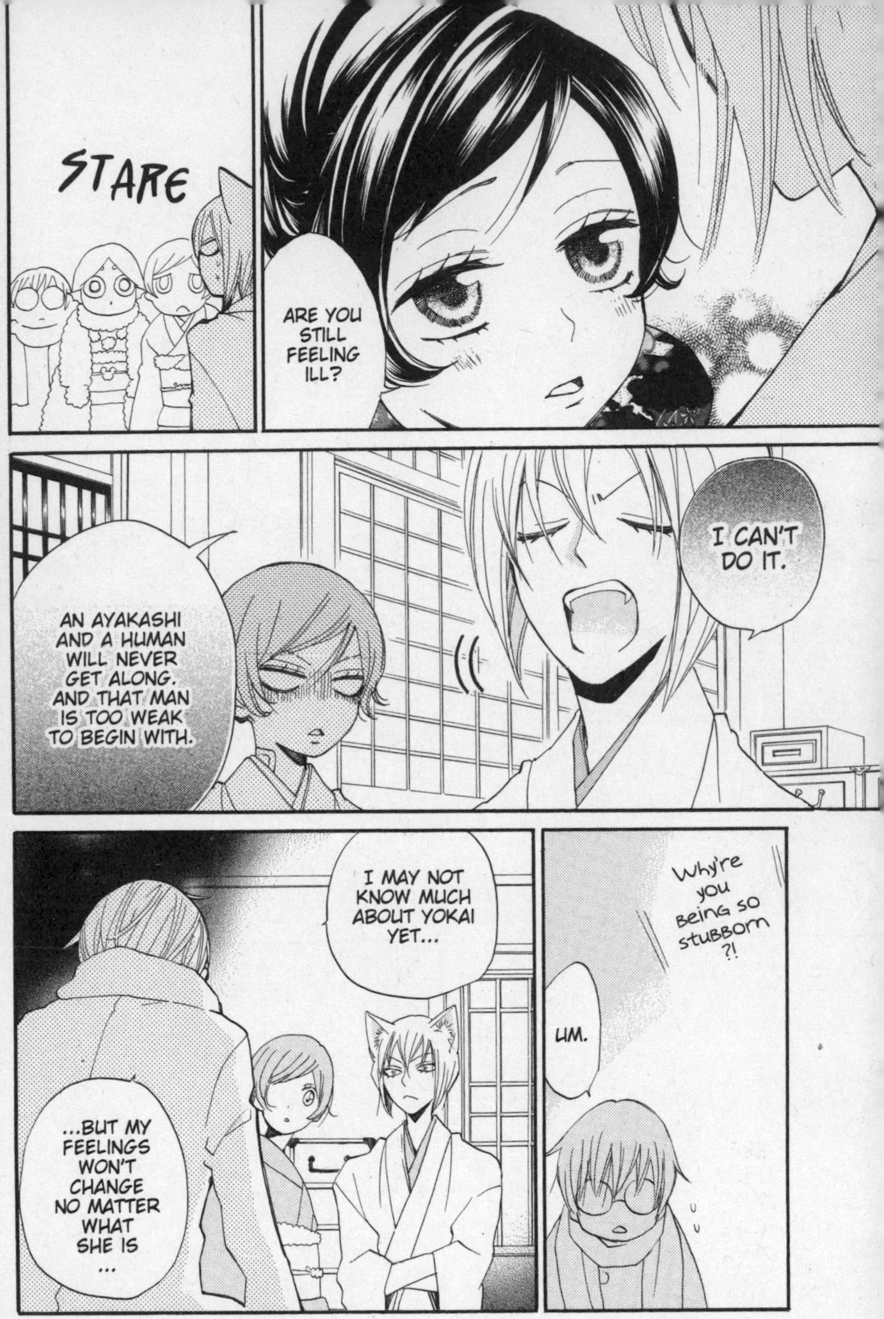
ARE YOU STILL FEELING ILL?
STARE
I CAN'T DO IT.
AN AYAKASHI AND A HUMAN WILL NEVER GET ALONG. AND THAT MAN IS TOO WEAK TO BEGIN WITH.
Why're you being so stubborn?!
UM.
I MAY NOT KNOW MUCH ABOUT YOKAI YET...
...BUT MY FEELINGS WON'T CHANGE NO MATTER WHAT SHE IS ...

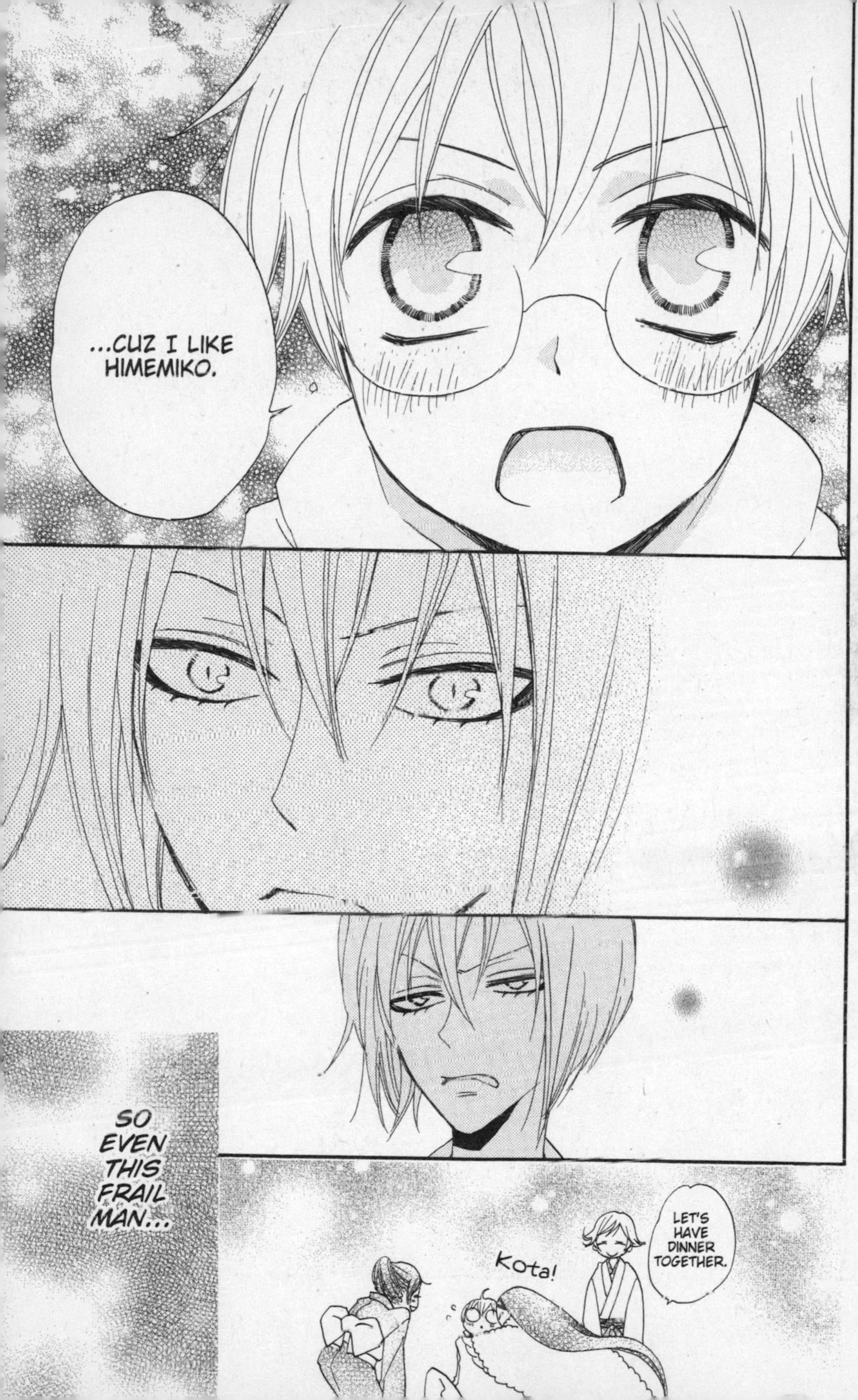
...CUZ I LIKE HIMEMIKO.
LET'S HAVE DINNER TOGETHER.
Kota!
SO EVEN THIS FRAIL MAN...

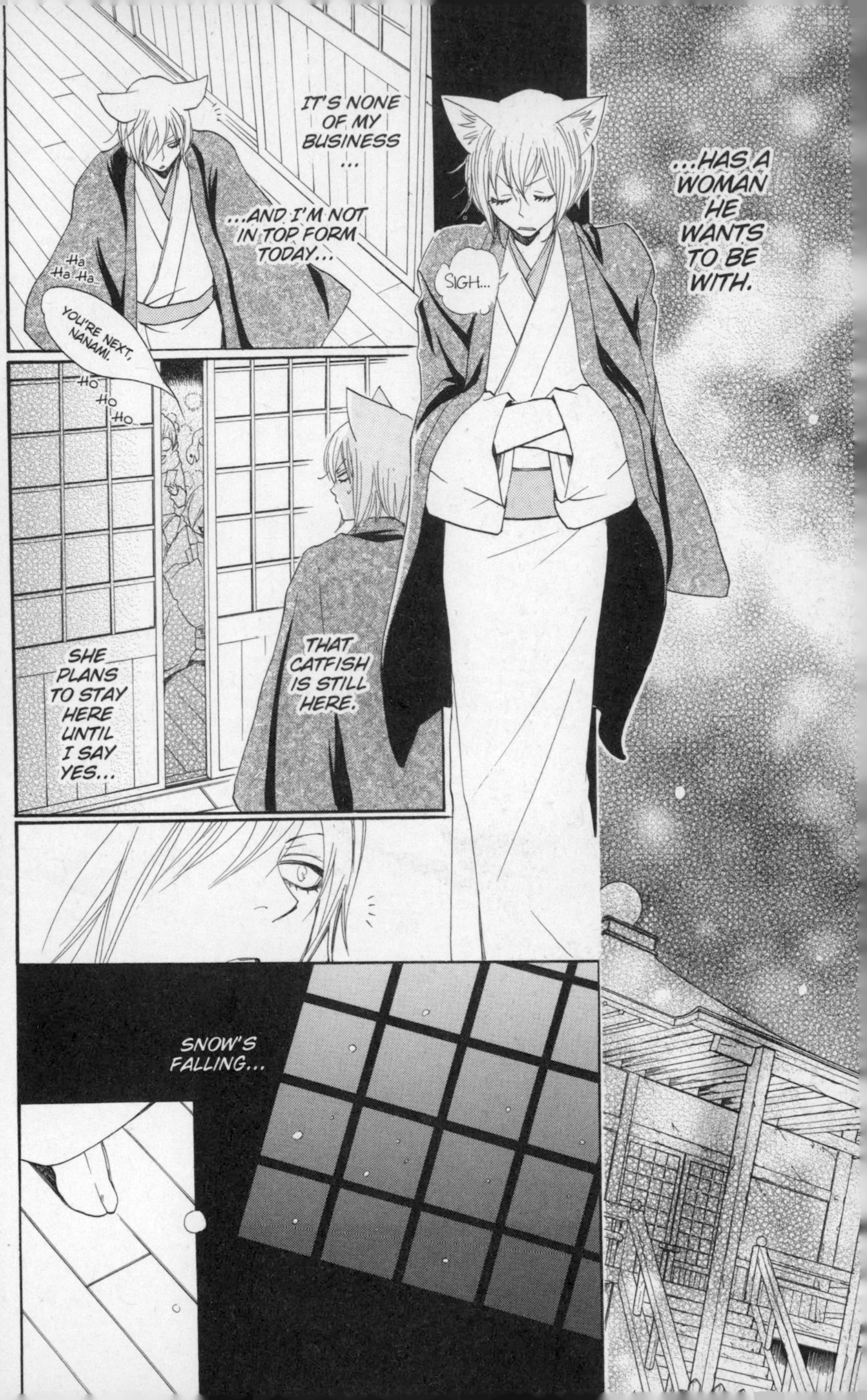
...HAS A WOMAN HE WANTS TO BE WITH.
SIGH...
IT'S NONE OF MY BUSINESS...
...AND I'M NOT IN TOP FORM TODAY...
Ha Ha Ha...
YOU'RE NEXT, NANAMI.
Ho Ho Ho...
THAT CATFISH IS STILL HERE.
SHE PLANS TO STAY HERE UNTIL I SAY YES...
SNOW'S FALLING...

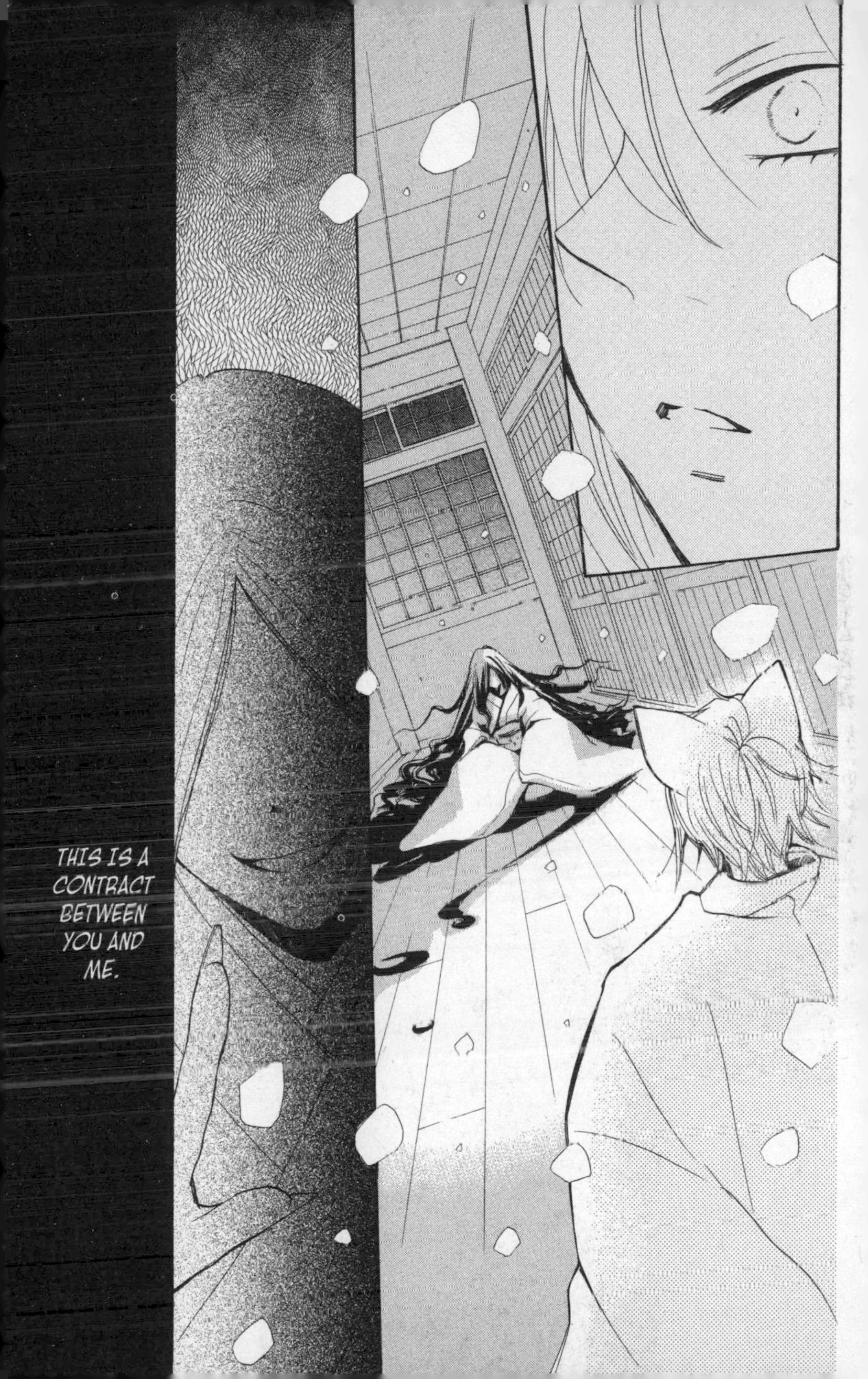
THIS IS A CONTRACT BETWEEN YOU AND ME.

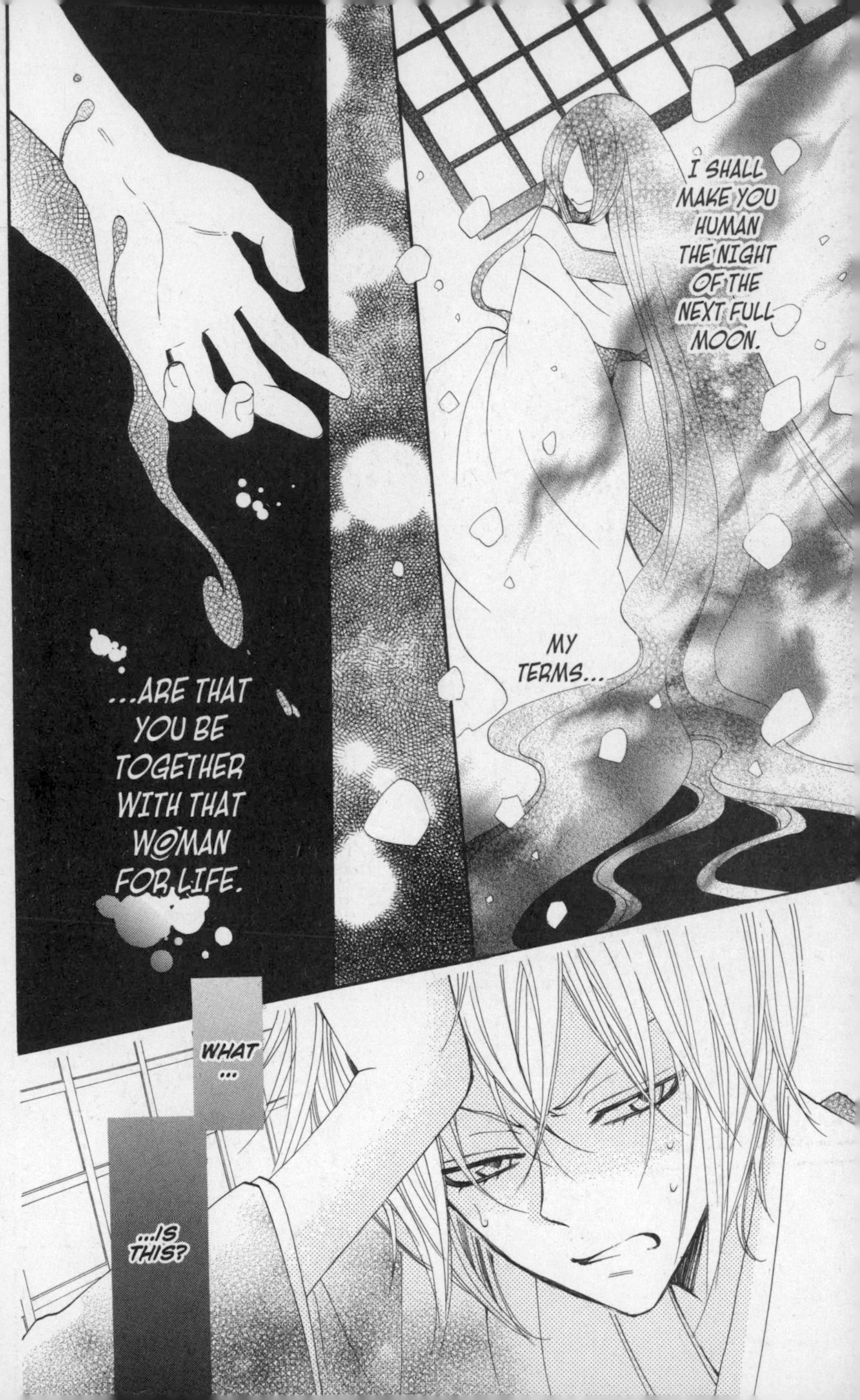
I SHALL MAKE YOU HUMAN THE NIGHT OF THE NEXT FULL MOON.
MY TERMS...
...ARE THAT YOU BE TOGETHER WITH THAT WOMAN FOR LIFE.
WHAT ...
...IS THIS?

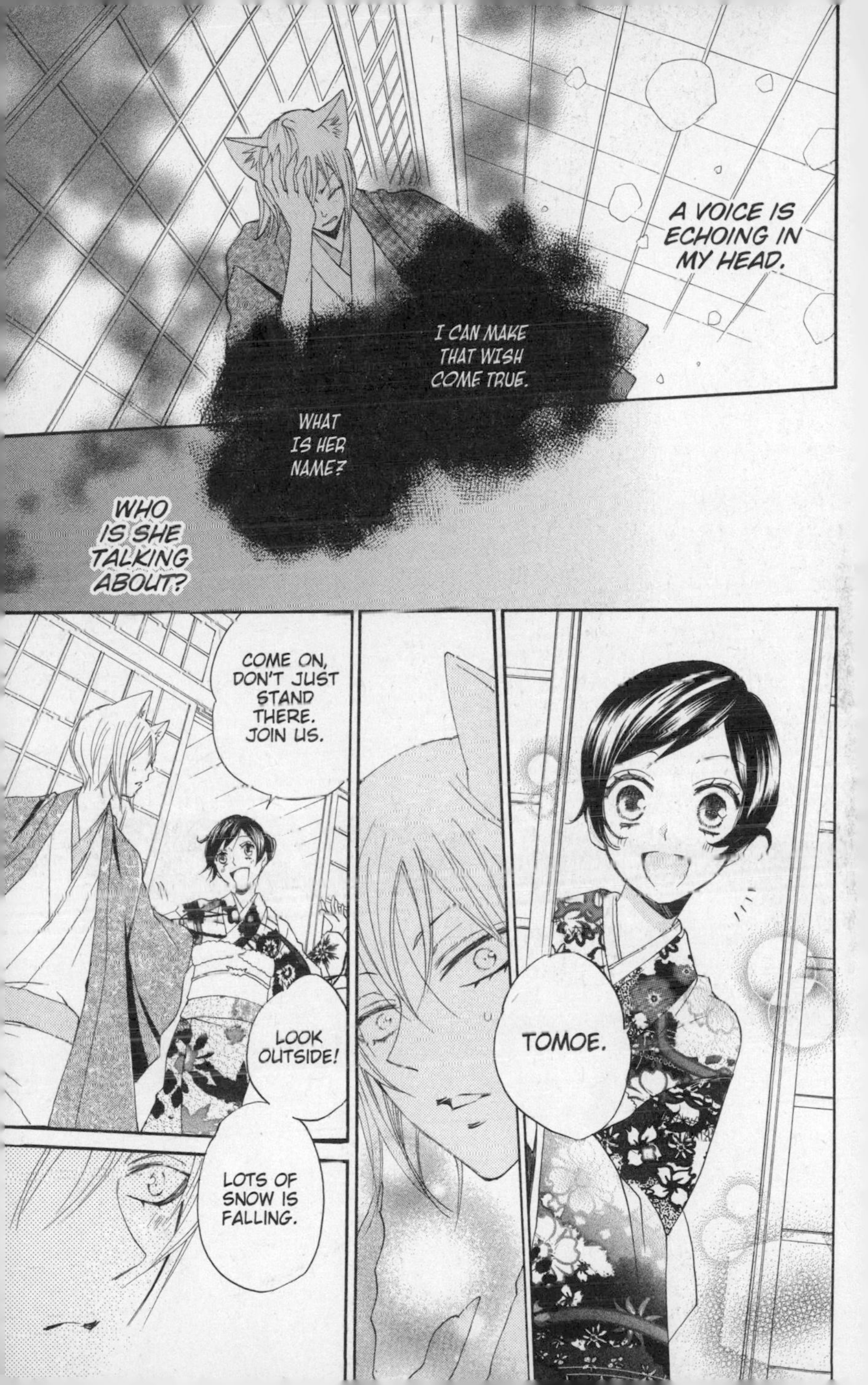
A VOICE IS ECHOING IN MY HEAD.
I CAN MAKE THAT WISH COME TRUE.
WHAT IS HER NAME?
WHO IS SHE TALKING ABOUT?
TOMOE.
COME ON, DON'T JUST STAND THERE. JOIN US.
LOOK OUTSIDE!
LOTS OF SNOW IS FALLING.

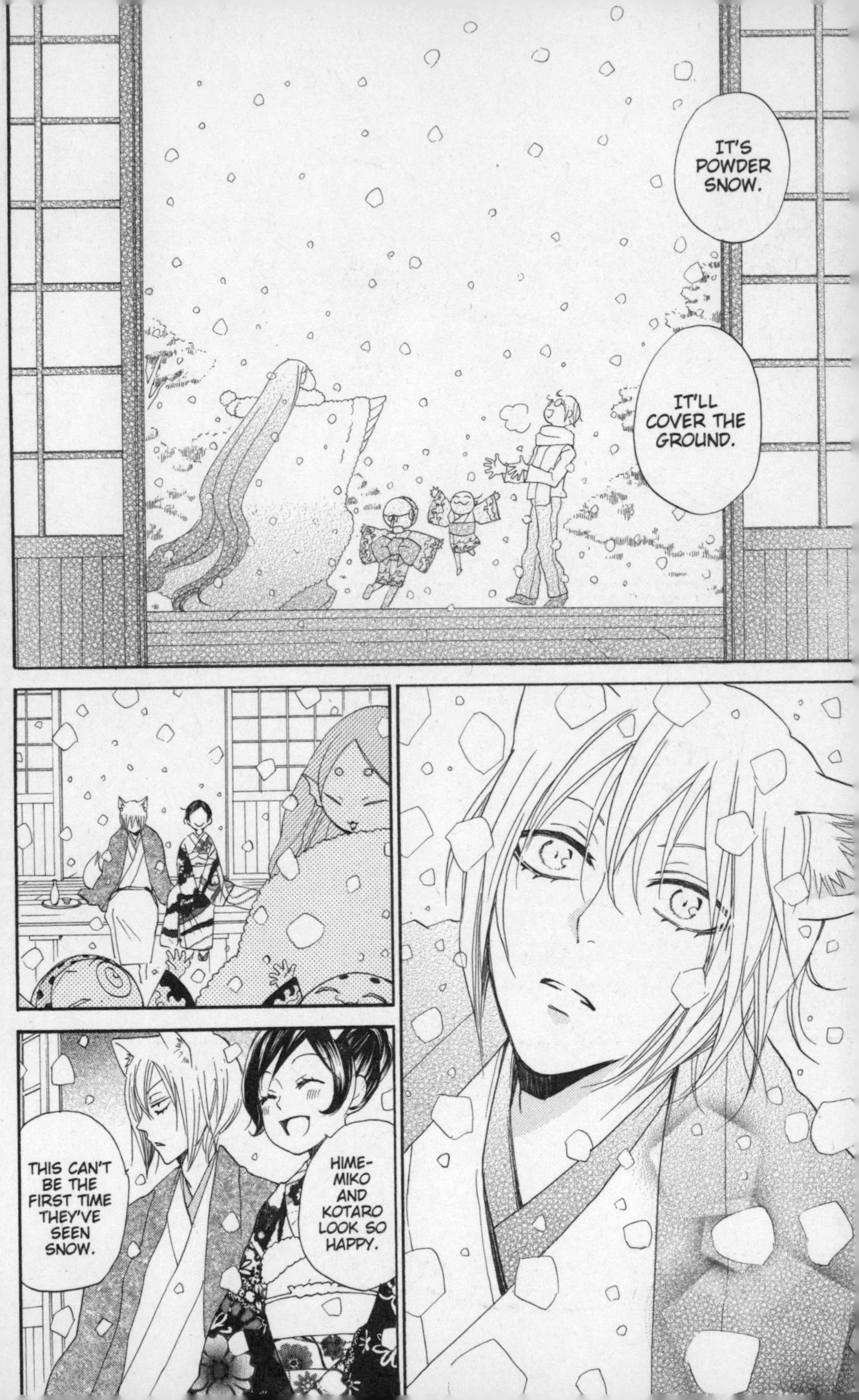
IT'S POWDER SNOW.
IT'LL COVER THE GROUND.
HIME-MIKO AND KOTARO LOOK SO HAPPY.
THIS CAN'T BE THE FIRST TIME THEY'VE SEEN SNOW.

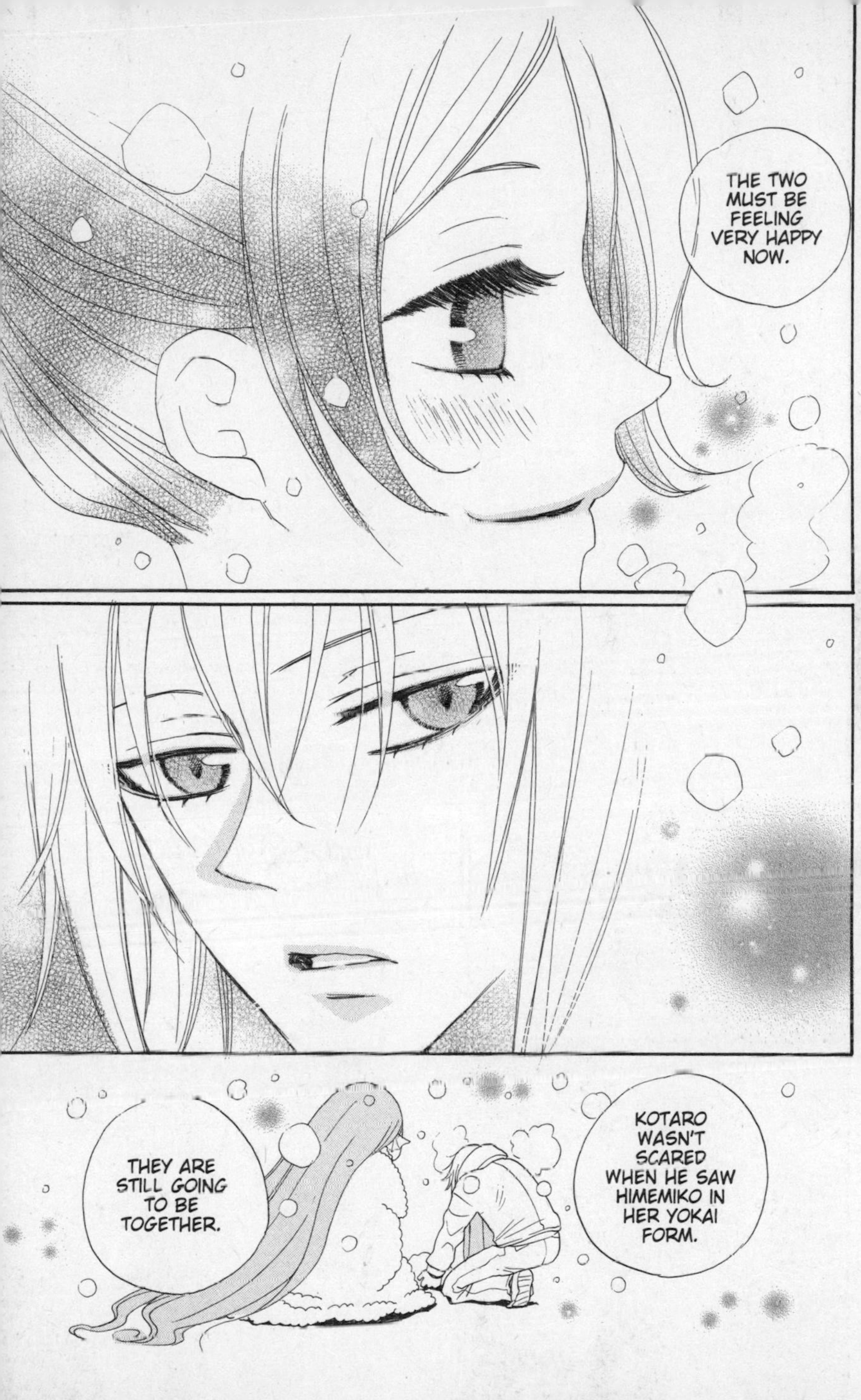
THE TWO MUST BE FEELING VERY HAPPY NOW.
KOTARO WASN'T SCARED WHEN HE SAW HIMEMIKO IN HER YOKAI FORM.
THEY ARE STILL GOING TO BE TOGETHER.

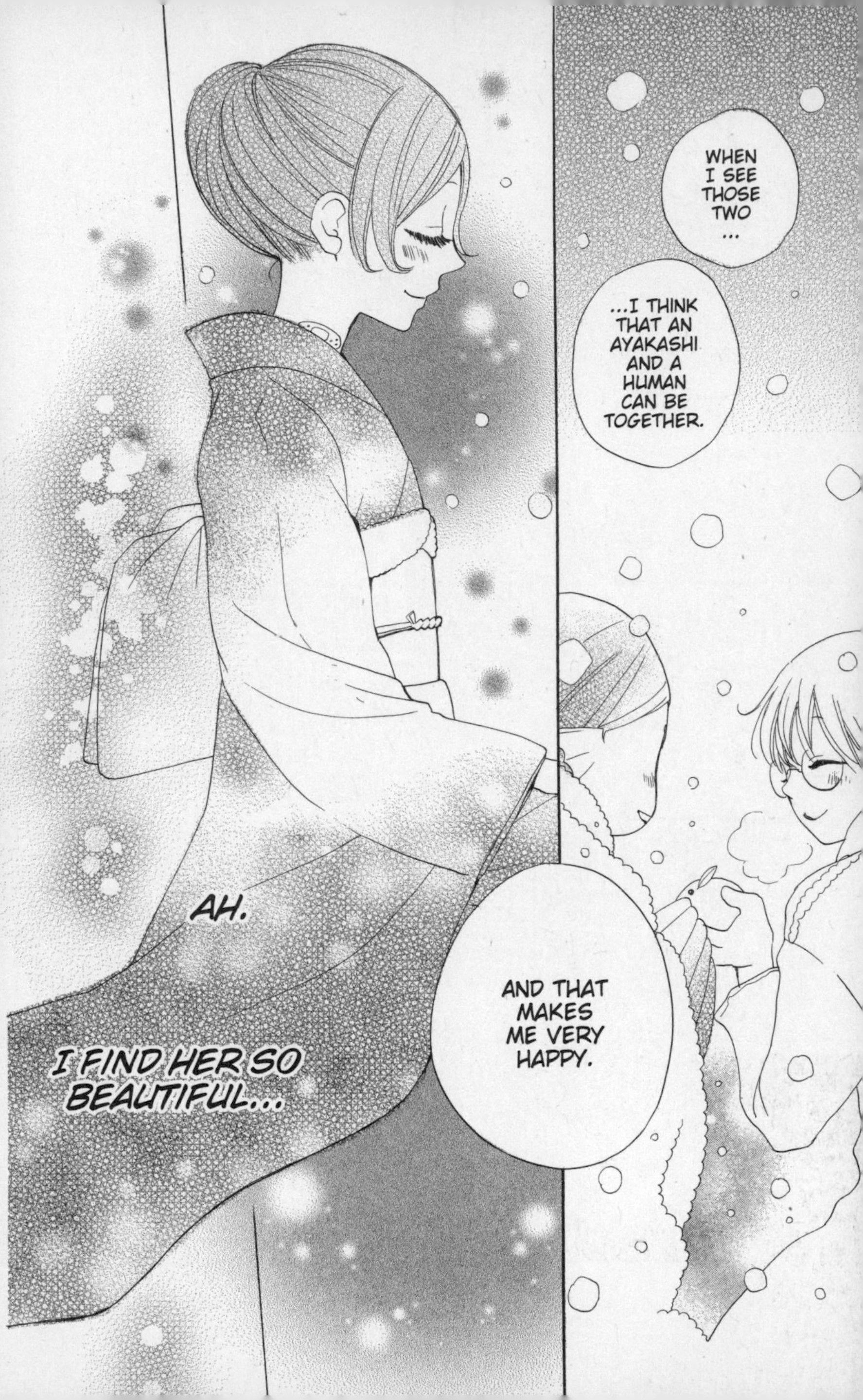
WHEN I SEE THOSE TWO ...
...I THINK THAT AN AYAKASHI AND A HUMAN CAN BE TOGETHER.
AND THAT MAKES ME VERY HAPPY.
AH.
I FIND HER SO BEAUTIFUL...

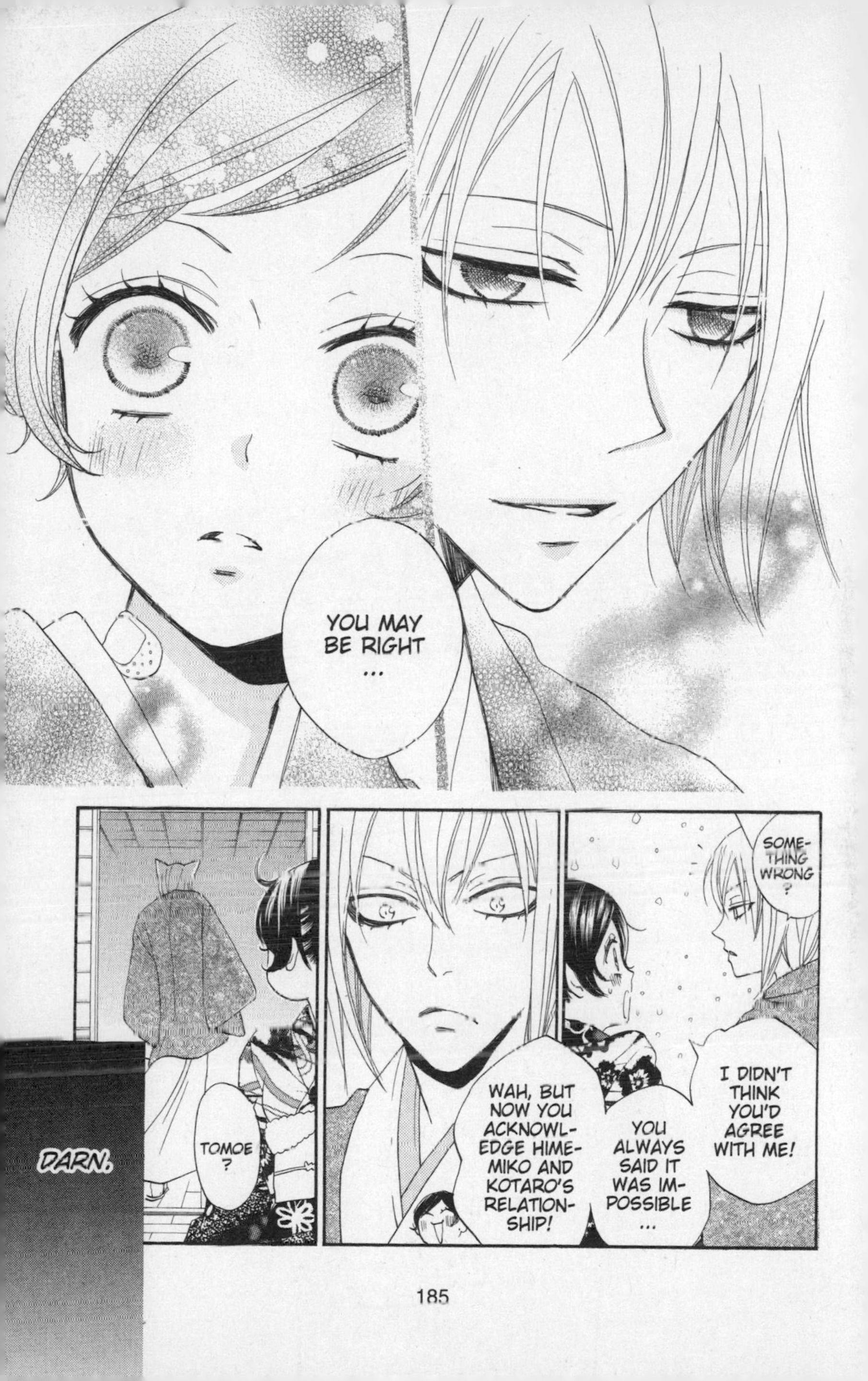
YOU MAY BE RIGHT ...
SOME-THING WRONG?
I DIDN'T THINK YOU'D AGREE WITH ME!
YOU ALWAYS SAID IT WAS IM-POSSIBLE ...
WAH, BUT NOW YOU ACKNOWL-EDGE HIME-MIKO AND KOTARO'S RELATION-SHIP!
TOMOE?
DARN.

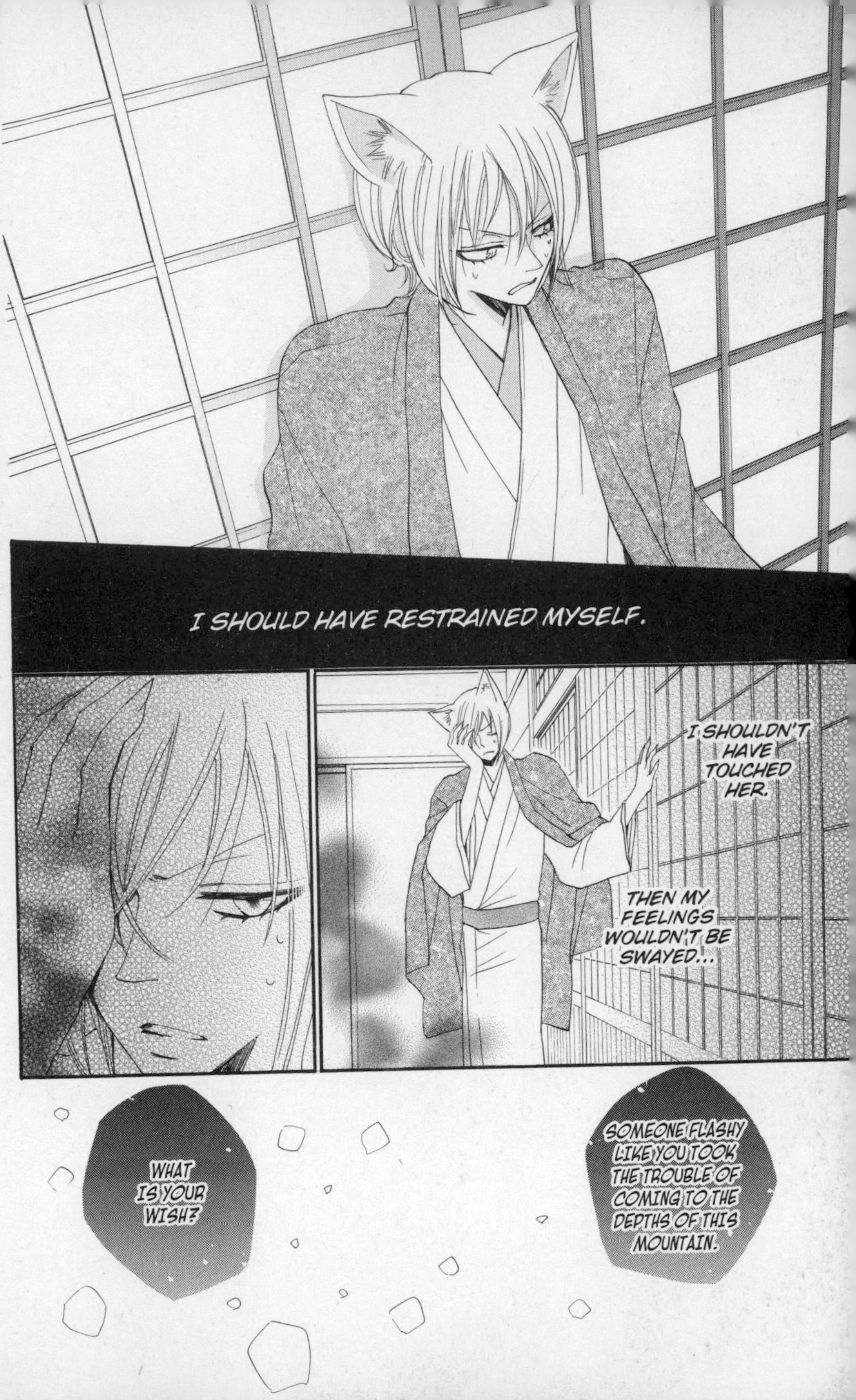
I SHOULD HAVE RESTRAINED MYSELF.
I SHOULDN'T HAVE TOUCHED HER.
THEN MY FEELINGS WOULDN'T BE SWAYED...
SOMEONE FLASHY LIKE YOU TOOK THE TROUBLE OF COMING TO THE DEPTHS OF THIS MOUNTAIN.
WHAT IS YOUR WISH?

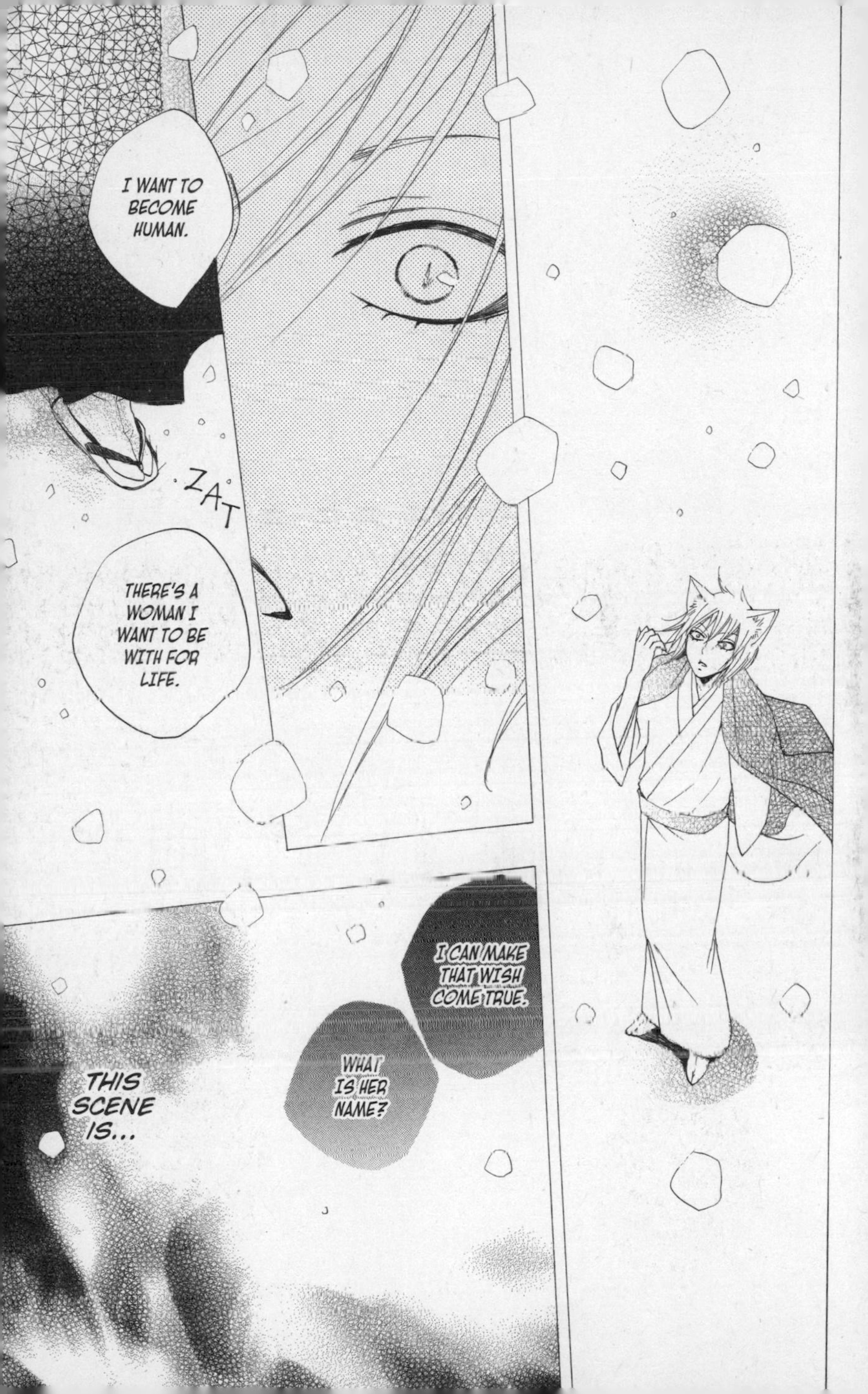
I WANT TO BECOME HUMAN.
ZAT
THERE'S A WOMAN I WANT TO BE WITH FOR LIFE.
I CAN MAKE THAT WISH COME TRUE.
WHAT IS HER NAME?
THIS SCENE IS...

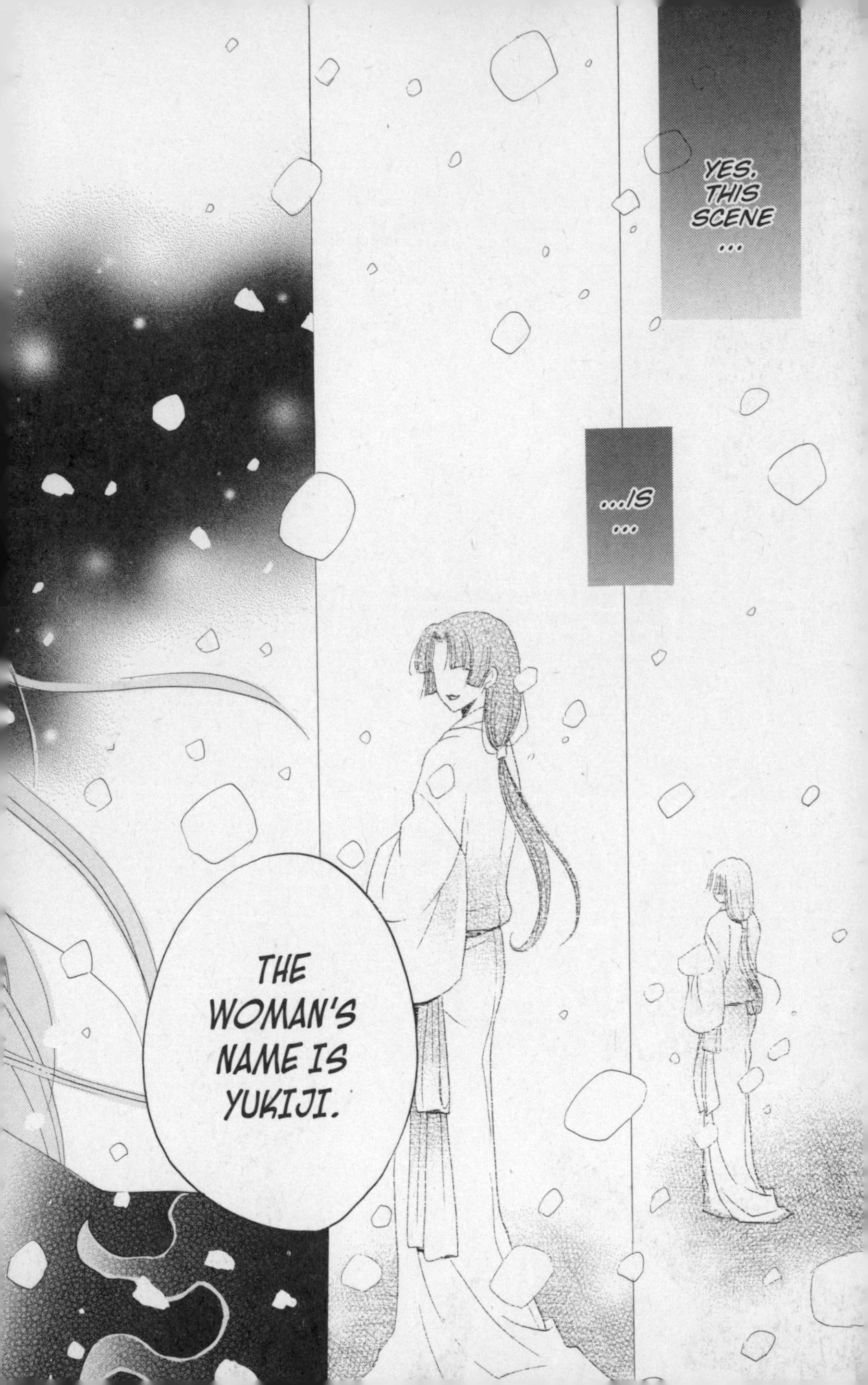
YES. THIS SCENE ...
...IS ...
THE WOMAN'S NAME IS YUKIJI.

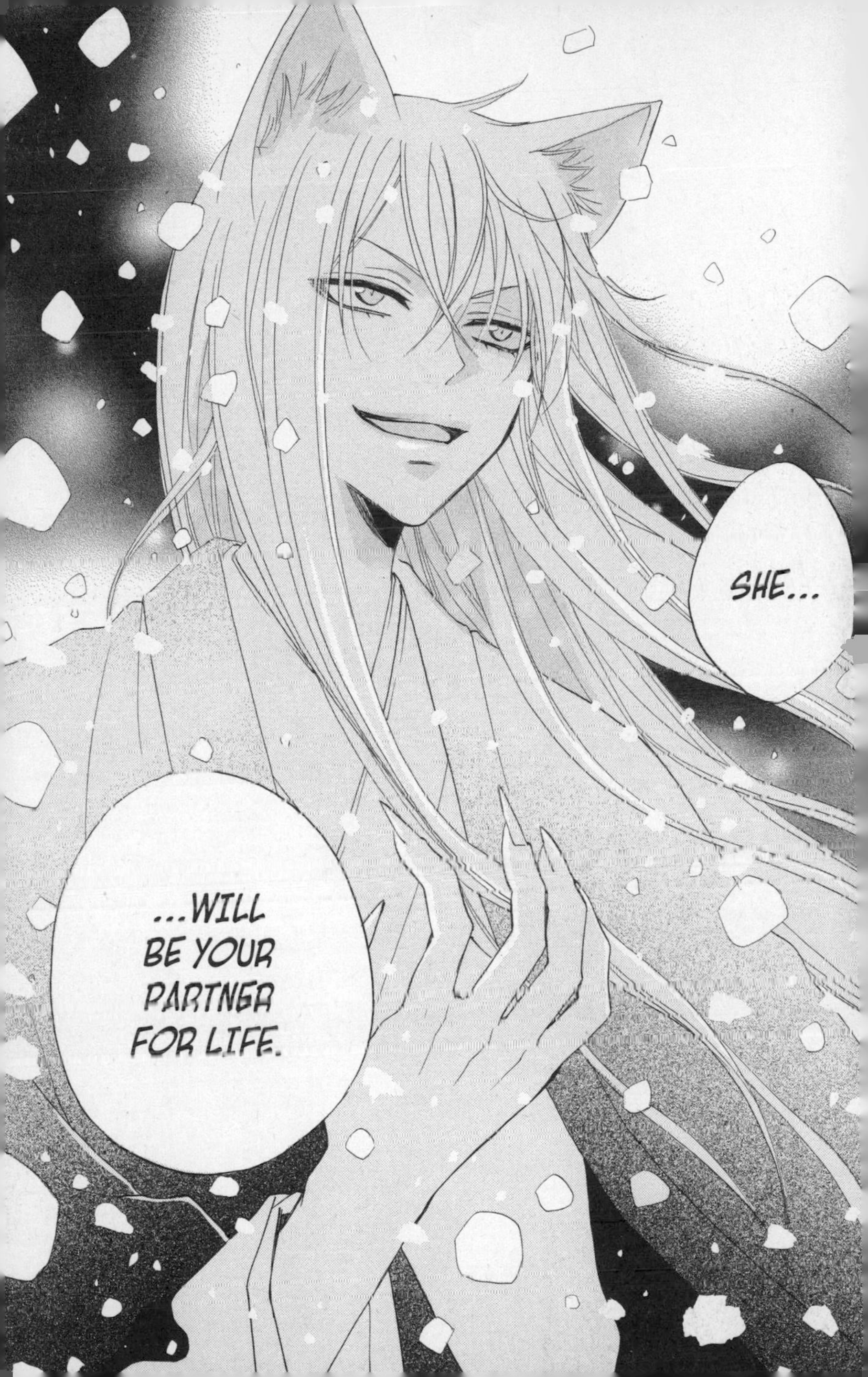
SHE...
...WILL BE YOUR PARTNER FOR LIFE.

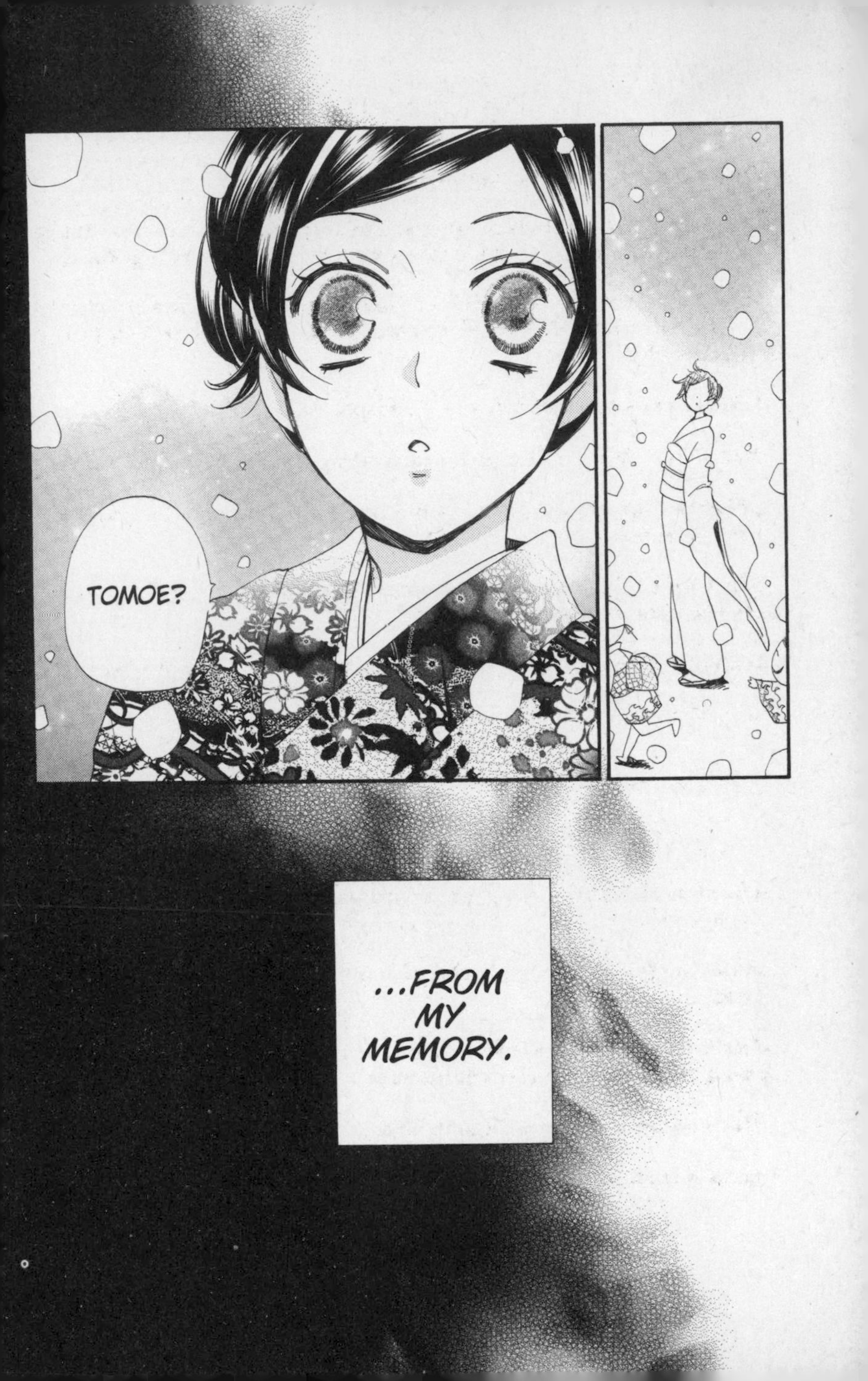
TOMOE?
...FROM MY MEMORY.

# The Otherworld

*Ayakashi* is an archaic term for yokai.

*Kami* are Shinto deities or spirits. The word can be used for a range of creatures, from nature spirits to strong and dangerous gods.

*Kotodama* literally means "word spirit," the spiritual power believed to dwell in words. In Shinto, the words you speak are believed to affect reality.

*Onibi-warashi* are like will-o'-the-wisps.

*Ryu-oh* is a title that literally means "dragon king."

*Shikigami* are spirits that are summoned and employed by *onmyoji* (Yin-Yang sorcerers).

*Shinshi* are birds, beasts, insects or fish that have a special relationship with a kami.

*Tochigami* (or *jinushigami*) are deities of a specific area of land.

# Honorifics

*-chan* is a diminutive most often used with babies, children or teenage girls.

*-dono* roughly means "my lord," although not in the aristocratic sense.

*-kun* is used by persons of superior rank to their juniors. It can sometimes have a familiar connotation.

*-san* is a standard honorific similar to Mr., Mrs., Miss, or Ms.

*-sama* is used with people of much higher rank.

# Notes

Page 90, panel 1: Sake cup vow
The bride and groom sharing sake is a traditional part of Japanese
wedding ceremonies and represents a formal bond.

Page 117, sidebar: *Yoriyori* are fried bread twists
and are based on a Chinese pastry called *mahua*.

Julietta Suzuki's debut manga *Hoshi ni Naru Hi* (The Day One Becomes a Star) appeared in the 2004 *Hana to Yume Plus*. Her other books include *Akuma to Dolce* (The Devil and Sweets) and *Karakuri Odette*. Born in December in Fukuoka Prefecture, she enjoys having movies play in the background while she works on her manga.

# KAMISAMA KISS
## VOL. 13
### Shojo Beat Edition

### STORY AND ART BY
## Julietta Suzuki

English Translation & Adaptation/Tomo Kimura
Touch-up Art & Lettering/Joanna Estep
Design/Shawn Carrico
Editor/Pancha Diaz

KAMISAMA HAJIMEMASHITA by Julietta Suzuki
© Julietta Suzuki 2012
All rights reserved.
First published in Japan in 2012 by HAKUSENSHA, Inc., Tokyo.
English language translation rights arranged with
HAKUSENSHA, Inc., Tokyo.

The stories, characters and incidents mentioned
in this publication are entirely fictional.

Printed in Canada

Published by VIZ Media, LLC
P.O. Box 77010
San Francisco, CA 94107

10 9 8 7 6 5 4 3 2 1
First printing, August 2013

www.viz.com     www.shojobeat.com

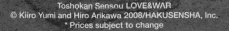

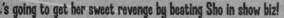

# This is the last page.

In keeping with the original Japanese comic format, this book reads from right to left—so action, sound effects, and word balloons are completely reversed. This preserves the orientation of the original artwork—plus, it's fun! Check out the diagram shown here to get the hang of things, and then turn to the other side of the book to get started!

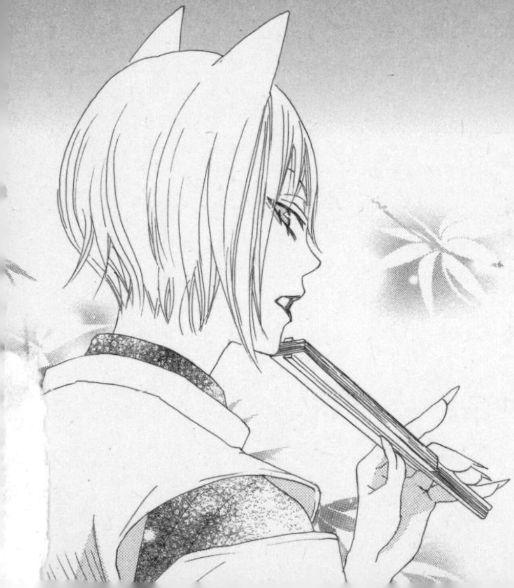

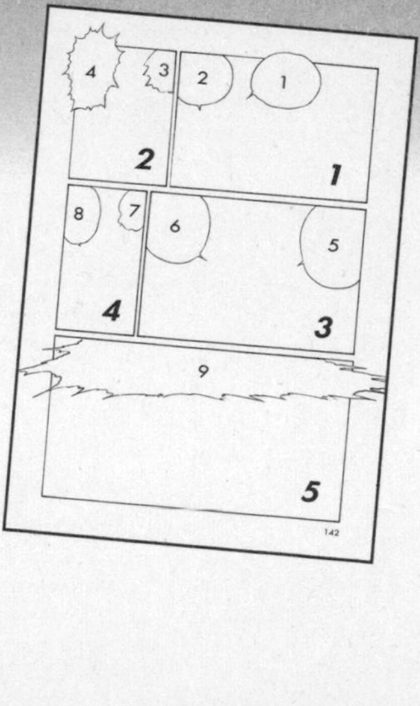
1
2
3
4
1
2
5
6
7
8
3
4
9
5
142